Ethnography at the Edge

Northeastern University 1898–1998

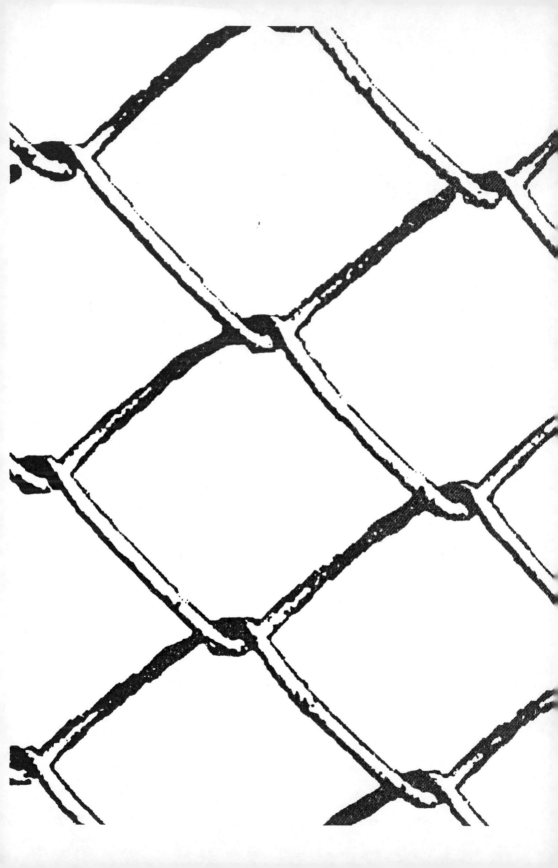

Ethnography at the Edge

Crime, Deviance, and Field Research

Jeff Ferrell and
Mark S. Hamm,

Editors

Northeastern University Press

Boston

Northeastern University Press

Copyright 1998 by Jeff Ferrell and Mark S. Hamm

Library of Congress Cataloging-in-Publication Data

Ethnography at the edge : crime, deviance, and field research / edited by Jeff Ferrell and Mark S. Hamm.
p. cm.
Includes bibliographical references and index.
ISBN 1-55553-341-8 (cl : alk. paper). — ISBN 1-55553-340-x
(pb : alk. paper)
1. Criminal anthropology—Research.   2. Criminal anthropology—
Field work.   3. Criminal behavior—Research.   4. Deviant behavior—
Research.   I. Ferrell, Jeff.   II. Hamm, Mark S.
HV6035.E74   1998
364.2'4—dc21   97—36683

Designed by Peter M. Blaiwas

Composed in Stone Serif by G & S Typesetters, Inc., in Austin, Texas.
Printed and bound by Thomson-Shore, Inc., in Dexter, Michigan.
The paper is Glatfelter Supple Opaque Recycled, an acid-free sheet.

Manufactured in the United States of America
08 07 06 05 04   7 6 5 4 3

To Thelonious Monk:
You play, I'll write.

JF

To The Grateful Dead (1965–1995):
Thanks for all the good stuff.

MSH

"To live outside the law, you must be honest."
—Bob Dylan, "Absolutely Sweet Marie"

"I broke the law for breakfast, break it again for lunch."
—Eugene Chadbourne, "Breakin' the Law Every Day"

Advisor in Criminal Justice to Northeastern University Press
Gilbert Geis

Contents

Foreword

Moving

Backward

Patricia A. Adler

Peter Adler

Ethnography has evolved in many ways. From its early beginnings in anthropology and sociology at the turn of the twentieth century, ethnography has advocated an approach to the study of human groups that rejects the more positivistic, objectivistic, and scientistic hegemony of its quantitative brethren. Though the first ethnographers were aware of philosophical and epistemological debates in the social sciences, and though later ethnographers eventually felt it necessary to codify the methodology to meet the demands of mainstream positivism, their approach has always been more impressionistic, humanistic, and artistic than any other social scientific methodology. *Ethnography at the Edge* comes at a distinct juncture in the history of fieldwork. As with movements in the art world, key figures and events have triggered revolutions in the way we conduct, teach, and read the ethnographic genre. At times drawing on the previous epoch, at other times reacting in contrast to what preceded them, ethnographers, like artists, have forged ahead to create their new styles. As such, the work in this volume both represents and counteracts what predates it.

Impressionism—Dating to the early Chicago School, sociological field researchers have studied criminal and deviant groups. In fact, some of the classics of the field, including Thrasher's study of gangs, Shaw's case study of the jack-roller, Landesco's studies of organized crime and pickpockets, Cressey's work on taxi dancehalls, and Anderson's research on homeless men, came out of this tradition.[1] Like the prisms through which their artistic counterparts saw the world, these first ethnographers interpreted early-twentieth-century urban life for us. Through their vision, we were able to get a clearer portrait of life in the ghetto, on the streetcorner, and among criminal mobs. Following Robert Park's edict to "go out and get your hands dirty in real research,"[2] these men (and a few women) were free to explore their worlds, unencumbered by legal restrictions, disciplinary codes, or stultifying customs. No one questioned their ethics, their veracity, or the seriousness with which they went about their work. Their legacy, which is still with us, is the decree to study social life *in situ*, looking at people in their natural habitats, embracing a world not abstractly but literally. The momentum they forged for this approach, though, went into temporary hibernation during the years of the Second World War. Sociology, gripped by the power of functionalism, was taken over by the departments at Harvard, Columbia, and Wisconsin, establishing the strong tradition of survey research that has held sway within the discipline ever since. While the proponents of the Chicago School still survived, their voices and contributions were not as strong.

Renaissance—It was during the early postwar years (1946–55) that the second generation of the Chicago School grew. These scholars, many of whom made an impact on criminology, were influenced by the need to study the oppressors as well as the oppressed. With an emphasis on amelioration, Chicago sociologists such as James Short, Lloyd Ohlin, and Albert Reiss turned attention toward studies of juvenile delinquency. Further, research by Howard Becker, Joseph Gusfield, Alfred Lindesmith, and Erving Goffman on moral entrepreneurs and other agents of social control eclipsed research on "disorganized" groups. This was a methodology that "held the student firmly to what he/she could see, hear, and experience at first-hand. . . . Abstractions and concepts ungrounded by the experience with concrete observations were suspect."[3] With this emphasis on realism, there was still no strict code of conduct, few rules to live by, and only a scattering of formal codes prescribing how ethnographers should conduct their business. In fact, guidance of any sort was minimal.

Abstract Expressionism—In the 1960s, with the movement of the ethnographic enterprise's sociological center to California, the study of deviant, alternative, countercultural, and illegal groups flourished. Free to go out and study those groups in close proximity, these ethnographers realized that the only sensible way to get information about hidden populations was to study them naturalistically. Disdaining the research endeavors that analyzed criminals as captured populations, these sociologists and criminologists went into bars, inside gangs, and into the inner sanctums of deviant populations to find out what constituted their realities. With broad strokes and vivid imagery, readers were treated to in-depth accounts of the underworld of horse racing, religious cults, skid row habitués, and those who frequented nude beaches.[4] It was within this general milieu that Ned Polsky decried: "This means—there is no getting away from it—the study of career criminals *au naturel,* in the field, the study of such criminals as they normally go about their work and play, the study of 'uncaught' criminals and the study of others who in the past have been caught but are not caught at the time you study them. . . . Obviously we can no longer afford the convenient fiction that in studying criminals in their natural habitat, we would discover nothing really important that could not be discovered from criminals behind bars."[5]

Along with this proclamation for naturalism, researchers were expected to rid themselves of the unnecessary handcuffs that bound them to being detached from those they studied. The classical approach to ethnography had taught that researchers should remain coolly detached from their subjects, lying back in the woodwork and not becoming too involved in their lives. It was Jack Douglas, in his landmark book, *Investigative Social Research,*[6] who laid to rest the fabrication that the exchange between researched and researcher was necessarily cooperative. Positing a conflict model of field research, he advocated techniques that would enhance the researcher's ability to get beyond the fronts and deceptions that characterized most fieldworkers' dilemmas. This radical approach, one that puts the burden of confidentiality and trust squarely on the shoulders of the ethnographer, did not meet with widespread approval among the moral entrepreneurs of academia and government. Instead, their response was to further tighten their grip over the research process.

The Dark Ages—Beginning in the late 1970s, but not fully taking hold until the 1990s, Institutional Review Boards (IRBs) at most colleges and universities have made ethnographic work on criminal and deviant groups almost impossible to conduct. Even the new Code of Ethics of the American Sociological Association yields to the decisions of these boards, claiming that if projects are disapproved by these local agencies, the research, in the association's eyes, is unethical.[7] Potentially gone, then, is any ethnographic research involving a covert role for the investigator (thus removing hidden populations further from view), any ethnographic research on minors that does not obtain parental consent (obviously problematic for youth involved in deviance or crime or who are victims of parental abuse), and any ethnographic research on vulnerable populations or sensitive (including criminal) issues without signed con-

sent forms that explicitly indicate the researchers' inability to protect subjects' confidentiality. This approach puts governmental and institutional
bureaucratic mandates ahead of the research bargains and confidences
previously forged by fieldworkers, denigrating the impact of critical dimensions of fieldwork techniques such as reciprocity, trust, evolving relationships, depth, shifting roles, and the relative weighting of research
loyalty (subjects versus society). Even though we have federal laws protecting the privacy of individuals that should be enough to cover research
exchanges, intrusion on research has grown recently. It was left to Rik
Scarce, a Washington State University graduate student at the time, to
alert us to how vigilant the government was willing to be. This lone
scholar, who was trying to uphold the legitimacy of research confidentiality, was jailed for six months in contempt of court because he would
not divulge information about the members of the radical environmental
movement he studied. Like those heretics muffled, denounced, and per-
secuted during the Dark Ages, Scarce was gagged for his "outlandish"
stance on the protection of human subjects.[8] For, in this era, governmental forces do not think that we researchers can police ourselves, but think
rather that we need to abide by the intrusion of their Philistine doctrines.
Amazingly, it is within this repressive atmosphere that the writers in this
volume have done their work.

The Enlightenment—The pioneering authors of the studies gathered
in *Ethnography at the Edge* will take us into the new century with renewed
verve for the criminological ethnographic enterprise. These intrepid,
brave souls are willing to reveal the trials and tribulations, the horrors and
joys, that faced them as they wove their way through both the institutional morass and subcultural environments they describe. Within these
pages is the latest research on such diverse subjects as skinheads, phone
sex workers, drug dealers, graffiti artists, and the homeless. Just at a time
when governmental and institutional agencies have made it difficult, if
not impossible, to conduct ethnographic research on criminal and deviant populations, the works found here are a beacon of light, giving us
hope that we can produce useful social scientific knowledge about hereto-
fore misunderstood or under-studied groups.

We are at a crossroads for depth criminological fieldwork. The efforts
of the scholars whose works are contained in this volume are therefore

Herculean. Since what counts as "moral" is constantly changing, a swing back may one day come. We cannot, however, let our toils stop during these Dark Ages. The works in this volume serve as the torch to keep the dream of unfettered research alive.

Notes

1. Frederic Thrasher, *The Gang* (Chicago: University of Chicago Press, 1927); Clifford Shaw, *The Jack Roller* (Chicago: University of Chicago Press, 1930); John Landesco, *Organized Crime in Chicago* (Chicago: Illinois Association for Criminal Justice, 1929); John Landesco, "The Criminal Gang," Report to the Local Community Research Committee, Charles E. Merriam Papers, University of Chicago Archives, Autumn 1925; Paul G. Cressey, *The Taxi Dance Hall* (Chicago: University of Chicago Press, 1932); Nels Anderson, *The Hobo: The Sociology of the Homeless Man* (Chicago: University of Chicago Press, 1923).

2. "Unpublished Statement Made by Robert E. Park and Recorded by Howard Becker While a Graduate Student at Chicago in the Twenties," in *Constructive Typology and Social Theory,* by John C. McKinney (New York: Appleton-Century-Crofts, 1966), 71.

3. Joseph Gusfield, as cited in John Galliher, "Chicago's Two Worlds of Deviance Research: Whose Side Are They On?" in *A Second Chicago School? The Development of a Postwar American Sociology,* ed. Gary Alan Fine (Chicago: University of Chicago Press, 1995), 183.

4. Marvin Scott, *The Racing Game* (Chicago: Aldine, 1968); John Lofland, *Doomsday Cult* (Englewood Cliffs, N.J.: Prentice-Hall, 1966); Jacqueline P. Wiseman, *Stations of the Lost* (Englewood Cliffs, N.J.: Prentice-Hall, 1970); Jack Douglas and Paul Rasmussen, *The Nude Beach* (Beverly Hills, Calif.: Sage, 1977).

5. Ned Polsky, *Hustlers, Beats, and Others* (Chicago: Aldine, 1967), 115-16, emphasis in original.

6. Jack D. Douglas, *Investigative Social Research* (Beverly Hills, Calif.: Sage, 1976).

7. American Sociological Association, *Code of Ethics* (Washington, D.C.: American Sociological Association, 1996).

8. Rik Scarce, "(No) Trial (But) Tribulations: When Courts and Ethnography Conflict," *Journal of Contemporary Ethnography* 23 (1994): 123-49.

Preface

Like the experiences on which it reports, *Ethnography at the Edge* is a work of human engagement. For the ethnographers of crime and deviance who are its contributors, this work represents a sort of collective confession, an honest accounting of the vivid pleasures and dangers which define their work. At the same time, this collection engages larger themes by exploring the dimensions of method, theory, politics, and meaning that intertwine with the day-to-day practice of field research. Ultimately, this book is meant to engage others—to serve as a warning, a challenge, and an invitation to undertake ethnographic research on crime and deviance. As this collection shows, such research is seldom safe, convenient, or professionally efficient; it is only necessary.

As with any work of scholarship, this book emerges from the flow of existing ideas and experience. Not surprisingly, then, certain names surface time and again throughout the pages that follow. Max Weber, Ned Polsky, James Agee, Alfred Lindesmith, Howard Becker—they and others have taught us to understand social research not as a set of technical skills, but as an attentive way of life. Just as important, they have demonstrated—as we hope to demonstrate here—that methodology is politics, that our decisions about research are inseparable from our decisions about honor, respect, decency, and justice. And so in this light we would mention one other scholar from whom we have learned a "methodology of attentiveness," as we have phrased it elsewhere: Allen Ginsberg. Ginsberg's incandescent life and work, and his death during the final stages of this book's preparation, remind us to live and write like it matters.

The flow of ideas and experience continues, of course, as does the support of colleagues. We thank especially our colleagues Gray Cavender, Bill Chambliss, Marilyn McShane, Ray Michalowski, Barbara Perry, Clint Sanders, Pat Sheehan, Gideon Sjoberg, Fred Solop, Neil Websdale, Trey Williams, and Nancy Wonders for the webwork of insights and inspiration they have provided. We acknowledge also Vic Kappeler, whose editorship of the journal *Justice Quarterly* has opened important intellectual space for the type of work found here; of the three previously published essays included in this collection, two appeared in *Justice Quarterly* under his tenure as editor. Similarly, we are grateful to Bill Frohlich, Scott Brassart, and the staff of Northeastern University Press, whose continuing commitment to first-rate scholarship benefits not just this work, but the larger community of critical inquiry. And we appreciate the support of Northern Arizona University, where work on this project was supported by an Organized Research Grant for 1996–97, and where the book's comprehensive bibliography was prepared with the able assistance of Matt Ade.

But none of this is enough. If we are to save ourselves and our ideas from becoming museum pieces—if we are to save ourselves and our disciplines from the dustbin of personal and intellectual history—we must keep ourselves unfinished, our ideas emergent and open to critique. To do so, we need, always, a next generation of scholars who will show us the proper disrespect. We thus urge younger scholars to examine this collection, to be inspired by moments of edgework and innovation, but at the same time to be disturbed by a certain consistency of identity and perspective. Read this collection not as orthodoxy, but as an invitation to heresy. Push back the edges; kick out the jambs; invent new sorts of field research, new dangers and pleasures, beyond what we can imagine.

James Agee said of his *Let Us Now Praise Famous Men,* "This is a book only by necessity. More seriously, it is an effort in human actuality, in which the reader is no less centrally involved than the authors and those of whom they tell." That is our effort here, also, and we look forward to your involvement.

Introduction

True Confessions

Crime, Deviance, and Field Research

Jeff Ferrell

Mark S. Hamm

We begin with the first of many true confessions on which this book is based. In 1993, each of this volume's editors published a book developed from intensive field research inside a criminal subculture.[1] One book was dedicated to the criminals, inside whose world the researcher had discovered not only a complex criminal dynamic but a remarkable experience of collective artistry and adventure. The other was dedicated to a victim of the criminals under study—a victim brutally beaten and killed by perpetrators caught up in their own sort of violent adventure. Where one research experience produced a converging sympathy between researcher and those researched, the other generated a diverging antipathy, a sentiment closer to Hunter S. Thompson's chilling conclusion to his edgy fieldwork inside the violent world of the Hell's Angels: "Exterminate all the brutes!"[2]

This book explores the lived politics of such seemingly dissimilar research processes—the experiential tension between them, but, more important, the methodological and experiential frameworks which unite them. Like other criminological and sociological field research projects recounted in this volume, these two entangled the researchers in a dangerous mix of legality and illegality, physical and professional danger, pleasure, excitement, and fear. And, as with other field research projects related here, this experiential tangle emerged as something more than a side effect; it came to exist as an essential component in the research itself.

In a real sense, then, this collection evolves out of the creative tension between two research experiences, out of the shared methodological space which produced one field researcher's profound affinity with his subjects of study and another's profound emotional outrage and disgust. As we shall see, in their lived intensity and in their emergence out of fieldwork methodology, these two opposite orientations couldn't be more alike.

2.

In another sense the idea for this collection was sparked in, of all places, the 1994 Awards Luncheon of the annual meeting of the Academy of Criminal Justice Sciences (ACJS). In the cavernous Grand Ballroom of the infamous Chicago Hilton—twenty-six years earlier a focal point of a different sort of meeting between Democratic politicians, Chicago police, and antiwar activists—a thousand or so criminologists had gathered for a free lunch. Above the din of clanking forks and conversation, James Inciardi was accepting an Outstanding Book Award for *Women and Crack-Cocaine*, the in-depth field study which he authored with Dorothy Lockwood and Anne Pottieger.[3] In his acceptance comments, Inciardi noted that it was certainly a long way from the dirty interiors of inner-city Miami crack houses and from his arrest by Miami police while doing research inside one of these crack houses to the elevated podium of the ACJS Awards Luncheon. Indeed, a reading of his methodological appendix to *Women and Crack-Cocaine* confirms just how great that distance is. There he considers issues which many criminologists and sociologists might prefer to ignore: his and other field researchers' vulnerability to grand-jury subpoenas and arrest, on the one hand, and crack-house violence or criminal threats, on the other. Worse, he raises some unanswerable ethical questions. What is the researcher's role when confronted with a "house girl"—a young, likely underage girl kept by the crack-house owner for sex with clients? What is the researcher to do when confronted—not in the abstract, but head-on, and day after day—with the "degradation, brutality, despair, injustice, and exploitation" which defines "the crack business" and many other arenas of field research as well?[4]

A number of us seated together—Mark Hamm, Jeff Ferrell, Ken Tunnell, Stephanie Kane—agreed that a remarkable space did in fact separate James Inciardi the field researcher, caught in the ambiguous ethics and questionable legality of his research, from James Inciardi the ACJS awards recipient. Further, we began to consider the equally great distance between our own field research—down graffiti-covered back alleys, among streetcorner skinheads and prostitutes, inside the cramped living rooms of ex-cons—and the safe, suit-and-tie respectability of an ACJS gathering. This book grows in part out of that moment of consideration. It seeks to demystify and define the distance; to bridge the distance with straightforward accounts of contemporary field research by criminologists and sociologists; and, ultimately, to explore the manifold connections and contradictions between fieldwork methodology, intellectual insight, and professional identity.

3.

As even a cursory glance through this collection will show, the interplay of professional identity and field research roles regularly leads criminologists and sociologists in a variety of directions less savory or acceptable than hotel luncheons and book awards. Certainly those who engage in field research share, to some degree, in whatever excitement or pleasure animates their subjects of study; and, as already suggested and as argued fully in subsequent chapters, these experiences may yield methodological and personal benefits. Moreover, field researchers regularly gain professional benefit from their fieldwork, and from the in-the-field cooperation of research subjects, by way of presented papers, published articles and books, and other prerequisites of career advancement. As Mark Fleisher will argue in this volume, skilled criminological field researchers might in this sense be thought of as successful pimps, selling dramatic accounts of crime and criminals to those unwilling or unable to acquire them on their own.

But if there exist disciplinary rewards for criminological and sociological field research, there exist some serious disciplinary dangers as well. To begin with, field researchers who share social and cultural space with crack "house girls" and street gang members, who intentionally place themselves in situations of shady legality and unconventional morality, push at the very boundaries of professionally acceptable scholarly inquiry. They risk having their research denigrated on grounds of bias, subjectivity, over-involvement, and "overrapport." They in turn risk informal censure from colleagues who feel that this sort of research, by directing close attention to criminal or deviant groups, in effect stamps these groups with an imprimatur of scholarly legitimacy[5]; even formal censure for violation of professional or university codes of conduct is possible.

Further, though in-depth field research may certainly lead to the publication of significant results, it hardly sets an agenda for rapid professional advancement. Field studies remain, in general, less attractive to funding agencies than do quantitative studies, which can produce at least the illusion of precise, measurable data. Given the long-term commitments of time and professional energy which they require, in-depth field studies are also unlikely to produce journal articles as quickly or as prolifically as hiring or tenure committees may require. Instead, they may lend themselves more to a sort of "book sociology" or "book criminology" in which long-term, detailed research findings can be presented and explored. Sadly, though, this is the very sort of scholarship that has, in many ways, been overtaken as a measure of contemporary academic success by what Feagin, Orum, and Sjoberg call "mainstream article sociology," or what we might call in the present context a convenient "criminology of correlations."[6] Morally and professionally, the fit between the disciplines of criminology and sociology, and field research as a criminological or sociological method, is uncomfortable at best.

Even field researchers who somehow navigate the disciplinary dangers of their work may still succumb to its legal and experiential perils. Inciardi's arrest while conducting crack-house research has already been noted; to this example we might add his accidental participation in a convenience-store holdup, the price put on his head by an angry crack-house owner, and other fieldwork adventures.[7] Similarly, police officers aggressively questioned Bourgois in the course of his field research into the crack economy; they arrested and threatened Armstrong during his field study of British soccer fans; and they arrested, abused, and threatened Small while he was conducting field research with black youth in London.[8] Humphreys was of course also apprehended during his (in)famous fieldwork in homosexual "tearooms." When asked his name by a police officer while he was outside a park tearoom, Humphreys responded, "I'm sorry, that's none of your business"; the officer responded by arresting him on charges of loitering.[9]

Recently, field researchers' refusals to provide information to legal authorities have generated equally dramatic and, in some cases, more longlasting consequences. In the early 1980s doctoral student Mario Brajuha was investigated by state and federal authorities and targeted by a grandjury subpoena because of the authorities' belief that portions of his field research information might be useful in solving a crime of arson.[10] Similarly, in 1993, Rik Scarce, then a doctoral student in sociology, was interrogated by FBI agents, subpoenaed to appear before a grand jury, and subsequently jailed for refusing to divulge information related to crimes allegedly committed by his subjects of study, members of the radical environmental movement. (It is also worth noting that Scarce's later request to conduct field research with inmates while in jail was denied by his university's Institutional Review Board.)[11] Around this same time, doctoral student Richard Leo was also subpoenaed in an attempt to force disclosure of field information he had gathered during research into police interrogation practices. (Again, it is worth noting that this research was approved only after three months' negotiations with the Human Subjects Committee at Leo's university — and that, ironically, these negotiations did not raise the possibility of Leo's vulnerability to subpoena.)[12] The resolution of the latter two cases reflects the broader, ambiguous status of criminological and sociological field research (and field researchers) vis-à-vis the law. Scarce never divulged his research information, but was finally released — with hugs and handshakes from fellow inmates — when the presiding judge felt that his confinement had "crossed the magic boundary" separating legal coercion from punishment. Leo did finally acquiesce to a judge's order to testify and notes: "I will always regret that decision."[13]

The accounts collected in this volume add to this compendium of legal, professional, and personal misadventures on the part of field researchers and further demonstrate that if legal authorities don't find fault with one's field research, subjects of study or colleagues likely will. Immersed in the ethnographic moment, Jeff Ferrell finds himself attempting (unsuccessfully) to outrun a patrol car in the course of late-night research with the graffiti underground. Bruce Arrigo confronts his increasingly blurry role as field researcher in a homeless community and colludes with members of the community to produce "contaminated" research findings. Mark Fleisher's field research among street gangs gives him nightmares, makes him "irritable, impatient, and cold," and forces him to question the efficacy of both criminological field research and criminal justice. Peter Kraska discovers, to his dismay, that he enjoys his fieldwork among aggressive, militarized police officers engaged in illegal, weapons-blazing "training" sessions. Mark Hamm drifts into a netherworld of paranoia and violence as he closes in on Timothy McVeigh and the "blue center-light of evil." Stephanie Kane finds her "ethnographic gaze" reversed, as she herself becomes a situated object of male scrutiny and desire in the course of her field research on prostitution and AIDS. Similarly, Christine Mattley's field research with phone sex operators produces significant insights into their lives, but at the same time generates disapproval and sexualized responses from male and female colleagues alike.

During Bruce Jacobs's research into crack dealers and crack dealing, the disapproval of a dissatisfied research subject takes a different and more violent form: robbery of Jacobs at gunpoint, followed by a long series of threatening phone calls. Alternatively, Ralph Weisheit discovers not violence and intimidation, but rather a wall of civility, honor, and silence which blocks all but the most careful of field researchers from access to the culture of rural marijuana growers. In the course of his field research with convicted property criminals, Kenneth Tunnell finds that turning off the tape recorder and turning on the marijuana produces invaluable research information, and in this and other research he is forced to explore deceptive strategies designed to ward off authorities' inquiries. Finally, and perhaps fittingly, Stephen Lyng explores his concept of the experiential and criminal "edge" by going over it—at 120 miles per hour on a cartwheeling, out-of-control motorcycle.

The accounts gathered here incorporate not only these sorts of "true confessions" regarding fieldwork danger and adventure, but thoughtful considerations of the various theoretical, methodological, and political issues embedded in these adventures as well. For now, though, two basic insights from these and other cases can be noted. First, the interconnections between deviance, law, crime, and field research are complex indeed, cutting back and forth between the investigation of deviance and criminality, the field investigator's involvement in deviant or criminal behavior, and the field investigator's subsequent vulnerability to legal, professional, and disciplinary disapproval. Second, and relatedly, if criminological and sociological field researchers are the beneficiaries of their field research, if they find there perhaps some measure of professional success and personal, thrill-seeking satisfaction,[14] they are equally the victims of this enterprise. In trouble with legal authorities and academic gatekeepers alike, vulnerable to charges of immodest behavior and outright immorality, forced into bad moments of personal and professional doubt, field researchers all too regularly confront the limits of methodology and identity in the course of their work.

Given this, the present volume seeks to explore not only field research's links to professional identity, but its interconnections with broader identities as well. If done well—if undertaken from inside the dangerous heart of deviance, crime, and criminality, from inside the interiors of crack houses and broken lives—field research risks more than the researcher's professional status. As the essays here will argue, effective field research demands that the researcher be submerged in the situated logic and emotion of criminality and deviance, and thus be willing to abandon in part the security of pre-existing personal and professional identities. In this sense, engaged field research doesn't just risk existential disorientation; it all but guarantees it.

At the same time, though, prior roles and identities are never fully abandoned; and, in fact, their existence shapes, to a large degree, the experience and the risk of such research. Reflecting on his arrest for tearoom loitering, Humphreys notes: "I suffered no harm and learned a great deal from my only experience with arrest and incarceration. I was not even forced to apprise the police of my research activities. The experience provided me with valuable data and some good conversation material. But that is because I was *who* I was and engaged in *what* I was doing. A different man, engaging in no more deviant activity than I was on that afternoon, could have been ruined."[15] Similar questions of who field researchers are and what they are doing remain at issue today. In what ways, for example, did Ferrell's adventure with late-night graffiti writers, Kraska's encounter with militarized male police officers, and Jacobs's violent battle with an angry crack dealer both result from and reproduce these researchers' own gendered identities? In what ways did the risks which Kane and Mattley encountered in their research reflect not just the research situation, but their and others' expectations regarding gender and professional identity? Many such questions are addressed in the following essays; many more remain.[16]

Finally, then, the subject of field research is not only the situated reality of crime and deviance, but the existential reality of the researcher.[17] In his gritty ethnography of "urban nomads," Spradley argues that "the foundation for *all* ethnography" rests in the "complex relationship" between field researchers and their subjects of study.[18] This collection explores that complex relationship by highlighting the contributions which the researcher makes to it and, at the same time, the profound consequences which the researcher carries away from it. And so, along with published research projects and ACJS luncheons, these are the starting points for the present volume: the dimensions of identity that exist beyond and in balance with one's research role, dimensions which shape and are shaped by the reality of field research.[19] The confessions which fill this book are meant to explore the dynamics of research experiences framed by danger and illegality; but as part of this exploration, they are meant to uncover and examine essential issues of researcher identity as well.

4.

But why bother?

Given the profound personal and professional dangers of field research into crime and deviance, why should criminology and sociology as disciplines, and criminologists and sociologists as individuals, support and engage in such research? And why, even if this sort of research is to be undertaken, should some researchers bother "confessing" the particulars of their involvement and their identities, and others bother reading and reflecting on these confessions?

Such questions take us to still other starting points for this collection, to basic frames of reference for both field research and reflexive accounts of it. One such starting point emerges from the long tradition of field research inside criminal and deviant subcultures, and from the newer orientation of "cultural criminology."[20] From these perspectives, field research remains, no matter what its risks, the essential research method for uncovering the situated meaning of crime and deviance, for exposing the emerging experiential web of symbolic codes and ritualized understandings which constitute deviance and criminality. In his classic field study of working-class kids, Willis pointedly notes, "The qualitative methods, and Participant Observation used in the research, and the ethnographic format of the presentation were dictated by the nature of my interest in 'the cultural.' These techniques are suited to record this level and have a sensitivity to meanings and values as well as an ability to represent and interpret symbolic articulations, practices and forms of cultural production."[21] Likewise, criminologist Jim Thomas draws on Spradley to describe contemporary ethnography as a "culture-studying culture," a body of method attuned to nuances of symbolism, discourse, and interpretation.[22] To the extent, then, that we understand deviance, crime, and criminality as taking shape within the shared codes of deviant and criminal subcultures, or within the subtle symbolic interplay that defines the foreground of deviant or criminal events, we must employ a "methodology of attentiveness" that can reveal something of these worlds to us.[23] As a wealth of field research has demonstrated, and as the following essays again confirm, research methods which stand outside the lived experience of deviance or criminality can perhaps sketch a faint outline of it, but they can never fill that outline with essential dimensions of meaningful understanding.[24]

Moving away from secondhand information and toward the immediate meanings of crime and deviance, we arrive at another starting point as well—a point outside the safe circles of legally sanctioned research and legal-system data. In Polsky's terms, we arrive at a point defined by the abandonment of "jailhouse sociology" or "courthouse sociology," sociologies founded in crime rates and crime reports, and in their place the pursuit of crime's dangerous reality as constructed by criminals in side streets, back alleys, and corporate offices.[25] As Hagedorn points out, this journey away from the safety of court records and crime reports and into the messy illegality of day-to-day criminality incorporates more than a researcher's personal methodological preference; it incorporates a significant shift in focus. In freeing our research from the courthouse, we begin also to free it from the "official definitions of reality" and of crime which are produced there.[26] By going into the field, we begin to understand crime by its own internal symbolism and logic, and not simply as a law enforcement issue, an embarrassment to community leaders, or a category of pre-condemned illegality. Polsky notes that, for "the great majority of criminologists . . . a central task of criminology, often *the* central task, is to find more effective ways to reform lawbreakers and to keep other people from becoming lawbreakers." Putting it more bluntly, Polsky argues that the central task is thus "making people obey current American criminal law."[27] If this is not the central task—if instead, like this volume's contributors, field researchers seek critical engagement with the subtle, ambiguous, and contradictory realities of both crime and criminal justice—they must have methods which can make this engagement possible.

In answering the question of why criminologists should bother with field research, we thus arrive at still another true confession. For at least one of this volume's editors, criminological field research and honest "confessions" of its dangerous allure interweave with the practice of a critical anarchist criminology and undergird one of anarchist criminology's basic goals: deconstructing the authority of law and carving out for ourselves and others critical distance from it.[28] Certainly this task can be undertaken by documenting the law's many internal contradictions and institutionalized abuses, by exploring its destructive effects on human communities, or by celebrating moments of creative resistance to it. But it can also be accomplished methodologically—by denying the presumed authority of courthouse criminologies and official crime reports, by weaning ourselves from their institutional authors and keepers, and by instead engaging in the sorts of grounded field research and "critical ethnography"[29] which can create independent understandings of crime and criminality.

In answering our first question regarding the usefulness of field research—namely, why bother with field research to begin with—we arrive also at the second: Why bother with field researchers' confessions of identity and involvement? Clearly, field researchers bring a culture and politics of crime and deviance to the research setting as much as they find them there; and when they engage in field research, they utilize a method which fits not just particular research settings, but particular researchers as well. This complex, homologous relationship between researcher and research setting is played out in a variety of ways. As previously seen, field researchers import pre-existing dimensions of professional and existential identity into the research setting and then find these dimensions reforged in the heat of ethnographic inquiry. As just implied, many of these field researchers in turn utilize the approach as both an attentive methodology and a sort of political prybar—a prybar which gains its progressive or critical leverage precisely because of its ability to document the unofficial, extralegal reality of crime and deviance. Similarly, as Williams et al. and others emphasize, effective field researchers work to understand the symbolic and stylistic universe of deviant or criminal situations as a subject of scholarly inquiry, but also as an important, practical technique for reshaping their personas, for gaining further research access, and for guaranteeing their own safety.[30] The situated symbolism and style which have meaning for research subjects thus become immediately meaning-ful for researchers as well; for field researchers, nuances of symbolism, style, and meaning come to constitute both an object and a method of study. As an excruciatingly human enterprise, field research at its best thus lays bare the political orientations, cultural codes, and existential predilections which researchers and research subjects alike bring to the enterprise, and which they collectively construct while together in it.

From this view, "true confessions" of field workers' identities and in-volvements serve more than academic self-indulgence; they serve as es-sential components in any full accounting of field research knowledge. In the context of sexuality and science, Foucault describes "the confession as one of the main rituals we rely on for the production of truth."[31] In the present context, we can understand the field researcher's confession as an emerging ritual designed to flesh out the fieldwork experience and to pro-duce situated understandings of field research and field research findings previously submerged under mythologies of researcher objectivity and distance. As will be discussed more fully in the following chapter, recent existential, ethnomethodological, feminist, and postmodernist perspec-tives on field research have set the context for such confessions by em-phasizing the essential place of field researcher roles and identities in shaping the research process. Together, these orientations have brought about what Van Maanen calls "an end to innocence"—a recognition that researchers must construct not only ethnographies, but "confessional ethnographies" and "ethnographies of ethnography" which are as atten-tive to researchers' identities, experiences, and emotions as they are to others'.[32] Certainly, in reintroducing ourselves into our research accounts, we must be careful lest these become accounts of little but ourselves. If we do take care to balance reflexivity with scholarly responsibility, though, we may well find that, in paying attention to ourselves, we are better able to pay attention to others as well.[33]

5.

In recognizing the situated meanings of crime and deviance, and the researcher's essential immersion and participation in these meanings, we arrive at a final starting point for this volume: a method which emerges inside the broader methodology of field research. This is criminological *verstehen.* As the following chapter will explicate, and as subsequent chapters will exemplify, criminological *verstehen* denotes a method which bridges the old dualisms of researcher and research situation, researcher and subjects of research, by utilizing the researcher's own experiences and emotions as avenues into the meanings of the situation and the experiences of the subjects. It implies a degree of subjective understanding between researcher and research subjects, an engaged methodological process such that researcher and research subjects come to share, at least in part, in the lived reality of deviance, crime, and criminality. Within this methodology, then, the experiences of field researchers matter, and matter profoundly. Ferrell's dash down an alley in the company of fleeing graffiti writers; Arrigo's collusion with members of a homeless community; Kraska's enjoyment of militaristic policing; Kane's entanglement in sexualized scrutiny; Jacobs's gunpoint assault—all are of consequence not simply as researcher confessions, or as accounts of researcher experiences, but as experiential insights into the situated dynamics of the deviant or criminal events under study. In such cases, as in others reported in this volume, the dualism of researcher versus research subjects gives way to a dialectic in which the experiences, understandings, and identities of researcher and research subjects blur and interweave. Framing the classic interactionist statement on crime and deviance, Becker insisted that "we look at all the people involved in any episode of alleged deviance . . . all the parties to a situation, and their relationships."[34] Criminological *verstehen* includes the researcher in that collective scrutiny.[35]

As a method of radical engagement with the subject of study, criminological *verstehen* all but assures the field researcher of physical, moral, and professional danger; it presumes deep involvement in criminal and deviant research situations, and thus fairly predictable involvement in the very sorts of problems outlined throughout this essay. Of perhaps greater importance, criminological *verstehen* in turn implies epistemic and existential frameworks profoundly different from those that have traditionally guided social scientific inquiry. In concluding their insightful, evolutionary account of fieldwork roles and methodology—an evolution over the past few decades away from detached objectivity and toward deep, experiential immersion—Adler and Adler argue that "We have removed some of the shackles placed upon us by the canons of science and objectivity. We are daring to act in terms of subjectivity, involvement, and commitment. We are allowing ourselves to be honest, not only to ourselves but to our readers. While we have paid 'lip service' to Weber's call for subjectivity for over a century, only now are we coming close to developing the methodology implicit in his call for *verstehen*."[36] As the following essay will argue more fully, the method of criminological *verstehen* does indeed contribute to this freeing of field research from the many shackles of science and objectivity. As a method of "subjectivity, involvement, and commitment," it frees field researchers to embrace the situated meanings generated by their subjects and themselves; to value the insights and understandings gained from shared emotion; to explore the lived politics of pleasure and pain, fear and excitement; to "think with the body"[37] as well as the mind. And, in this sense, criminological *verstehen* contributes to a project which has intertwined with the practice of criminological and sociological field research since its beginnings: the dismantling of dualistic epistemic hierarchies which position the researcher over and apart from research subjects, abstract analysis over and beyond situated knowledge, sanitary intellect over and outside human emotion and experience.

At the beginning of this essay, Thompson's damning conclusion to his intensive research inside the Hell's Angels—"Exterminate all the brutes!"—introduced the emotional intensity of field research. But the intensity of Thompson's experiences with the Angels carried him to other conclusions as well. Reflecting on his experiences with fast motorcycles, potent LSD, and the shifting "edge" of life and death, Thompson speaks of the "strange music" that begins to play at this "place of definitions," and adds: "The Edge. . . . There is no honest way to explain it because the only people who really know where it is are the ones who have gone over."[38] These contradictions—an ill-defined place of definitions, a hard-earned insight with no honest way to explain it—capture the heady mix of epistemic enlightenment and epistemic uncertainty, methodological potential and experiential danger, which defines this *verstehen*-oriented approach to field research. Out of this mix, we see emerging not simply a reconceptualization of field research, but radically new ways of living and knowing as criminologists and sociologists, ways of living and knowing which are at the same time more clear and more mysterious, closer than earlier methods to subjects of study and at the same time never close enough. We see, in place of a vain search for scientific objectivity, a dangerous poetic for criminology and sociology, an artistry and an artistic intensity in research and reporting that emerges somewhere beyond the careful constraints of courthouse criminology and arid academic discourse. Inside the shared intensity of criminological field research, we glimpse a terrible exuberance, a certain dark passion integrating the lives of criminals and criminologists alike.

In this sense the accounts gathered here constitute missives from beyond the edge of legality, notes from the underground of crime and deviance, attempts to communicate, if partially and imperfectly, the ineffability of field research and field research knowledge.[39] These essays are, by intention, not scientific reports. The lived reality of crime and deviance and the dangerous subtlety of method which can take us inside it exist beyond any easy language, beyond capture in data sets or statistical summaries. Instead, these accounts can perhaps best be understood as *translations,* as inherently incomplete efforts to transfer the immediacy of lived experience into narrative.[40] We close, then, with a final introductory confession. Measured by traditional standards of scientific objectivity or epistemic certainty, the "true confessions" gathered here are not true at all. Instead, they take shape as personal recountings of human situations, as complex and uncertain as the people and situations themselves, harboring a host of ineffable experiences and emotions while hiding in the illusory light of straightforward confession. This much, we confess.[41]

Notes

1. Mark S. Hamm, *American Skinheads: The Criminology and Control of Hate Crime* (Westport, Conn.: Praeger, 1993); Jeff Ferrell, *Crimes of Style: Urban Graffiti and the Politics of Criminality* (New York and London: Garland, 1993; Boston: Northeastern University Press, 1996).

2. Hunter S. Thompson, *Hell's Angels: A Strange and Terrible Saga* (New York: Ballantine, 1966), 348.

3. James A. Inciardi, Dorothy Lockwood, and Anne E. Pottieger, *Women and Crack-Cocaine* (New York: Macmillan, 1993). See also Avril Tayler, *Women Drug Users: An Ethnography of a Female Injecting Community* (Oxford: Clarendon Press, 1993).

4. James A. Inciardi, "Some Considerations on the Methods, Dangers, and Ethics of Crack-House Research," in *Women and Crack-Cocaine,* James A. Inciardi, Dorothy Lockwood, and Anne E. Pottieger (New York: Macmillan, 1993), 155.

5. Christine Mattley's chapter in this volume provides a particularly interesting example of these problems.

6. Joe R. Feagin, Anthony M. Orum, and Gideon Sjoberg, eds., *A Case for the Case Study* (Chapel Hill: University of North Carolina Press, 1991). See similarly Ted R. Vaughn, Gideon Sjoberg, and Larry T. Reynolds, eds., *A Critique of Contemporary*

American Sociology (Dix Hills, N.Y.: General Hall, 1993); John M. Hagedorn, "Back in the Field Again: Gang Research in the Nineties," in *Gangs in America,* ed. C. Ronald Huff (Newbury Park, Calif.: Sage, 1990), 254–55.

7. Inciardi, "Some Considerations," 151–54.

8. Philippe Bourgois, "In Search of Horatio Alger: Culture and Ideology in the Crack Economy," *Contemporary Drug Problems* 16 (1989): 619–49; Gary Armstrong, "Like that Desmond Morris?" in *Interpreting the Field: Accounts of Ethnography,* ed. Dick Hobbs and Tim May (Oxford: Clarendon, 1993), 3–43; Stephen Small, *Police and People in London: II. A Group of Black Young People* (London: Policy Studies Institute, 1983).

9. Laud Humphreys, *Tearoom Trade: Impersonal Sex in Public Places,* enlarged ed. (New York: Aldine de Gruyter, 1975), 94.

10. See Mario Brajuha and Lyle Hallowell, "Legal Intrusion and the Politics of Fieldwork: The Impact of the Brajuha Case," *Urban Life* 14 (1986): 454–78; Lyle Hallowell, "The Outcome of the Brajuha Case: Legal Implications for Sociologists," *Footnotes* 13 (1985): 1ff.

11. See Rik Scarce, "(No) Trial (But) Tribulations: When Courts and Ethnography Conflict," *Journal of Contemporary Ethnography* 23 (1994): 123–49; Rik Scarce, "Scholarly Ethics and Courtroom Antics: Where Researchers Stand in the Eyes of the Law," *American Sociologist* 26 (1995): 87–112.

12. See Richard A. Leo, "Trial and Tribulation: Courts, Ethnography, and the Need for an Evidentiary Privilege for Academic Researchers," *American Sociologist* 26 (1995): 113–34.

13. Scarce, "Scholarly Ethics," 96; Leo, "Trial and Tribulation," 128. See also Pamela J. Jenkins and Steve Knoll-Smith, eds., *Witnessing for Sociology: Sociologists in Court* (Westport, Conn.: Praeger, 1996); Gideon Sjoberg, ed., *Ethics, Politics, and Social Research* (Cambridge, Mass.: Schenkman, 1967).

14. See Raymond M. Lee, *Dangerous Fieldwork* (Thousand Oaks, Calif.: Sage, 1995), who notes that "researchers who enter difficult, dangerous, or unconventional research terrains are often accused by those who inhabit them of being thrill seekers" (5).

15. Humphreys, *Tearoom Trade,* 96, emphasis in original.

16. For more on issues of gender and research into crime and delinquency, see, for example, Meda Chesney-Lind, "Girls' Crime and Woman's Place: Toward a Feminist Model of Female Delinquency," *Crime and Delinquency* 35 (1989): 5–29.

17. See the insightful discussion of existential identity, existential sociology, and field research in Patricia A. Adler and Peter Adler, *Membership Roles in Field Research* (Newbury Park, Calif.: Sage, 1987). See also Joseph A. Kotarba and Andrea Fontana, eds., *The Existential Self in Society* (Chicago: University of Chicago Press, 1984).

18. James P. Spradley, *You Owe Yourself a Drunk: An Ethnography of Urban Nomads* (Boston: Little, Brown, 1970), 7, emphasis in original.

19. See, for example, Susan Krieger, "Beyond 'Subjectivity': The Use of the Self in Social Science," *Qualitative Sociology* 8 (1985): 309–24.

20. Jeff Ferrell and Clinton R. Sanders, eds., *Cultural Criminology* (Boston: Northeastern University Press, 1995); Jeff Ferrell, "Culture, Crime, and Cultural Criminology," *Journal of Criminal Justice and Popular Culture* 3 (1995): 25–42.

21. Paul Willis, *Learning to Labour* (New York: Columbia University Press, 1977), 3.

22. Jim Thomas, *Doing Critical Ethnography* (Newbury Park, Calif.: Sage, 1993), 10. See similarly James Diego Vigil and John M. Long, "Emic and Etic Perspectives on Gang Culture: The Chicano Case," in *Gangs in America*, ed. C. Ronald Huff (Newbury Park, Calif.: Sage, 1990), 57–58; John Van Maanen, "An End to Innocence: The Ethnography of Ethnography," in *Representation in Ethnography*, ed. John Van Maanen (Thousand Oaks, Calif.: Sage, 1995), 10.

23. On the foreground of criminality, see Jack Katz, *Seductions of Crime: Moral and Sensual Attractions in Doing Evil* (New York: Basic Books, 1988). On a "methodology of attentiveness," see Jeff Ferrell, "Urban Graffiti: Crime, Control, and Resistance," *Youth and Society* 27 (1995): 73–92. The following chapter in this volume also explores these issues more fully.

24. See Ferrell and Sanders, *Cultural Criminology*, 304–8, on linkages between cultural criminological perspectives and field research. See also the classic call to situated field research on crime and deviance in Howard S. Becker, *Outsiders: Studies in the Sociology of Deviance* (New York: Free Press, 1963), 165–76. More generally, see Jack D. Douglas, ed., *Research on Deviance* (New York: Random House, 1972), and especially Douglas's chapter "Observing Deviance" (pp. 3–34) in that volume; William B. Shaffir and Robert A. Stebbins, eds., *Experiencing Fieldwork: An Inside View of Qualitative Research* (Newbury Park, Calif.: Sage, 1991); Dick Hobbs and Tim May, *Interpreting the Field: Accounts of Ethnography* (Oxford: Clarendon Press, 1993).

25. Ned Polsky, *Hustlers, Beats, and Others* (Garden City, N.Y.: Anchor, 1969), 141. See also Richard Wright et al., "A Snowball's Chance in Hell: Doing Fieldwork with Active Residential Burglars," *Journal of Research in Crime and Delinquency* 29 (1992): 148–61.

26. Hagedorn, "Back in the Field," 244. Hagedorn adds: "In the final analysis, courthouse criminology and surrogate sociology give us questionable data. They are methods best suited to reinforcing the outlook of law enforcement and community agency bureaucrats" (250).

27. Polsky, *Hustlers*, 135–36. Emphasis in original. See the following chapter in this volume for more on these issues.

28. For more on critical anarchist criminology, see, for example, Ferrell, *Crimes of Style;* Jeff Ferrell, "Anarchism and Justice," in *Justice at the Margins,* ed. Bruce Arrigo (Belmont, Calif.: Wadsworth, forthcoming); Jeff Ferrell, "Against the Law: Anarchist Criminology," in *Thinking Critically About Crime,* ed. Brian MacLean and Dragan Milovanovic (Vancouver: Collective Press, 1997), 146–54; Jeff Ferrell, "Confronting the Agenda of Authority: Critical Criminology, Anarchism, and Urban Graffiti," in *Varieties of Criminology,* ed. Gregg Barak (New York: Praeger, 1994), 161–78.

29. Thomas, *Doing Critical Ethnography.*

30. Terry Williams, Eloise Dunlap, Bruce D. Johnson, and Ansley Hamid, "Personal Safety in Dangerous Places," *Journal of Contemporary Ethnography* 21 (1992): 348–50.

31. Michel Foucault, *The History of Sexuality, Volume 1: An Introduction* (New York: Vintage, 1990), 58.

32. Van Maanen, "An End to Innocence."

33. As Van Maanen points out, "Although often set apart from an ethnographer's realist accounts, confessional ethnography may nonetheless convey a good deal of the same sort of cultural information and speculation put forth in conventional realist work but in a more personalized and historically-situated fashion" ("An End to Innocence," 9). See also Kathleen Slobin, "Fieldwork and Subjectivity: On the Ritualization of Seeing a Burned Child," *Symbolic Interaction* 18 (1995): 487–504.

34. Becker, *Outsiders*, 183, 199.

35. In this context, Thomas notes that "the ethnographic experience can be seen as the exploration of a common, meaningful cultural world conducted by drawing on intuitive styles of feelings, perception, and guesswork. From these collective meanings we begin to create an understanding for the culture from the point of view of the other" (*Doing Critical Ethnography*, 15). Similar orientations are captured in Vigil and Long's notion of "emic understanding" as "empathic understanding of a way of life . . . from the viewpoint of the participants in that culture" ("Emic and Etic," 57), and Rochford's sense of the "subjectively meaningful world of members," in E. B. Rochford, Jr., *Hare Krishna in America* (New Brunswick, N.J.: Rutgers University Press, 1985), 41. See also Lee's discussion of subjective understanding in research on "unloved groups" and on groups caught up in violence, conflict, and danger, in Lee, *Dangerous Fieldwork*, 14–39; and Bruce DiCristina, *Method in Criminology: A Philosophical Primer* (New York: Harrow and Heston, 1995), 34–36. Adler and Adler note in this context that "our goal should be the integration and full use of ourselves as, simultaneously, complex human beings with unique individual biographies and trained and dedicated researchers" (Adler and Adler, *Membership Roles*, 86). See also broader discussions of these issues in the following chapter.

36. Adler and Adler, *Membership Roles*, 86, emphasis in original.

37. Nancy Scheper-Hughes, "Embodied Knowledge: Thinking with the Body in Critical Medical Anthropology," in *Assessing Cultural Anthropology*, ed. Robert Borofsky (New York: McGraw Hill, 1994), 229–42. As Scheper-Hughes says, much contemporary research is "theoretically driven by a concern with the overlapping domains of body, self, emotion, reflexivity, and resistance" (229). See also Slobin, "Fieldwork and Subjectivity."

38. Thompson, *Hell's Angels*, 345. For more on these issues, see Stephen Lyng's chapter in this volume.

39. See Stephen Lyng's chapter in this volume for more on the politics and methodology of ineffability.

40. See Van Maanen, "An End to Innocence"; Gary Allen Fine, "Ten Lies of Ethnography: Moral Dilemmas in Field Research," *Journal of Contemporary Ethnogra-*

phy 22 (1993): 267–94; James Clifford and George E. Marcus, eds., *Writing Culture: The Poetics and Politics of Ethnography* (Berkeley: University of California Press, 1986).

41. In prologue to his magnificent, attentive ethnography of southern share-croppers, James Agee allows that the book is meant to be "exhaustive, with no detail, however trivial it may seem, left untouched, no relevancy avoided, which lies within the power of remembrance to maintain, of the intelligence to perceive, and of the spirit to persist in." In the next breath, though, he warns that the book is "intended, among other things, as a swindle, an insult, and a corrective . . ." (Agee and Walker Evans, *Let Us Now Praise Famous Men* [New York: Ballantine, 1960], xiv–xv). This is the tension that animates this volume as well. Those who wish this tension resolved might do well to stay inside the prophylactic safety of "social science."

Criminological Verstehen Inside the Immediacy of Crime

Jeff Ferrell

Among the many methodological approaches that enrich criminology and sociology, one approach — direct field research inside the worlds of criminal life and criminal action — offers a particularly potent mix of problems and potential. In this chapter I explore the vivid and often dangerous dynamics of criminological field research. Specifically, I argue that the risky dynamics of field research offer criminologists not only access to criminals and criminal groups, but perhaps more importantly, an opportunity for partial immersion in the situated logic and emotion which define criminal experience. Moreover, while I focus on field research inside criminal worlds and illegal settings, I suggest that such field research immersion can provide equally important insights into the experiences of crime victims, crime control agents, and others. Put simply, I propose that experiential immersion on the part of field researchers can begin to unravel the lived meanings of both crime and criminal justice.

Such a methodological orientation embodies a troubling tangle of ethical contradictions and legal ambiguities. Researchers who pursue a strategy of deep engagement with criminal worlds (or even criminal justice worlds) must be prepared to face numerous personal and professional risks, to confront and acknowledge the human consequences of their research, and to make difficult decisions about personal and professional responsibility. Recent reconsiderations of research and researchers' roles, however, emphasize that such difficulties need not disqualify this or other methods from use; instead, they can provide important opportunities for investigating both the nature of scholarly inquiry and the nuances of the research subject. An excerpt from my own research can perhaps best introduce the odd mix of ethics and inquiry that informs a field researcher's immersion in the experience of criminality.

A Report from Inside the Immediacy of Crime

On a late August night, I head out—as I have done many times be-fore—for a night of wandering, drinking, and painting with members of the local hip hop graffiti underground. By this time I have engaged in al-most two years of intensive participant observation inside this under-ground—that is, inside the world of nongang graffiti "writers" who, drawing on the hip hop graffiti conventions first developed in New York City in the 1970s, organize themselves and their activities around illicit public displays of alternative artistry and style. Though my research fo-cuses on the subcultural dynamics that drive the underground, it also ex-plores the increasing criminalization of these writers and their activities under a legal/political campaign against graffiti begun in this city some years before. Given both my acceptance into the underground and my awareness of the aggressive legal measures directed against it, I have de-cided long before this night that, should I encounter police officers, gang members, or others, I will try not to hide behind the cloak of researcher or scholar, but rather participate as fully as possible in these risky social processes.

Since I am going out with one of the most acclaimed "kings" of the local scene—Eye Six, a talented artist known both in the graffiti under-ground for his brilliant murals and in the legitimate alternative art world for his innovative gallery shows—the night holds great promise. But it holds great danger as well. Many of the more experienced members of Syndicate, the graffiti "crew" to which Eye Six belongs, cannot go along this night; among the missing is another "king," Rasta 68, who often functions on outings as an important organizer, guide, and lookout. In their place we are accompanied by Toon, Frost, and other "toy" writers— young writers whose artistic inexperience is matched, we fear, by an un-bridled enthusiasm and relatively undeveloped street sense that may well draw unwanted attention. Moreover, we have decided to paint in the old lower downtown railyards, a popular graffiti setting and a place of dark-ness, automotive inaccessibility, and thus relative safety. On our way, though, plans change (as they regularly do in the underground), and we land in an old warehouse district on the edge of the yards—a district with brighter lights, better roads, and a larger population of street gang mem-bers. By this time I have been in the underground long enough to know the informal rules and street-level safeguards—but also to know how often these are broken in the haphazard contingencies of late-night adventure.

Settling into a narrow, half-lit alley between rows of warehouses, Eye Six and I begin the lengthy process of "piecing"—that is, of painting a large, graffiti-style mural. Having brought along the usual supply of "forties" (forty-ounce bottles of malt liquor), "shooters" (small bottles of Jack Daniel's and Yukon Jack), cigarettes, and Krylon spray paint, we and the other writers anticipate a long night in the alley. As the hours pass, the other writers tire of making minor contributions to the mural, or keeping watch. They begin to wander the alley, climb fences, "tag" (write their underground nicknames on walls and fences), and in general create a bit too much noise and movement. Eye Six and I remain busy with the piece; a vague commentary on a nearby nuclear weapons facility or, perhaps more broadly, on the aesthetics of modern science, it features hooded laboratory workers and stenciled images of gaseous bubbles. In these hours of piecing, we share not only work on the mural, but also an experience about which graffiti writers regularly talk: the tense excitement, the dangerous, almost intoxicating pleasure, of artistic production interwoven with illegality and adventure.

By 3:00 or 4:00 A.M., we are almost out of malt liquor, paint, and energy. Though the piece is not quite finished—Eye Six tags "6 B Back" on it to indicate its incompletion—we pack to leave. Suddenly, two cars round the corner into the alley a block and a half away and accelerate toward us at high speed. Having dealt with police officers, security guards, huffers (paint sniffers), and various street toughs on previous late-night graffiti excursions, I am overcome not only by a remarkably powerful rush of adrenalin and fear, but also by an awful uncertainty: Are these gangsters or police?

In any case, the other writers and I run for it. Eye Six and Frost stumble and fall, dive under a nearby loading dock, and thereby escape. I run out of the alley and down the street, intending to turn toward the dark salvation of the railyards, which lie only a couple of blocks to my left. A high fence blocks my way, though, and, as I continue down the street, I hear a high-performance engine closing on me, and at that moment I decide that it must be the police behind me. In the next instant, I am pinned against the fence by a policeman whose partner has caught up with Toon nearby. There follow a barrage of questions about my accomplices (which

I decline to answer), a seemingly endless string of derogations about the sort of university professor who would vandalize private property, threats of jailing, photographs of me and Toon, and finally a summons and complaint ordering me to court on charges of "destruction of private property." The police report notes that the "suspect had paint on hands matching colors on mural." It also includes — as I knew it would from my previous research — a special notation alerting the district attorney and judge that this is not a generic case of private property destruction, but rather the sort of "graffiti vandalism" case that the city now targets.

A month later, I appear in court. Engaging in the usual rituals of pretrial negotiation, my attorney meets with an assistant district attorney to work out a deal. He reports to me, however, that the assistant D.A. isn't willing to deal much on this case; the best he can get for me is a deferred judgment and sentence, dismissible on completion of one year's probation and payment of court costs. Though others in court that day seem to be negotiating less-stringent resolutions to domestic violence cases and other criminal situations, I agree, and enter the courtroom. But as the judge is reading the judgment, he pauses, threatening to reject the plea bargain unless arrangements have been made to remove this "graffiti vandalism." "Your honor," replies my lawyer, "we have no evidence that the property owner *wants* the mural removed." And, indeed, years later, the mural remains.

Some could surely argue that this incident exposes the thoroughly unprofessional nature of my criminological research, not to mention the dangers, to use the unfortunate phrase, of "going native." Others might argue that it transforms my status irrevocably from criminologist to criminal, and certainly I could have been charged that night with resisting arrest, public drunkenness, and contributing to the delinquency of a minor, along with destruction of private property. In another sense, though, the incident locates this sort of research alongside many of the fundamental works in criminology — due precisely (and only) to the research's odd interweaving of criminology and criminality.

For if we look again at Becker's field research among marijuana-smoking jazz musicians, Polsky's field experiences with hustlers and gangsters, Humphreys's work with the gay clientele of public bathrooms, Adler's participant observation with upper-level drug users and dealers, Padilla's field research with gangs and gang drug dealers, Wright and Decker's street-level work with residential burglars, and countless other cases of criminological field research, we realize that many of criminology's respected figures could well be considered a rogues' gallery of common criminals.[1] Whether through direct participation in illegal activities, the witnessing of criminal behavior, or simply the sort of "dirty knowledge" that constructs them as accomplices or accessories to crime, criminological field researchers have regularly crossed the lines of legality in developing important and influential accounts of crime and criminality. Put another way, criminology has consistently been enriched not only by case-study method and qualitative field research, but by case and field studies directly entangled in the experience of criminality and illegality.[2] In this light, the many past and present cases of engaged and illegal field research raise for criminology narrow issues of an individual's professionalism or propensity for illegality, but also broader issues concerning methodology, morality, and criminological insight.

A Methodological Framework

By first engaging in illegal field research, and then openly "confessing" this research strategy and my role in it, I situate myself and my research within established traditions of criminological fieldwork, but also within newer reconceptualizations of research methodology and scholarship. My research and this reporting of it take shape within recent feminist, postmodernist, and existentialist reconsiderations of research, and the role of the researcher, in criminology and elsewhere.[3] These perspectives emphasize the necessity of interpretive, ethnographic methods — methods that can help us "understand crime at close range," and thus "reveal parts of the social world that remain hidden by more traditional techniques."[4] Such perspectives further insist that these ethnographic methods are, and must remain, inherently personal, political, and partial endeavors. In so doing, they reintroduce the humanity of the researcher into the research process and make a case for critical, reflexive, autobiographical accounts and understandings — for "profound self-disclosures" and openness to the "subjective experience of doing research" — as part of the field research process.[5] They thus call for "true confessions" — that is, accounts of field research that in fact undermine absolutist notions of scholarly truth by incorporating situationally truthful representations of field researchers' lived and limiting experiences.[6]

These perspectives further emphasize that methodologies inevitably intertwine with theoretical stances, political choices, and the social situations in which they are practiced. Given this intertwining, criminological (and other) field researchers cannot conveniently distance themselves from their subjects of study, or from the legally uncertain situations in which the subjects may reside, in order to construct safe and "objective" studies of them. Instead, criminological field research unavoidably entangles those who practice it in complex and ambiguous relations to subjects and situations of study, to issues of personal and social responsibility, and to law and legality. This approach to research methodology thus serves as both a report and a manifesto, as evidence and argument that conventional canons of objectivity and validity are not, and indeed cannot be, followed in the everyday practice of criminological field research.[7] It also points to a situated, reflexive sociology of criminological field research—an accounting of the collective experiences, social relations, and webs of politics and power within which criminological field research unfolds.

A research agenda of engagement with subjects of study, a methodology that moves beyond objectivity to immersion in the actualities of daily criminality, forces, of course, new understandings not only of research methods, but of research morality as well. From inside a tradition of objectivity and scientific detachment, the lines of legality and illegality, of morality and immorality in research, may seem straight and clean. But as many criminologists know, these lines quickly become tangled and uncertain in the field—inside the lives of graffiti writers, gang members, drug users, or professional thieves. These newer perspectives on criminological research are distinguished from older ones in part by a willingness to acknowledge this moral and legal uncertainty—a willingness to abandon the myth of objectivist detachment, and instead to "confess" the inherently ambiguous morality and shady legality of criminological field research.[8]

As we step out from behind the facade of objectivity, we thus gain fresh insights into field research projects involved with illegality and crime. Objectivist perspectives would characterize illegality in field research as, at best, an unfortunate methodological side effect, and as, at worst, a personal and professional failure; in this new perspective, illegality can be more openly explored for its methodological potential. In the same way, a researcher's strict conformity to legal codes can be reconceptualized less as a sign of professional success than as a possible portent of methodological failure. For while close adherence to legality on the part of the field researcher doubtless shuts the researcher off from all manner of field contacts and social situations—and perhaps relegates the researcher to the role of "jailhouse or courthouse sociologist"[9]—a willingness to break the law may open a variety of methodological possibilities. To put it bluntly: For the dedicated field researcher who seeks to explore criminal subcultures and criminal dynamics, obeying the law may present as much of a problem as breaking it.

If, as already argued, these new perspectives on research are characterized by a more open and honest stance, we should also be honest about their potentially negative consequences. Within older scientific and objectivist models, the sorts of openly illegal approaches discussed here would likely have constituted professional suicide. They still may. A researcher who engages in illegal fieldwork may of course face jail time, court costs, betrayal of or by subcultural accomplices, and censure by colleagues. Moreover, any openly illegal research may generate negative public perceptions of the individual researcher and, more important, may produce the sort of negative media coverage and public imagery that contribute to broader contemporary attacks on the credibility and legitimacy of academic scholarship. Criminologists who consider this methodological path must also consider carefully which sorts of criminality are appropriate or inappropriate for study. In addition, they must weigh carefully their responsibilities to those criminals, crime control agents, and crime victims affected by their research, and they must anticipate for themselves a variety of personal, professional, and disciplinary consequences.[10]

Criminological Field Research and Criminological _Verstehen_

Despite the potential costs, participatory criminological field research is worth considering as a methodological strategy not only for broad reasons of subcultural access or experience, but also because of a distinctive methodological and epistemic issue—an issue that returns us to the alley and the criminal event in which I was caught. This is the notion of criminological *verstehen*.[11] As formulated by Max Weber and developed by later theorists, *verstehen* denotes a process of subjective interpretation on the part of the social researcher, a degree of sympathetic understanding between social researcher and subjects of study, whereby the researcher comes to share, in part, the situated meanings and experiences of those under scrutiny.[12] As Weber argues, within a sociology that "concern[s] itself with the interpretive understanding of social action . . . empathic or appreciative accuracy is attained when, through sympathetic participation, we can adequately grasp the emotional context in which the action took place."[13]

For Weber, this empathic understanding constituted a component in a larger science of sociology and was balanced with various rational understandings of social action and social meaning.[14] In the context of contemporary criminological field research, and within the emerging methodological orientations just considered, the concept of *verstehen* can be defined somewhat more narrowly and more modestly: as a situated strategy within the always partial and imperfect process of research into criminality. As utilized here, then, criminological *verstehen* denotes a researcher's subjective understanding of crime's situational meanings and emotions—its moments of pleasure and pain, its emergent logic and excitement—within the larger process of research. It further implies that a researcher, through attentiveness and participation, can at least begin to apprehend and appreciate the specific roles and experiences of criminals, crime victims, crime control agents, and others caught up in the day-to-day reality of crime.

The methodological utility and theoretical importance of criminological *verstehen* in turn hinge on a particular etiology of crime—an etiology that locates the origins and meaning of crime largely inside the criminal event.[15] An understanding of crime and criminality as constructed out of the immediate interactions of criminals, control agents, victims, and others, and therefore as emerging out of a tangled experiential web of situated dangers and situated pleasures, certainly refocuses theories of criminal causality on the criminal moment. It produces a second, methodological understanding as well: that criminologists must situate themselves as close to the (inter)action as possible—perhaps even inside the interaction—if they are to catch the constructed reality of crime.[16]

This etiology thus implies that criminologists will need the sorts of grounded ethnographic methods already discussed, a broad "methodology of attentiveness," in place of safely distanced survey research or statistical analysis.[17] It suggests that criminologists must develop a certain intimacy with illegality, a criminological *verstehen* through which they can begin in part to feel and understand the situated logic and emotion of crime. It means that criminologists, as best they can within limits of personal responsibility and professional identity, must be there in the criminal moment—in the dark alley described earlier and in many other situations as well—if they are to apprehend the terrors and pleasures of criminality. It means that criminologists must venture inside the immediacy of crime.

A variety of research findings and theoretical trajectories confirm the importance of situated criminal meanings and experiences, and thus the need for a criminological *verstehen* that can begin to explore them. Katz has broadly considered the "foreground" of criminality, the immediate, interactional interplay through which a criminal event takes shape, and specifically the "magical" excitement of shoplifting and other crimes.[18] As implied by my adventure in the alley and confirmed in a multitude of other research moments under bridges and down back alleys, my own work has likewise shown that graffiti writers piece and tag largely because of what they call the "adrenalin rush." Experienced and described by writers time and again, in graffiti undergrounds from Los Angeles to Berlin, this rush is an immediate, incandescent "high" that results from the execution of long-practiced art in dangerously illegal situations.[19] Lyng has similarly documented the experience of "edgework"—the exhilarating, momentary integration of danger, risk, and skill—that drives a variety of deviant, criminal, and noncriminal experiences.[20] Relatedly, Nehring has described the "outlaw emotions" that define both moments of cognitive insubordination and various deviant or insurgent subcultures.[21]

Other researchers—especially those investigating the day-to-day dynamics of juvenile delinquency and delinquent subcultures—have uncovered similar patterns. Miller's influential work listed "excitement"— that is, "sought situations of great emotional stimulation . . . the search for excitement or 'thrill' . . . sought risk and desired danger"—among the "focal concerns of lower class culture" that could precipitate gang delinquency.[22] In his study of British working-class delinquency, Willis found delinquency and youthful resistance to adult authority to be grounded in daily pleasure and experience; as one of his respondents reported in distancing himself from a less delinquent boy: "We've been through all life's pleasures and all its fucking displeasures . . . frustration, sex, fucking hatred, love and all this lark, yet he's known none of it. . . . He's not known so many of the emotions as we've had to experience. . . ."[23] Hamm describes the "emotional capacity" that neo-Nazi skinheads collectively develop as part of "going berserk" episodes aimed at outsiders; Vigil and others likewise note the collective emotion and experience developed by Latino gang members in "going crazy" (*loco, locura*) against rival gangs and others.[24] As Presdee reports, nongang delinquents also revel in the intense pleasure and excitement that accompany their participation in seemingly mundane forms of criminality such as "stealing objects" and "stealing travel."[25] Even some of the adult property criminals whom Tunnell studied, though operating within a rationalized "criminal calculus," report that stealing is "a high, now, I mean it's exhilarating. . . . I get off going through doors."[26] Similarly, Wright and Decker, in a reprise of Lofland's findings, report that many burglars are "committed to a lifestyle characterized by the quest for excitement and an openness to 'illicit action,'" and that some go so far as to burglarize occupied homes in order to make "the offense more exciting."[27]

Taken together, these criminological findings begin to address Riemer's concern about traditional conceptualizations of deviance: that deviance has "rarely . . . been considered a spontaneous, 'just for the hell of it' activity, in which the participants engage simply for the pleasure it provides."[28] And as O'Malley and Mugford argue, even where pleasure has been considered, it "has appeared in traditional criminologies as a more or less 'obvious' explanatory variable . . . the category and experience of pleasure . . . appeared to need no investigation."[29] Echoing Foucault's groundbreaking investigations of pleasure and its political frameworks, his demonstration that "power is in our bodies, not in our heads," these research findings in criminal and delinquent worlds demonstrate the importance of paying close attention to the situated sensuality, the definitive dangers and pleasures, of crime.[30] Together these perspectives demonstrate that if we are to make sense of any number of deviant and criminal experiences, we must understand them to be, in Weber's terms, "affectually determined" and must therefore find ways to partake in part of the immediate emotions and perceptions that define them.[31] We must develop a criminological *verstehen* that can begin to take us inside the many specific moments of illegality. This methodological stance in turn implies not only that criminologists must be present in criminal (and criminalized) subcultures and situations, but also that they must be present *affectively;* that is, they must share, to whatever extent possible, in the dangers, pleasures, emotions, and experiences that constitute criminal activity as part of their understanding of it.

In this sense, the notion of criminological *verstehen* employed here necessitates, along with a grounded methodology that transcends objectivity and distance, new epistemic frameworks that transcend the rationalist assumptions embedded in traditional objectivist methods. Given the sense of sympathetic understanding incorporated in the notion of *verstehen,* making sense of immediate criminal experiences means not just "understanding" them by locating them within exterior intellectual or analytic models, but appreciating the specific sorts of situated logic and emotion that emerge within them.[32] Moreover, and perhaps most radically, criminological *verstehen* implies a certain emotional empathy, a notion that pleasure, excitement, and fear can teach us as much about criminality as can abstract analysis.[33] It embodies a sense that adrenalin rushes and outlaw emotions matter to criminals and criminologists alike, that our understanding of criminal experiences may come to us as researchers as much in the pits of our stomachs, in cold sweats and frightened shivers, as in our heads.[34]

Given this talk of shivers, sweats, and emotions, it is worth noting that the subject of study remains social, and that the method of criminological *verstehen* remains sociological. The sorts of edgework and adrenalin-rush experiences that define joyriding, drug taking, shoplifting, graffiti writing, and gangbanging are to large degree constructed collectively, out of the common experiences of subcultural participants and out of the shared cultural codes of criminal groups.[35] Their meaning is likewise constructed linguistically, as graffiti writers or gangbangers give shape to their experiences by encasing them in the collectively meaningful argot of the subculture. Following Mills and Cressey, what might first appear as isolated, individual, or impulsive experiences thus reflect a shared "vocabulary of motive," a repertoire of meanings common to those involved in them.[36] Because of this, the practice of criminological *verstehen* does not require that criminologists somehow mystically penetrate the heart or mind of the criminal, but rather that they engage in sociological research—that they participate in the collective experiences, emotions, and meanings of those they study.

Yet, even as the collective construction of criminal pleasure and excitement opens these experiences to a method such as criminological *verstehen,* it closes them to some degree as well. To begin with, different criminologists occupy different positions within structures of social class, gender, age, and ethnicity, and often they occupy distinctly different positions in these structures than those they seek to study. Because of these differences in identity, some criminologists who pursue membership and participation in a criminal subculture may not succeed; and even those who do can never succeed more than partially, no matter how attentively they go about the process. To the extent that membership in the subculture shapes the collective experience of criminal pleasure and excitement, then, the criminologist's ability to achieve criminological *verstehen* is limited at best, even where she or he encounters the same situations as others. And thus, given that the meaning and appeal of these criminal experiences reflect not only subcultural dynamics, but larger structures and one's location within them, a criminologist who partakes in criminal events may neither fully experience nor fully understand the seductions that others leading different lives find there.

Moreover, the very nature of these collective experiences as dangerously illegal events further limits the criminologist's participation in them. Activities such as graffiti writing, illegal cruising, motorcycle gang "runs," and even drug and alcohol use may lend themselves to some degree of direct participation by certain criminologists, and thus to some degree of direct criminological *verstehen.* Other activities which a criminological researcher judges to incorporate intolerable degrees of threat, violence, or moral danger—or which simply stay closed to the researcher because of differences in age, gender, ethnicity, or social class—may be accessible only through intensive interviewing and other techniques that can perhaps to some degree imaginatively reconstruct the experience of criminological *verstehen.* As before, the very strength of criminological *verstehen*—its volatile mix of insight and immersion—demands caution in its application.[37]

Even as an inherently dangerous and imperfect method, though, criminological *verstehen* remains an important component of research. If we understand that many forms of criminality are grounded in the immediate experiences of excitement, pleasure, and fear, we must also imagine methods that can explore these experiences. In discussing his research on skydiving as edgework, Lyng notes that "many edgework enthusiasts regard the experience as ineffable" and adds: "[T]he data collected in my study of the skydiving group were not easily acquired. In the early stages of the study, I was constantly frustrated in my attempt to get sky divers to talk about the jump experience. The typical response to my probing questions was, 'If you want to know what it's like, then do it!' It was only after the respondents became convinced that I shared their commitment to edgework that they were willing to try to articulate their feelings about the experience."[38] My ethnographic research into urban graffiti writing followed a similar pattern. I gained entry into the subculture of graffiti writers through a series of informal tests of my willingness to participate in the dangerous pleasures and excitement of graffiti writing: all-night wandering, social drinking, illegal painting, and (mostly successful) strategies for the avoidance of legal authority. My participation in these activities, in turn, created a level of collective trust and experiential camaraderie essential to intensive interviewing and other aspects of long-term criminological fieldwork. Here, then, we see the necessity of criminological *verstehen* inside particular research situations, and also the positive secondary effects of shared or sympathetic understanding in opening other avenues of grounded research into crime and criminality.

Finally, the concept of criminological *verstehen* as an essential component in criminological fieldwork returns us to the particular dangers faced not only by criminals (and their victims), but also by those who conduct this sort of research with them. Indeed, criminological *verstehen* constitutes in a sense the researcher's deepest sort of submersion in the dangers of criminality, a submersion that takes the researcher both inside the setting and inside the emotions and experiences that animate it. Moreover, a field researcher immersed in adrenalin rushes or edgework may well be immersed at the same time in a net of police surveillance or may face arrest by legal authorities for whom this sort of research, quite understandably, constitutes a simple case of criminal misconduct — or worse, a clear case of sympathy for the devil. Even a criminological field researcher who attempts to stay somehow inside the boundaries of legality, or who chooses to conduct research not with criminals but with criminal justice practitioners, may risk later redefinition by crime control agents or others as a criminal accomplice or accessory.[39]

And it is here that we encounter an essential issue in criminological field research and criminological *verstehen*. As all criminologists know, criminality is decided as much by legal and political authorities and by their strategies of criminalization, enforcement, and control as it is by criminals themselves. Given this fact, the nature and limits of criminological field research and criminological *verstehen* are determined in part by the field researcher and those under study, but also by legal and political decision makers, shifting and selective law enforcement and prosecution, and the broader political climate of crime control. To engage in (potentially) illegal field research, to pursue the insights afforded by criminological *verstehen,* is therefore to engage a larger set of moral issues and political dynamics and to confront one's own theoretical and political responses to them.

In this sense, a field researcher's participation in illegal activities and criminological *verstehen* dramatically resurrects the question posed by Becker in the sociology and criminology of the 1960s: Whose side are we on?[40] Within the lived dynamics of criminological research situations, as Polsky and others have shown, neutrality is seldom an option.[41] Where conflict between legal authorities and criminals not only predates the researcher's participation, but pervades the situations and decisions within which the researcher operates, there is little chance of having it both ways, of working honestly, openly, and empathically with both criminals and legal control agents. By the design of the fieldwork, the dynamics of its evolution, and the demands of its shared experiences and emotions, researchers must time and again align themselves more with one group than with the other, and then must live out, at least temporarily, a decision as to whose side they are on.

Field research that stretches or breaks conventional boundaries of legality or morality thus calls into play, along with important methodological issues, essential theoretical and political affiliations of the researcher.

To the extent that a criminological researcher understands the law to be a relatively fair and just representation of social concerns and shared values, violation of the law or empathic participation with criminals in the course of research may constitute an inexcusable breach of professional ethics, and of the larger social contract of which the researcher is a part. To the extent, though, that the researcher works from within the fundamental assumption of a more critical criminology—that the law in part reflects, incorporates, and perpetuates social privilege and social injustice—such field research may still pose professional problems, but will hardly present itself as a desecration of the social contract. Indeed, such research may instead take on positive theoretical and political connotations that mirror its methodological possibilities, and that come to serve as a lived affirmation of the researcher's theoretical and political convictions. Whatever a researcher's affiliations, though, criminological field research and criminological *verstehen* constitute profound, if impermanent, processes of confrontation both with criminality and with a researcher's own criminological orientations. And whatever a researcher's affiliations, these methodologies appear to hold promise and danger both in the sorts of situations just described, and in a variety of emerging contexts as well.

The Future of Criminological Field Research and Criminological Verstehen

The always changing contours of law, enforcement, and public debate around crime and justice continually reshape the methodological and political contours of criminological field research and criminological *verstehen.* As moral entrepreneurs and political leaders work to criminalize new areas of social and cultural life, as crime is portrayed as a pervasive problem and crime control constructed as social salvation in the contemporary political climate, criminologists of all sorts face a double set of consequences.[42] These changing circumstances certainly guarantee an ever-expanding domain of criminological inquiry, with each newly criminalized identity or situation, each new crime control controversy, offering fresh opportunities for research. Yet, they also promise more and more research situations in which field researchers may find themselves crossing over into illegality and perhaps also into public excoriation by concerned criminal justice officials, outraged moral entrepreneurs, or others.

Field researchers who run back alleys with graffiti writers, loiter with gay men in Humphreys's public tearooms, or hang with heroin users in backlot shooting galleries have traditionally been at risk.[43] But as other social situations and cultural activities are criminalized, so, potentially, is field research on them. As young people's everyday (and every-night) activities come under the purview of expanded curfews, anti-cruising laws, and other anti-delinquency measures, for example, those who would conduct field research with young offenders increasingly risk charges or accusations of contributing to youthful delinquency.[44] As new legal regulations of urban space and urban life increasingly criminalize the lives and actions of homeless people and dislocated urban populations, field researchers engaged in participant observation with them face more and more situations in which their own activities may also be construed as violating numerous new or newly enforced ordinances relating to vagrancy, loitering, curfew, trespass, panhandling, public lodging, and public nuisance.[45] As anti-immigrant policies fuel harsher controls on undocumented workers at the U.S. border and elsewhere, those conducting research among them may increasingly face charges of harboring fugitives, abetting escape, or encouraging illegal immigration.[46]

While these and other contemporary trends point to the increasing likelihood and necessity of conducting illegal criminological field research, they also point to new efflorescences of criminal danger, excitement, and pleasure, and thus to new occasions for criminological *verstehen.* Lyng, for example, locates the drive toward the voluntary risk taking of legal and illegal edgework within a "social system associated with class conflict, alienation, and the consumption imperative" and within "conditions of trivialized, degraded labor."[47] Under such general conditions, the development and application of precise survival skills in edgework situations generate for those involved the sorts of purposeful meanings and grounded identities unavailable in everyday life and work. Similarly, the "adrenalin rush" of graffiti writing results from the pleasures of practiced artistry, as amplified within the dangerous illegality of the act. For graffiti writers, as for other edgeworkers, the excitement of the act provides immediate gratification, but also a framework for inventing an identity, a sense of crafted self, that resides to some degree outside the usual limits of youthful status degradation, low-end wage work, and enforced legality.[48] The combination of two contemporary trends—the growth of marginalized, low-status work, especially among the young, and the increasing push toward punitive crime control policies — suggests, then, that the appeal of criminal pleasure and excitement can only increase. The spreading disintegration of the work process, the growing confinement of kids and adults in fractured and relatively meaningless situations of work (when they can find work at all), will surely continue to heighten the seduction of edgework and adrenalin-rush experiences as moments of cleansing terror and desperate rehumanization. The growing criminalization of social and cultural life, especially among young people, ethnic minorities, and the poor, will of course further close off avenues of legitimacy, construct more opportunities for criminal edgework and adrenalin, and in turn amplify and enhance the edgy pleasure and excitement that these experiences contain. As criminologists, we can anticipate more situations of illegal field research and more situations in which criminological *verstehen* will be needed as an avenue inside the dangers and pleasures which define them.

The changing and expanding dynamics of social, cultural, and criminal life thus demand that field researchers in all sorts of situations — even in those not traditionally thought of as criminal — remember Polsky's cautionary maxim: one had best consider the personal and professional limits of law, crime, and field method *before* beginning field research. "In field investigating, before you can tell a criminal who you are and make it stick, you have to know this yourself. . . . You need to decide beforehand, as much as possible, where you wish to draw the line. . . ."[49] More generally, the increased likelihood and necessity of conducting field research in criminalized contexts require that criminology as a discipline — as taught to students, discussed at conferences, and displayed to the public — incorporate an awareness and consideration of law, crime, and field research in its day-to-day operations. Most generally, these emerging issues suggest that we as criminologists may now want to begin considering other possible futures of criminological field research and criminological *verstehen*. What sort of field research, for example, would be appropriate if abortion were again made illegal? If gay and lesbian life were in effect outlawed, what would be the role of the field researcher immersed in the experiences and emotions of that life? If homeless and other inner-city populations continue to be marginalized and criminalized, where will we as criminologists draw the line between ethnography and activism, legality and illegality?[50]

Illegal criminological field research and criminological *verstehen,* then, would seem to be important methodological strategies not only in a variety of current situations, but also in research on various forms of criminality that may emerge out of developing social and political arrangements. Whatever the extent of these methodologies' wider applicability in the future, though, they would seem also to have a wider utility in the present than I have sketched so far. For an attentiveness to situated danger and excitement, in revealing something about contemporary criminality, also suggests insights into the broader relationships between crime, crime victimization, and criminal justice.

As a starting point, it seems likely that adrenalin and excitement, pleasure and fear animate not just the experiences of everyday criminals, but equally so the experiences of other everyday participants in crime, crime control, and criminal justice. Police officers involved in high-speed automobile pursuits, foot chases, or undercover/sting operations certainly experience—and to some degree savor—these situations as adrenalin-charged adventures, and in this sense they may find in their day-to-day lives the same sorts of hyped pleasures as do those they seek to control.[51] In the middle-of-the-night chase down a dark alley, a degree of tense excitement surely energized not only my experience, and that of the scattering graffiti writers, but the experience of the pursuing police officers as well. The often anxious and aggressive excitement of police work, as played out in day-to-day operations and reproduced within the language and values of police subcultures, may in turn help to explain the close social and emotional bonds that regularly develop among police officers. It may also help to explain the ferocity of certain encounters between police and citizens (who may well be caught up in their own swirls of excitement and fear) and to account for the sorts of situated dynamics that at times transform these encounters into eruptions of violence and brutalization.[52]

Similarly, victims of crime seem regularly to experience victimization not as a rationally calculable loss of property or safety, but as an overwhelming moment of terror and despair that haunts them long after property or safety is restored. Attention to the lived reality of crime victimization can thus lead us closer to a *verstehen*-oriented victimology, a sympathy and support grounded in interpretive understanding and shared experience. For the many criminologists who have been victimized by crime, an understanding of crime's costs can perhaps emerge as much from an examination of their own emotional experiences—and from a contextualization of these experiences within those of others—as from an objective examination of crime victims or crime-victimization rates. This understanding may in turn begin to explain the ease with which public hysteria over crime is constructed and to uncover the ways in which political leaders and others are able to anchor crime control policies not in rational evaluation but in experiential anxiety. Adrenalin and excitement, terror and pleasure seem to flow not just through the experience of criminality, then, but through the many capillaries connecting crime, crime victimization, and criminal justice. And as these terrors and pleasures circulate, they form an experiential and emotional current that illuminates the everyday meanings of crime and crime control.

Given this complex current, the methodological utility of criminological *verstehen* may well extend beyond the sorts of field research described here and into all sorts of criminological and criminal-justice research. If the experiences of criminals, crime victims, crime control agents, and others are shaped by terror, pleasure, and excitement—and shaped differently according to their location within networks of crime and criminal justice, and within larger structures of social class, gender, age, and ethnicity—researchers must work toward particular forms of criminological *verstehen* attuned to these differences. As part of a larger methodology of attentiveness and engagement, criminological *verstehen* can, at its best, take criminologists at least partially inside the tangle of lived situations which constitute crime and crime control. It can perhaps also begin to take criminologists inside the many meanings and emotions that emerge there and, finally, inside the immediacy of crime for all involved.

Notes

An earlier version of this chapter was published in the journal *Justice Quarterly* 14 (1) (1997), under the title "Criminological *Verstehen*: Inside the Immediacy of Crime." It is reprinted here by permission of the Academy of Criminal Justice Sciences.

1. Howard S. Becker, *Outsiders: Studies in the Sociology of Deviance* (New York: Free Press, 1963); Ned Polsky, *Hustlers, Beats, and Others* (Garden City, N.Y.: Anchor, 1969); Laud Humphreys, *Tearoom Trade: Impersonal Sex in Public Places,* enlarged ed. (New York: Aldine de Gruyter, 1975); Patricia A. Adler, *Wheeling and Dealing: An Ethnogra-*

phy of an Upper-Level Drug Dealing and Smuggling Community (New York: Columbia University Press, 1985); Felix Padilla, *The Gang as an American Enterprise* (New Brunswick, N.J.: Rutgers University Press, 1992); Richard T. Wright and Scott Decker, *Burglars on the Job: Streetlife and Residential Break-ins* (Boston: Northeastern University Press, 1994). Interestingly, Wright and Decker obtained a prior "agreement with the police that they would not interfere in our research" (28).

2. Adler, *Wheeling;* Gilbert Geis, "The Case Study Method in Sociological Criminology," in *A Case for the Case Study,* ed. Joe R. Feagin, Anthony M. Orum, and Gideon Sjoberg (Chapel Hill: University of North Carolina Press, 1991), 200–223; Polsky, *Hustlers.*

3. Patricia A. Adler and Peter Adler, *Membership Roles in Field Research* (Newbury Park, Calif.: Sage, 1987); Michael Burawoy et al., *Ethnography Unbound: Power and Resistance in the Modern Metropolis* (Berkeley: University of California Press, 1991); Susan Caulfield and Nancy Wonders, "Gender and Justice: Feminist Contributions to Criminology," in *Varieties of Criminology,* ed. Gregg Barak (Westport, Conn.: Praeger, 1994), 213–29; James Clifford and George E. Marcus, *Writing Culture: The Poetics and Politics of Ethnography* (Berkeley: University of California Press, 1986); Patricia Ticineto Clough, *The End(s) of Ethnography: From Realism to Social Criticism* (Newbury Park, Calif.: Sage, 1992); Kathleen Daly and Meda Chesney-Lind, "Feminism and Criminology," *Justice Quarterly* 5 (1988): 497–535; Gary Alan Fine, "Ten Lies of Ethnography: Moral Dilemmas of Field Research," *Journal of Contemporary Ethnography* 22 (1993): 267–94; Mary Margaret Fonow and Judith A. Cook, eds., *Beyond Methodology: Feminist Scholarship as Lived Research* (Bloomington: Indiana University Press, 1991); Loraine Gelsthorpe, "Feminist Methodologies in Criminology," in *Feminist Perspectives in Criminology,* ed. Loraine Gelsthorpe and Allison Morris (Milton Keynes, UK: Open University Press, 1990), 89–106; Clinton R. Sanders, "Stranger Than Fiction: Insights and Pitfalls in Post-Modern Ethnography," *Studies in Symbolic Interaction* 17 (1995): 89–104.

4. Daly and Chesney-Lind, "Feminism and Criminology," 517; Caulfield and Wonders, "Gender and Justice," 223.

5. Adler and Adler, *Membership Roles,* 86; Gelsthorpe, "Feminist Methodologies," 93; Adam Begley, "The I's Have It," *Lingua Franca* 4 (1994): 54–59.

6. Fine, "Ten Lies."

7. Howard S. Becker, "Whose Side Are We On?" *Social Problems* 14 (1967): 239–47.

8. See Sanders, "Stranger." These newer perspectives, then, not only privilege grounded field research over more abstract or objectivist methods, like survey research and statistical analysis, but also conceptualize fieldwork accounts as personal and incomplete representations rather than as objective or definitive reports.

9. Polsky, *Hustlers,* 141; see John Hagedorn, "Back in the Field Again: Gang Research in the Nineties," in *Gangs in America,* ed. C. Ronald Huff (Newbury Park, Calif.: Sage, 1990), 240–59.

10. Here we see the public and professional dangers of role confusion and status

inconsistency as described in various contexts by Adler and Adler, *Membership Roles;* Gary Marx, *Undercover: Police Surveillance in America* (Berkeley: University of California Press, 1988); and others.

11. Jeff Ferrell and Clinton R. Sanders, eds., *Cultural Criminology* (Boston: Northeastern University Press, 1995), 312–13; Mark Hamm and Jeff Ferrell, "Rap, Cops, and Crime: Clarifying the 'Cop Killer' Controversy," *ACJS Today* 13 (1994): 29.

12. Max Weber, *The Methodology of the Social Sciences* (New York: Free Press, 1949); Max Weber, *Economy and Society* (Berkeley: University of California Press, 1978); Adler and Adler, *Membership Roles,* 85–87; William Outhwaite, *Understanding Social Life: The Method Called Verstehen* (New York: Holmes and Meier, 1976); Marcello Truzzi, *Verstehen: Subjective Understanding in the Social Sciences* (Reading, Mass.: Addison-Wesley, 1974).

13. Weber, *Economy,* 4–5.

14. Weber, *Economy,* 3–24.

15. Jack Katz, *Seductions of Crime: Moral and Sensual Attractions in Doing Evil* (New York: Basic Books, 1988).

16. Jeff Ferrell, "Making Sense of Crime," *Social Justice* 19 (1992): 110–23; Jeff Ferrell, *Crimes of Style: Urban Graffiti and the Politics of Criminality* (Boston: Northeastern University Press, 1996).

17. Jeff Ferrell, "Urban Graffiti: Crime, Control, and Resistance," *Youth and Society* 27 (1995): 87.

18. Katz, *Seductions.* Alternatively, Bill McCarthy, "Not Just 'For the Thrill of It': An Instrumentalist Elaboration of Katz's Explanation of Sneaky Thrill Property Crimes," *Criminology* 33 (1995): 519–38, argues that a multitude of background factors impinge on the magically sensual foreground of "sneaky thrill property crimes" like shoplifting.

19. Ferrell, "Urban Graffiti"; Ferrell, *Crimes.*

20. Stephen Lyng, "Edgework: A Social Psychological Analysis of Voluntary Risk Taking," *American Journal of Sociology* 95 (1990): 851–86; Stephen Lyng and Mitchell L. Bracey, Jr., "Squaring the One-Percent: Biker Style and the Selling of Cultural Resistance," in *Cultural Criminology,* ed. Jeff Ferrell and Clinton R. Sanders (Boston: Northeastern University Press, 1995), 235–76.

21. Neil Nehring, *Flowers in the Dustbin: Culture, Anarchy, and Postwar England* (Ann Arbor: University of Michigan Press, 1993), 7.

22. Walter Miller, "Lower Class Culture as a Generating Milieu of Gang Delinquency," *Journal of Social Issues* 14 (1958): 5–19. As Lyng, "Edgework," notes, though, this embracing of danger and excitement may in fact not be confined to the lower class, but may be distributed throughout contemporary social systems.

23. Paul Willis, *Learning to Labour* (New York: Columbia University Press, 1977), 16.

24. Mark S. Hamm, *American Skinheads: The Criminology and Control of Hate Crime* (Westport, Conn.: Praeger, 1993); James Diego Vigil, *Barrio Gangs: Street Life and Identity in Southern California* (Austin: University of Texas Press, 1988); James Diego Vigil

and John M. Long, "Emic and Etic Perspectives on Gang Culture: The Chicano Case," in *Gangs in America,* ed. C. Ronald Huff (Newbury Park, Calif.: Sage, 1990), 55-68.

25. Mike Presdee, "Young People, Culture, and the Construction of Crime: Doing Wrong versus Doing Crime," in *Varieties of Criminology,* ed. Gregg Barak (Westport, Conn.: Praeger, 1994), 179-87.

26. Kenneth Tunnell, *Choosing Crime: The Criminal Calculus of Property Offenders* (Chicago: Nelson-Hall, 1992), 45.

27. Wright and Decker, *Burglars,* 117; John Lofland, *Deviance and Identity* (Englewood Cliffs, N.J.: Prentice-Hall). Additionally, although the research findings reported here focus on the sorts of pleasures and excitement that construct the criminal experience, certainly other experiences and emotions—economic desperation, anger, revenge seeking, even compassion—drive other sorts of criminal events, and therefore merit investigation through criminological *verstehen* as well.

28. Jeffrey Riemer, "Deviance as Fun," *Adolescence* 16 (1981): 39.

29. Pat O'Malley and Stephen Mugford, "Crime, Excitement, and Modernity," in *Varieties of Criminology,* ed. Gregg Barak (Westport, Conn.: Praeger, 1994), 209.

30. Michel Foucault, *The Use of Pleasure* (New York: Pantheon, 1985); Michel Foucault, *The History of Sexuality, Volume 1: An Introduction* (New York: Vintage, 1990); Nancy Fraser, "Foucault on Modern Power," in *Social Control: Aspects of Non-State Justice,* ed. Stuart Henry (Aldershot, UK: Dartmouth), 11.

31. Weber, *Economy,* 9.

32. Katz, *Seductions;* Weber, *Economy,* 7.

33. Fonow and Cook, *Beyond Methodology,* 9-11.

34. As Adler and Adler, *Membership Roles,* note in reference to "existential sociology": "[I]ts proponents believe that people have strong elements of emotionality and irrationality, and often act on the basis of their situated feelings or moods. . . . This view of society has profound ramifications for existentialists' methodology. The only way to penetrate people's individual and group fronts is to become an insider, thereby gaining deep and direct personal experience in their worlds. Fieldworkers should . . . draw on their observations, experiences, and feelings as primary sources of data" (20-21). In these terms, what is being proposed here might thus be thought of as a sort of existential criminology.

35. Becker, *Outsiders;* Stephen Lyng and David Snow, "Vocabularies of Motive and High-Risk Behavior: The Case of Skydiving," in *Advances in Group Processes,* ed. E. J. Lawler (Greenwich, Conn.: JAI, 1986), 157-79.

36. C. Wright Mills, "Situated Actions and Vocabularies of Motive," *American Sociological Review* 5 (1940): 904-13; Donald Cressey, "The Differential Association Theory and Compulsive Crime," *Journal of Criminal Law and Criminology* 45 (1954): 49-64.

37. Instances of these sorts of issues played out in specific field research situations are reported by Adler, *Wheeling;* Padilla, *The Gang;* and Wright and Decker, *Burglars.* These and other "membership role" issues in field research are also discussed by

Adler and Adler, *Membership Roles*. And as Weber notes, "the more radically" human values and actions "differ from our own ultimate values . . . the more difficult it is for us to understand them empathically" (*Economy*, 5–6).

38. Lyng, "Edgework," 861, 862n.

39. Richard Leo, "Trial and Tribulations: Courts, Ethnography, and the Need for an Evidentiary Privilege for Academic Researchers," *American Sociologist* 26 (1995): 113–34; James Marquart, "Doing Research in Prison: The Strengths and Weaknesses of Participation as a Guard," *Justice Quarterly* 3 (1986): 15–32; Rik Scarce, "Scholarly Ethics and Courtroom Antics: Where Researchers Stand in the Eyes of the Law," *American Sociologist* 26 (1995): 87–112. In these instances, a labeling theory of crime becomes also a labeling theory of research into crime. The meaning of the research resides not (only) in the research act itself, but in the web of official and unofficial reactions to it; see Becker, *Outsiders;* Polsky, *Hustlers.*

40. Becker, *Outsiders;* Becker, "Whose Side."

41. Polsky, *Hustlers.*

42. Becker, *Outsiders.*

43. Humphreys, *Tearoom Trade.*

44. William Ruefle and Kenneth Reynolds, "Curfews and Delinquency in Major American Cities," *Crime and Delinquency* 41 (1995): 347–63.

45. Gregg Barak, *Gimme Shelter: A Social History of Homelessness in Contemporary America* (New York: Praeger, 1991); Gregg Barak and Robert Bohm, "The Crimes of the Homeless or the Crime of Homelessness?" *Contemporary Crises* 13 (1989): 275–88; Mike Davis, *City of Quartz* (New York: Vintage, 1992); June Kress, "Homeless Fatigue Syndrome: The Backlash Against the Crime of Homelessness in the 1990s," *Social Justice* 21 (1994): 85–108.

46. Artists' studios, art galleries, and museums are also at times reconstructed as locations of crime and criminalization; see Ferrell and Sanders, *Cultural Criminology.* Raymond Lee, *Dangerous Fieldwork* (Thousand Oaks, Calif.: Sage, 1995), explores the broader range of dangerous field research situations.

47. Lyng, "Edgework," 869, 871.

48. Ferrell, "Urban Graffiti"; Ferrell, *Crimes.*

49. Polsky, *Hustlers,* 118, 127.

50. We might wish to reconsider the past in this light as well. For example, what sort of (illegal) field research would we now consider to have been appropriate in a time when "racial mixing" was outlawed in the American South and elsewhere?

51. Marx, *Undercover.*

52. Victor Kappeler, Richard Sluder, and Geoffrey Alpert, *Forces of Deviance* (Prospect Heights, Ill.: Waveland, 1994); Peter Kraska and Victor Kappeler, "To Serve and Pursue: Exploring Police Sexual Violence Against Women," *Justice Quarterly* 12 (1995): 85–111.

Homeless and Marginal Populations
Streets and Shelters

Ethnographers, Pimps, and the Company Store

Mark S. Fleisher

I confess. I have had impure thoughts about the effect criminology has had on crime policy and the effect that the criminal justice system (police, courts, jails, and prisons) has had on criminals' behavior. This chapter is based on these impure thoughts and conveys the following ideas. The first idea is that there is a major difference between ethnography and criminology. This difference influences what students of criminology and criminal justice, but also the general public, know about crime and criminals. Furthermore, this understanding of crime and criminals then influences policymakers' decisions about crime intervention and the treatment of criminals.

The second idea is that today's criminal justice system exploits criminals as socioeconomic capital. These criminals are investments, fertilizer for the growth of criminal justice agencies (police, court services, prisons). With agency growth comes hiring more employees, issuing higher salaries to managers and administrators (with retirement and medical benefits), and, of course, employing consultants who are often university professors and former agency employees.

However, enormous expenditures to expand the criminal justice system have made few substantive strides toward, say, lowering rates of violent and property crime and "rehabilitating" criminals. Why? Voters have learned to believe that the criminal justice system is designed to combat street crime, slow the genesis of young criminals, and redirect the lives of convicted offenders. At the same time, voters have been deceived by criminologists, criminal justice professionals, and politicians who suggest either that the construction of prisons can deter criminal behavior or that, once built, prisons ("correctional institutions") can effectively rehabilitate ("correct") criminals, if these institutions receive sufficient public support (a euphemism for large budgets) for inmate treatment (drug and alcohol therapy) and programs (remedial education and vocational education).

These are empty and expensive promises. The criminal justice system is merely a warehousing service, and surely is not the place to look for crime's cause or cure. Crime and criminals are products of much more complicated cultural issues. What's more, an ebbing of crime would mean a slowing in the economic upsurge of the criminal justice industry.[1]

I am not a criminologist, although for many years I have studied prisoners and adolescent and adult street criminals. Most of my friends are either criminologists or practitioners in the criminal justice system. I was once a senior administrator in an agency of the U.S. Department of Justice. But, alas, I am an anthropologically trained ethnographer and have done research in many places around the world for more than twenty-five years. In this light, I explain below what an ethnographer does and how he or she does it, and how the process of the ethnography of crime is different from the criminological study of crime.

Over those twenty-five years of anthropological research, I have slept peacefully on Salish and Nootkan Indian reservations on the northwest coast of North America, in the central valley of Mexico, in the highlands of Guatemala, on the islands of Java and Sulawesi in Indonesia, and in dozens of hotels and motels near state and federal prisons all over America. But my peaceful nights were disturbed in the summer of 1995 when I began spending my days with the Fremont Hustlers, a group of adolescent boys and girls, in Kansas City, Missouri.[2] The Kansas City Police Department calls this group a "gang." But what the Fremont Hustlers are called by police and the courts isn't important here. What is important is this: after I began hanging out at the intersection of Fremont Avenue and 13th Street, a corner "owned" by the Fremont Hustlers, my restful nights ended and were replaced by sleeplessness or nightmares.

I spent months thinking about why the Fremont research had such troubling personal effects and talking about these effects to my closest friends, some anthropologists, others criminologists. What I discovered was that I am angry: angry at myself, angry at criminologist colleagues, and, most of all, angry at the criminal justice system itself.

Don't misunderstand. I am not angry because someone forced me to study the Fremont Hustlers. After all, I asked the Harry Frank Guggenheim Foundation for research funding to do this research and received a grant. It doesn't bother me to hang out in a dangerous neighborhood where there is a youth gang, drive-by shootings, and drug sales. I enjoy the risks and the excitement that comes with them. I enjoy the company of Fremont Hustlers and prefer the Fremont neighborhood to my campus. But the enjoyment I derive from hanging out with these kids and the pleasure of writing about them does not compensate for the pain I feel as I watch their slow self-destruction.

To many adolescents, gang life must look like fun. Believe me, it isn't. Most Fremont kids are drug addicts. Many are violent. Some are killers. A few have made it to Kansas City's Most Wanted list, a kind of honor roll for school drop-outs and adolescent miscreants who enjoy hurting people. Fremont kids have taken handguns and rifles and assault weapons and have shot other kids who are just like themselves: poor, uneducated, drug-addicted, violent kids who were abused and neglected by their mothers and fathers. They shoot at and kill people for reasons we think are trivial, such as verbal insults and jealousy over girlfriends. But, most of all, these kids do violent things because it feels good to them. The excitement of pointing a nine-millimeter semiautomatic handgun at someone and then pulling the trigger is like nothing else in the world, they say. Not only do I abhor this violent behavior, I despise the parents of the Fremont Hustlers for perverting and transforming children into teenage urban predators. Worse yet, the parents of these kids were perverted by *their* parents. And when it comes to the intergenerational transmission of violence, I refuse to fall into this trap: *tout comprendre, c'est tout pardonner.*[3]

At a time when most kids are entering junior high school, Fremont kids are in juvenile detention centers, prisons for kids. To watch Fremont kids sublimate their own pain into killing and maiming other kids, commit suicide by ingesting noxious drugs, and put themselves in life-threatening situations makes me angry.

But what causes my anger? It's simple. Youth gangs are the single most dangerous law enforcement problem in America today, say law enforcement officials. To combat this growing danger, there are national gang conferences held in fancy hotels. At these sessions, gang researchers, gang prosecutors, gang police, gang consultants, and gang interventionists lecture at one another, gather for cocktail parties and dinners, and then go home — to arrest, prosecute, and imprison young gangsters. Gang researchers, and I'm included among them, go about the business of interviewing gang kids who are in jails and juvenile detention centers and publishing the results in dust-covered journals. Gang interventionists seek out young gangsters to offer them an alternative lifestyle; and I have done this too.[4] Mind you, the alternative lifestyle we offer adolescent offenders is a lifestyle these teenagers know nothing about and are ill-prepared to accept. A lawful lifestyle would require, say, that Fremont Hustlers give up all their current street companions, find new "straight" companions, and begin another lifestyle from scratch. Can you imagine any teenager suddenly giving up all of his or her friends at the request of an adult?

Here is a central irony in the criminal justice system, as well as in the "gang research, suppression, and intervention industry": the hundreds of millions, if not billions, of dollars spent by gang researchers, gang cops, and gang probation and parole officers are allegedly meant to effect radical changes in the behavior of the most inadequately socialized and poorly adjusted adolescents. Yet, they are the ones least able to make drastic lifestyle changes. When these adolescents (and this applies to adult offenders too) don't change, we get angry and "throw the book at them." Imagine a supercilious judge, a pompous probation officer, or a condescending cop lecturing a seventeen-year-old gang member who's been on his own since he was eleven: "Now even though your parents beat the hell out of you, your mother's lovers sexually molested you, and no one ever read a book to you or showed you by example that education is valuable, we now want you to go to school, get a job, and be responsible like we are. So there. Now do it."

Juvenile justice officials engage in the business of imprisoning kids as if these criminal justice practitioners and their advisors—the criminologists—did not in fact know the tragedy of kids' lives, and more generally how difficult it is for any child to grow up in America today. The superficiality of the criminal justice system and of banal interventions oftentimes causes more pain to damaged kids than it resolves. This angers me.

I don't believe that evil forces, such as pornographic literature and violent movies, lurking in American culture compel men like Ted Bundy and John Wayne Gacey into doing truly evil things. Perhaps those who argue that violent movies cause violent behavior have never seen inside a violent family. I have seen inside households where preschool children watch their mother being "humped" by her boyfriend on the living-room couch, while in the next room young gangsters smoke marijuana and rock cocaine and fiddle with handguns. These kids' real lives should be rated PG 18, V (for graphic violence), L (for filthy language). Where are the social workers? Where are the interventionists? Where are the conservatives who preach family values?

I am unwilling to defend violent Fremont Hustlers like Chucky D, who at age fourteen took a baseball bat and beat homosexuals, robbed them, stole their cars, and burglarized their houses. Cara, a Fremont Hustler and one of Chucky D's girlfriends, said, "Chuck's evil." And he didn't get that way by watching Hollywood movies and reading pornographic books. Evil and violence engulfed Chucky D in his early life family, and for some reason criminal justice professionals and the courts believed that sending him to adult prison at age fifteen, again at age seventeen, and yet again at age nineteen would teach him a lesson.

Over many years of hanging out with Chucky D and others like him, I have learned how to describe with objective clarity what I see. But descriptive clarity doesn't mean I must be neutral about Chucky D and other violent Fremont Hustlers as they inflict pain on other kids. What these kids do to themselves is awful to see.

What Fremont Hustlers have done to others is illegal and it's immoral. But we, the voters, the criminal justice professionals, the criminologists, the ethnographers let it happen — and then when blood is spilled, we jump into the ring and offer after-the-fact interventions or propose more survey research to help us find the "correct" independent variables that predict the violence surrounding us.

Americans have become accustomed to politically correct talk. We hear it from elected officials who dance around sensitive social issues such as poverty and racism and their link to crime. Neutrality helps protect us, the onlookers, from the horror of the real lives criminals live, and from the real-life devastation wreaked on others by criminals of all colors and on criminals themselves by their culture via parents and street companions.

America has a long history of political correctness and cover-ups. Cover-ups rename things, and when that happens we lose sight of the problem. Schoolchildren study the westward expansion of the railroad in the nineteenth and early twentieth centuries. Our children have learned to call this expansion the "conquering of the West." What does that expression mean? Strip away the neutrality and get beyond the political correctness, and, lo and behold, we find that "conquering of the West" means killing American Indians, stealing their land, and stripping them of their language and culture. Why did the American government sanction and encourage westward expansion? It did so to benefit wealthy businessmen. Here, entrenched in the history of American culture, is what I call metaphorically "the company store." The company store is a place where financially influential and thus powerful people trade on the social and financial disadvantages of the poor and powerless.

In our midst today, there is yet another company store. This one relies on the neutrality of criminology and its pretense that "science" is, by its very nature, better than and preferable to real-life images. The business of criminology is the manufacture of crime statistics. While useful for understanding crime trends nationwide, crime statistics transform flesh-and-blood people into "people-free" variables and categories, such as delinquents, at-risk and high-risk youth, and suppression targets. A fourteen-year-old "boy" who has been involved in street crime for years may engender your compassion, but a fourteen-year "suppression target" goes straight to prison.

By transforming "people" into "criminals" and then into people-free events—that is, crime trends—criminology conjures the image that crime has no face. Then, of course, faceless agents of crime ("offenders") can be mistreated any way lawmakers wish. And victims become faceless statistics too. I can't be emotionless about the boys and girls, and the men and women, who inflict pain and misery on others. If teenagers do violent things, put them in prison. Yet I can't be silent about a criminal justice system, social service agents, and elected officials who act only to punish and imprison lawbreakers and do virtually nothing to prevent the genesis of predators like Chucky D.

The core of anthropology and the central difference between a criminologist's and an ethnographer's approach to crime is captured in the expression: *Homo sum: humani nil a me alienum puto.*[5] In the context of crime policy, this means that if we reduce human beings to crime trends, we can then do whatever we wish to the generators of crime statistics. When human behavior is aggregated into trends, we can easily neglect the specific social and cultural conditions which have produced millions of criminals.

In the end, however, crime control can only be truly effective if we face the specific conditions that produce adolescent deviants like Chucky D.

A principal cause of adolescent deviance is serious child abuse. Harsh socialization has the same effects on children in so-called primitive (non-western, nonliterate) societies as it has on children in industrialized societies like the United States.[6] Every predatory, self-destructive Fremont Hustler who is enmeshed in burglary, robbery, car theft, carjacking, and drug peddling has been reared by drug-addicted, violent parents, many of whom are convicted felons.[7]

The standard crime explanations criminologists offer have to do with poverty, joblessness, and structural inequalities between the "haves" and "have-nots." The truth is, adolescents don't kill one another because they are unemployed or because they have black or brown skin. Poverty never made Chucky D beat anyone with a baseball bat nor forced Skizzy to steal a boy's athletic jacket and slash the victim's stomach just for fun. These acts require a choice. Gang boys who shoot and stab people have made the wrong choices. This choice isn't the result of being poor; it's the result of being sick. And should you look deeply into these boys' families, you'll find these violent kids to be like their parents.

Why has it been so difficult for criminologists, judges, social workers, and politicians to say publicly and loudly that parents must be stopped permanently from beating children?[8] Facing serious parental abuse and neglect and then doing something about it is quicksand for politicians and would force scholars out of hiding. Instead of the simple truth, politicians tell voters, and scholars tell one another, that adolescent deviance and youth gangs are caused by racial marginalization, structural victimization,[9] weak ties to legitimate institutions, inadequate opportunities, and subcultural learning.

These are traditional scholarly aphorisms: they injure no one, help no one. The smart way to stop a parent from beating a child black-and-blue is to remove a battered child from that parent's custody. The imprudent choice, at least for the protection of a battered child, is to fund yet another "parenting" program. Kids who are beaten need security, protection, and treatment. Adults who beat kids need to be in a prison cell, not on a therapist's couch. It's that simple.

We know how to stop child abuse. How do we stop racial marginalization? Show me a step-by-step action plan that will end structural victimization. Line up and then count all of the community members in your town who are willing to spend evenings and weekends tutoring and welcoming into their own homes "high-risk" children from "racially marginal" groups. The line will be short. And, finally, will someone please describe in detail how state or federal government officials are supposed to stop the detrimental effects of subcultural learning?

When it comes to racial justice, the United States has a problematic record. In the last one hundred years, Native Americans were slaughtered on American soil by federal government fiat, and, before that, businessmen sold and bought slaves in what is now midtown Kansas City, Missouri. Today's version of racism (a worldview that sorts some people from other people with the use of glib and convenient rationalizations) allows the overlords of the criminal justice system to imprison hundreds of thousands of minority offenders and, at the same time, to let children starve in households where parents barter food stamps for drugs.

In the last century the federal government, unfettered by loyal Americans, allowed soldiers to slaughter Native Americans, exiled the survivors to reservations, and imprisoned in Bureau of Indian Affairs (BIA) jails Native American parents who spoke native languages to their children. The BIA is still a federal monument to racial marginalization and gross social injustice developed and implemented by the federal government.

The criminal justice system is today's version of government self-interest. Given the track record of state and federal government officials, I wouldn't take seriously any plan to fix structural victimization or racial marginalization. Be realistic: how would any political party reconstruct the socioeconomic fabric of America?

Politicians have no real plans to achieve social and economic parity for minority groups or anyone else on the fringes of American society. But elected officials talk about it, especially near election time, and policymakers spend billions of tax dollars on social development and criminal justice programs whose alleged intent is to improve the lives of marginal folks. Even a cursory reading of the cross-cultural literature on politics and economics tells us that all societies, from simple to complex, have marginal people. Marginality is a natural occurrence in human cultures.[10] Nevertheless, state and federal programs offer fantasy images of social justice, which in reality tender thousands of jobs for citizens employed in the prison-industrial complex and allied businesses.[11] As I see it, many jobs in the prison industry, in law enforcement, and in lucrative, though fundamentally valueless, anticrime programs like DARE, would be un-necessary if parents were adequate caretakers of children.

We can stop parental abuse, but we don't. And we have plenty of ex-cuses for not doing so: crowded family courts, overworked social workers, limited budgets, corrupt foster care, and the ultimate conservative battle cry—"protecting the family" at all costs. I have seen child abuse over and over again. If I can see it, why can't the policymakers and judges? If I can see adolescent drug dealers and prostitutes, why can't their parents? More important, why don't their parents do something to stop their children's illegal and self-destructive behavior?

Scholars and politicians of all colors have been guaranteeing their own paychecks while boys and girls are beaten, sexually molested, and al-lowed to sell drugs and themselves on the streets. Government paychecks can be accepted with a clear conscience only if black-and-blue boys and girls are ignored in favor of colorless crime statistics.[12] Until criminolo-gists learn how to translate the statistics of crime into visual images that have impact on policymakers' likelihood of being (re)elected, criminol-ogy will have a minor role in crime policy.

Crime intervention may not work well, because it is based on incom-plete social science and on interventionists' romantic notions of how to save the poor. Like Bourgois, I feel no need to forgive violent people for in-juring victims and inflicting pain.[13] Poverty, marginalization, and lack of education are bad apologies for violence. I do, however, feel the need to lift the blame for deviance and crime from the shoulders of "poverty," "racism," and "marginalization" and put it where it belongs. It belongs on the shoulders of parents. If parents did their jobs well, kids would stay in school and wouldn't grow up hating anyone. Well-educated, unbiased kids wouldn't find themselves on the social and economic margins of America.

Ethnography as I See It

Ethnography is the systematic collection of observations and inter-view data.[14] The data we collect in ethnographic research are, for the most part, not the same as the data collected by survey researchers, who use self-report crime surveys and so-called in-depth or intensive interviews. I have little patience with researchers who call a thirty-minute interview "in-depth" or "intensive." No one, especially a criminal, would divulge innermost secrets to a stranger, even a stranger offering a fee, for a conversation that lasts less time than a Sesame Street episode.

Gaining rapport is a prerequisite to interviewing. There are levels of rapport. We are familiar with levels of rapport from dating experiences. What you see and hear and learn about someone on a first date is a far cry from what you know after a year. Good research, like dating that leads to choosing a marriage partner, takes time, patience, and endurance. Criminals conceal and distort information about themselves. How many "nice guys" turn out to be batterers and date rapists? The truth is, it takes time, as well as deception and "impression management" on the part of a researcher,[15] to study the liars and manipulators we call criminals.

Gathering data in what ethnographers calls "white-room" interviews—that is, in the researchers' environment, not the criminals'—takes very little time and commitment on the part of a researcher. Ethnographers don't work that way. When we enter a scene, we stay there, for months or years. I met two core members of the Fremont Hustlers in July 1994 and spent seven days a week, ten to twelve hours a day, for six weeks with them in June and July 1995. I then hung out with them two to three times a month, for three to four days at a time, for more than a year. The days we spent together were long, almost never less than ten hours; sometimes the days lasted fourteen hours. We hung out on porches and in rental houses and apartments, stood on sidewalks and in convenience stores, drove in cars to kill time or get a thrill by cruising in enemy gang territory. When they sold drugs and used them, I was there. When they were high and decided to shoot off their handguns, rifles, shotguns, and assault weapons, I was there. When they tried to assault and steal things from other kids, I was there and often intervened to stop it.

No ethnographer worth his or her salt would believe for a moment that informants' words spoken in thirty-minute, white-room interviews are even close to being sufficient to understand the complexities of and motivations for real-life behavior. But the discipline of criminology is founded on the idea that data collected with scientifically constructed samples and survey instruments are more valuable to the study of crime and criminals' behavior than detailed ethnographic narratives about real-life behavior. Sounds strange, but it's true.

Doing ethnography has its advantages; but it has real disadvantages and ethical dilemmas, which have caused me to have nightmares. It's difficult to know informants as real people. I know as I sit there talking to them, sharing their lives from day to day and winning their trust, that I will write unflattering things about their behavior. Criminologists don't have this problem.

I question my own motives late at night, after I have returned from being immersed in poverty, from being surrounded by teenagers high on drugs and pregnant teenage girls who smoke marijuana, and from having seen black-and-blue toddlers who were beaten for one stupid reason or another by an angry gang boy or one of the toddler's mother's lovers. I watch, doing nothing, knowing that if I interfere I will harm my rapport with my informants, or, worse yet, I will end up black and blue myself. So I let the awfulness of gang life happen all around me, because I want to collect data, publish another book, get another salary increase, improve my life.

Ethnographers who study crime and criminals face decisions that influence their own—as well as their informants'—lives and personal safety. Should I report the names of Fremont drug dealers to the police? Should I report abusive parents (gang members who abuse their children) to social service agencies? I once had a senior Kansas City police official whom I met at a gang conference ask me questions about the illegal activities of the Fremont Hustlers. He said that if I were arrested with gang members who were selling rock cocaine and marijuana and carrying firearms I could call him and he'd see to it that I was released from jail without charges being filed. "That's great," I thought, "but what's the price?"

Genuine ethnography, spending six months to a year with informants in natural settings, effects a sort of "marriage" between a researcher and the researched. When I commit myself to a neighborhood and its people, that commitment obtains the right to see things other researchers never see, ask questions others never ask, get answers others never get. But that privilege has a dark side. That dark side is the personal damage that seeing kids in pain who inflict pain on others has caused me. I see child abuse and teenage prostitution, drug addiction and drug dealing, and have even heard murder contracts and street-to-prison drug smuggling being arranged over the phone. For this privilege I pay a heavy price.

At night when my eyes close I see the horrible scenes of the day. I ask myself, "To get this story written, how much of my soul do I have to sell?"

I have no answer. To this day, the nightmares continue. But guilt is cheap, and anguish, however real, is the comforting swamp of morality. My research and my bad dreams are worth it only if my writing results in a better life for these people. But that's not up to me.

An Ethnographer Looks at Criminology

Philippe Bourgois, a street ethnographer and an anthropologist, wrote that "[c]ollege-educated intellectuals are usually too elitist or too frightened to be capable of treating unemployed, drug-addicted, violent criminals with the respect and humanity that ethnographic methods require for meaningful dialogue to occur."[16] It takes courage to tell the truth.

The data of any social science are words and behaviors. But collecting accurate and truthful data depends in large part on the social setting. Imagine, if you will, a famous cultural anthropologist like Margaret Mead flying a plane full of native people from highland New Guinea to a "human behavior laboratory" in New York City and then writing a book about New Guineans' behavior and culture. Imagine also that, because of Mead's reputation as world-class scholar and anthropologist, professionals and the public automatically accept what she says about these New Guineans as truth.

Criminological theories are abstract constructions about behavior that criminologists have, for the most part, never seen. What criminologists know about crime and criminals has come from studying criminals in captivity (jails, prisons) and from crimes reported, though frequently not observed, by local police and other law enforcement agents. The validity of criminological theories is then tested with measurements (statistics) collected by instruments (surveys, interviews) used on criminals who have been removed from native environments. This sanitized style of studying criminals and crime has brought us dozens of criminological theories and dozens more strategies to intervene in criminal behavior. If any of these theories were correct and interventions effective, we wouldn't need so many of them.

Criminologists think of themselves as social scientists (with emphasis on "scientist"); however, they are unlike "real" scientists, the physicists, the chemists, the geneticists, the engineers who create experiments and replicate experimental results over and over. Criminologists can't perform real scientific experimentation with human beings; instead, they insist on scientific objectivity. They use random samples and statistical methods rather than nonrandom samples and narratives as ethnographers do. And it's the ethnographers' use of nonrandom samples and their personal involvement with informants that causes criminologists to disqualify ethnographers as scientists and to devalue ethnographic analyses as fundamentally flawed and useless. To many criminologists, ethnography is anecdotal and entertaining reading but little else. From here, many criminologists go on to claim that insights into the causes of crime and crime intervention based on ethnographic data are unfit for use in anticrime policies.

Can you imagine the irrationality of a social science that proclaims that knowing criminals well is less useful than not knowing criminals at all? I can. This is the essence of sociology and social psychology. And it's this style of research that perpetuates the company store.[17]

As "crime experts," criminologists report crime trends to politicians and policymakers, who then use these numbers to manipulate taxpayers' perceptions of crime by claiming that, for instance, longer prison terms do in fact make for safer streets. But when it comes to what criminals actually do, and why criminals do those things, criminologists' rendering of reality is, in fact, based largely on guesses about behavior. Yet, because the cost and scope of grounded policies likely to do any good are too great, policymakers who don't *want* to know anything more than crime trends accept these guesses. Consequently, when crime policies are developed and implemented, these policies usually fail. They fail because a vision of crime conjured in the computer laboratory is a long way from drug houses and from households where preschoolers are transformed into predators.

The Company Store

Criminologists who advise criminal justice officials, mayors and governors, and state and federal government leaders are very happy to keep a safe distance from flesh-and-blood criminals. The reality is that many criminologists and criminal justice practitioners don't care whether or not crime control programs make better lives for anyone but themselves.

The bottom line is the governmental paycheck, and ensuring that the paycheck continues to come.

A fundamental irony in the criminal justice system thus emerges: if the criminal justice system did lower rates of street crime and rehabilitate offenders, hundreds of thousands of well-paid public servants and consultants, like myself, would be put out of work.

When the West was being conquered, railroad companies had company stores. Laborers did back-breaking labor all day to earn a low wage, which was then spent at the company store to purchase the goods needed to survive so that they could do more back-breaking work tomorrow. The company profits; the laborers toil. America's criminal justice system works the same way.

Taxpayers employed outside the criminal justice system work hard and pay taxes. These taxes support an ever-expanding, albeit largely ineffective, criminal justice system. But, at the same time, taxpayers are frightened by public servants into believing that because crime rates are skyrocketing and streets are unsafe (both allegations are false),[18] more tax dollars are needed to expand the criminal justice system. Of course, those public servants' incomes depend on the fears of the taxpayers. In the end, taxpayers lose: the criminal justice system expands, more jobs are offered to new company employees, more tax dollars are invested, and the quality of other publicly funded services (schools, roads, parks) diminishes.

How can this happen? It's simple. The primary goal of any institution (in this case, the criminal justice system) is its own continued well-being. And to ensure that well-being a lack of true accountability is maintained at key positions in the criminal justice system. Mind you, the company store (the criminal justice system and its benefactors) needs to keep itself open. Here is how accountability operates, or doesn't operate, in the criminal justice system.

Accountability has two parts. First, accountability ensures that the goods and services allegedly generated by state and federal government agencies are actually produced and delivered. Second, accountability enables this production and delivery system to be changed, if necessary, by modifying the system itself and replacing ineffective staffers and policies with effective ones.

Think carefully about accountability in a criminal justice system whose stated purpose is to reduce crime and rehabilitate offenders. Say a juvenile court judge releases a fourteen-year-old killer to the street, arguing that this young predator needs "another chance." Back on the street the youngster kills someone else. Does the judge lose her or his job? Does a state's attorney prosecute the judge for knowingly contributing to the death of the victim? Can the victim's relatives file a wrongful death civil suit against the judge, requesting a remedy of compensatory and punitive damages for the loss of a family member? Will the community organize a recall election and push the judge off the bench? Of course not.

Say a social worker overlooks an abused child and leaves the preschooler with an abusive, neglectful mother who continues deliberately to maim the child. Will the social worker lose his or her job? Is that social worker charged with a crime by the state's attorney? Is that social worker fired? Of course not.

Say crime rates soar in the inner city of Chicago, New York, Los Angeles, Detroit, Cleveland, Minneapolis, Miami, or any other American city. Is that city's police chief fired? Is the mayor expelled from office in a recall election? Of course not. These officials will simply ask some other politician, perhaps the president of the United States, for a few hundred of the one hundred thousand more police officers President Clinton promised taxpayers in the 1997 State of the Union address.

Say a prison warden oversees an institution with two thousand male inmates, most of whom are members of violent street gangs and who, once released, continue to slaughter citizens. Is the warden of that prison fired, reprimanded, or reassigned because he or she didn't effect some miraculous cure on these criminals? Of course not.

Say elected state and federal officials pass bills allowing the construction of hundreds of new prisons at a cost of hundreds of millions of dollars. And once these institutions are filled to the brim, the streets are no safer than they were before these prisons were constructed. Do these publicly elected officials resign out of shame? Do they voluntarily relinquish their retirement benefits as compensation for wasting tax dollars? Do the voters seek a social remedy, such as imprisonment, for these officials who mismanaged public funds? Of course not.

Where, then, in the criminal justice system do we find genuine accountability? We don't. We don't because criminal justice officials design and operate the company store, are recipients of its benefits, and, as such, don't allow themselves to be held accountable. The worst that can happen to a lousy politician or police chief is to be voted out or kicked out of office. Should that happen, she or he will receive retirement and other benefits and go fishing. American workers toil, criminals get arrested, criminal justice officials and politicians reap the profits.

To be sure, any elected officials who told the public the truth about the criminal justice system would lose the public trust and would without doubt lose a re-election as senator, representative, mayor, or governor. Imagine for a moment a candidate for governor saying these words in a speech delivered at a political rally: "Prisons have not and will not stop criminals from committing crimes. We are imprisoning too many people and compounding this error by imprisoning at a very high cost convicted criminals whose crimes are not a threat to public safety. Drug dealers, purveyors of marijuana, cocaine, heroin, for instance, would not be a problem to the community if working people—that's right, taxpaying citizens who are the community's blue-collar and white-collar workers—stopped smoking marijuana, shooting and snorting heroin, and inhaling cocaine! We must shorten prison terms for drug peddlers and send fewer of them, not more of them, to prison." Social science tells us these words are for the most part true, but these words also are a prescription for a lost election.

I hung out on the streets of Kansas City for a long time. Never once did I see a city official other than gang detectives in the Fremont neighborhood. No social workers, no elected politicians, no criminologists ever walked around talking to the gang members and their parents about school, vocational training, and medical care for pregnant teenagers. The only way for these kids to obtain an education, job training, and medical services was to commit a crime and go to jail. And so the company store perpetuates itself for the good of the educated elite.

No one cares what academics write to one another in articles published in refereed journals. Few people outside the company store read these journals. The dilemma arises when criminologists' opinions are wrong and still are used to develop crime policies and intervention programs. Worse yet, the company store shields mistakes and perpetuates them. If one hundred prisons have not stopped criminal behavior, then politicians tell taxpayers we need one hundred more prisons, rather than rethinking the use of prisons as a crime intervention and rehabilitation device.

So many American families now depend on the company store for income that an economic panic would hit the land if someone actually had the "cure" for crime. Crime means jobs for practitioners, tenure for professors, books published by authors, political speeches, and lucrative contracts for anyone who can weasel his or her way into the company store. In the end, what works to end or slow crime doesn't matter. What matters is who gets and controls the anticrime money.

Those whose livelihoods depend on criminals will deny these accusations vehemently, no doubt in loud voices. But the test of devotion comes when the funding ends. How many intervention do-gooders and crime researchers find new areas of study when the company store closes its doors by denying a university researcher a federal grant?

Who's the Pimp?

A pimp brokers something of value (sex), which belongs to someone else (the prostitute), to a third party (the "john"). Pimping, some people would say, is immoral because the service being sold is sex. Selling sex doesn't bother me. To me, pimping is immoral because pimps receive a greater return at lower risk than the prostitutes. Plain and simple, pimping is capitalist exploitation.

I am a pimp, of sorts. I sell a product (tales about criminals) to those who have never seen criminals up close. Selling the painful experiences of other people has made me a tenured professor and author of two well-known books, with a third book forthcoming which will exploit the Fremont Hustlers.[19] I have transformed gang life into narratives that educate and entertain readers. My work has benefited some Fremont gang members more than others, but, in the end, I will benefit the most.

I am not the only university professor who has pimped or is currently pimping research subjects. Everyone of us who has bought into the company store benefits more than our research subjects. Plain and simple, we are pimps.

There are limits to what I sell, however. In my ethnography about street criminals and youth gangs I create a picture of these people and the things they do. Fremont kids do illegal things: they sell rock cocaine, bags of marijuana, "dank sticks" (cigarettes dipped into a mixture of PCP diluted, or cut, with either formalin, brake fluid, or nearly pure alcohol); burglarize houses and sell and buy the property, such as drugs and weapons, garnered from burglaries; buy stolen vehicles to be used in drive-by shootings; engage in shootings; commit armed assaults and homicide with stolen weapons. But writing about these activities doesn't bother me at all. What bothers me most is the image of these kids I will create in my ethnographic narrative. Will I create loathsome characters? Or will I remain neutral, offer facts about their lives, but conceal their awful behavior from public view? A few Fremont Hustlers have killed people, beaten criminal cases filed against them, and now freely walk the streets. In the ethnographic narrative, do I transform these killers into despicable people, or create an image of them as victims of poverty, structural inequality, and racism? Do I mention details about crimes which Fremont members have shared with me for which criminal charges have not been brought? What should I do if the Kansas City Police Department subpoenas me to testify against a Fremont Hustler?

Forgive Me Someone for I Have Sinned

Criminologists do "clean" lab research, wearing the white coat of science. We street ethnographers "get our hands dirty." Both of these types of research have their own ethical issues. Truthfully, I don't think either research style is entirely right or wrong. Each has its own advantages, limitations, and disadvantages. I do think, however, that it is the responsibility of the researcher to make certain that his or her audience knows these dilemmas and shortcomings and is conscious of the tension between different styles of research. I don't think that's being done. But, in the end, it's the pimping, or publishing, of crime narratives and crime statistics that's truly immoral.

At a multiday conference on juvenile crime, a panel of invited presenters was paid five hundred dollars each for a short presentation. At dinner after the first day, one of my colleagues said that each of the six people at the table should donate his or her honorarium to the representative of a particularly interesting youth program operating in one of America's most troubled inner cities. What an idea. We stared at one another, wondering who would do it. My outspoken colleague said he would stand up the next day in front of an auditorium full of hundreds of distinguished presenters and guests and ask each presenter to relinquish his or her honorarium. He was serious, but we talked him out of doing it, knowing that the presenters would look at him as if he were crazy. In the end, he would have been embarrassed and ridiculed. Of course each one of us kept our honorariums and had good reasons to do it. One person said bills needed to be paid; another that his spouse would "kill" him if he came home without a check.

My three books and the journal articles, newspaper and magazine stories, and book chapters I've written about gangs and prisons are "stock" in the company store. But I tell myself, at least in my book about the Fremont Hustlers, I will be writing about adolescents doing horrible things to one another and maybe that book will effect some change, someday. Perhaps that effort will balance the immorality.

It may be unrealistic to think this way, but personally I am hopeful that my writing about real life will change the climate of crime control, at least in a small way, so that the lives of some of the Fremont Hustlers will improve. And if their lives can't be improved now, let's hope the lives of their children will be better. Winning the hearts and minds of conservatives and their children is one of my main goals. If winning over these policymakers means spending years watching the pain of others and more years writing about it, then I'll do it. But until then, I will preach to my students about their responsibilities as parents and as criminal justice practitioners and teach them as well about the horror of child abuse and the desperation of life on the street.

Since I began studying the Fremont Hustlers in 1995, I have sworn to colleagues over and over again that I'll never again do another long-term study of delinquents on the street because it's too painful for me to watch them suffer. But when I think about leaving behind street research, I feel as if I will abandon the teenagers who trusted me by sharing the details of their lives. I owe them something. At least I can return to see them, feed them, and offer advice when they're arrested and jailed. These are small things to offer, but these gestures help me sleep more peacefully.

Notes

This essay benefited from the advice of H. Russell Bernard (University of Florida), Nancy McKee (Washington State University), and Jill Seymour (Binghamton University). The opinions expressed in the essay are mine and do not reflect the opinions and policies of any local, state, or federal law enforcement agency.

1. See Steven Donziger, *The Real War on Crime* (Harper Perennial, 1995), and Mark S. Fleisher, "How to Break the Criminal Lifestyle," *USA Today Magazine,* in press.

2. See Mark S. Fleisher, "Guns, Drugs, and Gangs: Kids on the Streets of Kansas City," *Valparaiso Law Review* 31, in press.

3. This expression means "to understand everything is to forgive everything." Are we willing to forgive the violent behavior of a teenage criminal just because he or she was abused by his or her parents? And then are we willing to forgive a mother's or father's abuse of a child because we know that parent was abused by his or her parents? I am absolutely unwilling to forgive egregious violence inflicted on children by anyone under any circumstances. There can never be an acceptable reason to damage children.

4. In my forthcoming book, *Dead End: Lives of Urban Gang Kids* (University of Wisconsin Press), I describe in detail my failing effort to pull one adolescent girl out of the Fremont Hustlers and guide her into an alternative school and community college.

5. This expression means "I'm a man: I find nothing human foreign to me."

6. Ronald P. Rohner, *They Love Me, They Love Me Not: Worldwide Study of Parental Rejection* (New Haven, Conn.: HRAR Press, 1975); Robert A. LeVine, *Culture, Behavior, and Personality* (Chicago: Aldine, 1973).

7. Terence Thornberry wrote: "Sixty-nine percent of youths who had been mistreated as children reported involvement in violence as compared to 56 percent of those who had not been maltreated . . . a history of maltreatment increases the chances of youth violence by 24 percent" ("Violent Families and Youth Violence," Office of Juvenile Justice and Delinquency Prevention, Fact Sheet #21 [December 1994]).

8. One anonymous reviewer of this chapter was terribly angered by my writing and criticized this sentence in particular. The reviewer wrote, "[D]eclarations are declared right and left, totally without evidence. . . . [One of the declarations offered without evidence is] everybody knows that the cause of crime is child abuse, but everybody is afraid to grant this obvious fact." Had the reviewer read the entire paragraph, he/she would have read that I wrote "deviance" is an outcome of parental abuse; crime, on the other hand, is a sociolegal classification of behavior. Decades of anthropological and criminological research have clearly shown that harsh childhood socialization has its effect in adolescent and adult deviance (see n. 7).

9. Philippe Bourgois, "Confronting Anthropology, Education, and Inner-City Apartheid," *American Anthropologist* 98 (1996): 249–58.

10. Robert B. Edgerton, *Sick Societies: Challenging the Myths of Primitive Harmony* (New York: Free Press, 1992).

11. Donziger, *Real War,* chap. 3.

12. Since the decline in manufacturing over the last twenty years, industrial jobs have moved overseas where labor is cheap, and America has shifted to a service-and-information economy. Many employees of today's prisons and other criminal justice agencies have too little education for the high-tech industry. Because manu-

facturing jobs are scarce, these workers moved into secure positions in criminal justice agencies. In the state of Illinois, the only criteria for a job as a correctional officer in a state prison are a GED and no criminal history. If it weren't for state prisons, where would these men and women find secure jobs with medical benefits and a retirement plan? See Marvin Harris, *Why Nothing Works* (New York: Touchstone, 1981), for an anthropological interpretation of the economics of American life.

13. Bourgois, "Confronting Anthropology," 249–58.

14. This research technique has spawned a number of classic studies of American urban life. These include the following: Elijah Anderson, *Streetwise: Race, Class, and Change in an Urban Community* (Chicago: University of Chicago Press, 1990); Elliot Liebow, *Tally's Corner* (Boston: Little, Brown, 1967); James Spradley, *You Owe Yourself a Drunk: An Ethnography of Urban Nomads* (Boston: Little, Brown, 1970); William F. Whyte, *Street Corner Society: The Social Structure of an Italian Slum* (Chicago: University of Chicago Press, 1943).

15. H. Russell Bernard, *Research Methods in Cultural Anthropology* (Newbury Park, Calif.: Sage, 1994), 136–37.

16. Bourgois, "Confronting Anthropology," 249.

17. Actually, though, the statistical outcomes and scientific persona of criminology are just window dressing. Citizens' fear of crime and revenge toward criminals perpetuate the company store, just as fear and revenge led to the extermination of Native Americans. "Crime control" is today's version of "conquering the West." Criminology helps make fear and revenge look modern, legitimate, and antiseptic.

18. Donziger, *Real War.*

19. See Fleisher, *Dead End.*

Shattered Lives and Shelter Lies?
Anatomy of Research Deviance in Homeless Programming and Policy

Bruce A. Arrigo

One of the most pressing and persistent social problems confronting American society during the past two decades has been homelessness. The emphasis on this more recent time frame is not to suggest that documented cases of vagrancy did not predate the 1970s. Indeed, the historical roots of American homelessness can be traced to the colonial era.[1] Moreover, since that period researchers have chronicled the development of homelessness, linking it to notable changes in the political, economic, and social fabric of the early to mid-nineteenth century,[2] the post–Civil War era,[3] the early twentieth century,[4] and the post–World War II years.[5] Nonetheless, the recent past (i.e., the late 1970s through the early 1990s) marked the birth of a certain consciousness in which "observers of the American social scene began to notice with increasing frequency the presence of people without homes, wandering city streets, and sleeping in doorways and depots."[6]

It is difficult to say with precision what factors cause homelessness and therefore what forces were responsible for its re-emergence in the late 1970s. Most experts agree, however, that the economic recession of the early 1980s,[7] the decline in affordable housing for the poor,[8] reforms in the Social Security Disability Insurance Program,[9] the massive deinstitutionalization movement,[10] and individual and social system factors (e.g., family issues, substance abuse, criminality) contributed to the troubling reappearance of homelessness.[11]

It was with this sense of history and of the recent past that my own

encounters with homelessness began. In 1985, while residing in Pitts-
burgh, Pennsylvania, I became acquainted with a nonprofit agency called
Community Human Services Corporation (CHSC). First as a volunteer
and later as an employee, I learned about the cultural rhythms of urban
vagrancy. Nearly all of my experiences were in the field; thus, I was immersed in a way of life reflecting the needs and aspirations of the poor and
disenfranchised. Very quickly I became interested in single room occupancy (SRO) housing for the homeless. It was within this setting, between
the years 1985 and 1991, that I experienced how a sense of community
could be created for displaced people by embracing the ideals of peer support, environmental autonomy, and empowerment. Looking back on
these occasions, I recall how some of my fieldwork methods as a site counselor, program director, and policy analyst were shaped by practices that
many researchers would today find questionable and undisciplined, if
not altogether scurrilous and self-serving.

In this chapter I attempt to explore the intersections of field research,
homeless studies, and investigator deviance. The aim is to deepen our
(my) understanding of experiential scholarship (i.e., ethnography) by focusing upon the theoretical and methodological presuppositions of the
researcher. I begin with a brief description of the Wood Street Commons
(WSC) SRO. It was within this housing facility that much of my fieldwork
occurred. Some attention is paid to my journey of fellowship and belonging, as well as to my unique role as program investigator and policy director. In addition, some consideration is given to the two stages of
fellowship and community that structured WSC's evolution, my position
in this organization, and the levels of aggregate tenant deviance that were
subsequently identified. Next, I sketch the development of radical views
on membership roles in field research, emphasizing a more postmodern
orientation in such endeavors. In this section Adler and Adler's work on
ethnomethodological and existential paradigms is extended.[12] This conceptual analysis is deliberately placed after my observations on the building's ecology, as my experiences of Wood Street Commons occurred
prior to my identification of any established theoretical model on field
research. I then discuss the application of a deconstructive-chaotic
methodology to homeless studies, single room occupancy housing, and
community-based research. I explore how postmodern field research is
dependent on the local, positional, and provisional understanding of re-

ality that individual and collective members voice and live. I conclude with several speculative statements on the relationship between field research in the postmodern age, homeless studies featuring SRO communities, and deviant investigatory behaviors and practices.

SROs, Wood Street Commons, and Membership in a Community

Single room occupancy facilities are not a contemporary phenomenon.[13] Having undergone considerable change in the twentieth century, they can be traced to the urban dweller's perception of the city as both a marketplace and a home.[14] This perception is important in that it can contribute to the daily functioning and stability of an SRO, much as it did in Wood Street Commons.

Single room occupancy communities can be distinguished from other forms of low-rent housing (especially shelters) on the basis of several criteria. These structures have the look and feel of apartment-style buildings, but with a scaled-down level of tenant amenities and services. In the WSC community there were 259 units. Each resident occupied his or her own unit or room. The rooms included a single bed, a sink and mirror, a sitting area with chair, and a walk-in closet. There were between three and five full, private bathrooms per floor. In WSC, there were ten floors tailored for residential purposes. Six other floors were leased for commercial use and helped defray operating costs for the building's residential component. Each of the ten tenant floors contained twenty-six units.

An additional feature found in most SROs is a congregate space. This convening area in WSC was designed for recreational activities (e.g., parties, generic hobbies, special events) as well as advocacy initiatives (e.g., the tenant newsletter, cottage industries, and resident council meetings). The congregate space was also the location where cafeteria-style breakfast and dinner meals were prepared and served. This convening area was situated in the lower level of the building.

As a collection of citizens, the urban poor who lived in SROs during the late 1970s through the early 1990s represented an array of disparate groups. Popularly referred to as the "new homeless," these collectives included the following previously unheard of or under-represented social outcasts: the chronically and acutely mentally ill,[15] young children and families,[16] displaced day laborers,[17] AIDS victims,[18] and Vietnam-era veterans. Each of these subgroups in varying numbers was represented in WSC. Intake documents in the facility also indicated that a sizable number of residents were chemically dependent and/or had cycled through the criminal justice apparatus.[19]

All WSC tenants possessed their own room keys. Access to the ten residential floors was simplified through use of two elevators, and thus tenants could visit others freely. Important resident demographics further distinguished this SRO from other comparable facilities. Among the residents 70 percent were male and 30 percent were female; the median age was forty-one; 50 percent of the residents worked at least part-time; and 35 percent represented racial minorities.[20] Many shelters accept applicants on a first-come, first-serve basis. The administrative staff of WSC, however, believed that careful "profiling" of tenants as cataloged above was essential to ensuring a stable, safe, and secure community.

Staffing patterns within SROs represent another criterion distinguishing them from other low-income housing communities. Shelter staffing is generally distributed along several continua reflecting a clearly articulated division of labor: caseworkers provide generic counseling services; security workers maintain the integrity of the property and the safety of the tenants; clerical staff manage the front desk and administrative needs pertaining to residents; housekeeping and janitorial workers see to all the hygiene and sanitation concerns of the building. Wood Street Commons followed a similar division of labor but encouraged reasonable and responsible tenants to fill many of these positions.

The SRO I encountered during the mid-1980s through the early 1990s was organized according to the ecological, demographic, and operational factors described above. I was responsible for developing and maintaining these crucial building features. As an outsider, moreover, much of my membership in and affiliation with the WSC setting occurred gradually— often after much labor and strife, followed by intense, seemingly endless interaction and negotiation, usually resulting in compromise and accommodation. It was in these moments, however, that I cultivated a fieldwork praxis conducive to safe urban living in a densely populated SRO neighborhood. In what follows, I sketch the process of my participation in the evolution of Wood Street Commons first as a housing resource for the homeless, and then as a sustainable community for low-income consumers. Delineating my role in these dichotomous phases is important given that residents, staff, volunteers, and administrative personnel underwent an existential process of self and communal discovery—one which precipitated both structural change and programmatic variance. This measure of transformation was the impetus behind the developing postmodern and deconstructive field research method that subsequently emerged out of it.

Housing the Homeless—Elsewhere I have described the two stages of Wood Street Commons' evolution as a *needs-based* philosophy of human service intervention (Phase I) followed by a *strength-based* philosophy of social welfare practice (Phase II).[21] During the Phase I period (1985–87) my role in the SRO mostly consisted of supporting residents with their unmet needs. Often I functioned as a broker who facilitated the delivery of essential human services: entitlement assistance, literacy training, housing referrals, job placement, psychological counseling, and parenting classes. As both program director and site counselor, I was primarily concerned with increasing the delivery of assistance to the urban poor residing within the facility.

During this period I was also WSC's principal researcher. With a focus on tracking tenant assimilation within the SRO community, I closely monitored weekly reports pertinent to intake statistics, incident reports, tenant demographics, and evictions, as well as any noticeable changes in staffing patterns, resident participation in community events, and house rules. Throughout Phase I of the building's development, I regarded my membership role as *ancillary* to the social fabric of the community. Tenants knew that I worked for Community Human Services Corporation. They chided me by pointing out that I merely "did my job" or that I "completed tasks" while in the building. I felt detached from the residents and from Wood Street Commons. In short, I sensed that I had fashioned myself into an outsider; my fieldwork was more about methodically producing and carefully interpreting data and less about fostering meaningful community relationships.

My research (in the area of program and policy analysis) assumed that most, if not all, WSC tenants were the product of social forces that had catapulted them into poverty and vagrancy. The operating assumption was that tenants needed to be benignly helped by specialists and experts; that is, residents were incapable, without some targeted staff direction, of resolving their personal crises or social condition. The production of empirical and measurable data supported this contention. Thus, I sustained a dispassionate, impartial, and nonpartisan fieldwork/researcher attitude in the hope of accumulating information which would reflect how ongoing, professionalized social services rendered to the tenants of Wood Street Commons would make a meaningful difference in preparing them for autonomous living.

Community for Consumers—During the course of this Phase I intervention, the building sustained two fires set by disgruntled tenants. Further, the average weekly occupancy figures during this period were low (only 54 percent). Comparable data on evictions and incident reports were high (sixteen per week and fifteen per week respectively). Tenants were not assimilating into the community's culture. Vandalism and other forms of theft were rampant. Staff members were dissatisfied with their work, and employee retention suffered because of it. By all accounts, change was sorely needed in my (our) fieldwork practice. Many of the staff felt that our style of community intervention was related to the building's fires, low occupancy rate, and high eviction/incident figures. Discussions ensued in which the method of fieldwork practice became a subject of careful evaluation.

During the Phase II period, from 1987 to 1991, a major transformation took place in Wood Street Commons which affected the staff's interpersonal exchanges with residents and our (my) field research praxis. This transformation was related to our ongoing examination of which community intervention techniques did or did not work. The change focused on the role of *chaos* in contributing to the vitality of the community. Briefly stated, chaos theory holds that all systems (including communities) tend to natural states of order and disorder; that is, there is a mix of predictability and unpredictability that accounts for the mapping of individual behavior within a social environment.[22]

Initially, many of us who frequented Wood Street Commons as CHSC community organizers, counselors, and social workers felt that the emphasis on chaos would undermine the integrity of our needs-based philosophy of human service intervention. We understood that chaos meant that tenants would assume a greater role in the direction and tone of the facility: they would decide to meet or not to meet with SRO counselors; they would decide to address or not to address their social deficiencies or life crises; they would determine what experiences, persons, things, and places mattered or did not matter to them. In short, residents would carve out their individual identities within the building and, therefore, would contribute to the structuring of a residential identity more compatible with their collective sense of neighborhood in an SRO facility. Staff members were now charged with cultivating tenant competencies; that is, we were responsible for fanning the flames of each tenant's specialized skills and strengths.

We also understood that the predictability associated with our established and routinized community-organization practices would no longer govern our relationships with the residents, nor would such ritualized exchanges themselves assume a prominent place in our interaction with community members. Actively brokering on behalf of residents for social resources or networking with other professionals to acquire much-needed client assistance was no longer crucial to our involvement with residents.

As a sociologist-criminologist with some training in social work and social welfare, I confronted the Phase II strategy with trepidation. The obvious uncertainty associated with any organizational chaos and the significance given to it in structuring the ecology of Wood Street Commons meant that my role would be blurred; I was no longer merely the Director (i.e., the program setter, policymaker, and field researcher). I would need to become part of the social fabric that was to be the more effusive and more fluid WSC community as envisioned by the building's social architects, including the Community Human Services Corporation.

Blurring fieldwork boundaries affected many facets of my interpersonal exchanges within the SRO. In particular, the accurate collection and interpretation of tenant data—so essential to the continued funding of several initiatives within the facility—were simply not meaningful to the residents and to the character of the community they were creating. Thus, my recording of tenant data became less formal, less objective, and less dispassionate.

Understanding and cultivating tenant competencies assumed a larger portion of my time. I was motivated by a desire to learn more about the capacities of the urban poor inhabiting WSC—especially how *they* described their strengths and actualized their skills. Many residents actively formed groups promoting their desire for *advocacy and self-governance* (e.g., tenants who produced a monthly newsletter, a tenant council, residents who engaged in public speaking), for *celebration* (e.g., they organized theme dances, fashion shows, picnics), for *consumerism* (e.g., they created food service and janitorial maintenance cottage industries), for *art* (e.g., they formed a performing arts collective that featured homeless musicians, co- medians, dancers, and vocalists), and for *recreation* (e.g., they organized a homeless sports league composed of men and women from area soup kitchens and other shelters that played organized basketball, softball, vol- leyball, and touch football).

In order to sustain the chaos flourishing in WSC, a constant re- engagement with residents (mostly on a group basis) was required. As a field researcher, this meant that I participated in most of the events and activities developed by residents, regardless of how these experiences structurally changed (e.g., addressing the confusion of newly initiated participants, cycling through different tenant leadership groups, or mov- ing impetuously from unfinished projects to still more innovative ones). Senior SRO inhabitants indoctrinated newer tenants. Recently hired staff workers were introduced to the building by resident council members. These forms of interaction were always unconventional, never staged, and routinely subject to the evolving sensibilities of the tenants. There was a great deal of unpredictability and disorder at the micro-interac- tional level; yet, because of this, there emerged a great deal of predictabil- ity and order at the macro-institutional level. Weekly occupancy figures during Phase II dramatically improved (to 95 percent). Tenant evictions and incident reports improved as well (only five per week and six per week respectively). Staff attrition was no longer a major concern, as many real- ized that the building was now functioning well and the change in orga- nizational tone had exceeded anyone's expectations.

At times during this strength-based period, I questioned whether the building was producing shelter lies; field research was undisciplined and data collection was unsystematic. Often, tenants actively assisted in the research process—thus raising obvious questions regarding contamina- tion in the findings, sample bias, and researcher fraud. On one particular occasion, residents participated in a self-report survey on alcohol con- sumption in the facility. Both the participating community members and I were aware of the implications the data would hold for the continued funding of our chemical recovery and shelter program operating within the SRO. Further, we understood that without the continued funding several addicts legitimately attempting recovery while in the building would become homeless. In this instance, tenants reported levels of alcohol consumption in the SRO that were vastly lower than what we all knew to be the "reality."

On these and other similar occasions I did not challenge residents to tell "the truth." I am not suggesting that tenants blatantly lied, nor that I engaged in some form of deliberate deceit; rather, I am suggesting that *residents intersubjectively determined what reality expressed their uniquely felt experience of the situation confronting them, and they spoke and responded accordingly.* Throughout Phase II, one thing remained constant: beyond individual staff or resident behaviors and practices, the SRO had become vital. The building was now sustaining and fostering a growing sense of community.

Radical Field Research Paradigms: From Existentialism and Ethnomethodology to Postmodern Deconstructionism

The development of radical views on researcher roles in the field can be traced to French and German traditions of existential phenomenology. The investigative paradigm of existential sociology rejected the absolutism and positivism implied in the natural scientific approach, particularly the way in which scientific methodological pursuits dismissed the role of the researcher in co-constituting reality. The German mathematician and philosopher Edmund Husserl spent considerable time unraveling the essential identity of social phenomena and the stance individuals took with respect to phenomena they observed when in and out of the *natural attitude.*[23] Martin Heidegger, a student of Husserl's, furthered this epistemological interest by exploring the meaning of being, or *Dasein,* and, more specifically, what it meant to be a *Being-in-the-world.*[24] The French philosopher Merleau-Ponty contributed as well by suggesting that truth, reality, and meaning were intersubjectively verifiable; that is, that they were dependent on the joint effects of the phenomenon's objective presentation to the world and our subjective encounter of it.[25]

Along with others (particularly the philosophy of Jean-Paul Sartre and the hermeneutics of Wilhelm Dilthey), the epistemology of existential phenomenology and sociology suggested that there was something more to discover about everyday life and individuals in it than what could be discovered through detached, "scientific" investigatory practices. Getting back to the "things themselves" and the people who fashioned them required a more involved stance when in the field. Thus, researchers were to "experience the setting as much as possible like any new participant."[26]

This investigatory process was critical because dual realities governed social spaces and the behavior of their inhabitants. Goffman identified these dual realities as frontstage (i.e., polite, conversational, superficial) and backstage (i.e., instinctual, uninhibited, natural) impressions that allowed for variance in group interaction.[27] Thus, following the existential-phenomenological fieldwork paradigm, the researcher became "socialized to the setting, [able] to learn the taken-for-granted assumptions, to grasp the setting as insiders [did] and, as much as possible, to feel the way insiders [did]."[28]

The related ethnomethodological model of investigatory roles in the field was an outgrowth of the existential phenomenology of Alfred Schutz. Schutz endeavored to understand the everyday dimensions of social life and human interaction.[29] He emphasized a careful and detailed description of the individual's conscious experiences. Freeman has described this process as encountering the "contours of consciousness."[30] Schutz felt that this deliberate activity would deepen our understanding of the reality individuals experienced and the meaning they assigned to it.

During the 1950s and 1960s, Harold Garfinkel championed the cause of ethnomethodology in field research.[31] Combining ideas contained in the writings of both Husserl and Schutz, Garfinkel focused on how people, in their routine encounters, came to know, define, and construct the world through a process of continual negotiation and interpretation.[32] As an investigatory science, then, ethnomethodology is descriptive in nature, attending both to a deeper appreciation for our interactions with one another through a method of conversational analysis[33] and to our use of pragmatic reasoning in taken-for-granted encounters through a method of situational analysis.[34]

In ethnomethodological field research it is crucial for the investigator to gain a valid sense of the context which situations create for subjects. Ethnomethodologists refer to this phenomenon as *indexicality*. The interpretation of language, behavior, motives, objects, and events in a given environment is subject to manifold meanings unless the environment of those who inhabit it is understood from the members' unique perspective. Thus, field researchers are to index this community of meaning. This requires immersion in the rhythms, customs, and practices of the membership group.

Ethnomethodological field work is also concerned with how community members make sense of their environment.[35] In other words, what are the cognitive processes employed to interpret the social world? This activity is reflexive or reciprocal in nature: interpretations of social living are dependent on the indexical meanings assigned to speech, phenomena, objects, and emotions, and the indexical meanings themselves in turn reflect back onto the speech, phenomena, objects, and emotions once they are produced. This is akin to the co-constitutive dynamic alluded to earlier when discussing the work of existential phenomenologists. Ethnomethodological field researchers must be cognizant of the duality implicit in the interpretation of the everyday world, and of the ways in which investigatory methods contribute to the very phenomena they seek to understand.

Postmodern deconstructionism as a method of inquiry has undergone considerable revision but can be traced to the work of several French social critics,[36] "second wave" feminist scholars,[37] Frankfurt School neo-Marxists,[38] and continental semioticians.[39] Similar to existential phenomenology and existential sociology, postmodernism represents a historical and epistemological split from traditional interpretations of the world that are based on an encoded logic privileging empirical, objectifiable science.[40] For postmodernists, no fundamental truths exist because the world cannot be essentially retrievable, reducible, controllable, and, therefore, knowable. The absence of any permanent or fixed markers structuring society is an outgrowth of our very existences, which depend on the multiple and mutable interpretations we assign to them. Thus, it is *language* which structures our thoughts in ways that are not neutral, and in ways that signify an accenting of preferred meanings for social living and social reality.

Deconstructionism represents a method of interpreting the meanings we assign to persons or events in the world. It is a deliberate process of teasing out the warring factions communicated in and through the speech we employ. Deconstructionists maintain that there is always something more—or something other—we communicate in our encounters with people or with the social order. Deconstructionists do not believe that we can ever know all the meanings conveyed in our interactions; however, we can come to understand some of them as interpreted from a series of given perspectives and in a constellation of given contexts.

One strain of postmodern deconstructive analysis not well developed in the social science literature is chaos theory. Chaos theory resists all universal and totalizing principles of thought, judgment, and meaning.[41] The theory fundamentally questions the veracity of Newtonian physics, Euclidean geometry, Aristotelian logic, and indeed any approach guided by deterministic and positivistic principles of science. The essence of chaos theory can be conceptualized on the basis of several interdependent propositions. The most relevant of these follow:

Non-linearity—There are no essential structures and no permanent stabilities governing space or time.[42] Thus, the social order is situated in unpredictability (disorder), and natural systems are understood to maintain themselves steadily "precisely because they are 'unprincipled,' i.e., they behave nonlinearly."[43] Thus, minor or incremental changes (inputs) can produce major or substantial results (outputs). For example, residents of Wood Street Commons were able to dramatically shed their perceived public identities as lazy and unmotivated social outcasts by volunteering to participate in a relatively small number of cable access and radio shows describing the lives of the sheltered homeless.

Fractal Space—Natural scientific interpretations of space and the plotting of movement in space are based upon whole integers. Chaologists recognize the fractional dimension of space.[44] Extending this rationale to social life and field research in Wood Street Commons, sound investigatory practices were measured in degrees. In other words, contrary to the binary formula found in Aristotelian logic, chaos theory posits that fieldwork is more appropriately about fractal values; it is not an all (completely objective and detached) or nothing (completely subjective and involved) equation. The tenant culture regarding drug use is illustrative of this point. During the Phase II period of WSC, residents and staff acknowledged that being "chemically free" was a process in which different individuals would be at different points in the recovery continuum. Thus, many building members spoke of addiction and recovery in this way, which contributed to a healthier, less hostile drug climate in the facility.

Attractors—Chaologists envision the mapping of dynamic systems (e.g., the ethnography of community SROs) in a nonlinear fashion.[45] Attractors are cumulative patterns of behavior or trajectories that plot out and point to movement tendencies in a system. There are maps which depict linear trajectories. These are called *limit* or *point* attractors. Other maps portray nonlinear movements. These are called *torus* or *strange* attractors. These latter trajectories behave in ways contrary to Newtonian physics and conventional science. They represent both order and disorder, predictability and unpredictability.

The Tenant Advocacy Group (TAG) is a representative example of how this chaos principle functioned in the SRO. Although TAG representatives convened weekly, there was usually a great deal of uncertainty about who would attend, whether agenda items would be addressed or not, or which debates would ensue between parties. Over time, however, we found that there was structuration (predictability) at the macro- (institutional/global) level, stemming from conditions of flux (unpredictability) at the micro- (situational/local) level. In other words, although the weekly TAG meetings were routinely fraught with high levels of disorder, cumulatively these gatherings pointed to an organizational pattern of TAG resident behavior and interaction. Thus, order emerged out of chaos.

The Torus and Iteration—In chaos theory, the torus attractor is depicted by a tubelike structure. Cross-gaps of the torus are called Poincare sections. They represent events isolated at a particular time. At the macro-level or in terms of global/institutional system movement, there is overall order. This predictability is the tubelike torus itself. However, at the micro-level, or in terms of local, positional system movement, there is indeterminability. In other words, "pinpointing specific occurrences within this slice (Poincare section) with exactness is an illusory exercise."[46] In speech we can appreciate this process through *iteration*.[47] Every word or phrase has a multitude of indexicalities. Meaning explodes and scatters. It is not fixed, static, or closed. At best there are only approximations. There is no *precise* fit.

Assigning meaning to the residents' decision to report lower levels of building infractions (house rule violations) illustrates the effects of the torus and iteration. At the macro-level providing intentionally false and incomplete data may be wrong and deviant. However, at the situational level, the defining of "building incidents" was unstable; it depended upon the person to whom the question was put, as well as the situation, position, and context in which a tenant's interpretation was proffered. The same may be said regarding all aspects of communal living in Wood Street Commons. There was a range of possible meanings for "building incidents." The slightest variation in *factual* circumstances could have altered the iterations that were given preferred meaning. This is an instance of postmodern, nonlinear dynamics at work.

Far-from-Equilibrium Conditions—According to chaologists, dynamic systems continually break down but are spontaneously reconstituted. Chaologists term such conditions *dissipative structures*.[48] These structures are characterized by their sensitivity and responsiveness to variation, contingency, perturbation. Dissipative structures are receptive to change, chance, indeterminacy, and flux. The generating mechanisms for such fluid systems are *far-from-equilibrium* conditions.[49] These conditions make possible the establishment of new meanings or replacement narratives (ways of knowing) wherein the speech actions of an individual find greater expression and legitimacy.

Systems which tend toward stasis and closure (including entire communities) promote predictable interactions, restrictive discourses, and circumscribed truth claims held out as universal realities. Individual and collective differences (characterized as deviations) are quashed. However, systems governed more by randomness, continuous variation, and unpredictability ready the way for alternative truths—that is, replacement realities compatible with the contingencies, spontaneities, contradictions, ironies, ambiguities, fantasies, and absurdities of social living. As an open-ended system of communal interaction, multiple expressions of being human would be embodied: various discourses understood as provisional, positional, and relational, as well as truths subject to iterative variation, would find legitimate voice and acceptance.

During Phase II, the fieldwork practice in Wood Street Commons established new vistas of meaning for many facets of the building's internal ecology. For example, consistent with both postmodern thought and chaos theory, the very choice of how staff defined residents (as consumers of services rather than troubled clients), how interaction was structured (inclusively rather than exclusively), and how decisions were made (cooperatively rather than hierarchically) altered the texturing of the field practice. Again, there was more unpredictability at the situational level, but, over time, a pattern of communal identity emerged.

In chaos theory, the most celebrated "strange" attractor is the butterfly attractor. It appears with two wings called outcome basins. The strange attractor is much more sensitive to contingencies than is the torus. At the macro-level, order and predictability prevail; however, at the micro-level, disorder is pervasive. In other words, within each basin, accurate, precise prediction is impossible. Notwithstanding, with repeated iterations (the repetition of certain meanings) a pattern emerges; that is, the butterfly wings appear. The instances in which undecidability and indeterminacy prevail are moments of open-endedness and receptiveness. They are periods in which stasis and closure are resisted. These are crucial points of decision making, crucial points of knowing. They are not identically fixed even in situations reflecting similar circumstances.

From the perspective of chaos theory, in fieldwork practices the researcher must be open to variance in individual and collective interpretations of social space and social order. This very openness is an invitation to embrace the truth claims of members *from their unique communicative perspectives*. The attention to multiple languages (and meanings) is therefore essential.

The fieldwork praxis during Phase II of the Wood Street Commons experience was about hearing the voices of its members. Their language, their knowledge, and their desire were fundamental to the structuring of the community. Further, by stressing chaos, the opportunity for multiple knowledges—always understood as positional, provisional, and relational—ensured that various expressions of resident realities were embodied at the local or micro-interactional level. Notwithstanding, through divergent encounters and through changes in tenant membership, a deracinated cultural identity emerged at the macro-interactional level.

Field Research, Homeless Studies, and Investigator Deviance: Some Speculations in the Age of Postmodernity

The role of deconstructionism and chaos as linked to my postmodern fieldwork method at Wood Street Commons raises some interesting questions concerning the presence of investigator (and tenant) deviance. If, following the theoretical and methodological presuppositions of chaology, SRO behaviors and practices were contingent upon the local and relational knowledges of its members, then my policy and programming conduct was compatible with the communal social reality. Does it therefore follow that there is no possibility for engaging in researcher deviance when in the postmodern attitude? Or, to put it differently, does this mean that any fieldwork activity is permissible in light of the deconstructive and chaotic researcher paradigm outlined above? In the case of Wood Street Commons the answer to these questions was dependent upon the SRO itself, and upon individual tenant interpretations of ethical behavior in particular instances and interactions among specific members.

Clearly, then, there is room for investigator deviance; but it must be categorically understood on the community's terms and put into the language of the community itself. To do otherwise promotes a victimization of the residents and their uniquely encoded understanding of their social rhythms and congregate attitudes. During my Phase II experiences at Wood Street Commons, I did *not* fashion researcher deviance from the tenant's perspective, but I did so from some outsiders' point of view. While in the community and in the residents' attitude, there was, nonetheless, a haunting and gnawing suspicion that my field practice behavior was questionable and unsophisticated. In the face of the facility's commitment to chaos, however, what the residents taught me was something meaningful about the power of their words, their way of doing things, their truth. This is precisely what postmodernism has to offer field research methods in general and investigatory practices in particular. It is not merely enough to return to "the things themselves" or to "become the phenomenon." Both must occur in that specialized discourse (and from that behavior) which gives meaning to those persons and places whom field workers study.

Summary

This chapter has provisionally explored several techniques of postmodern field research relevant to homeless studies and investigator deviance. By describing two separate developmental phases of an urban single room occupancy, the practical results of chaos in promoting unstable micro-social and stable macro-institutional realities were presented. Membership roles in the community were transformed in the face of the unpredictable social arrangements that materialized.

My participation in Wood Street Commons, particularly my policy and programming research, was similarly affected. In both instances, open-ended communal interaction promoted the articulation of multiple expressions of shelter life. In theory, deconstructive chaology endeavors to give voice to these replacement ways of knowing. The methods of postmodern fieldwork must therefore do the same. The question of investigator deviance under such circumstances is positional, provisional, and relational. In other words, what matters most are the words, the meanings, and the behaviors of those who are the subjects of observation and study. To ignore this challenge in field research is to promote, knowingly or not, the oppression of those very members whose styles of existence would otherwise slumber in despair.

Notes

1. Albert Deutsch, *The Mentally Ill in America: A History of Their Care and Treatment from Colonial Times* (New York: Columbia University Press, 1937); Gerald Grob, *Mental Institutions in America: Social Policy to 1875* (New York: Free Press, 1973); Madeline Martin, "Homeless Women: A Historical Perspective," in *On Being Homeless: Historical Perspectives,* ed. Rick Beard (New York: Museum of the City of New York, 1987), 112–43.

2. David Rothman, *The Discovery of the Asylum* (Boston: Little, Brown, 1971); David Rothman, "The First Shelters: The Contemporary Relevance of the Almshouses," in *On Being Homeless: Historical Perspectives,* ed. Rick Beard (New York: Museum of the City of New York, 1987), 83–104.

3. Samuel Wallace, *Skid Row as a Way of Life* (Totowa, N.J.: Bedminster Press, 1965); Peter Ringenbach, *Tramps and Reformers 1873–1916: The Discovery of Unemployment in New York* (Westport, Conn.: Greenwood, 1973).

4. Andrew Solenberger, *One Thousand Homeless Men* (New York: Russell Sage Foundation, 1911); Nels Anderson, *The Hobo: The Sociology of the Homeless Man* (Chicago: University of Chicago Press, 1923).

5. New York City Welfare Council, *Homeless Men in New York City* (New York: Welfare Council, 1949); Donald Bogue, *Skid Row in American Cities* (Chicago: University of Chicago Press, 1963); Donald Bogue, *The Homeless Man on Skid Row* (Chicago: Tenants Relation Bureau, City of Chicago, 1961); Howard Bahr, *Homelessness and Disaffiliation* (New York: Columbia University Bureau of Applied Social Research, 1968).

6. Catherine Caton, *Homeless in America* (New York: Oxford University Press, 1990), 12.

7. Mario Cuomo, *1933–1983—Never Again* (Portland, Maine: Report to the National Governors' Association Task Force on the Homeless, 1983).

8. Paul Kasinitz, "Gentrification and Homelessness: The Single Room Occupant and the Inner City Revival," *Urban and Social Change Review* 17 (1984): 3–18.

9. "Proposals for Mentally Disabled Would Ease Eligibility for U.S. Aid," *New York Times,* December 9, 1984, A1.

10. David Rothman, *Conscience and Convenience: The Asylum and Its Alternatives in Progressive America* (Boston: Little, Brown, 1980).

11. John Wright, *Address Unknown: The Homeless in America* (New York: Aldine de Gruyter, 1989), 81–93.

12. Patricia Adler and Peter Adler, *Membership Roles in Field Research* (Newbury Park, Calif.: Sage, 1987), 20–32.

13. See, for example, Harvey Siegal, *Outposts of the Forgotten* (New Brunswick, N.J.: Transaction Books, 1978); Jan Smithers, *Determined Survivors: Community Life Among the Urban Elderly* (New Brunswick, N.J.: Transaction Books, 1985); Charles Hoch and Richard Slayton, *New Homeless and Old: Community and the Skid Row* (Philadelphia: Temple University Press, 1989).

14. Bruce Arrigo, "Rooms for the Misbegotten: Social Design and Social Deviance," *Journal of Sociology and Social Welfare* 24 (1994): 96; Kim Hopper and Janet Hamberg, *The Making of America's Homeless: From Skid Row to the New Poor, 1945–1984* (New York: Community Services Society, 1985).

15. Wright, *Address Unknown;* Richard Lamb, "Deinstitutionalization and the Homeless Mentally Ill," *Hospital and Community Psychiatry* 35 (1984): 899–907.

16. Bruce Arrigo, "A Preliminary Investigation of the Modest Needs Homeless Family Phenomenon: Agenda for Research, Policy, and Practice," unpublished manuscript, 1996; Sonja Redmond and Joan Brackman, "Homeless Children and Their Caretakers," in *Homelessness in the United States,* ed. Jamshid Momeni (New York: Praeger, 1990), 64–81.

17. Richard Williams, *Hard Labor* (Atlanta, Ga.: Southern Regional Council, 1988).

18. Robert Bayer, *Private Act, Social Consequence: AIDS and the Politics of Public Health* (New York: Free Press, 1989).

19. Bruce Arrigo, "Recommunalizing Drug Offenders: The 'Drug Peace' Agenda," *Journal of Offender Rehabilitation* 24 (1996): 83–106.

20. Arrigo, "Rooms," 101.

21. Arrigo, "Rooms," 98–100; Arrigo, "Recommunalizing," 83–88.

22. T. R. Young and Bruce Arrigo, *Chaos and Crime: From Criminal Justice to Social Justice* (Albany: SUNY Press, 1997).

23. Edmund Husserl, *Phenomenology and the Crisis of Philosophy* (New York: Harper and Row, 1965); Edmund Husserl, *Ideas: General Introduction to Pure Phenomenology* (New York: Collier, 1962).

24. Martin Heidegger, *Being and Time* (New York: Harper and Row, 1962).

25. Maurice Merleau-Ponty, *The Structure of Behavior* (Bloomington: Indiana University Press, 1983); Maurice Merleau-Ponty, *Phenomenology of Perception* (New York: Humanities Press, 1962).

26. Adler and Adler, *Membership Roles,* 22.

27. Erving Goffman, *The Presentation of Self in Everyday Life* (Garden City, N.Y.: Doubleday, 1959); Erving Goffman, *Interaction Ritual* (Garden City, N.Y.: Doubleday, 1967).

28. Adler and Adler, *Membership Roles,* 22.

29. Alfred Schutz, *Collected Papers I: The Problem of Social Reality* (The Hague: Martinus Nijhoff, 1962); Alfred Schutz, *Collected Papers II: Studies in Social Theory* (The Hague: Martinus Nijhoff, 1964); Alfred Schutz, *Collected Papers: Studies in Phenomenological Philosophy* (The Hague: Martinus Nijhoff, 1966); Alfred Schutz, *The Phenomenology of the Social World* (Evanston, Ill.: Northwestern University Press, 1967).

30. Charles Freeman, "Phenomenological Sociology and Ethnomethodology," in *Introduction to the Sociologies of Everyday Life,* ed. Jack Douglas (Boston: Allyn and Bacon, 1980), 114–30.

31. Harold Garfinkel, *Studies in Ethnomethodology* (Englewood Cliffs, N.J.: Prentice-Hall, 1967).

32. Adler and Adler, *Membership Roles,* 25; Jeremy Heritage, *Garfinkel and Ethnomethodology* (Cambridge: Polity, 1984).

33. Aaron Cicourel, *Cognitive Mappings* (New York: Free Press, 1971); Edward Schegloff and Howard Sacks, "Opening Up Closings," in *Ethnomethodology,* ed. Robert Turner (Baltimore: Penguin, 1974), 147–68.

34. Michael Pollner, "On the Foundations of Mundane Reason" (Ph.D. diss., University of California, Santa Barbara, 1970); David Sudnow, ed., *Studies in Social Interaction* (New York: Free Press, 1972).

35. William Handel, *Ethnomethodology* (Englewood Cliffs, N.J.: Prentice-Hall, 1982).

36. Jacques Derrida, *Of Grammatology* (Baltimore: Johns Hopkins, 1976); Jacques Derrida, *Speech and Phenomena* (Evanston, Ill.: Northwestern University Press, 1973); Michel Foucault, *Madness and Civilization: A History of Insanity in the Age of Reason* (New York: Pantheon, 1965); Michel Foucault, *The Archeology of Knowledge* (New York: Pantheon, 1972); Roland Barthes, *The Semiotic Challenge* (New York: Hill and Wang, 1988); Jean Baudrillard, *Simulacra and Simulations* (New York: Semiotext[e], 1983); Jean Baudrillard, *Selected Writings,* ed. Mark Poster (Stanford: Stanford University Press, 1988); Jacques Lacan, *Encore* (Paris: Edition du Seuil, 1975); Jacques Lacan, *Ecrit: A Selection* (New York: W. W. Norton, 1977).

37. Luce Irigaray, *This Sex Which Is Not One* (Ithaca, N.Y.: Cornell University Press, 1985); Luce Irigaray, *Je, Tu, Nous* (New York: Routledge, 1993); Julia Kristeva, *Desire in Language* (New York: Columbia University Press, 1980); Julia Kristeva, *Revolution in Poetic Discourse* (New York: Columbia University Press, 1984).

38. Jürgen Habermas, *Legitimation Crises* (Boston: Beacon Press, 1975); Jürgen

Habermas, *The Theory of Communicative Action, Vol. 1, Reason and the Rationalization of Society* (Boston: Beacon Press, 1984); Jürgen Habermas, *The Theory of Communicative Action, Vol. 2, Lifeworld and System: A Critique of Functionalist Reason* (Boston: Beacon Press, 1987); Theodore Adorno, *The Jargon of Authenticity* (New York: Continuum, 1967); Theodore Adorno, *Negative Dialectics* (New York: Continuum, 1976); Louis Althusser, *Lenin and Philosophy* (New York: Monthly Review, 1971).

39. Algirdas Greimas, *On Meaning* (Minneapolis: University of Minnesota Press, 1987); Algirdas Greimas, *The Social Science: A Semiotic View* (Minneapolis: University of Minnesota Press, 1990); Umberto Eco, *Semiotics and the Philosophy of Language* (London: Macmillan, 1984); Umberto Eco, *Theory of Semiotics* (Bloomington: Indiana University Press, 1984).

40. Jean-Francois Lyotard, *The Postmodern Condition: A Report on Knowledge* (Minneapolis: University of Minnesota Press, 1984); Peter Dews, *Logics of Disintegration: Post-Structuralist Thought and the Claims of Critical Theory* (New York: Verso, 1987); Anthony Giddens, *The Consequences of Modernity* (Stanford: Stanford University Press, 1990). See Bruce Arrigo, "The Peripheral Core of Law and Criminology: On Postmodern Social Theory and Conceptual Integration," *Justice Quarterly* 12 (1995): 447–72; Bruce Arrigo, *The Contours of Psychiatric Justice: A Postmodern Critique of Mental Illness, Criminal Insanity and the Law* (New York: Garland, 1996).

41. Lyotard, *Postmodern Condition,* 53–67; Bruce Arrigo and T. R. Young, "Chaos, Complexity, and Crime: Working Tools for a Postmodern Criminology," in *Thinking Critically About Crime,* ed. Brian MacLean and Dragan Milovanovic (Vancouver: Collective Press, 1997), 77–84.

42. See, for example, John Briggs and F. David Peat, *Turbulent Mirror* (New York: Harper and Row, 1989); James Gleick, *Chaos: Making a New Science* (New York: Penguin Books, 1987); Benoit Mandelbrot, *The Fractal Geometry of Nature* (New York: W. A. Freeman, 1983). For applications to criminology and law see, for example, Bruce Arrigo, "Legal Discourse and the Disordered Criminal Defendant: Contributions from Psychoanalytic Semiotics and Chaos Theory," *Legal Studies Forum* 18 (1994): 93–112; Bruce Arrigo, "New Directions in Crime, Law, and Social Change: On Psychoanalytic Semiotics, Chaos Theory, and Postmodern Ethics," *Studies in the Social Sciences* 33 (1995): 101–29; Bruce Arrigo, "Dimensions of Social Justice in an SRO: Contributions from Chaos Theory, Policy, and Practice," in *Chaos, Criminology, and Social Justice,* ed. Dragan Milovanovic (New York: Greenwood, 1997), 139–54.

43. T. R. Young, "Chaos Theory and Human Agency: Humanist Sociology in a Postmodern Age," *Humanity and Society* 16 (1992): 445.

44. T. R. Young, "Chaos and Crime: Nonlinear and Fractal Forms of Crime," *The Critical Criminologist* 3 (1991): 3–4, 10–11; T. R. Young, "The ABC's of Crime: Attractors, Bifurcations, Basins, and Chaos," *The Critical Criminologist* 3 (1991): 3–4, 13–14.

45. Gleick, *Chaos,* 119–53.

46. Dragan Milovanovic, "Lacan, Chaos, and Practical Discourse in Law," in

Flux, Complexity, and Illusion in Law, ed. Roberta Kevelson (New York: Lang, 1993), 324.

47. Jean M. Balkin, "Deconstructive Practice and Legal Theory," *Yale Law Journal* 96 (1987): 743–86.

48. Ilya Prigogine and Isabelle Stengers, *Order Out of Chaos: Man's New Dialogue with Nature* (New York: Bantam Books, 1984).

49. Prigogine and Stengers, *Order,* 12–14.

Militarism, Terror, and the State

Enjoying Militarism Political/ Personal Dilemmas in Studying U.S. Police Paramilitary Units

Peter B. Kraska

Traditionally, both positivistic and interpretive inquiry required researchers to bracket or suppress their own beliefs, values, or subjective reactions to the research experience. The researcher played the role of analytical empiricist, no matter how intimate he or she became with the social setting. Legitimate knowledge could be acquired only from research "subjects." Twenty-five years of scholarship in a variety of human science disciplines have called into question our empirical-analytical notions of what constitutes legitimate acquisition of knowledge, as well as the validity of the scientific belief in severing the objective from the subjective. This critique has reached a crescendo in the last five years, sounding the death knell for the "objective" researcher and for the distinction between researcher and subject.[1]

Reactions to this shift range from protectiveness among positivists to nihilistic euphoria among skeptical postmodernists.[2] Critically oriented qualitative researchers in sociology and cultural anthropology embrace certain aspects of the shift. Emerging methodological norms, for instance, now welcome researchers to apply their own critical analysis of personal experiences and reactions to those experiences when appropriate, as a legitimate source of knowledge. This personally grounded approach is characterized as "self-reflexive."[3] The term is slightly misleading, however; it gives the impression that researchers reflect only from the perspective of their own personal impressions. In actuality, the *shared experience* of the critical ethnographer and the subject allows dual insight into the subject's culture as well as the researcher's experience. In transcending the traditional objective/subjective ideal, this approach has the potential to link personal ironies and contradictions experienced during the research process with their larger theoretical, cultural, and political implications.

Studying Militarism: Enacting Self-Reflexivity

The critical criminological ethnographer distrusts the state's definition of an activity as a crime. A central objective in researching crime violators, therefore, involves understanding, without legal or moral condemnation, the meaning of the activity for the subject from her or his perspective. *Verstehen,* or interpretive understanding, requires intimacy with the subjects and their activity.[4] In some cases the researcher actually becomes the subject by engaging in the "deviant" activity itself.[5] Yet, blurring the distinction between researcher and subject to the point of engaging in the deviance under study, as compelling a methodology as it may seem, obviously has certain moral limits. Smoking marijuana with jazz musicians or spray-painting murals with graffiti artists may be relatively safe undertakings morally compared to a host of other criminal activities such as rape, assault, burglary, or embezzlement. Is experiential-based understanding in these latter examples desirable, or even possible?

A different sort of moral dilemma for some ethnographers arises from researching subjects with whom the researcher cannot and does not want to relate—whose activity is, at least on the surface, morally or ideologically reprehensible. For these researchers, it may seem best to leave the subjects' activity condemned rather than understood, let alone participated in for the sake of research.

For the researcher who disdains *militarism*—the glorification of the tools and bureaucracies which perpetuate organized state violence—few research activities could be as distressing as active participation in the collaboration of the military and police in their development of domestic police paramilitary units. This research does not examine criminal behavior or a fascinating slice of deviance; instead, it focuses on the microsocial construction of coercive state power. It pursues the same objective as Ferrell espouses—"confronting and exposing the law as the machinery of centralized authority." Yet, it approaches this objective not from examining those who are regarded as lawbreakers, as Ferrell emphasizes, but rather from examining the wielders of law. Paramilitary practitioners' activities, unlike conventional forms of criminality, include the creation and enforcement of governmental power with its most crude tools and methods—the threat and use of militarized violence.

Ironically, my struggle in conducting this research had little to do with any inability to develop an understanding of the subjects; the disturbing aspect was the ease with which I succeeded. The macro-political/social implications of this research event should alarm most readers. How could someone who had thought out and condemned militarism have enjoyed many aspects of experiencing it? Here, blurring the researcher/subject distinction illustrates the expansive and addictive powers, even in these "postmodern" times, of a deeply embedded ideology of violence—*militarism,* and its accomplice, *hypermasculinity.*

In this essay I first examine this ethnographic experience and its enjoyment. I then cross-contextualize my personal experiences with larger social, political, and cultural forces. Finally, I attempt to make sense of this irony of enjoying militarism by linking personal experience with broader political and cultural influences, drawing on Bourdieu's theory of practice. The purpose of this chapter is not exclusively methodological, theoretical, or practical, but all three. Explaining the irony of enjoying militarism necessitates a theoretical and epistemological discussion about the relationship between the unresolved dualities of agency versus structure, micro-social versus macro-social, and personal versus political. Describing the irony provides a forum for exposing the practical, criminal justice implications of this micro-research event: intensifying processes of militarism, hypermasculinity, and militarization in policing and the crime control industry as a whole. Finally, enacting "self-reflexivity" as a methodological approach suggests its broader utility.

Experiencing Militarism: Weekend Warriors and Their Weaponry

Conducting field research, especially in criminology, requires the researcher to loosen inhibitions—to bump along the unpredictable and spontaneous path of social events. Working at the whim of natural social settings requires flexibility, patience, and a willingness to explore the unknown and possibly dangerous. The research event described here required that I step out of my professional and personal comfort zone. I was invited to observe an ad-hoc "training session" of police officers and military soldiers. This was an "ask no further questions" invitation; my attempt to gain more information resulted only in vague references to "tactical operations training." Despite my discomfort, I knew this was a good opportunity to meet police officers who were also military soldiers in the National Guard or military reserves. As part of my research into the emerging relationship between police and military forces in the post–cold war era, I welcomed the chance to witness the overlap firsthand.

I knew two of the participants well (I refer to them here as "Mike" and "Steve"). They approached me after hearing of my interest in the military's role in policing the drug problem. Over the course of a year we developed a relationship that included numerous in-depth conversations and approximately sixty hours of fieldwork. The scenario described here was the first of my eight field experiences with Mike and Steve's police soldier acquaintances. Mike and Steve were excellent informants because of their amiable personalities and their awareness of the broader implications of their activities. They also filtered the world through a peculiar set of presuppositions. Both of these highly trained soldiers completely lacked respect for the military bureaucracy, disdained the government as an institution (although, as the bumper sticker says, they "loved their country"), and had an attitude of irreverence toward authority and mainstream society which would make any good leftist smile. At the same time, they were highly respected and trusted within the military, and they revered military weaponry and tactics. Both had served in active duty and were now in the military reserves. They planned to enter police work immediately after their "time served in college."

I arranged to meet my informants at a supermarket parking lot. They motioned me excitely to the trunk of their car, removed several black canvas attaché-type cases, assured me that all of this was legal, and showed me several semiautomatic and fully automatic military weapons. Most of the weapons were actually owned by the military and had been lent to these soldiers over the weekend for "training." The men were eager to get to the "training site" and insisted, despite my protests, that I ride with them.

On the ride to the site, I asked Mike and Steve about their connection to training police officers. They explained that they worked regularly with several different departments interested in "tactical" operations. These officers either served currently on a tactical operations team (commonly referred to as SWAT) or were attempting to create such a team. The group we were meeting, they continued, included two ex-military soldiers who were now in the reserves. They had just begun to organize an ERU (emergency response unit) that would include selected officers from several small police departments. These officers strongly believed that small municipalities and county police were being left behind by not having special tactics teams, even if only for contingencies. According to Mike, "This shit [creation of ERUs] is going on all over. Why serve an arrest warrant to some crack dealer with a .38? With full armor, the right shit [pointing to a small case that contained a nine-millimeter Glock] and training, you can kick ass and have fun." True to their irreverent nature, Steve added: "Most of these guys just like to play war; they get a rush out of search and destroy missions instead of the bullshit they do normally."

The "training site" was an unregulated piece of land containing a vertical, eroded hillside, which made an ideal backdrop for stopping bullets. Debris from previous shooting sessions was scattered everywhere—glass, water jugs, paper targets, shell cases, and household appliances. I knew this sort of setting well. As a youth, having lived all over the country, it seemed to me that every community had somewhere an abandoned piece of land where the noise and destructiveness of guns were tolerated—although I suspect such sites have become less available over the last fifteen years.

I followed my companions to a half circle of trucks and cars, where seven police officers were laughing and talking. Our arrival silenced their conversation, and they met my escorts with smiles and outstretched hands. Mike introduced me as a professor of policing who believed in the Second Amendment. I could tell instinctively from their looks that I needed to take the lead in defining myself to them. Although these processes were not conscious at the time, I remember that a tall, lean officer used profanity when I walked up; almost instantaneously, the "f-word" casually came out of my mouth. When they inquired into my past, I managed to include my roots in Alaska and the fact that I had been a bush guide. These attempts at what Goffman calls "impression management"[6] were only the beginning of a long performance that solidified my position in the group as "fitting in" with their normative system (conservative, adventurous, hypermasculine, militaristic)—a convincing performance that disturbs me to this day.

A quick semiotic analysis of each of these friendly men's clothes told volumes about their culture: several had lightweight retractable combat knives strapped to their belts; three wore authentic army fatigue pants with T-shirts; one wore a T-shirt which carried a picture of a burning city with gunship helicopters flying overhead and the caption "Operation Ghetto Storm"; another wore a tight, black T-shirt with the initials "NTOA" (for National Tactical Officers Association). A few of the younger officers wore Oakley wraparound sunglasses on heads which sported either flattops or military-style crew cuts.

As part of their full tactical uniforms, these officers sometimes wear Oakley brand goggles designed to fit inside their Kevlar helmets or over their "Ninja"-style hoods. During previous fieldwork, I have observed the popularity of this style of wraparound sunglasses among the younger and more paramilitary-minded officers. Their image is part of a futuristic style that emphasizes a full covering of the body, hands, and face with black or urban camouflage clothes and paraphernalia. Along with very short haircuts, these police strive for a cold, fearless, mechanistic look. The Oakley goggles, along with facial masks (referred to as "balaclavas") and/or helmets, are critical to this techno-warrior image. One company labels its tactical armor as the "Cyborg 21st" line.

Steve suggested that they should line up their vehicles with tailgates or trunks facing the hillside. Once in position, each of the men laid out on mats or gun cases the various weapons and ammunition he had brought. I was awestruck, ceased to be a reflective observer, and entered the moment with fascination and alarm. Each weapon was unsheathed with care; some of the officers wiped down their already spotless weapons with silicone-impregnated rags. There were at least fifty firearms, including fully automatic urban warfare guns (H&K MP5, MP5/40), modified tactical semiautomatic shotguns, and numerous Glock- and Barretta-brand pistols. There was also a wide array of firearm paraphernalia, including noise suppressors, special-use shotgun shells, laser sights, clip-on flashlights, and, Mike and Steve's pride, a newly issued night-vision scope. I became anxious and looked around nervously, especially at the highway in our view, as if we were doing something illegal. Then I recalled a calming bit of folklore from an old Western: "Who would complain? And so what if they did? Hell, they were the law." Without reflecting on the broader implications, I felt at ease in the moment.

The men held a short discussion as to how they would go about their "training." By now I knew that the term "training" was likely only the "frontstage talk" used to legitimate and professionalize this group's activities.[7] One of the men (I'll call him "Mel") didn't participate in this discussion or in the presenting of the arms ritual. He was aloof and dispassionate; initially, I misinterpreted this behavior as apathy. Finally, once the group had reached consensus about how to proceed with the "training," Mel coolly unsheathed a Weatherby bolt-action rifle with a 3×9 power scope, walked diagonally another 150 yards from the vehicles, and set his weapon on a six-foot-long mat with a small bipod. I realized then that Mel, who had quite a bit of experience in "tactical operations," was the sniper.

I didn't recognize the high status of the sniper position until I later began to read about elite special forces units within the military. Police paramilitary units are to policing what the Navy Seals or Army Rangers are to the military. These small cadres of warriors delineate each member by some special skill or expertise. Many police paramilitary units now have, for example, one member who is an expert in the sort of explosives which allow quick entry into a fortified building or residence. The military and police special operations subculture holds the sniper in especially high reverence. The subculture glorifies the skill, discipline, endurance, and mind-set necessary to execute people from long distances in a variety of situations. Some of the most popular items available to the police in numerous police catalogs are the videos and manuals on "sniping," usually authored by ex-military special operations snipers.

The group decided to begin by shooting pistols. For the next twenty to thirty minutes they shot at silhouettes of "bad guys," employing an array of maneuvers and tactics that required speed and skill to perform. The group was particularly impressed with Steve: he was able to draw his ten-millimeter Glock 20 handgun and rapidly fire four rounds each into three "bad guys" spaced about twenty-five feet apart. All twelve shots were deemed "kill shots"; the group found it remarkable that he managed, despite the speed with which he fired, to save his last three shots for the unseen "bad guy." Later I discovered that Steve had special status among his paramilitary policing peers, aside from his superior weapons skills, because he had served in combat in Operation Desert Storm.[8]

Next came the Heckler and Koch (H&K) MP5s. My first exposure to this line of weapons came from an H&K advertisement in a policing magazine. The advertisement exploited the hierarchy of status in militaristic thinking with regard to "elite" military special forces units. The message was: "This weaponry will distinguish you, just like the revered Navy Seals, as an elite soldier in the war on "drugs. . . . *From the Gulf War to the Drug War. . . .* Winning the war against drugs requires some very special weapons. Weapons that law enforcement professionals can stake their lives on. The MP5 Navy model submachine gun was developed especially for one of America's elite special operations units. Battle proven in the Gulf War, this model is now available for sale to the police at a special low price."

The MP5 series is the pride and the staple of police tactical operations units and holds a central place in the paramilitary police subculture. Its imposing, futuristic style overshadows its utility as a superior "urban warfare" weapon. Numerous pencil drawings, paintings, sculptures, and jewelry available for sale to paramilitary police officers depict the ultimate "tactical operations" officer; the weapon of choice is almost always some version of the MP5. The popularity of these weapons is enhanced by a multitude of accessories, including laser aimers, sound suppressors ("silencers"), and training programs sponsored by H&K.

The training of police paramilitary officers by for-profit corporations appears to be a lucrative and growing industry. Both paramilitary policing magazines—the *Tactical Edge* and *S.W.A.T.*—contain advertisements from numerous training organizations. Some are restricted to police and military personnel; others admit anyone with the five-hundred- to three-thousand-dollar tuition. One paramilitary training facility operates under the auspices of Eastern Michigan University. The Heckler and Koch "training division" not only trains the police in the use of their high-tech weaponry and tactics, but actively promotes the paramilitary subculture. This company commissioned an artist who specializes in drawing military special operations teams and now offers for sale twelve prints of highly detailed pencil drawings of police paramilitary forces in action. I have seen these drawings used as wall art in police departments, on police officers' business cards, and in public-relations brochures.

The MP5s clearly altered the tone of this "training session." The controlled, methodical approach to firing the pistols vanished, and I realized that the pistol practice was only a prelude (or, for those who prefer a psychosexual link, the foreplay) to a less restrained form of "play." Targets filled with water and sand were placed in front of us, and for the next thirty minutes the officers fired almost nonstop except for the brief moments needed to reset targets and to imagine new ways to prove their destructiveness. I could not help noticing how "playful" and unrestrained these men were while shooting these deadly projectiles. Sharing this activity, at least within the moment, also softened the barriers between them and fostered group solidarity.[9] They even felt compelled to bring me into their experience.

A young, small-town police officer ("Mitch"), who also served in the Army Reserves, walked over to where I was watching, presented his MP5 with outstretched arms, and said in a subtly challenging manner, "Give it a try." I tried to avoid his provocation, but both Mike and Steve gave me covert sideways jerks of their heads, urging me to go along. Once in position, Mitch insisted that I fire it on the fully automatic setting, stressing that I was a "big boy" and "should be able to handle it." I fired at a body-sized target, and, just as this officer surely anticipated, I made all the mistakes of someone who had never fired an automatic before. I held the trigger too long, and the muzzle rose after several rounds, causing me to shoot completely over the target. I emptied an entire thirty-clip magazine in a virtual flash. Everyone enjoyed this process of affirming their own proficiency in weapons by setting up the academic "egghead" for failure.

My unreflective reaction came right out of a paramilitary movie script: "I've never shot this high-tech crap before. I prefer a good 'side-by-side' [a shotgun]." I explained that I had spent a significant part of my youth shooting and hunting with shotguns. Because Mitch had instigated this masculine game of one-upsmanship, he tested my assertion by loading and handing me a Remington 1187 tactical-unit shotgun. I gave a personally satisfying demonstration of my shotgun skills, which more than proved my worth to these aspiring warriors. Tactically, as a researcher, participating in this status-legitimating contest furthered my research objectives. At the same time, however, the incident raised some troubling questions about the authenticity of my intellectual convictions, and the powerful interplay between paramilitary culture and masculine ideology.

Next the group armed itself with shotguns and several boxes of odd-looking shotgun ammunition. One of the officers fired a round into a junked clothes dryer. The explosion was unbelievably loud, despite ear protection; simultaneously, a large flash was visible in the dwindling daylight.[10] The men also experimented with other "special event" shells, including a shredder round, which cuts the locking mechanism out of doors. After witnessing its effect on a metal file cabinet, a younger officer said jokingly that he might load up with these shells on his next crack raid.

The high-tech shotgun ammunition entertained these military and police personnel for almost an hour. During this pyrotechnics frenzy, even I ceased to connect the technology with its use on real people and their residences. The loud, bright explosions, the destructiveness, and the laughter took me back to a youth filled with bottle-rocket wars, imaginative uses of firecrackers, and a tacit belief that the bigger and more destructive the explosion, the better. As with these police and military personnel, however, this fun-filled activity often was not benign. Frequently my objectives as a youth were to destroy other people's property and to terrorize despised neighbors and school officials.

I later mentioned to the group that I did not understand the utility of the high-tech weaponry aside from its recreational value. Several of the men explained that these new technologies, and tactical units in general, were mostly the result of the "out of control drug and crack problem." Serving arrest and search warrants and conducting drug raids in crack-infested neighborhoods, they explained, required a well-trained, well-equipped tactical operations unit. (Until quite recently, police paramilitary units have been limited to hostage or barricaded suspect situations.) They also pointed out that these neighborhoods were "powder-kegs" ready to explode. For them, tactical operations personnel were the front-line defense for the inevitable emergence of civil disturbances.

Mel concluded the "training" with an exhibition of his sniping skills. The group was awed and mentioned instances of Mel's uncanny ability to remain calm and disciplined under pressure. I never asked whether Mel had actually killed anyone as a sniper; the group's admiration of his ability and apparent willingness to kill was unsettling enough.

Personal Enjoyment and Distressing Implications

Mel the sniper, and his accompanying status, coincide with long-running scripts rooted in militaristic thinking. His demeanor and training—calmly shooting "head-size" jugs of water behind plates of glass—were poignant reminders of the potential danger represented, both symbolically and physically, by these civilian police acting as military soldiers. Thus, my ethnographic experience is more complex than the characterization "enjoying militarism" might suggest. In actuality, I drifted back and forth between enjoyment and alarm. I felt enjoyment when I forgot myself and became fully immersed in the intensity of the moment, unintentionally bracketing my ideological filters. Schutz believed that in the realm of the experienced moment, meaning lies suspended for subsequent application.[11] Discomfort and sometimes distress came at those times of broader consciousness where even split-second moments of reflection allowed for impositions of meaning. As discussed later, these tensions, between the moment and conscious reflection, between enjoyment and aversion, may be instructive as to the role of cultural/ideological influences in constructing our personal ideological frameworks, and in clarifying possibilities of reconstruction.

Several aspects of the research experience, then, were pleasurable or satisfying. The most difficult confession, in view of my pro-feminist orientation, is that I enjoyed gaining the acceptance of a group of male police/soldiers by using hypermasculine signifiers ("Alaskan," "Bush Guide," "Shotgun Warrior," "One-Upsmanship," "Gun Worshiper"). Many of these men were repulsive ideologically, but (outside my research objectives) I enjoyed their approval as filtered through their hypermasculine standards.

I also enjoyed observing and using the weaponry, explosives, and associated technology. In my youth, two older brothers and I searched continually for more efficient ways to launch projectiles to destroy, vandalize, or inflict pain on someone or something. This quest ranged from hurling dirt clods, spears, and inner tubes, to shooting "wrist rockets" (slingshots), blowguns, BB guns, pellet guns, bow and arrows, and, when available, fireworks. We routinely attempted to approximate the "war experience" by engaging in painful and often terrifying BB-gun and pellet-gun wars, complete with casualties. This quest for more powerful weapons peaked when we smuggled a .22 rifle out of the house and shot it in our suburban backyard with a homemade silencer. I found myself, twenty-five years later, holding the ultimate projectile-hurling technology, fitted with a "sound suppressor" that actually worked. The quest was complete.

Power played a role as another enjoyable aspect of this experience. I had an intense sense of operating on the edge of legitimate and illegitimate behavior. Clearly much of the activity itself was illegal, although reporting it would never have resulted in its being defined as "criminal." As mentioned earlier, I felt at ease and in some ways defiant. I've had this experience in the past when field-researching police officers, and I realize that in a sense I am basking in the security of my temporary status as a beneficiary of state-sanctioned use of force. This is likely the same intoxicating feeling of autonomy from the law that is experienced by an abusive police officer, corrupt judge, or politically wired corporate executive.

Other aspects of this research experience were less disturbing. In a society that lures us into depthless lifestyles and in which a complex web of implicit regulations increasingly predetermines our choices, stepping out of the safe halls of academe into unregulated, original experience was exhilarating.[12] It was also instructive: I discovered, in unmasked form, the link between the police and military, the state's two primary use-of-force entities. Mainstream police academics routinely reassure themselves about the recent turn toward community service, accountability, and responsiveness. This research constituted a first step in realizing that the coercive dimension of policing is probably expanding in the very shadow of community policing rhetoric and imagery.

Cultural and Macro-Political Implications

At this point I contextualize my enjoyment of this experience within its more distressing social, cultural, and macro-political implications. As Thomas states, "[C]ritical ethnography takes seemingly mundane events, even repulsive ones, and reproduces them in a way that exposes broader social processes of control, taming, [and] power imbalance. . . ."[13] With proper substantiation, then, this ethnographic study can be used as a window from which to view larger societal trends, ideological influences, and the nature of the state's construction and maintenance of power.

The most immediate trend, which has gone largely unnoticed despite the Waco and Ruby Ridge incidents, is the rise and change in the nature of U.S. police paramilitary units since the mid- and late-1980s. With little effort, my background research for this chapter uncovered six police departments in a small geographical area which had established within the last four years autonomous, fully staffed "tactical operations" units. Mike and Steve knew of five additional units in the process of forming.

The drug war fury of the 1980s and 1990s has seen not only an increase of paramilitary police units but also a significant change in their character. The present research, along with two national studies,[14] demonstrate that these paramilitary units are expanding their previously limited functions—apprehending the occasional barricaded suspect or dealing with the even rarer hostage and terrorist situation—to include such policing mainstays as serving arrest and investigatory search warrants, conducting crack raids, and patrolling "high crime" areas in both large and small U.S. cities.

The Fresno, California, police, for example, have implemented a militaristic form of "proactive policing." In a popular police magazine, Fresno police claim that the streets have become a "war zone"; they have responded by deploying their SWAT team, equipped with military fatigues and weaponry, as a full-time patrol unit to "suppress" the crime and drug problem. The department has deemed the experiment an unqualified success, deployed a permanent unit, and now is encouraging other police agencies to follow suit. "The general consensus has been that SWAT teams working in a pro-active patrol-type setting does work. Police officers working in patrol vehicles, dressed in urban tactical gear and armed with automatic weapons are here—and they're here to stay."[15]

Just as the officers in this ethnography claimed, the "epidemics" of crack and inner-city gangs are seen to justify a full militarization of police operations.[16] Research substantiates that this use of paramilitary police units is not limited to the Fresno police department. Agencies of varying sizes and types—about 18 percent of all departments serving communities of twenty-five thousand or more—routinely deploy their units in similar fashion.[17]

Even by mainstream standards, establishing "civilian" police and clearly delineating police and military activities and personnel have been unquestioned hallmarks of democratic governance. A central characteristic of the participants in this research was the lack of delineation between the police and military not only culturally, but also in terms of material hardware, technology, training, operations, and especially personnel. A clear feature of the post–cold war era is the increasing overlap between the military and police (internal and external security functions) and, even more broadly, between the military industrial complex (MIC) and the rapidly expanding "criminal justice industrial complex" (CJIC).[18]

My examination of police paramilitary units is an appendage of my earlier research which examines the "police-ization" of the military rather than the militarization of the police. The military, with strong urgings from the U.S. Congress and Presidents Reagan and Bush, has been attempting since about 1988–90 to become more "socially useful." This usefulness includes international and domestic policing activities. The social and health problem of substance abuse, for example, was declared by presidential directive to be a "threat to national security." All branches of the military, including National Guard units, have engaged in a full range of policing activities both domestically and abroad.

Just as "Mike" and "Steve" train civilian police and hope to become police officers themselves, and just as the other tactical officers in their group work for the state as both military soldiers and police, recent events in national politics illustrate the overlapping connections between the CJIC and MIC. Attorney General Janet Reno, for example, while speaking to a mixed crowd of military, law enforcement, intelligence, and defense-industry officials, compared the monumental effort and will demonstrated during the cold war to the war on crime as follows: "So let me welcome you to the kind of war our police fight every day. And let me challenge you to turn your skills that served us so well in the Cold War to helping us with the war we're now fighting daily in the streets of our towns and cities."[19]

Shortly after Reno issued this challenge, the Department of Justice (DOJ) and the Department of Defense (DOD) agreed upon a five-year "partnership" to share intelligence gathering and "use of force technology." In addition to weaponry and technology, the military and police are also being encouraged to share personnel. Just as Law Enforcement Assistance Administration money was pumped into the CJIC at the end of the Vietnam War, military downsizing of personnel in the post–cold war era has brought calls for hiring more police officers. As part of the pledge to hire one hundred thousand new police officers, the Clinton administration recently passed legislation termed "Troops to Cops." Under a grant from both the Department of Defense and the Department of Justice, police agencies are encouraged to hire ex-military soldiers by providing them with five thousand dollars per "troop" turned "cop."

Perhaps what C. Wright Mills referred to as the "newly emerging means of violence" during his time, the military industrial complex, is becoming partially transmuted into a more subtle but still threatening form of paramilitarized violence—the criminal justice industrial complex.[20]

To understand these developments, we must examine also the role of militarism and militarization in contemporary society. Enloe provides a useful definition of militarization: "Militarization is occurring when any part of a society becomes controlled or dependent on the military or on military values."[21] As illustrated by the T-shirt worn by one of the officers in this research (with the motto "Operation Ghetto Storm"), the militaristic nature of the discourse on crime and drug control—wars on crime and drugs—constitutes more than ineffectual media and political rhetoric. Filtering solutions to the complex social problems of crime and substance abuse through the "war" metaphor helps to structure our values-in-use, our theories, and most important, our actions.[22] Consider how the metaphor and associated discourse of war have materialized, for example, in urban and small-town police departments deploying paramilitary police groups to patrol U.S. neighborhoods.

The value and belief system that underpins the process of militarization is militarism. Ironically, criminology as a whole has not employed this concept to any appreciable extent, despite the obvious militaristic presuppositions underlying the operations of the CJIC.[23] Militarism is defined as an ideology which stresses aggressiveness and the use of force and the glorification of military power, weaponry, and technology as the means to solve problems. Militarism underlies the tendency of states throughout history, even those preceding industrialization and capitalism, to approach perceived problems, either external or internal, with military violence or the threat thereof.

As illustrated by my ethnographic experience, militarism does not remain encapsulated within militaries; militarization requires militarism to be an integral part of society's value and belief systems in order to provide moral support, young people as warriors, and material resources. This militaristic dimension to culture is particularly acute in those societies that place strong emphasis on military superiority, such as the United States. Gibson develops an instructive thesis on the consequences of the pervasiveness and continued addictiveness of militarism in recent U.S. popular culture since the "loss" of the Vietnam War. In referring to what he terms the "New War Culture," Gibson explains the resurrection of martial culture during the 1980s and 1990s as a reaction to losing the Vietnam War. He continues: "It is hardly surprising, then, that American men—lacking the confidence in government and the economy, troubled by the changing relations between the sexes, uncertain of their identity or their future—began to *dream,* to fantasize about the powers and features of another kind of man who could retake and reorder the world. And the hero of all these dreams was the paramilitary warrior." [24]

Through film, politics, media, and field research Gibson documents how the new culture of paramilitarism, which emphasizes the lone warrior or small, elite groups of fellow warriors, pervaded young males' minds during the 1980s. This pervasive ideology of paramilitarism helps explain the contemporaneous rise in police paramilitary units within federal and local law enforcement agencies, as well as the paramilitarism found in right-wing militia and hate groups and in violent urban gangs. It also provides the larger cultural context from which to situate and make sense of Mike's, Steve's, and the rest of the group's paramilitary praxis.

As shown by my reaction to the MP5 scenario, another cultural force—hypermasculinity—provides the "seeds" and "fuel" which sustain militarism: "In most cultures that we know about, to be manly means to be a potential warrior." [25] The interwoven scripts of militarism and masculinity provide the cultural foundation for organized forms of violence by militaries and police to further state power, and these scripts furnish a more diffuse but still pervasive social network of threatened and real violence among individual men. In a sense, then, this research experience was a continuation of centuries of pre-scripted masculine thinking and power building—a history of militarized praxis still vital in the 1990s, and one in which I re-emerged as a participant.

Structure versus Agency: Overcoming or Overwhelmed by the Habitus

In this section I attempt to demonstrate how my enjoyment of militarism connects with larger cultural and structural forces. Readers accustomed to conventional forms and formalities of scholarly discourse may misinterpret this self-reflexive analysis as self-indulgence or self-therapy. On the contrary, the purpose of this self-reflexive endeavor is to examine from a personal level of analysis my experiences as contained within the "training session" and my paramilitary peers' experiences. Such analysis can perhaps shed light on such issues as the possibilities for agency overcoming structure, the micro-dynamics involved in the theory/practice dialectic, the deep-rooted nature of militarized masculinity, and the possibilities for academic research to be politically relevant.

I am therefore attempting an explanation of my "practice," as it relates to larger social processes. French sociologist Pierre Bourdieu provides a compelling and instructive "theory of social practices," which is relevant here because of its ability to wed individual practices (enjoying militarism) with social structure (macro-political/cultural implications).[26]

The central concept used by Bourdieu in forming his approach is the *habitus,* "a set of dispositions which incline agents to act and react in certain ways. The dispositions generate practices, perceptions and attitudes which are 'regular' without being consciously co-ordinated or governed by any 'rule.'"[27] These dispositions develop throughout a person's biographical history; they are formed out of and contain the effects of social structure. In referring to the habitus as a "system of dispositions," Bourdieu views these dispositions only as "orienting" an individual's thoughts and practices rather than as being deterministic: "The habitus is a product of conditionings which tends to reproduce the objective logic of those conditionings while transforming it. It's a kind of transforming machine that leads us to reproduce the social conditions of our own production, but in a relatively unpredictable way. It's adjustable and adaptable to new and unforeseen situations, not a destiny pre-determined."[28]

Bourdieu identifies some features of these dispositions that are germane for understanding the irony of enjoying militarism. First, the habitus is more than an unconnected conceptual framework from which to interpret the world. It imbues the physical body and becomes an unconscious part of how we carry ourselves, react to others, and employ language. The habitus actually "molds the body" and becomes second nature. Second, given that the habitus "reflects the social conditions within which it is acquired," a feature Bourdieu terms *structured,* social structure itself becomes *corporealized* within individuals. Third, it would follow that these structured dispositions are also *durable:* "They are ingrained in the body in such a way that they endure through the life history of the individual, operating in a way that is pre-conscious and hence not readily amenable to conscious reflection and modification."[29] In light of my youthful experiences with militarism and its tools, Bourdieu's notion of corporealization of social structure helps explain the ease with which I blended into and enjoyed paramilitarism, despite my academically attained disdain for such an orientation. I suspect that I even "carried myself" (i.e., engaged in corporealization) differently when interacting with my paramilitary peers not only to fit in but also to measure up to their warrior standards.

The fourth and final feature of the habitus concerns its ability to generate a multiplicity of practices and ways of thinking within social settings other than those in which the habitus is formed. Bourdieu refers to these varying social settings as *fields:* "Hence particular practices or perceptions should be seen, not as the product of the habitus, as such, but as the relation between the habitus, on the one hand, and the specific social contexts or 'fields' within which individuals act, on the other."[30] In these terms, this research involved the intersection of my "habitus of militarism" with an extremely militarized field.

Although Bourdieu uses his theory to explain class differences in linguistic practices, it seems equally well-suited for understanding my practice as it relates to broader cultural and structural forces. Given the durable and structured nature of militarism throughout history, we might think, for instance, of the "habitus of hypermasculinity," the "habitus of militarism," or, more generally, the "habitus of violence." In other words, the culture of militarism and paramilitarism is manifested not only in macro-political form (the rise and normalization of paramilitary policing) but also in micro-personal form (in my case, acting out through my own habitus of violence); each form transforms and generates the other (i.e., the politics of the personal). The power of militarized masculinity lies in this transformative dialectic between agency and structure, the personal and political. Because Bourdieu's conception of the habitus is corporealized and hence is "not readily amenable to conscious reflection," it privileges the macro-influence of militarism and its macro-political forms over the power of personal agency—a proposition substantiated by the enduring nature of militarism across time, and my own experience of engaging in and enjoying militarized rituals, which I had assumed were for myself a "thing of the past."

Personal Ironies/Political Problems

In sum, my enjoyment of militarism while immersed in a militarized "field" can be viewed as the temporary educement of my incorporated, biographical history of masculinity and violence. Critical ethnography, particularly that which blurs the distinction between researcher and subject, provided me with the professional license to engage in experiences that I would normally condemn. This license also created conditions enabling me to self-reflexively recognize the interplay and tension between my response to immersion in a paramilitarized field (the micro-personal level) and the larger processes of militarism and militarization occurring in the post–cold war era (the macro-political level). The research experience illustrates how engaging the social fabric of crime and criminal justice—as uncomfortable, difficult, and ethically problematic as this may seem—can reveal volumes about the intertextuality of theoretical, political, and personal fields.

On the practical side, this ethnography provides a window from which to view broader processes of militarism and militarization as they relate to the criminal justice apparatus. The identities of Mike and Steve are at least a partial product of a long-standing cultural environment, idealized during the Reagan-Bush era, which actively promotes the notion that a "man's" worth increases in proportion to his ability to be a warrior. This influential spirit of militarism during the 1980s, and now in the 1990s, is unmistakable in "boys'" video and computer games, toys, television shows, and home videos. The appeal of these pedagogical devices derives from their *recreational* nature. As with my own ethnographic experience, militarism is enjoyed and embraced, as well as imposed. Through learning, enjoying, and internalizing the tenets of militarism, the habitus for many of our youths (including myself) as they approach "manhood" is pre-constructed for violence and war—whether with other nations, other gangs, drug law violators, or the police. Growing older, for many, only changes and amplifies the organization, the hardware, and the consequences.

The mutually reinforcing elements of "militarism," "industry," and "war" are uniting in a historically proven scenario for the unrestrained growth of the criminal justice industrial complex. Nils Christie asks repeatedly where we might find limits.[31] A potential answer stems from feminist theory, one of the few bright spots within a growing nihilism in academia. The consciousness raising and resulting political-personal action within the feminist movement demonstrate the emancipatory potential of what the Frankfurt School termed the "subjective individual."[32] If traditionally constructed forms of masculinity are the seeds and the fuel of militarism, redefining masculinity in a way that de-emphasizes the tenets of militarism may expose the seeds and restrict the fuel on which the industry depends.

To conclude on a more pessimistic note, however, the "subjective individual" is awakened and enacted in a social context more ambiguous than this analysis might suggest. Again, militarism has been and continues to be a seductive, pleasurable, and embedded component of social life. To make matters worse, militarism and its consequences, although pervasive, are for most people less apparent and overt than in the past. Christie argues that conditions of heightened modernity—formal rationality, corporate interest, scientific authority, managerialism, and, especially, moral indifference—mask and decouple from its source the offensiveness of the policies and consequences of the war-on-crime industry.[33] This same genre of critique is developed in the policing literature. Manning has clarified how police imagery, symbolism, and rhetoric, particularly within the "community policing" movement, mask the historical and political realities of policing in the United States.[34] According to both Christie and Manning, then, overt state coercion, violence, and militarization become subsumed, reformulated in symbolic form, and sanitized by a hypermodern veil.

Christie and Manning clarify the cloaking power of the veil; this ethnography peers firsthand at the undeniable police activity occurring behind it. As this chapter has demonstrated, this unique mode of knowledge acquisition provides the researcher a powerful method by which to tear through the veil of surface appearances, rationalizations, and taken-for-granted rhetoric. It allowed this researcher to observe and participate in the ground-level reality of state agents enjoying militarism—that is, the micro-processes of training to be soldiers of organized violence, whether in the service of the police, the military, or both. More generally, it positions the researcher/participant to appreciate and make sense of the unique "trialectic" between the micro-social event, its macro-sociological context, and the unsettling yet instructive place of her or his own "self."

Notes

An earlier version of this chapter was published in the journal *Justice Quarterly* 13 (3) (1996), under the title "Enjoying Militarism: Political/Personal Dilemmas in Studying U.S. Police Paramilitary Units." It is reprinted here with permission of the Academy of Criminal Justice Sciences. The author would like to thank Mark Hamm and especially Jeff Ferrell for providing the inspiration and many of the ideas for this piece.

1. For more thorough discussions of this critique, see Seyla Benhabib, *Critique, Norm, and Utopia: A Study of the Foundations of Critical Theory* (New York: Columbia University Press, 1986); Richard Bernstein, *The New Constellation: The Ethical-Political Horizons of Modernity/Postmodernity* (Cambridge: MIT Press, 1992); Wilfred Carr and Stephen Kemmis, *Becoming Critical* (London: Falmer Press, 1986); Raymond A. Morrow, *Critical Theory and Methodology* (Thousand Oaks, Calif.: Sage Publications, 1994).

2. Pauline M. Rosenau, *Post-Modernism and the Social Sciences: Insights, Inroads, and Intrusions* (Princeton: Princeton University Press, 1992); Andrew Sayer, *Method in Social Science: A Realist Approach*, 2d ed. (London: Routledge, 1992).

3. See, for example, Pertti Alasuutari, *Researching Culture: Qualitative Method and Cultural Studies* (Thousand Oaks, Calif.: Sage Publications, 1995); James Clifford and George E. Marcus, *Writing Culture: The Poetics and Politics of Ethnography* (Berkeley: University of California Press, 1986); Jeff Ferrell, "True Confessions: Law, Crime, and Field Research," paper presented at the Academy of Criminal Justice Sciences meetings, Boston, Mass., 1995; Clifford Geertz, *Works and Lives: The Anthropologist as Author* (Stanford: Stanford University Press, 1988); Peter Reason, *Participating in Human Inquiry* (Thousand Oaks, Calif.: Sage Publications, 1994).

4. Max Weber, *The Methodology of the Social Sciences* (New York: Free Press, 1949).

5. Howard S. Becker, *Outsiders: Studies in the Sociology of Deviance* (New York: Free Press, 1963); Jeff Ferrell, *Crimes of Style: Urban Graffiti and the Politics of Criminality* (Boston: Northeastern University Press, 1996).

6. Erving Goffman, *The Presentation of Self in Everyday Life* (London: Allen Lane, 1959).

7. Harold Garfinkel, *Studies in Ethnomethodology* (Englewood Cliffs, N.J.: Prentice-Hall, 1967).

8. Steve embodied the ultimate warrior in that he had experienced war firsthand, and, more important, had killed. Killing in combat is the ultimate mark of military bravado. Interestingly, Steve never discussed having killed an Iraqi soldier as far as I knew. Everyone simply assumed he had done so because of his combat role in the war and because of his silence on the matter.

9. Male solidarity is an essential part of the police and militaristic subcultures. For a more complete discussion of their inner workings, see James W. Gibson, *Warrior Dreams: Manhood in Post-Vietnam America* (New York: Hill and Wang, 1994).

10. A popular device used by paramilitary police units is referred to as a "flash-bang grenade." The general purpose is to distract, disorient, and administer "less-

than-lethal" pain to the occupants of a building. Most of the devices produce a very loud explosion and a flash; some incorporate rubber pellets, or CS gas. The Department of Justice and the Department of Defense have entered into a joint venture to develop for the civilian police an entire line of these types of what they term "less-than-lethal technologies."

11. Alfred Schutz, *The Phenomenology of the Social World* (Evanston, Ill.: Northwestern University Press, 1967).

12. With regard to "depthless lifestyles," see Chris Rojek and Brian S. Turner, *Forget Baudrillard?* (New York: Routledge, 1993). On the ascendence of the regulatory society, see Ben Agger, *The Discourse of Domination: From the Frankfurt School to Postmodernism* (Evanston, Ill.: Northwestern University Press, 1992); Herbert Marcuse, *One-Dimensional Man* (Boston: Beacon, 1964); George Ritzer, *The McDonaldization of Society: An Investigation into the Changing Character of Contemporary Social Life* (Thousand Oaks, Calif.: Pine Forge Press, 1993).

13. Jim Thomas, *Doing Critical Ethnography* (Newbury Park, Calif.: Sage Publications, 1993), 9.

14. See Peter B. Kraska and Louis J. Cubellis, "Paramilitary Policing in Small U.S. Localities: A National Study," *Justice Quarterly* (forthcoming); Peter B. Kraska and Victor E. Kappeler, "Militarizing American Police: The Rise and Normalization of Paramilitary Units," *Social Problems* 44 (1997): 1–18.

15. Charles D. Smith, "Taking Back the Streets," *Police Magazine* 19 (1995): 36, 82.

16. The SWAT team in Chapel Hill, North Carolina, conducted a large-scale crack raid of an entire block in a predominantly African American neighborhood. The raid, termed "Operation Redi-Rock," resulted in the detention and search of up to one hundred people, all of whom were African American. (Whites were allowed to leave the area.) No one was ever prosecuted for a crime. See *Barnett v. Karpinos*, 460 S.E.2d 208 (N.C. App. 1995).

17. Kraska and Cubellis, "Paramilitary Policing"; Kraska and Kappeler, "Militarizing American Police."

18. See Peter B. Kraska, "Militarizing the Drug War: A Sign of the Times," in *Altered States of Mind: Critical Observations of the Drug War*, ed. Peter B. Kraska (New York: Garland, 1993), 159–206; Richard Quinney, *Criminology* (Boston: Little, Brown, 1975).

19. National Institute of Justice, "Technology Transfer from Defense: Concealed Weapon Detection," *National Institute of Justice Journal* 229 (1995): 1–6.

20. C. Wright Mills, "The Power Elite and the Structure of Power in American Society," in *Power in Societies*, ed. M. Olsen (New York: Macmillan, 1970), 241–61.

21. Cynthia Enloe, *Police, Military and Ethnicity* (New Brunswick, N.J.: Transaction, 1980), 132.

22. See George Lakoff and Mark Johnson, *Metaphors We Live By* (Chicago: University of Chicago Press, 1980); Gareth Morgan, *Images of Organization* (Beverly Hills, Calif.: Sage, 1986).

23. The major exception is Richard Quinney, who employed the military metaphor as an ideological referent for critiquing the criminal justice system. Quinney's original connection of military with criminal justice ideology continues today

in "peacemaking" criminology; see Harold E. Pepinsky and Richard Quinney, *Criminology as Peacemaking* (Bloomington: Indiana University Press, 1991). One of the more perceptive and direct discussions of militarized masculinity in a criminological context is found in Larry Tifft and Lynn Markham, "Battering Women and Battering Central Americans: A Peacemaking Synthesis," in *Criminology as Peacemaking*, ed. Harold E. Pepinsky and Richard Quinney (Bloomington: Indiana University Press, 1991), 114–53.

24. Gibson, *Warrior*, 11. See also Mark S. Hamm, *American Skinheads: The Criminology and Control of Hate Crime* (Westport, Conn.: Praeger, 1993).

25. Cynthia Enloe, *The Morning After: Sexual Politics at the End of the Cold War* (Berkeley: University of California Press, 1993), 52.

26. Pierre Bourdieu, *Outline of a Theory of Practice* (London: Cambridge University Press, 1977); *Language and Symbolic Power* (Cambridge, Mass.: Harvard University Press, 1991).

27. Bourdieu, *Language*, 12.

28. Pierre Bourdieu, *Sociology in Question* (Thousand Oaks, Calif.: Sage, 1993), 16.

29. Bourdieu, *Language*, 12.

30. Bourdieu, *Sociology*, 14.

31. Nils Christie, *Crime Control as Industry: Towards Gulags, Western Style* (New York: Routledge, 1994).

32. Marcuse's "subjective individual" embodies the emancipatory potential of all individuals; see Herbert Marcuse, *Counterrevolution and Revolt* (Boston: Beacon, 1972). Agger draws from Marcuse's work in developing what he terms a "dialectical sensibility." He calls for a repoliticalization of critical theory — one which avoids the academic tradition of "disengaged intellectuality." He would replace the latter with dialectical sensibility which "does not separate theory and practice, envisaging instead a radical intellectuality that itself contributes to social change" (*Discourse*, 265, 271). See also Susan Caulfield and Nancy Wonders, "Personal and Political: Violence Against Women and the Role of the State," in *Political Crime in Contemporary America: A Critical Approach*, ed. Kenneth Tunnell (New York: Garland, 1994), 79–100; Brian Fay, *Critical Social Science: Liberation and Its Limits* (New York: Cornell University Press, 1987).

33. Christie, *Crime Control*.

34. Peter K. Manning, *Police Work: The Social Organization of Policing* (Cambridge: MIT Press, 1977); "Community Policing as a Drama of Control," in *Community Policing: Rhetoric or Reality*, ed. J. R. Greene and S. D. Mastrofski (New York: Praeger, 1988), 27–46; "Economic Rhetoric and Policing Reform," *Criminal Justice Research Bulletin* 7 (1992): 1–8.

The Ethnography of Terror

Timothy McVeigh and the Blue Centerlight of Evil

Mark S. Hamm

I shambled after as I've been doing all my life after people who interest me, because the only people for me are the mad ones, the ones who are mad to live, mad to talk, mad to be saved, desirous of everything at the same time, the ones who never yawn or say a commonplace thing, but burn, burn, burn like the fabulous yellow roman candles exploding like spiders across the stars and in the middle you see the blue centerlight pop and everybody goes "Awww!"
—Jack Kerouac, *On the Road*

I'm the same way. That's my first confession: I am what you might call a janitor for academic criminology. I study the people that everybody loves to hate, but on whom nobody wants to spend the time, energy, or money to figure out why they became so dangerous in the first place—men who kill their wives, Cuban "Marielitos," assassins, skinheads, Charles Manson; and corrupt public officials like Edwin Meese, or the grievously naive, like Janet Reno.[1]

In fact, more than anyone in recent years, Attorney General Reno and the Federal Bureau of Investigation have taught me to be far more worried about what government does to protect us from criminals than about the criminals themselves. The seeds of that lesson were planted in my mind some twenty years ago in a chance but truly fortunate encounter I had with Mother Teresa, who said, "I do not fear Satan half as much as I fear those who fear him." She has a point. If you study great acts of evil in this world you find that they are often perpetrated by our protectors.

Here is another confession: I know that exploring the roots of evil is not the safest of jobs. It takes time to explore these roots. It is sometimes frightening and forever lonely. Beyond that, it leads to spiritual and intellectual obsessions. Yet, to borrow a term from another semihazardous profession, there's always a gig.

So that—for better or worse—is what has led me to this dangerous, godforsaken stretch of highway running southbound down through the Black Mountains of the Mojave Desert, where Nevada meets Arizona at the Hoover Dam. Anyone who has ever traveled this hard road knows that this place is unimaginably immense.

More than a mile below me the powerful Colorado River is gouging through mountain blocks the size of the Astrodome. Above lies a moonscape of huge, black volcanic mountaintops against a pure blue sky. But that is only part of what makes this place so godforsaken. There are the winds. They have whipped across this land for five million years, blowing away every grain of sand and silt, killing everything in their path but the deformed Joshua trees and yucca plants. The winds have left behind granite, stone pebbles, and a desert varnish darkening the mountains and the sloping aprons surrounding them.

That's where I'm standing, on a silent mountainside. As the wind lashes my face, I pick up the sweet but deadly scent of a rattlesnake nest just over the cliff. I know one thing for damn sure: I am alone out here, profoundly alone, and I must be careful. I reach to my chest and feel the cross that hangs there, hoping to affirm that good will overcome evil.

While there may be something evocative about nature's evolution on this mountainside, in social terms there is also something down that ravine in front of me which illustrates just how far humankind has failed to come. I spent most of the 1970s and 1980s living in Arizona. I've hiked the bosoms of her canyons, drunk in her honky-tonks, and worked the cellblocks of her meanest prisons. I know well that this land has always drawn the strong, the outspoken, the hard-headed, and the imminently criminal. For years, this part of the Mojave has been a place where things can be stashed out of sight. Things like homicide victims, bags of robbery money, methamphetamine laboratories, and, since Janet Reno unleashed the black beast at Waco, composite materials for constructing homemade bombs.

That's what I'm searching for as I head down the ravine, past the rattlesnakes. That and the blue centerlight of evil.

Trouble, Nothing but Trouble

Social scientists have long debated the strengths and weaknesses of ethnography as a research method.[2] While ethnography offers researchers sensitizing strategies for understanding the experiential setting of criminal and deviant behavior, ethnographic studies are often limited in their ability to provide findings that can be generalized to similar populations. Recently, however, social scientists have begun to acknowledge a more urgent problem associated with ethnography: the enormous personal toll that this method can take on the researcher, a toll that can potentially transform the research process itself.

Recent examples of such confessions can be found in studies of street gangs, the homeless, political prisoners, and people with AIDS.[3] Similar issues have also been recounted in the literature on new social movements. In her ethnographic study of civil disobedience waged by a California anti-nuclear group in Nevada, sociologist Josepha Schiffman confessed that

> Most [activists] were ecstatic at the beauty of the desert. I, on the other hand, was none too fond of the radioactive dust and the cactus thorns that pierced my shoes. . . . I reproached myself with the memory of all those researchers who troop off to face unknown dangers in hostile field sites. But as I was throwing up in a cheap Las Vegas motel . . . from drinking contaminated water, I resolved that my next participant observation project would be studying the leisure habits of the very wealthy. . . . I knew then that I had reached a turning point. . . . It was a wrenching experience, and one for which I was totally unprepared. . . . I never anticipated how much I would be affected personally by the experience of doing participant observation.[4]

Thus comes my next confession: while I have known thousands of criminals in my life and have studied hundreds of crimes, I was completely unprepared for what I would find in this ravine, and in my larger research on the Oklahoma City bombing. Put as succinctly as possible, here is what I found.[5]

Timothy McVeigh, a young methamphetamine-addicted and highly decorated veteran of the Persian Gulf War, became obsessed with what he saw as the mass murder of seventy-eight men, women, and children by the FBI at the Branch Davidian compound outside Waco, Texas, on April 19, 1993. On Easter Sunday 1995, McVeigh parked a battered yellow 1977 Mercury Marquis in a vacant lot about one hundred yards from the Alfred P. Murrah Federal Building in Oklahoma City and placed a cardboard sign in the windshield reading "Broken Down, Do Not Tow." Three days later, on April 19, McVeigh returned to the site in a twenty-four-foot Ryder rental truck carrying a bomb weighing more than two-and-a-half tons. Due to his methamphetamine use, McVeigh was anorexic. He stood six feet, two inches tall, yet weighed only 155 pounds. His hair was fashioned in a military crew cut; he wore black combat boots, black jeans, and a blue windbreaker over a white sweatshirt emblazoned with these words from a speech made famous by Thomas Jefferson more than two hundred years ago: "*The Tree Of Liberty Must Be Refreshed From Time To Time By The Blood Of Tyrants And Patriots.*" Timothy McVeigh had come to avenge the sins of Waco.

He parked the Ryder truck across the street from the city post office, walked to the Mercury, and drove it to a parking space directly across the street from the Murrah building. Then McVeigh walked back to the Ryder, started the engine, and lit a ten-foot fuse running through a hole connecting the cab to the cargo bay and the bomb. He slowly pulled the truck in front of the federal building, shut off the engine, put the keys in his pocket, and ran to the Mercury. As he made his getaway down Interstate 235, the detonation system kicked in.

In one imperceptible instant, the bomb killed 167 men, women, and children; it grievously injured another 500. Because the truck bomb was placed directly beneath the Murrah building's day-care center, some 20 infants took the full force of the blast in their faces. They never had a chance. Their human remains — tiny arms and legs — were found a block away.

From what universe beyond the one that most of us inhabit does this kind of evil arise?

I have struggled with that question every day since the bombing; yet, I have found little guidance in the literature on domestic terrorism. To begin with, most studies of terrorism are wholly derivative of official documents and journalistic sources. As such, these studies represent secondhand observations of the criminal event, observations that are simply passed from one source to the next without the benefit of serious criminological inquiry. I agree with Howard S. Becker that "the basic operation in studying society is the production and refinement of an *image* of the thing we are studying."[6] No amount of secondary analysis can enhance the criminological image of McVeigh killing those babies.

In fact, most studies of terrorism ignore victims altogether.[7] Not only do such descriptions do a shameful disservice to the victims, but they also completely overlook the impact of terrorism on the community. As a consequence, we learn little about the individual suffering caused by terrorism, and even less about how a community copes with such extraordinary loss. I have vowed not to make that mistake in telling the story of the Oklahoma City bombing.

I have therefore relied on an ethnography of terror, beginning with a study of the bomb site itself. The ghastly remains of the Murrah building were demolished in May 1995, and the site was converted to a memorial. An estimated two million people have visited this memorial. I have gone there six times. Each time, I have been reduced to tears—not only by the monumental suffering that occurred on that sacred ground, but also by the remarkable strength and resilience of the people of Oklahoma City. I have used this situated ethnography to move beyond the surface examination of the bombing offered by journalists and government bureaucrats. The bombing has led to unprecedented counterterrorism legislation recently enacted by the U.S. Congress. This ethnography of terror, then, can be conceived as a deliberate attempt to honor the victims of Oklahoma City by paying attention to what Michel Foucault called "the blood that has dried on the codes of law."[8]

I have followed one simple rule in this ethnography: God gave us two ears and one mouth for a reason—we should listen twice as much as we talk. I have had to ask few questions, then; simply being there is enough. While many visitors to the memorial site have been locked in their own silence, others have been more than willing to express themselves voluntarily to me. I have been especially moved by several Vietnam veterans who made pilgrimages to the memorial. McVeigh detonated his truck bomb one week before the twentieth anniversary of the fall of Saigon. In the weeks following the bombing, counselors across the nation reported that these vets experienced increased flashbacks, nightmares, and signs of "hypervigilance"—a feeling of being in constant danger. But here in this windblown ravine, I remember that perhaps the most poignant stories have come from those at life's extremes: the very old and the very young. For me, one of these stories shall always stand as an exemplar of the power and the pity of the ethnography of terror.

It's Labor Day 1996, and I'm walking through the vacant lot where McVeigh hid the Mercury. In contrast to media portrayals of the bomb site, this section of Oklahoma City is not part of an urban metropolis. Rather, it is that part of town where the muffler shops are found, where the weeds are never cut, where empty crack vials and whiskey bottles line the gutters, and where a broken-down old Mercury would go unnoticed.

Two black children approach on foot. They can't be more than eight years old. One of them, missing his two front teeth, asks me, "What you doin'?"

"I'm lookin' for where that man parked his car," I say gently. "The man that blowed up the building. You know."

"Yeah. My cousin died in there."

"Jesus, I'm sorry little man. How old was he?"

"Two."

"Two years old?"

"Yeah. It was his birfday. It's sad you gotta die on your birfday."

Just then, the second kid points toward the memorial and asks, "How'd you like to live with yourself after you did that?"

I can't answer that question down in this ravine. I've got to get out of this place; there's nothing down here anyway, except more rattlesnakes. I'm heading to Kingman, Arizona, and what will no doubt be even more trouble.

Paint It Black

The first problem, of course, is that Timothy McVeigh is no longer in Kingman. As of this writing, he sits alone in a specially designed cage in Denver awaiting execution for the worst act of terroristic mass murder in American history. I have been in contact with McVeigh, though, through his attorney, and I am currently awaiting my chance to interview him in a holding pen outside his cell. In the meantime, I am left with the task of analyzing McVeigh through what Michael Burawoy calls the "virtual participation in the lives of those one studies."[9]

Kingman is important because McVeigh lived here off and on with his former army buddy, Michael Fortier, in a brown-and-white house trailer on McVicar Avenue.[10] The two worked together for a while at the True Value hardware store on Stockton Hill Road, and later McVeigh used Kingman as his home base when he worked the southwestern gun-show circuit.

The plan to bomb the Murrah building fell into place two weeks before Christmas in 1994. That was when McVeigh and Fortier—while en route from Arizona to Council Grove, Kansas, to take possession of firearms stolen from gun dealer Roger Moore—stopped in Oklahoma City and cased the Murrah building to assess what it would take to destroy it. McVeigh believed (incorrectly) that some of the FBI agents responsible for the Waco disaster were housed there. Over the next three months, McVeigh—aided by another army buddy, Terry Nichols of Herington, Kansas—set about the task of gathering composite materials for the bomb. These materials included two tons of ammonium nitrate fertilizer, acetylene tanks, plastic barrels, mixing paddles, blasting caps, TNT, detonator cord, fuses, and diesel fuel. By the first week of March 1995, most of these materials were stored in Nichols's basement and in rental lockers in rural Kansas.

On March 11, McVeigh returned to Fortier's Kingman trailer. By all accounts, he was furious. Essentially, Fortier had decided that he would have nothing to do with the bombing plan, and now Nichols had backed out as well. McVeigh then began searching for a "silent brother" to help him deliver the reckoning. First he sent a message to a small group of neo-Nazis who ran a crystal methamphetamine lab in Oatman, twenty miles southwest of Kingman, asking them to join the conspiracy.

On March 23, McVeigh rented the video *Blown Away*. In this 1993 film, actor Tommy Lee Jones plays a rogue Irish terrorist named Ryan Gaerity—a lone-wolf bomber too violent for even the Irish Republican Army. After breaking out of a Northern Ireland prison with a plastic explosive, Gaerity moves to Boston where he delivers the "gift of pain" by wreaking havoc upon the police department's bomb squad as part of a long-ago vendetta associated with the Troubles. The body of the film then works along two dimensions: the protagonist's bombing of public facilities (climaxing in the attempted mass murder of thousands at a Fourth of July Boston Pops Concert) and the inability of law enforcement to do anything about it.

Meanwhile, in Hot Springs, Arkansas, Roger Moore was growing livid with the Garland County Sheriff's Department. Back on November 5, 1994, Moore had stepped out his back door to feed the ducks when he was suddenly confronted by a man wearing camouflage, a black ski mask, and gloves. In his hands were a pistol-grip shotgun and a garrote wire. The assailant bound and blindfolded Moore with duct tape and made off with 66 firearms, $8,700 in cash, bars of silver and gold, pieces of jade, and the key to a bank safety-deposit box (much of this loot was later found in a Las Vegas storage locker rented by Terry Nichols). Moore told the Garland County sheriff, in no uncertain terms, that he knew a young army vet from the gun shows who might have been involved. His name was Tim McVeigh. The reason for Moore's anger? The sheriff had failed to pursue the lead on McVeigh.

On March 25, McVeigh began to put his personal affairs, such as they were, in order. He began by writing a hurried letter to his sister, Jennifer, warning her not to write to him after April 1. "Watch what you say back to me," Tim wrote. "Because I may not get it in time, and the G-men might get it out of my [mail]box, incriminating you." The letter ended with Tim telling Jennifer to burn all his other letters to her. McVeigh then drove to a Kingman storage locker he had rented in October and loaded its contents into his 1983 Pontiac Sunbird. He drove to a rattlesnake-infested wash in the Black Mountains, where he wrapped several bundles of dynamite and more than five hundred blasting caps in an army poncho and buried it in a gravel scrub.

Four days later, with no word from the neo-Nazis in Oatman, McVeigh grew desperate for a silent brother. So he turned to Fortier's neighbor — a stocky, long-haired, twenty-eight-year-old petty criminal named Jim Rosencrans, also a methamphetamine user. McVeigh asked Rosencrans if he would be willing to drive for "14 or 20 hours" to an unspecified place and drop McVeigh off. Then Rosencrans was to go to the nearest airport and "leave the car there." For this, McVeigh offered to pay him "about $400." But Rosencrans didn't have the mettle for terrorism, and he declined the offer.

It was then that Timothy McVeigh made his last stand. On March 31, McVeigh drove his Sunbird over to the Imperial Hotel on Route 66 in Kingman. Using his own name, but giving a Fort Riley, Kansas, address, he paid $245 for thirteen days' lodging and settled into Room 212. "I thought he was in the Reserves because of the way he came in here all dressed up in his camouflage and black boots," said the proprietor, Helmut Hofer. According to Hofer, McVeigh "stayed in the room and minded his own business" for nearly two weeks. McVeigh was on a solitary vigil; waiting, it seems, for word from someone.

Now, a little more than a year later, I have just paid Helmut Hofer $42 for two nights' lodging and have checked into Room 212 of the Imperial Hotel myself. My plan is to conduct a virtual ethnography of McVeigh's last stand. I walk across the asphalt parking lot with a bag over my shoulder, my guitar in one hand, and the room key in the other. Looking up at Room 212, I'm suddenly frozen in my tracks. Maybe I'm too absorbed in this research. Maybe I'm still shaken by the rattlesnakes back in the Black Mountains. I close my eyes, take a deep breath, and look again. I can't believe what I'm seeing. There, surrounding the door frame of 212, is a black aura.

Spirit of Place: No More Kicks on Route 66

All writers have what Rudolfo Anaya calls "a room of their own," meaning that the writer's place is, for the writer, the center of the universe.[11] The center of my universe is not inside Room 212. I am merely a traveler here, collecting lumber for a story that I will write in my own room, a room not of darkness, but of light.

Because every area is inhabited by the spirits of the place, stories about that place must be guided by the soul of the community and the land. In this regard, it is unlikely that Timothy McVeigh could have acquired the emotional impetus to carry out the Oklahoma City bombing back in his hometown of Pendleton, New York. Nor could he have forged it at Terry Nichols's house in Herington, or in Waco. Those places do not possess the soul of evil required by terrorism. But that evil can be found along Route 66.

Once known as the "Main Street of America," by the time McVeigh checked into the Imperial Hotel, Route 66 had become one of the nation's

darkest alleys. The stretch of Route 66 running through Kingman is deso-
late, primarily because of the winds, which have invested the place with
what one expert on the Mojave refers to as "the bewitching allure of
beauty and disaster."

The Imperial is one of those cheap, prefabricated structures of Arizona's 1970s building boom. Stepping to the door of Room 212 and looking out at the massive, black granite Haulapai Mountain Range—ragged
cliffs, buzzards soaring in the blue sky—you quickly gain a sense of perspective: the feeling that you are a very small human being in a very large
and brutal landscape. This creates a paradox. On one hand, there is the
visible desert—the vast, incomprehensible space that kills much and sustains little. On the other, there is the desert that people perceive. It is this
perceptual dimension that will evoke the true confession in any lone traveler. For the Mojave is so mighty that it defies human understanding. Rational thinking disappears and is replaced with existential fear.

You can see that fear in the eyes of the losers down on Route 66. But
you have to look closely; the fear is often hidden beneath a truculent, bel-
ligerent exterior. Below the Haulapais are four cheap hotels, a tavern, the
Town Restaurant, and Smith's Family Restaurant—though you'd be hard-
pressed to see a family there. These establishments cater to the losers, outcasts from the fringes of American society—skinheads from California
and Idaho, alcoholics, drifters, derelicts, crackheads, Elvis impersonators,
and legions of truck drivers and impoverished young single women, their
diapered babies walking through the broken glass of motel parking lots.
Many are drawn to the place by the availability of crystal methamphetamine; other attractions are few.

Less visible is the evil of the Haulapais. It is there, at a ranch beneath
Penitentiary Mountain, that it all began. McVeigh recently told a reporter
from the London *Times* that he was inspired by the Arizona Patriots, a vi-
ciously racist and anti-Semitic group founded in the mid-1980s by Jack
Maxwell Oliphant, the spiritual godfather of the Patriot movement. In
December 1986, FBI agents from Phoenix arrested Oliphant and six con-
federates for plotting to hijack an armored car leaving the Laughlin,
Nevada, gambling casinos. With proceeds from the robbery, the Patriots
planned to blow up federal buildings in Phoenix and Los Angeles and
then launch a mortar and machine-gun attack on the huge IRS complex
in Ogden, Utah. Agents foiled the plan, however, sending Oliphant and
several others to prison.

Upon his parole in 1989, Oliphant returned to Penitentiary Mountain, where he raised rattlesnakes and read the Scriptures over shortwave radio. During World War II, Oliphant had broken his back in a bombing mission over Germany. At the age of seventy, he got into an argument over his rights to a gold mine in California and accidentally blew his right arm off with a shotgun. After the Oklahoma City bombing, Jack Oliphant was one of the first persons interviewed when the FBI brought several dozen agents to Kingman. I had arranged to interview the legendary one-armed old bigot while staying here at the Imperial. But three weeks before, he died. This research is nothing but trouble.

In downtown Kingman, the winds seem to have swept away any pretense of culture. There is no bookstore. There is no record store, art gallery, coffee shop, beauty parlor, or even strip joint. In fact, there are almost no people at all. It is certainly an Arizona anomaly. Unlike Phoenix, Tucson, and Flagstaff, descendants of the Pueblo Indian and the Mexican Hispano have never been allowed to assimilate into the identity of Kingman. It is, instead, a white man's town, full of white man ways.

As far as I can tell, there are only two downtown establishments that do any business. One is Heavy Metal, a weight-lifting gym. The other is Archie's Bunker, a survivalist outlet that specializes in Desert Storm cammos, assault rifles, and bomb-making manuals. Both businesses cater to angry white men juiced on steroids and crystal methamphetamine. For modern paramilitary warriors like Tim McVeigh, these places represent more than business establishments. They are cultural artifacts that form the mainstay of what Pierre Bourdieu identified as *symbolic violence.* This cultural transformation is achieved through a process that Bourdieu called *misrecognition,* or "the process whereby power relations are perceived not for what they objectively are but in a form which renders them legitimate in the eyes of the beholder." [12] In Kingman, this process of misrecognition is aided and abetted by the local political culture—a culture that marches in lockstep with the legacy of iniquity created by Jack Oliphant a decade ago out in the Haulapais.

Even the names of local politicians seem to bespeak the presence of evil. A man named Tom Thate (T-hate) is the Mohave County sheriff. Nathan Pagan is a county commissioner. But the most successful politician is Joe Hart, owner and manager of a local radio station. Hart's station broadcasts a nonstop talk show that routinely rails against President Bill Clinton ("the Slick One"), Attorney General Reno ("Butch Reno"), and the Bureau of Alcohol, Tobacco, and Firearms (BATF), nicknamed "Burn All Toddlers First." Hart, a Republican, is an influential Arizona legislator. He is currently chairman of the state's powerful Public Institutions and University Committee. His primary accomplishments in this capacity have been to slash spending for higher education, to encourage gambling on Indian reservations, to draft laws that tax those gambling proceeds, and to appropriate millions of dollars for the expansion of Arizona's juvenile correctional system. Joe Hart is related by blood to Lori and Jason Hart. Lori is married to Mike Fortier, who is currently facing a twenty-five-year sentence for his part in the Oklahoma City bombing. Jason Hart is a two-bit burglar and drug dealer. It was he, in fact, who supplied Fortier and McVeigh with a constant stream of crystal methamphetamine.

The Ghost of Earl Turner

Only Timothy McVeigh knows for sure what happened inside Room 212. Evidence gathered at the time of his April 19 arrest indicates that he entered this room with a .45 Glock revolver loaded with hollow point "cop killer" bullets, a shoulder harness with several more clips of cop killers, a five-inch Buck knife, political documents about Waco, a copy of the Declaration of Independence, stories on the battles of Lexington and Concord (which took place on April 19, 1775), and selected writings of Thomas Jefferson and seventeenth-century political philosopher John Locke, who once wrote that it should be "lawful" to kill those "who would take away my liberty." Also in McVeigh's possession was a telephone calling card, some antacid tablets, a cassette player, the tape *Pretty Hate Machine* by Nine Inch Nails, and, of course, a vial of crystal meth.

It is likely that McVeigh neatly placed these items beside the telephone on the small Formica-topped writing desk that sits next to the television set. There is a flimsy plastic chair in front of the desk, which sits on a worn green carpet with several blackened cigarette burns on it. A few steps from the bed is a cramped little kitchenette and a tiny refrigerator that contains the slightest scent of disinfectant. This is where McVeigh kept his plastic bottles of Pepsi and—for those occasions when he was moved to eat—his spaghetti noodles, sauce, bread, butter, and bags of junk food. On the nightstand next to the bed, McVeigh kept several packs of Rolaids to calm the nervous, fiery backwash of tomato sauce and Pepsi. A Gideon Bible lies in the drawer. I expect to find some evidence of

McVeigh's reading of the Book of Revelation, but the Bible has had little use. The room is completed with dingy, yellow-striped wallpaper. At several spots on that wallpaper, there is dried snot. Room 212 is a despicable place. It smells musty, foul, and strange.

I am primarily concerned with three objects in this room: the telephone, the bed, and the TV.

As late as the second week of April, McVeigh was still a loner in search of a silent brother who would somehow "emerge from the shadows" at the last minute to join the bombing conspiracy. According to the FBI, he made dozens of phone calls from Room 212, but four were especially important. The first came on April 5, when McVeigh called Elliott's Body Shop in Junction City, Kansas, to reserve the Ryder truck that would later carry the bomb. The second occurred moments later when he called a neo-Nazi commune in the remote mountains of eastern Oklahoma, looking for a German Ku Klux Klansman. The third and fourth came sometime between April 5 and April 11 when McVeigh called a message center operated by the National Alliance of Hillsboro, West Virginia. These calls were allegedly patched through to the unlisted number of the National Alliance leader, William Pierce, author of *The Turner Diaries*. McVeigh had been obsessed with this book for years.

Briefly, *The Turner Diaries* is a science fiction novel about a white-supremacist guerilla force led by the book's protagonist, Earl Turner. During the 1980s, *The Turner Diaries* served as the blueprint for a reign of terror—assassinations, bank robberies, and bombings—committed by two legendary terrorist groups, the Covenant, the Sword, the Arm of the Lord and the Order. In the book, a new law dubbed the Cohen Act has invested police patrols with the power to confiscate firearms from all white Americans—an act termed the Gun Raids. *Two years to the day* after the Gun Raids, Earl Turner and his followers retaliate by driving a truck carrying a homemade bomb made of five thousand pounds of ammonium nitrate fertilizer and diesel fuel inside FBI headquarters shortly after 9:00 A.M. one morning, blowing off the front of the building, collapsing the upper floors, and killing more than seven hundred people.

While this written text is extremely important, in true white man fashion, nothing informs life in Kingman better than television. During my stay here, the fifty-unit Imperial Hotel appears to be about half full. Yet, morning, noon, or night, I rarely catch a glimpse of anyone. The residents are inside, out of the wind. McVeigh lay alone on this bed for thirteen days, presumably watching TV for hours on end. There are more than fifty programs available at any given time. These include programs carried by HBO, the Movie Channel, and Spice, a porno station. Spice was probably of little interest to McVeigh. As best as I can determine, Timothy McVeigh was a twenty-six-year-old virgin. Similar to the themes expressed on *Pretty Hate Machine,* there is a strong misogynistic streak running through McVeigh's biography.

But it is likely that the Movie Channel and HBO held his attention, day and night, while the winds wailed outside his door. These channels are designed to appeal to the interests of local viewers. From Kingman to Barstow, California, that means the constant showing of obscure B movies with distinctly antigovernment, anti-intellectual, and antifeminist motifs. The 1985 made-for-cable movie *The Park Is Mine*—starring Tommy Lee Jones as an embittered war veteran who plants explosives in a public park to draw Congressional attention to the plight of Vietnam vets—was shown twice during McVeigh's last stand in Room 212. *Sniper,* starring Tom Berenger as a U.S. Marine gunnery sergeant who assassinates a left-wing guerilla leader in Latin America, was shown four times during the period.

For two days now, I have lain in this bed, watching the movies and trying to understand what inspired McVeigh to carry on with the bombing plot when everyone else had abandoned him. This has been one of the most difficult, gut-wrenching experiences of my life. Essentially, I've been chasing the ghost of Earl Turner. And chasing ghosts, I have come to discover, is an assignment for which I am totally unprepared.

Down Where the Vultures Feed

The encroaching evil doesn't help. Yesterday, to break the monotony, I went for a run down Route 66 at sunset. Even though I ran about five miles, because of the winds I couldn't break a sweat. Add to this the bad food of this ghost-town-in-waiting, and you have some idea of how confused the body becomes. Just as I was returning to the Imperial, four white teenagers in a pickup truck pulled up beside me, and one of them shouted, "Get the fuck out of town, freak!" Quickly weighing my options, I decided to ignore them and go on my way.

That's typical of my experience in Kingman. Elijah Anderson defines a streetwise researcher as one who "neither takes the streets for granted nor recoils from them but becomes alive to dangerous situations, drawing on a developing repertoire of ruses and schemes for traveling the streets safely."[13] I have tried to connect with people here, hoping for an interview or two, but all my ruses and schemes have come up short. I've walked into several stores and bars, looking for someone with whom to talk, but have only been met with icy glances. That's understandable, I suppose. After the bombing, journalists from every major news organization in the world descended on Kingman, filing one negative story after another about this town. And there are still dozens of undercover FBI and ATF agents here, investigating tips on McVeigh, Fortier, and the militias. The whole town is spooked. And that has created enormous research problems.

Today I tried to catch the eye of a swastika-tattooed skinhead several doors down from Room 212. I've interviewed dozens of skinheads over the years, in the United States and abroad, and have only once found myself in what I'd call a compromising situation.[14] But this skinhead was different. He was older, about thirty, and prison-hardened; he was six feet tall and close to two hundred pounds, with massive shoulders, a tiny, angular shaved head, and eyes that were hard as mountain granite. He didn't turn those eyes away from me when I looked at him. Instead, he "bull-dogged" me—prison argot for intense staring. His eyes were filled with righteous hatred. I got the distinct impression that he wanted to kill me. I slowly returned to 212 and closed the door, breathing heavily.

Just then, I felt something wet in the center of my chest. Taking my shirt off and looking down, I see that the red pen in my shirt pocket has broken. The cross I wear is covered with red ink, dripping bloodlike onto the foul carpet of Room 212. For the first time in years, I am afraid.

Shine a Light on Me

I can almost hear the ghost of Earl Turner laughing at me. I've reached the blue centerlight of evil, and it is not a pleasant experience. It has shaken me to my core. I wash the red off my chest, lay the cross aside, pick up my guitar, and begin gently strumming a Bob Dylan song. I'm looking for something deep, some spiritual connection to get me through this awful ethnography of terror. I think of those black kids back in Oklahoma City and arrive at my truest confession.

I am not a religious man, if you think of religion in terms of suffering, sin, guilt, and redemption. But I am spiritual. And that spirituality comes from the same source that inspires my work in criminology—from the angelheaded hipsters. I would never have become a criminologist were it not for the writings of Jack Kerouac and the great musicians who put the beat in the Beat—namely Dylan and the Grateful Dead. I'm certainly not the only one whose career has been influenced by these artists. For millions of us who came of age during the sixties, these angelheaded hipsters shined a light on the path to all things beautiful and right. I looked to them for inspiration because they spoke in an accessible language about a world I recognized—something that few sociologists have ever done. It has been said that the so-called hippie generation was basically a spiritual generation. I know that to be true, and right now that's all that matters, because it is that spirituality that guides me in my struggle with the ghost of Earl Turner. Other criminologists in this situation would rely on their own particular survival skills; this is what I rely on.

The hipsters saw ghosts too. Their words and music are replete with visions of the meaninglessness of human life in the face of existential pain.[15] These visions prompted them to ask spiritual questions, often by "slumming it" among those who live outside the law—just as I'm doing now. Special reverence was accorded to these outlaws—the "desolation angels"—because they were supposedly open to revelations that the law-abiding couldn't have. Kerouac discovered these angels in the seams of a vanishing American West. And they excited his imagination, just as they did—appropriately, perhaps, for this ethnography of terror—when Kerouac first heard Bobby Troup's early fifties hit song, "Route 66" ("Get your kicks/On Route 66").

What separated the hipsters from other popular artists was the pace, the attack, and the emotion of their work. Theirs was not the voice of the detached observer. It was instead the voice of honest confession, or what Kerouac called "the song of yourself" that is written for your "own soul's ear." This led to authentic artistic creations gushing with Biblical imagery, drug-induced surrealism, street visions, playfulness, hipster talk, and—thanks to the cosmic sizzle of Jerry Garcia's guitar—a dazzling array of jazz, blues, and rock licks.

Lying at the core of this artistic Zeitgeist was an intensely spiritual longing for a personal god in the face of an intensely impersonal world. That is what I draw on now, as I sing Dylan's "Desolation Row" and fill Room 212 with the angelheaded spirits of tenderness, compassion, and the holiness of life. This momentarily heals me by confirming an ideal I have cherished for years: That it is far more important—indeed, far more noble—to be true to one's vision of goodness and beauty than to succumb to the darkness of fear and evil.

Working through my existential pain in this way has increased my commitment to telling the story of McVeigh and Oklahoma City as clearly as possible. The research has been an attempt to achieve what Buddhists call *dharma*. For me, that means the human spirit required to dig deeply into my soul in the belief that, once that far down, others will understand what I'm saying—because that far down, they and I are the same. For future generations of criminologists who must struggle with fear as I have, I therefore leave this gift from Verse 22 of Kerouac's *The Scripture of the Golden Eternity*: "Stare deep into the world before you as if it were the void: innumerable holy ghosts, buddhics, and savior gods there hide, smiling. All the atoms emitting light inside wavehood, there is no personal separation of any of it. A hummingbird can come into a house and a hawk will not: so rest and be assured. While looking for the light, you may suddenly be devoured by the darkness and find the true light." [16]

The Blue Centerlight of Evil

Ethnomethodologists refer to the sort of analysis which I am attempting in terms of *indexicality*—the interpretation of language, behavior, motives, objects, and events in a given environment. [17] To this list we can add *research danger*. For danger affects the researcher's ability to interpret language, behavior, motives, objects, and events. Here, then, from within this dangerous research, is as close as I've been able to come to explaining McVeigh and his blue centerlight of evil.

Here in Room 212, the fictional world described by William Pierce informed the delusional world of Timothy McVeigh. This is a world of paranoid conspiracies that, by their nature, defy empirical testing. They are locked and loaded mental constructs about the human struggle that face down all contradictory evidence.

At the center of all this are three important forces. The first is an interlocking of historical events that confirms the validity of the conspiracy theory. The more these events connect with one another, the greater the proof that there is a diabolical enemy to be annihilated. The second is the sense that a historical clock is ticking toward an end-time struggle. This is the omen of apocalypse, the sense that the cosmic human struggle is about to enter a new phase. And the third is cultural misrecognition brought about by the spirit of place.

In this lonely and isolated world, there is no coincidence or happenstance. Here, Waco, the American Revolution, *The Turner Diaries,* and the plot to bomb the Murrah building are connected via crystal meth to the date of April 19. To McVeigh, in his paranoia, that date was a beacon guiding him toward his chosen destiny.

In Room 212 McVeigh threw himself into martyrdom for the American radical right. This occurred at the dangerous crossroads of popular culture, paranoid politics, and the spirit of place — a crossroads where decisions are made, decisions about the link between ideas and action. From those crossroads stepped the living embodiment of Earl Turner and Ryan Gaerity, all rolled into one Pretty Hate Machine. "Tim is very, very committed to justice, whatever his definition," said Phil Morawski, an antitax protestor who knew McVeigh from the gun-show circuit. "He is the kind of person that would lay down his life for his comrades."

Yet in a sense the true disaster of this story lay not in the spirits of Room 212, the Haulapais, Archie's Bunker, Heavy Metal, or cable television. The true disaster lies at the intersection of Route 66 and Harrison Road, less than a mile north of the Imperial. There sits the Arizona Highway Patrol post. Officers from the post routinely passed McVeigh's Sunbird as it sat in front of Room 212 during his two-week stay there. The officers were able to see it as they drank coffee at the Town Restaurant. But because Arkansas law enforcement and federal authorities had failed to investigate the Roger Moore robbery, Arizona troopers were unaware of McVeigh's extraordinary criminality, and he was allowed to go free.

McVeigh checked out of Room 212 on April 12. He was now a lone wolf and the Day of the Rope was at hand. In a final spasm of meth-induced delusion, he stopped by Mike Fortier's trailer and made one final attempt to enlist the assistance of Fortier. When Mike refused, McVeigh got angry and declared that he was "going back to Kansas" to seek Terry Nichols's help in mixing the fertilizer and fuel oil. Then McVeigh headed east, toward the apocalypse in Oklahoma.

Notes

1. Mark S. Hamm and John C. Kite, "The Role of Offender Rehabilitation in Family Violence Policy: The Batterers Anonymous Experiment," *Criminal Justice Review* 16 (1991): 227–48; Mark S. Hamm, "State Organized Homicide: A Study of Seven CIA Plans to Assassinate Fidel Castro," in *Making Law: The State, The Law, and Structural Contradictions,* ed. William J. Chambliss and Marjorie S. Zatz (Bloomington: Indiana University Press, 1993), 315–46; Mark S. Hamm, *American Skinheads: The Criminology and Control of Hate Crime* (Westport, Conn.: Praeger, 1993); Mark S. Hamm, "No Sense Makes Sense: The Paradox of Prosecuting Bias-Motivated Cult Crime," *American Journal of Criminal Justice* (1994): 145–60; Mark S. Hamm, *The Abandoned Ones: The Imprisonment and Uprising of the Mariel Boat People* (Boston: Northeastern University Press, 1995); Mark S. Hamm, *Apocalypse in Oklahoma: Waco and Ruby Ridge Revenged* (Boston: Northeastern University Press, 1997).

2. See Michael Burawoy et al., *Ethnography Unbound: Power and Resistance in the Modern Metropolis* (Berkeley: University of California Press, 1991); Charles C. Ragin and Howard S. Becker, *What Is a Case? Foundations of Social Inquiry* (New York: Cambridge University Press, 1992); Ned Polsky, *Hustlers, Beats, and Others* (Garden City, N.Y.: Anchor, 1969).

3. Respectively, these works include Mark S. Hamm, "Doing Gang Research in the 1990s," in *Gangs: A Criminal Justice Approach,* ed. J. Mitchell Miller and Jeffrey P. Rush (Cincinnati: ACJS/Anderson, 1996), 17–32; Martin Sanchez-Jankowski, *Islands in the Street: Gangs in American Urban Society* (Berkeley: University of California Press, 1991); Hamm, *The Abandoned Ones;* Kate Millett, *The Politics of Cruelty: An Essay on the Literature of Political Imprisonment* (New York: Norton, 1994); Joshua Gamson, "Silence, Death, and the Invisible Enemy: AIDS Activism and Social Movement 'Newness,'" in Burawoy et al., *Ethnography Unbound,* 35–57.

4. Josepha Schiffman, "'Fight the Power': Two Groups Mobilize for Peace," in Burawoy et al., *Ethnography Unbound,* 78–79.

5. See Hamm, *Apocalypse in Oklahoma.*

6. Howard S. Becker, "Cases, Causes, Conjunctures, Stories, and Imagery," in Ragin and Becker, *What Is a Case?,* 210.

7. Mark S. Hamm, *Terrorism, Hate Crime, and Anti-Government Violence* (Washington, D.C.: National Research Council, 1996).

8. Quoted in James Miller, *The Passion of Michel Foucault* (New York: Simon and Schuster, 1993), 290.

9. Michael Burawoy, "Introduction," in Burawoy et al., *Ethnography Unbound,* 4.

10. All information on the bombing conspiracy is based on Hamm, *Apocalypse in Oklahoma.*

11. Rudolfo Anaya, "Foreword: The Spirit of the Place," in *Writing the Southwest,* ed. David King Dunaway (New York: Plume, 1995), x.

12. Pierre Bourdieu and Jean Claude Passeron, *Reproduction in Education, Society and Culture* (London: Sage, 1977), xiii.

13. Elijah Anderson, *Streetwise: Race, Class, and Change in an Urban Community* (Chicago: University of Chicago Press, 1990), 6.

14. Hamm, *American Skinheads;* Mark S. Hamm, "Hammer of the Gods Revisited: Neo-Nazi Skinheads, Domestic Terrorism, and the Rise of the New Protest Music," in *Cultural Criminology,* ed. Jeff Ferrell and Clinton R. Sanders (Boston: Northeastern University Press, 1995), 190–212.

15. See Steve Turner, *Angelheaded Hipster: A Life of Jack Kerouac* (New York: Viking, 1996).

16. Jack Kerouac, *The Scripture of the Golden Eternity* (New York: Corinth, 1970), 25–26.

17. Harold Garfinkel, *Studies in Ethnomethodology* (Englewood Cliffs, N.J.: Prentice-Hall, 1967).

Sex Work and Gender Work

Reversing the Ethnographic Gaze

Experiments in Cultural Criminology

Stephanie Kane

Loki's Toast

The first change of mind happened in 1991. I was about to analyze a toast, an African American oral narrative about a pimp and prostitute. The toast was recited to me from memory by Loki, a man I did some AIDS intervention with in 1988 on the South Side of Chicago.[1] He told it to me one cold day, when the going was rough. The night before I left town, he let me record it, along with several others from his repertoire. What struck me about the toast was that although it was clearly a fiction, the reality the fiction indexes doesn't exist in the same way or degree anymore. I thought I'd talk about the changes in the prostitution industry brought about by the drug trade, especially cocaine, and AIDS. Pimping as a way of organizing "the life" has been eclipsed to a large degree by the intensification of the drug trade, and the implications of the pimp and pro (prostitute) relationship have been altered by the risk of HIV infection. Thus, I would use the toast as a sort of myth that I could then demystify by relocating its poetically portrayed gender-role stereotypes within local social history. I thought the toast would make an interesting point of departure for a feminist analysis of prostitution, one that would allow me to give a toast of a different sort to Loki.

I thought about what I would actually say, for although the toast said about the pro that *"She ranked with the best, from the east to the west,"* it set her up to be used in a way that doesn't exactly show a sensitive appreciation for womanhood. In fact, like most poems of this genre of folk poetry, the toast is terribly misogynist, as noted by the mostly white male authors who wrote about such poems in the 1960s and 1970s.[2] It is also wonderful, which made it an appropriate gift. This was the contradiction—signaled by my bursts of laughter at certain points on the tape, immediately followed by waves of guilt for taking pleasure in even a neat turn of phrase that compliments a whore by reminding us that a dog is a man's best friend.

So, yes, in the back of my mind, I settled on a theme of analyzing misogyny and how it is possible for me as a woman to take pleasure in it when it is elevated to art. When the time came to actually write the piece, though, it hit home to me that as a white woman writing this piece about the exploitation of a black woman by a black man, I was walking on questionable ground.

To help me out of this jam, I turned to three African American feminist writers — Hortense Spillers, bell hooks, and Michele Wallace — whose essays, I'm ashamed to say, I'd never read whole before, but whose generic "women of color" label, together with acknowledgments of the profound impact they've had on critical thinking, I've been hearing and seeing so much of lately in Anglo and French feminist writings.

And I quickly realized that they weren't going to help me out of this jam, because they'd rather I stop and look at what the jam itself might mean.

In her essay "Interstices: A Small Drama of Words," Hortense Spillers uses toasts as an example in building her argument that images of super-sexed black women, together with images of unsexed black women, "embody the very same vice, cast the very same shadow, inasmuch as both are an exaggeration — at either pole — of the uses to which sex might be put."[3] My focusing on these images, then, even if it is to deconstruct them, might nevertheless contribute to the "invisibility blues," to borrow the title of Michele Wallace's book, that black feminists feel when they see and hear these exaggerated representations of women that are repeated everywhere "from pop to theory."[4]

In her essay "Critical Interrogation: Talking Race, Resisting Racism," bell hooks examines the crucial issues that are involved when "a member of a privileged group 'interprets' the reality of members of a less powerful, exploited, and oppressed group,"[5] and how these crucial issues are often disguised with valorizing notions such as intellectual freedom. She ends the essay with this paragraph: "If much of the recent work on race grows out of sincere commitment to cultural transformation, there is serious need for immediate and persistent self-critique. Committed cultural critics — whether white or black, scholars or artists — can produce work that opposes structures of domination, that presents possibilities for a transformed future by willingly interrogating their own work on aesthetic and political grounds. This interrogation itself becomes an act of critical intervention, fostering a fundamental attitude of vigilance rather than denial."[6] I think this statement is key to the endeavor of analyzing folk poetry in terms of crime. In this, if we make a commitment to address issues of gender, we cannot elide issues of race. But, by addressing the problem of a universalized misogyny, this is of course what I would have effectively and unconsciously done had I ignored the problem of racial difference between myself and the black woman figure in the toast.

Then I wondered: How do we adequately theorize race and sex together? How do we, as bell hooks suggests,[7] include an analysis of white ethnicity, so as to denaturalize that category that is left to stand while we are busy with our mind's hands all over the so-called other? Where in my fieldwork can I discover a point of departure for such an analysis?

I found two points at which a white male gaze of a certain negative kind, directed at me, made me feel the sickness that is racism and sexism, and feeling it, I knew it in a way that book learning and participant observation in the usual mode couldn't begin to communicate. The phenomenology of knowledge — how we come to know, what it is we can know — depends on who we are, even when we're standing in the same place, looking at the same thing. This jam is getting deeper, the foundations of social science shakier. The very idea that we can go into the field and experience what it's like to live in another culture, to become competent as a native, to be warned even of the dangers of going native, whatever that might be, seems a bit fantastical. Unless we do something to change our methods, I don't believe we can ever come close to achieving those goals, for the mediations that predate our arrival abound, guiding our exchanges down well-worn colonialist paths (both within and without the United States). Unless we allow ourselves to be more vulnerable to the effects of power as they are directed at the powerless, I don't think we professionals will be effective in making power more compassionate. Most frightening to me, I now realize, is that the global structures that are always already there, because they are just large enough, and because some privileged "we" have been placed at their center and have not tested their walls, have fooled some of us into thinking we are free to learn, to move about, to love.

In her book *Woman, Native, Other,* Trinh Minh-ha writes: "Trying to find the other by defining otherness or by explaining the other through laws and generalities is, as Zen says, like beating the moon with a pole or scratching an itching foot from the outside of a shoe. There is no such thing as 'coming face to face once and for all with objects'; the real remains foreclosed from the analytic experience, which is an experience of speech."[8]

In this attempt to talk about how women are defined—how prostitutes in particular are defined—I'm going to make a couple of moves away from a more straightforward analysis of the toast as text.

First, I'm going to relocate the site of analysis to a scene in Belize, an Afro-Caribbean nation of Central America, where I also did fieldwork.[9] The move helps me work against the stereotypical notions indexed in the toast by resituating them in an analytic context wherein race is not hooked up to gender and power in quite the same way as it is in the urban United States. This may boost the effect of demythologizing the gender/race stereotypes, because instead of posing the toast's myth against a history that is constructed by those same stereotypes, I pose it against a history with different ideological bases. More specifically, Belize is a context in which blacks are the majority and not the minority, and they are not in the subordinate position within local power hierarchies to the same extent as African Americans are in the United States. As a result, the image of black women there is not usually linked to prostitution in discourse the way it frequently is in the United States.

Also, I attempt to problematize the gap between my identity as a white woman ethnographer and the black woman figure in the toast by using a substitute text which conflates my professional identity as an ethnographer with the identity of a prostitute, creating an ambiguity productive of ethnographic knowledge in a different key.

But before I share my fieldnotes, I mention one more change of mind. After I published the first version of Loki's Toast,[10] of which this piece is a variant, I met a folklorist named Dotson who studied toasts and who specialized in collecting women's toasts (of which people said there weren't any). Dotson told me that the charge that toasts are misogynist is untrue, an error drawn from the misreadings of people who are not players in "the game."[11] He explained that the language of toasts is inverted: the poetics of toasts play with the basic structure of hustling and gender relations in the straight world—that is, a pimp's actual dependency on women is transformed by his magnetic rap. When recited to the appropriate audience, players cognizant of the rules of "the game," the toast is an art form that draws its emotional power from love, humor, and adventure, *not* degradation. It's taken me years to be comfortable with the disjuncture between my gut reaction to the image of woman in the toast and the understanding that, when told to an appropriate audience, toasts do not *mean* misogyny. So in the spirit toast tellers originally intended, I offer you some lines from one of Loki's toasts interspersed with ethnography.

It was Thirsty Thursday at the club in downtown Belize City. I was there doing ethnographic fieldwork that would provide background information for a national AIDS intervention project, should such a project be set in motion. More specifically, I was identifying and describing situations of risk in regard to HIV transmission. The most obvious of these was the prostitution trade organized to service British military personnel. Doing this work solo was rough, so when the Belize government hired a new man to coordinate AIDS intervention and surveillance in the country, I was pleased we had overlapping goals and suggested we try to do some fieldwork together. We set a date to meet at the bar on Thirsty Thursday. I was anxious about going alone, so I went to his office the morning we were to meet to remind him of our appointment. When he began apologizing in advance for not showing up, I suspected he had no intention of coming that evening. But I went ahead with the plan, even though I knew the time he'd proposed, 9:00 P.M., was way too early. I wore the unsexiest tropical clothing I could find and asked some of my white creole, middle-class friends to drop me off—they wouldn't be caught dead in the place. They wanted to know what I was doing, so I told them I needed to check out the prostitution scene, and they were quite taken aback that I thought that what was going on there was prostitution. "Those are Belizean women who go there. Belizean women aren't prostitutes. They're just out for a good time, some free drinks, you know, partying." Hmmm, I thought. I'd been there before, and it sure looked like prostitution to me, taking note of the gap between our perceptions.

I walked upstairs to confront the two bouncers at the door, who said something like, "Hey lady, do you know this is Belize?" I said, with a bravura I did not really feel, "Yes, thank you, I know where the fuck I am." The club was pretty empty. The white soldiers, mostly boys still wet behind the ears—"limies" as they're called—were bunched up outside on the balcony and inside not far from the bar. At the bar, watching CNN, probably post–Gulf War propaganda, sat a few black creole women and black and white creole men. On the balcony with the limies were a few black creole women and one obviously gay black creole man. I got a beer and sat down at a table where I had a good view of everything and watched and waited. Everyone else was watching and waiting, too; as I say, it was early. The women, dressed up and looking pretty, began to stake out positions at the tables against the wall. The band started setting up. This AIDS coordinator fellow looked to be a no-show for sure. And people started to wonder what I was doing there, and came up with the obvi-ous—I needed some bread, I was either new at the game, or new in town, but I was making a go for it. There was some tension and some polite cu-riosity, but no one actually asked me. After appraising my person for a time, the light-skinned creole man started making pimping moves, send-ing over beers, which it turned out I could not refuse, and so was trying to drink slowly, figuring I couldn't afford any sloppy mistakes this night. I re-called Loki's toast: *"So it wasn't by chance, that I caught her glance. I intended to steal this dame. And I thought with glee, Holy Jesus. It's time for me to gain."* More people started coming, and, by the time the band started playing, the place was jumping. The black gay man was the most boisterously sex-ual person in the place. The life of the party, he moved round and round, teasing the soldiers, enlivening the subtext of homoeroticism among them, getting the women worked up, and being friendly to me, for which I was grateful. The Chinese owners, flanked by three black creole, one Latina, and one Chinese woman, sat as still as statues along the wall op-posite me, also watching the scene.

The limies started getting drunker, louder, and more integrated. The women who'd staked out positions at the tables early were now squeezed in by men. The dance floor became the focus. I began training my atten-tion on the conditions which would shape the enactment of risk—more particularly, the sexual and ethnic identities of the people, the geography and rhythm of activities, and the sexualization of this social interaction. When the pimp wanted to dance with me, I began to weigh my chances of getting out of there without a problem, and I figured I still had some leeway. So I danced with him, and he looked me up and down, telling me I was going to do all right, not to worry—the cherries and oranges ringing up in his eyes like a slot machine. Perhaps he was dreaming of Loki's heroic whore: *"She tricked with Frenchmen, torpedoes and hitsmen. To her they were all the same. She tricked with Jews, Apaches and Sioux. And some breeds I can't even name."*

He wasn't too sticky, though, and I was on my own again when I struck up a conversation with a woman, a soldier in the Belize Defense Forces, who came from the same small town in the south where I was living at the time. She introduced me to another older woman, who seemed to be there looking out for the younger women at the scene, and I told them what I was doing there. One of them said, "Oh, you're the public health lady!" Belize is a small country. It happened that her cousin was the secretary of the man who was supposed to meet me there, and they had spoken about me.

Meeting these women, and having them know who I was, reassured me and allowed me to stay longer. By midnight, the scene was really hopping. The gay man was doing some wild maneuvers with a black creole woman on the dance floor, pretending to have sex with her, acting out the bisexual possibilities for the limies, who were now mostly paired off with local women. Other Belizean locals started coming out, and even some men from the Belize Defense Forces, who weren't supposed to frequent this place set up for the Brits. The crowd was loosening up, intermingling. The sex trade was by now effectively indistinguishable from the regular nightlife of the city.

At some point, I don't remember exactly when, a white guy crossed my path. He was an American who owned some ramshackle hotel by the water. He was there dancing with his wife. I'd met him before, once, when I was looking for a place to stay, but he was full up, and I was just one more gringa passing through. My presence in this context apparently struck him somewhat differently, though, for he looked at me with a glance of utter disgust. I'd felt that glance before—because when you are the object of it you don't just see it, you feel it, it's visceral. This conjures Loki's hellish whore: *"You can cop her lid, for the lowest bid. You can set her ass on fire. You can dig in her cunt, for a mother-fucking month. She's the cheapest bitch you can hire."*

Where I'd felt that glance before was in Chicago, on 47th Street, just west of Martin Luther King Boulevard, to be exact. I'd left the field station where I worked as an ethnographer on the AIDS intervention project because I had to bring some shoes to the shoemaker, and George, one of the older generation of IV drug users who were regulars at the station, insisted that he accompany me. I put on this slightly worn, floor-length gray coat—trying to stay warm and look like I had no money—but apparently I'd gone overboard, because George started laughing riotously at my down-and-out appearance. On this day, the incredibly narrow space of the shoe store, lined with the old-time banks of high wooden seats, was filled with mostly black men talking, hanging out, staying warm, getting their shoes shined. When George introduced me, my name, Dr. Kane— carried along by its popular connotation—rippled through the house with merriment. Then George wanted to take me in to meet the people in the pawnshop, where he said he did some work—he swept their floors. He took me to the back to introduce me to the white managers, who were sitting at desks behind bars. That was the first time I felt the glance, from them, like I was a piece of slime on the floor.

According to my ethnographic analysis, inspired in part by Annette Kuhn's analysis of photographs in her book *The Power of the Image*,[12] this glance and its repetition were elicited by a certain configuration of features which fixed the meaning of my person within a regime of representation. My identity, from the perspective of these white males, was determined by the context in which they read me. In this context, the white woman-ness of me disrupted the circuit of power and/or pleasure that the white men had come to expect: in these situations, I was the wrong mirror for their masculinity. Because of my disruption, I suffered a glance that left no room for ambiguity, a glance that repositioned me in their circuit of power, a glance that taught me some things.

One thing I learned is how professional identity, when recognized, is like a glass box, through which participant observation takes place in a shielded manner, and how the quality of data, like the glance viscerally perceived, produces a knowledge effect on the ethnographer that is not necessarily present when that knowledge is mediated by another's experience. If I saw this happen to somebody else, or somebody told me about it, as I'm telling you, it would not intrude upon my analyses in quite the same way. In respect to methodology, then, we might want to highlight such accidental breakthroughs, so that the clarity of the situational dynamics obtained can align our more systematic descriptions. I suspect we all probably do this as a matter of course, but I think it offers a variation that may constructively mix into the stance of critical self-reflection that feminists like Trinh Minh-ha have been cultivating. We might even want, in some cases, to engineer such moments, which do not necessarily have to be negative. For as Hortense Spillers has written, "[W]e are not always properly attuned to the deep chords of deception that sound through the language and the structures of thought in which it fixes us."[13]

The glance I twice encountered is a racist glance, because I was a white woman playing the part carelessly, ruthlessly, and in a way regularly assigned to the feature of black woman-ness by white men. But it's a slippery thing, because, in the South Side case, had I met those guys in, for instance, Friday night services at the synagogue, I would never have seen it. And because it could be dangerous for me to be misidentified as a prostitute on 47th Street, I went back the next day dressed in professional garb, carrying my professional card. I told the managers that they had no right to look at a person like they looked at me yesterday and that I didn't want there to be any confusion about what I was doing out on the street. They acted as if things could not possibly have been as I perceived. Their racism and sexism were recuperated in the discourse of politeness. On the other hand, as a white woman in Belize, there are situations in which I might have engaged in prostitution that would have been more in line with what that American white hotel owner would find acceptable in his scheme of things. For instance, if he'd seen me on some yacht, bought for the day, I might have elicited, instead of the glance of disgust, a lucre-promising leer. Sex work, it seems, is highly coded according to the linked features of race and class.

Twice glanced, I was shown how my identity as a middle-class white woman is so loosely bound to my body, that if I am inhabiting a social space in which white middle class-ness is not evident through context, if I do not fulfill the conditions required to represent white middle class-ness, the privileges will be immediately withdrawn. In other words, the freedom which I have been led to expect as a fundamental right of bourgeois citizenship is only extended if I uphold the sex, class, and race contracts to which I have been trained. In fieldwork, such a glance thus blurs the lines between personal and professional, causing the ethnographer a certain amount of productive turmoil. The glance, repeated, keyed me in to the importance of determining the particular ways in which race structures the organization of sex work. Once I was keyed in, the ambiguities and recuperations no longer shielded my observations and analysis as completely.

Through all these peregrinations, believe it or not, I really was hoping still to find a way to use the toast more fully, and other toasts that Loki gave me as well. But, alas, it eludes me. You know, it wasn't easy for me to get the toast in the first place. That day when things were going rough, Loki said, "Come on out to the car," and we turned on the motor for the heat, and he recited it to me. He knew I'd really like it. Offering me something that he knew I'd dig professionally was his way of letting me know he cared about me as a friend. And he apologized for not having recorded it, saying that he had tried to the night before, but his kid was making too much of a ruckus or something. I set up a couple of other dates with him to record it, but it always happened that when he showed up and was in a toasting kind of mood, there was no tape recorder. He told me a lot of great stories, too, especially about pickpocketing. He said he'd like me to write a book about his exploits someday. He did tell me that he'd put the toast together with a bunch of guys while he was in jail in Lexington, Kentucky, doing a three-year sentence for selling drugs (that was before the jail was changed from a Narcotics Farm to a women's prison). *"And you pay a price, when you deal in vice. We all know it takes a steady grind,"* the toast recalls. Suspicious folklorist that I am, I asked him if they had put it together from pieces of other things. And he said, "Well, it wasn't so much pieces from other things, as, it's just the guys' heads, see, it's a co-existent thing." Loki explained that the toast was composed by himself and his fellow inmates (who included some well-known musicians and criminals) as they lay about on mattresses, locked in otherwise empty rooms for hours on end. Later, in the library, I came across an article that quoted some key lines of a toast the authors called "The Fall."[14] They matched up roughly with Loki's.

Loki's toasted whore eventually fails him. *"Now the real trouble began when the girl took sick and quit gin. She had the piles and inflamed biles. For a month she couldn't pee. When her ovaries failed I was shocked to hell. Cause things really looked bad to me. When lockjaw set in, believe me friend. The Chinaman took his toll. Her head was dead, her ass was red. And the lips on her cunt was cold."* When Loki, as the pimp in the toast, saw the woman couldn't make it anymore, he went to get another. The heroine-turned-hellion got mad and had him thrown in jail for pimping. This takes him out of circulation, but doesn't stop the game. The toast ends with the toaster—sitting in jail: *"Farewell to the nights and the neon lights. Farewell I say to it all. Farewell to the game, may it still be the same. Next year, when I'm through doing this fall."*

While Loki and his prison mates certainly keep the toast alive, and add their own names and twists, the toast isn't what you'd call strictly "original." But that doesn't change anything, does it? I do wonder about the circulation of these images of prostitutes: the way they are encoded in artistic forms like toasts and pornographic photographs, how they are authored, and how they reproduce a circumscribed set of racial conventions that organize the circuit of money and pleasure that is sex work and the circuit of money and pleasure that is not sex work, but academics.

In closing, I'll tell you this little joke played on me down on the South Side of Chicago. It was Milton, another old regular at the field station, who came up to me and said: "I had a dream last night and you were in it."

And I said: "I hope it was beautiful."

And he said: "It was beautiful all right. As a matter of fact, I owe you some money."

When Ethnographic Field Time Intersects History

Data foraged in the borderlands between illicit nightlife and public health call for a scholarly search between disciplines, and the idea of a "cultural criminology" seems to fit.[15] This essay considers the status of ethnographic knowledge collected in the field and library by drawing ideas from feminist anthropology, critical race theory, and cultural studies to analyze the meaning and structures of power embedded in the transnational prostitution industry. In a strategic move to displace the objective gaze of the researcher as professional who is outside the deviant subculture she studies, I blur the boundary between observer as good citizen and observed as deviant—a boundary which structures so much criminological understanding.

As an alternative structure of understanding, consider those moments when field time intersects historic events. These may be large-scale events, such as getting caught up in the Los Angeles riots while studying race relations, or small-scale, personal events, such as getting arrested along with the people you are studying.[16] In these moments, the normal distinctions between fieldworker and subjects of study may well be confused and abandoned, leading to cases of mistaken identity—a process not unlike "going native," but more evanescent—and, in studies of illegal or deviant acts, potentially more dangerous. Ethnographers have always experienced such events. Indeed, war stories are traded with relish in the interstices of professional conferences. Rarely, however, are these stories brought into formal presentations. In this essay, I suggest that it is well worth the effort of bringing our personal experiences of such events into our social science texts, for in moments of shocked surprise we may find some good ideas.

Of course, we take a chance by incorporating such events into academic texts, especially if they are personal. Introducing an observer's subjectivity challenges the objectivity claims made on the basis of more systematic dimensions of fieldwork. On some level, this weakens our scholarly authority, but, on another level, it has the potential to increase the power of our texts to speak *to,* not just *from,* events. There is no reason why ethnographic texts cannot explicitly work on dual levels simultaneously, offering systematic analyses and, at the same time, showing how moments of extreme or unusual conditions render systematicity impossible. What happens in those moments when systematic methods become useless, when chaos transforms our usual work into a mere professional fetish? The accident of our being there, the sudden unpredictability brought on by a rush of events: such conditions may precipitate an erasure of professional privilege. And yet, we may maintain our documentary and analytical expertise in this process, enabling us to capture and decode the experience—*our* experience—on a phenomenological level.

In sum, I ask not that we abandon the systematic, empirical mode of observation, but rather that we take the risk of challenging the illusion of a totalizing scientific control that privileges most ethnographic and criminological discourse. We can use serendipity. We may even be able to engineer incidents of mistaken identity—not all of which need be negative—so that we can begin to account for those dimensions of social control and resistance that have not yet been considered.

Notes

The section of this chapter entitled "Loki's Toast" was published in an earlier form by Stephanie Kane as "Race, Sex Work and Ethnographic Representation; Or, What to Do about Loki's Toast," *Canadian Folklore canadien* 15 (1993): 109–18, and is reprinted here by permission of the journal. It was first presented at the annual meeting of the American Anthropological Association, November 1991, Chicago, as part of the session sponsored by the Association for Feminist Anthropology entitled "Defining Women: Images of Women in Folklore, Ritual, and Popular Culture." It was written while I was in residence at the Rockefeller Foundation Humanities Fellowships Program at the State University of New York at Buffalo. Research in Chicago was funded by the National Institute of Drug Abuse (NIDA Grant No. 5R18 DAO 5285) and in Belize by Fulbright and the Council for International Exchange of Scholars.

Above all, I dedicate this essay to the memory of George Lewis, alias "Loki," for his friendship and artful speech. I would also like to thank the people in Chicago and Belize City for everything they taught me, and Pauline Greenhill, Kristin Koptiuch, Joanne Lukitsh, Bruce Jackson, Elizabeth Kennedy, and Theresa Mason for comments and discussion.

1. For in-depth discussion of this research, see Stephanie Kane, "AIDS, Addiction and Condom Use: Sources of Sexual Risk for Heterosexual Women," *Journal of Sex Research* 27 (1990): 427–44; Stephanie Kane, "HIV, Heroin and Heterosexual Relations," *Social Science and Medicine* 32 (1991): 1037–50.

2. See, for example, Roger Abrahams, *Deep Down in the Jungle: Negro Narrative Folklore from the Streets of Philadelphia* (Chicago: Aldine, 1963); Michael Agar, "Folklore of the Heroin Addict: Two Examples," *Journal of American Folklore* 84 (1971): 175–85; Bruce Jackson, "Circus and Street: Psychological Aspects of the Black Toast," *Journal of American Folklore* 85 (1972): 123–39; Dennis Wepman, Ronald Newman, and Murray Binderman, "Toasts: The Black Urban Folk Poetry," *Journal of American Folklore* 87 (1974): 208–24; Bruce Jackson, *Get Your Ass in the Water and Swim Like Me: Narrative Poetry from Black Oral Tradition* (Cambridge, Mass.: Harvard University Press, 1974); Anthony Reynolds, "Urban Negro Toasts: A Hustler's View from L.A.," *Western Folklore* 33 (1974): 267–300; Bruce Jackson, "A Response to 'Toasts: The Black Urban Poetry,'" *Journal of American Folklore* 88 (1975): 178–82; Dennis Wepman, Ronald Newman, and Murray Binderman, *The Life: The Love and Folk Poetry of the Black Hustler* (Philadelphia: University of Pennsylvania Press, 1976); David Evans, "The Toast in Context," *Journal of American Folklore* 90 (1977): 129–49.

3. Hortense Spillers, "Interstices: A Small Drama of Words," in *Pleasure and Danger: Exploring Female Sexuality,* ed. Carole Vance (London: Pandora, 1984), 75–76.

4. Michele Wallace, *Invisibility Blues: From Pop to Theory* (New York: Verso, 1990).

5. bell hooks, "Critical Interrogation: Talking Race, Resisting Racism," in *Yearning: Race, Gender, and Cultural Politics* (Boston: South End Press, 1990), 55.

6. hooks, "Critical Interrogation," 55.

7. hooks, "Critical Interrogation," 55.

8. Trinh Minh-ha, *Woman, Native, Other: Writing Postcoloniality and Feminism* (Bloomington: Indiana University Press, 1989), 76.

9. For an in-depth discussion of this research, see Stephanie Kane, "Prostitution and the Military in Belize: Planning AIDS Intervention in Belize," *Social Science and Medicine* 36 (1993): 965–79.

10. Kane, "Prostitution."

11. Jason Dotson, personal communication, 1993.

12. Annette Kuhn, *The Power of the Image: Essays on Representation and Sexuality* (New York: Routledge and Kegan Paul, 1985).

13. Spillers, "Interstices," 83.

14. Wepman, Newman, and Binderman, "Toasts."

15. I first saw this term used by Redhead, and it is attributed to academic commentators such as Stanley. See Steve Redhead, *Unpopular Cultures: The Birth of Law and Popular Culture* (Manchester and New York: Manchester University Press, 1995), 44; Chris Stanley, "Outwith the Law" (Ph.D. thesis, University of Kent, n.d.). See also Jeff Ferrell and Clinton R. Sanders, eds., *Cultural Criminology* (Boston: Northeastern University Press, 1995).

16. For example, Ferrell analyzes his own arrest in the course of studying graffiti crews in Denver, in Jeff Ferrell, "True Confessions: Law, Crime and Field Research," paper presented at the annual meetings of the Academy of Criminal Justice Sciences, Boston, March 1995.

(Dis)Courtesy Stigma

Fieldwork among Phone Fantasy Workers

Christine Mattley

More than thirty years ago Erving Goffman trenchantly revealed to us not only the sociological concept of stigma, but that of courtesy stigma as well.[1] In discussing courtesy stigma he suggested that when an individual is related through the social structure to a stigmatized individual that relationship leads the wider society to treat both individuals in some respects as one. A courtesy stigma is then accorded the previously unblemished individual.

Subsequently, the topic of courtesy stigma has received scant attention in the literature. Birenbaum detailed the process of managing courtesy stigma when it results from familial ties to mentally retarded children, and he offered adaptations to courtesy stigmas.[2] Herman and Reynolds likewise noted that the families of the mentally ill may spend much of their time "attempting to mitigate the stigma potential of mental illness through the employment of information management techniques."[3] Kirby and Corzine discussed the dangers of studying deviant groups. Based on observations of others' reactions to their research on the "gay subculture," the authors exposed the contagion of stigma in the attitudes and opinions of professional colleagues and suggested ways of managing or deflecting such courtesy stigma.[4]

It is the courtesy stigma resulting from research that is of interest in this chapter. During my field research I experienced a variant of courtesy stigma that I have chosen to label *(dis)courtesy stigma.* Kirby and Corzine suggest that the application of a courtesy stigma is more of a problem with nonacademics than with academics—that "the labeling that occurs in academic settings is usually less direct than that in the larger society."[5] Yet I found labeling of me just as problematic—if not more—among academics than among nonacademics. Moreover, in that the label was applied to me in a particularly discourteous way, I refer to the stigma as (dis)courteous stigma.

The Research Site

Before turning to my research and the subsequent (dis)courtesy stigma which emerged there, let me describe how I came to do field research on phone fantasy workers. This research originated from an ongoing interest in the sociology of emotions. The increasing sociological interest in the commercialization of emotion includes the ways in which people are trained to manage their own emotions as well as the emotions of their customers or clients. Virtually all of the literature on occupationally related emotional labor focuses on mainstream occupations such as flight attendants, bill collectors, therapists, missionary wives, or supermarket clerks.[6] As this list of occupations indicates, most workers in post-industrial society now interact with other individuals rather than operating machines. Fewer than 6 percent of workers now work on assembly lines; voice-to-voice or face-to-face delivery of services has become prominent in our culture. A capacity to deal with people is the requirement of most jobs.[7] Moreover, service-sector jobs are far more likely to demand emotional labor of employees.

Hochschild observed employee training at the Delta Airlines' Stewardess Training Center in Atlanta, Georgia, and also interviewed Delta flight attendants.[8] Through her observations she was able to detail the company's official rules, regulations, and guidelines regarding the attendants' emotional labor. Such demands are important because they provide workers the norms with which they are expected to comply; they define normative emotions in the workplace. For instance, new attendants were constantly told that their smiles were their biggest asset. There were also appeals to modify actual feeling states—specifically, the trainee was expected to act as if the airplane cabin were her home. Trainees were asked to think of a passenger "as if he were a personal guest in your living room."[9] Thus, company rules dictated how the employee was to feel and was to express emotion.

I decided to conduct research into telephone fantasy workers for two reasons. First, as mentioned previously, the existing literature on emotional labor focuses on mainstream occupations. While that research is invaluable, research focused on more marginal occupations such as those in the emerging phone sex industry is necessary for a fuller understanding of emotional labor. I use the term "marginal" here because the phone sex industry occupies an intriguing position relative to other legal occupations. On the one hand, it is part of the sex industry; that is, it shares the social/cultural space occupied by prostitution and pornography. On the other hand, it is a segment of the larger phone industry that sells services and goods more generally. Therefore, investigation into the phone sex industry helps fill the gap in our current understanding of occupations and emotional labor.

Second, I decided to study work in which the commodity sold is emotion—work which is *characterized* by emotional labor, rather than work in which emotion work is simply a component. It seemed to me that the prototype of work characterized by emotional labor was the selling of fantasy—specifically the selling of sexual fantasy over the telephone. Callers are not, for instance, buying transportation from one physical location to another, but are actually *buying emotions* from a faceless voice. The issue of emotional labor is thus critical to an understanding of the work and of the worker and, in turn, provides an opportunity to investigate the ways in which workers manage their own emotions and those of the customers. Although customers buy sexual fantasy, and could therefore be thought of as purchasing arousal, I found the primary commodity sold was emotion. Callers' arousal hinged on affect, and talk included conversations ranging from their feelings about themselves, to feelings about their lives, to their feelings about calling phone fantasy lines. Thus, the emotion sold was broader than (but also included) arousal.

Choice of Method

The research reported here is based on participant observations conducted over a nine-month period. I chose participant observation because I feel that the sociology of emotions requires a methodology of emotion; in this case, a firsthand, involved investigation of emotional labor. Recently sociologists have recognized the importance of attending to emotions during the research process, rather than bracketing them.[10]

Ellis has argued for an emotional sociology that describes, embodies, and interprets lived emotional experience. Specifically, she suggests that as sociologists we can "examine emotions emotionally, feeling for the people we study. We can view our own emotional experience as a legitimate sociological object of study, using our feelings as a way of understanding and coping with what is going on emotionally in our research. Finally, we can concentrate on studying how emotions feel in the context, and by the narrative terms, of people's everyday lives."[11]

In the same way that we cannot ignore participants' feelings and expect to understand their social groups, then, we cannot omit our feelings as participant field researchers. Attending to *our* feelings in the field helps us to understand how members construct meaning and understandings. Researchers who are aware of their feelings in the field and who consciously respond to those feelings and feeling norms thus become what I have called "sentient researchers."[12]

The Data

My research was conducted over a nine-month period during which I spent between three and five days per week, for a minimum of six hours per day, working for an adult phone fantasy telephone line in a large city about one hundred miles from where I live. Not only did I keep a field journal including data on the callers, workers, and daily activities; I also kept a field journal that included my own emotions and reactions throughout the entire experience, from trying to locate such a business, to trying to acquire funding for my project, to trying to gain access, and on throughout the time I spent in the field. I was fortunate to have two colleagues who acted as sounding boards for me, and I often included their comments and documented their support of me in my emotion field journal. During the time I worked the phones, I took about two thousand calls, got to know other workers and the management, and spent many hours talking with the people working there. Some of the women became friends with whom I occasionally socialized after working hours; others were merely acquaintances. What I wish to describe here is the stigma I felt as a result of my research and, more broadly, my feelings about it throughout the entire research process.

(Dis)Courtesy Stigma

One of the first steps in this research process was, of course, trying to obtain funding to offset the costs of research (particularly my travel and living expenses). I applied for a modest amount of grant money available from my university. One of the reviewers of my grant proposal, a feminist I know well, objected to the research site, suggested that there must be another occupation to study, and wondered whether I chose the proposed site simply because it was titillating. Of course, the implication was that somehow my perverted, voyeuristic tendencies led me to this research topic and site. (Needless to say, I received no funding.) I wrote in my field journal at the time, "I am so disappointed in her, I feel betrayed by her. . . . I guess I expected more from her as a woman and as a feminist. This is obviously part of the sex industry which clearly exploits women. Isn't this a feminist issue? Is she provincial enough to think this research is 'dirty'?" I know that field researchers are often questioned about their choice of topics, so although I felt a bit wounded, I didn't take the criticism too seriously. I knew that my research was worthwhile.

I was undaunted. While I was planning my faculty fellowship leave, I happened upon a help-wanted ad for a phone fantasy business in a large city nearby. I called, they asked me to come in for an interview, and within several days of finding the ad I was hired. I was ecstatic! The owner knew that I was an academic; I had told him that I needed a part-time job, and he had no problem with that. It also worked out well, since I told him that I would prefer weekends, and they badly needed those shifts covered. If the other workers asked what I did for a living, which of course they did, I told them; and although they were intrigued, they didn't seem to care. They readily accepted me and treated me as they treated the other women.

During the time I was in the field, I became friends with many of the women; we socialized with one another away from work and talked about our lives, our problems, and our families. We also talked occasionally about the stigma associated with the work we did. The women consciously chose which people in their lives to inform about their work. Often one or more family members knew and colluded in not telling other family members. Typically boyfriends, lovers, and husbands knew, but not always. One of my co-workers, "Jamie," was married to a trucker who did not know that she was working the phones. She had told him that the business she worked for was in a building that had four stories, and that on the first three floors telephone marketing was the primary activity, including selling magazines and taking mail orders for household objects. On the fourth floor, however, women worked as phone fantasy workers. She would tell me that he often said to her, "Now, stay away from the fourth floor Jamie!" The women whose husbands or lovers knew often talked about how the men felt about their work. Generally, they did not want to know what the women said to the callers, nor were they particularly curious about the work; they viewed it as "just a job."

Without exception, though, there were people in all the women's lives who did not know about the women's work. The identity of those people varied from woman to woman, but all the women anticipated disapproval and/or stigma from someone in their lives. They sometimes discussed their ambivalence about whether or not to reveal their work to others. In response, other women talked about experiences they had had when they told friends or acquaintances about their work. The reactions they recounted ranged from surprise to disbelief and acceptance. One woman, "Blair," told me about one of her male friends who reacted by first saying, "No way! You're making this up!" Later this same man told her, "I'm not surprised. It's totally cool that you do that." Additionally, some women described the reactions of men (other than husbands or boyfriends) as a salacious curiosity and a decided change in tone of the interaction. Finally, women talked about the attitude of the owner toward the workers. Though he was typically described as seeing us as "phone ho's," his reaction was not taken too seriously because he also occasionally took calls from men who wanted to talk to a man. Consequently, he was seen, to some degree, as one of us.

Talking to other workers about the stigmas they endured helped me recognize the one applied to me. The stigma I felt and want to describe here came from other academics. While I didn't recognize what was happening early on as a stigma, I knew that reactions to my research seemed unusual and were worth noting. It seemed as though people around me were not seeing my work as *research*. They couldn't see the research because they couldn't see beyond the research site. For instance, some of my early journal entries read as follows: "I'm fascinated by other people's reaction to this research. T is incredulous. (He thinks that 'This is the ticket to Donahue.') G wishes she was going to be a fly on the wall. F is dying to know what happens, and wants me to call her immediately. L is also curious and 'is dying to know how it goes.' I'm not sure if they are really fascinated by the idea of doing something forbidden or what. They seem to be interested in what I'll say or need to do. It's as though they're more interested in the data site than the data." From the day of my job interview: "S calls later that night and I tell her about the interview. She is intrigued by it all, but seems not to take it very seriously. She is laughing and teasing me about it, she keeps saying 'Oooh, baby!' R calls on the next day, I talk to her about it and she is amused by it. Likewise, when I talk to D he is amused. Why do all these people think this is funny?" From a couple of days later: "Tonight I talked with B and told her my concerns about this research not being taken seriously, about my fears that I have maybe given off messages about not being serious about this research. She allayed my fears and told me that I have been open about this work, and that I have presented this as serious research. She suggested that maybe people think of whether they would be able to talk 'dirty.' She said that she would not be able to do this work."

Clearly, some of my acquaintances reacted by laughing and perhaps by being embarrassed, making me feel that they were not taking this research seriously and that they saw themselves as different from me. One of my colleagues who acted as a sounding board for me continued to reassure me that the research was valid and worthy of being taken seriously. As an experienced field researcher and a feminist, he was a tremendous resource for me. He helped to keep me focused throughout the entire time I was in the field, asking sociological questions about the work itself: we spent many hours over coffee while he listened to me sort out analytic categories. Another of my colleagues was very helpful as well. One day I heard secondhand a description of my work he had given to someone asking about my research. He was not only supportive of me and my work, he also emphasized the fundamentally sociological nature of the research; he essentially "cooled out" a salacious inquirer.

In general people seemed to be very interested in my research. I chose not to pursue conversations about my research aggressively with people because I was in the field covertly, and I simply didn't want to take any chances. However, often a colleague would ask me about my faculty fellowship leave or would introduce the topic around other academics. After this happened a few times I began to be aware of the pattern of reactions

I received. I recognized the pattern as stigma—in part because of my discussions with other phone sex workers about people's reactions to them.

First, the reactions to my research were (and are) gendered. After listening to a description of my research into the emotion work of phone sex workers—always a rather abstract and academic description—men generally first responded by saying (always smiling), "Well, you have a great voice for it!" Then, "So, what do you say? What do you talk about?" I usually answered, "Just exactly what you would think." Not being deterred, they continued, "Like what?" I never told them, never described calls to them, but rather tried to steer them away from such questions by saying, "That is not the point of my research." If they persisted, I told them, "It costs $1.25 a minute to find out."

Callers also often told me what a great voice I have, so I have come to know what that phrase means. When colleagues say it, I always walk away from the situation feeling as though I am no longer a sociologist, but have been reduced to a "great voice." A field journal entry illustrates the point: "My identity as an academic is leveled. The talk about my research has become talk about talk—metatalk. Within the department I have also noticed that some men who were previously respectful toward me or treated me like 'one of the guys' now sometimes giggle, make double entendres, and allude to things like dirty movies, etc., in my presence. I have become sexualized to them." To treat me in such a way is to do me a discourtesy; consequently, mine is not only a courtesy stigma resulting from my field research association, but also a (dis)courtesy stigma.

Chancer observed a similar phenomenon when discussing with her colleagues her theoretical piece on prostitution. Her male colleagues reacted in an embarrassed or ridiculing way. After reading her article, three colleagues even asked if she had herself been a prostitute.[13] She refers to this reaction as ambivalence. "To analyze prostitution unavoidably raises both the ongoing specter of gendered oppression in patriarchal societies and our often schizophrenic—part-acknowledged, part-tabooed—passions about sex: in combination the two may evoke highly ambivalent and disconcerting sets of reactions."[14] Chancer and I received analogous reactions from men; but what about women?

Women had two types of reactions to my research. Most seemed to be interested in the women with whom I worked, the people for whom I worked, and the actual physical site. They generally asked questions about the age of the workers, the social class of the workers, the number of women who worked there, what the owner was like, whether I felt safe, if I could hear other women on calls, and if the other women were friendly. They seemed genuinely curious about the research and the research site.

A second reaction took me totally by surprise. Sometimes when I was talking to women, a couple of whom I know to be feminists, they would listen and ask me the same genre of questions other women asked. Suddenly, it was as though a curtain had fallen over their faces and they would say, "I could *never* do that sort of work." Or they might ask, "How can you do that? How can you sell something so intimate? Something so private?" Or "Don't you feel like you're selling part of yourself?" I've even been asked if I became aroused while doing calls. These questions and comments were usually delivered in such a way as to make it clear to me that while they could never do "that sort of work," there must be something about me that made it easy for me to do the work. Once again I was accorded a (dis)courtesy stigma.

Why did this take me by surprise? First, I assumed that they understood that this was research, not some voyeuristic jaunt. Second, I suppose I expected more from women, and from those few feminists who reacted in that way. Clearly, my research investigated a part of the sex industry which exploits women; it investigated an important feminist issue. Third, this seemed like a classist response to me. They could never do this sort of work; the implication is that it was beneath them. Perhaps they have never had to make the choices working-class women have. Chancer has recognized the class-based nature of sex work—that women who become sex workers are economically motivated.[15] I agree with Chancer in suggesting that feminism must recognize that the marginalization of sex workers is inconsistent with the interests of representing all women.[16]

How is this (dis)courtesy stigma different from a courtesy stigma? As discussed by Birenbaum and by Herman and Reynolds, courtesy stigma is a result of an affiliation with someone possessing what Goffman identified as a physical stigma (mental illness) which is not generally perceived to be voluntary.[17] The stigma accorded sex workers is, of course, a moral stigma and is thought to be voluntary in nature. This distinction is an important one because of the resulting reactions associated with these courtesy stigmas. In the first instance, the accompanying reaction is sympathy or concern for what seems to be a "legitimate problem." Likewise, the courtesy stigma associated with the researcher in this case is a consequence of studying a legitimately marginal group.

In the second instance, the courtesy stigma associated with sex work has connotations of voluntary behavior. Kirby and Corzine faced a courtesy stigma because of their research into gay subcultures.[18] However, they suggested that the stigma was less of a problem among academics than the general population, that academics were more tolerant. Neither Chancer nor I found this to be the case.[19] More important, the courtesy stigma was applied in a most discourteous manner, unlike the way Kirby and Corzine describe. Consequently, the stigma we endured is a variant of courtesy stigma: (dis)courtesy stigma.

My (dis)courtesy stigma is similar to the stigma endured by other sex workers. In explaining the whore stigma, Pheterson suggests that women are allowed to give free sex, but not to negotiate sex without defying a host of laws.[20] A woman who earns money through sex is defined as selling her honor. In concrete terms, she does not negotiate her honor as the word "selling" implies; however, as a result of negotiating her sexuality she does officially lose civil liberties and human rights. "Among the activities generally subsumed under the whore dishonor by straight society, i.e. society identified as legitimate, lawful, and necessarily unassociated with prostitution is . . . *a woman using one's energy and abilities to satisfy impersonal male lust and sexual fantasies. . . .* Socially, thus, female dishonor is attached to whore *identity. . . .*"[21] My (dis)courtesy stigma was attached to my identity. I had voluntarily used my energy to satisfy impersonal male lust and therefore I was accorded a whore identity.

(Dis)courtesy stigma, then, is bound up with notions of illicit sex and sex work, and it is related to the debate about sex materials. I prefer the term "sex materials" to the usual binary opposition of erotica/pornography.[22] The use of "sex materials" allows us to expand the discussion to include all cultural representations and constructions used sexually. The usual debate about pornography, and the sex industry in general, hinges on an invocation of the centered self with a singular identity as constituted by thinking and rationality, enabling our ability to decipher an objective world. Such an invocation ignores multiple realities, contexts, histories, and power relations. It is undergirded by an assumption that sex materials are constant, that they are a part of an "objective reality." The implication is that sex materials are always interpreted in the same way.

By dichotomizing sex into good and bad, we can then dichotomize activities and cultural constructions into good and bad as well. But this dualism fails to recognize context, social production and usage of materials, or relations of power. It also assumes a unified subject, a centered subject, and, consequently, a unified object or Other.

The construction of the stigmatized Other, then, ignores multiple realities of sex workers and the context of creation and consumption of sex work. It reduces the sex worker to a singular identity: an Other who is a "bad girl." Constructing me as an Other invoked a (dis)courtesy stigma — the Other constructed in a particularly discourteous way. My identity was a "great voice," a phone worker, nothing else — all else receded. My being reduced to a single identity made me feel dehumanized. However, it helped me understand and empathize with the stigmatization of the workers I knew and with whom I worked. As a matter of fact, I found myself identifying with and being an advocate for them — defending them and sex workers in general. The women I worked with weren't weird or perverted but were "normal" women with the same kinds of everyday problems in their lives as the academic women I know. They were complex and interesting women not deserving of being reduced to a single dimension.

While the reactions of men generally and some women to my research seem to be dissimilar, I believe they emanate from the same source. The general discourse surrounding sex materials *leads* people to dichotomize these materials into good and bad and the people involved into good and bad. However, such binary oppositions lead to an impasse in discussion. They short-circuit discussion, leaving us unable to analyze sex materials sociologically, to analyze their social construction, the varied contexts of their production, the cultural climate that encourages their production, the changing power relations embedded in them. By dichotomizing, we are left with nothing to say, nowhere to explore. Moreover, the logical conclusion to such an opposition is a dichotomous hierarchy of self and Other. Such a hierarchy especially keeps women divided, and impedes understanding or empathy.

Finally, this good/bad dichotomy has implications for us as sociologists in terms of what is seen as legitimate research. The dichotomy truncates understanding and restricts space for critical inquiry. An arena of interaction and behavior is ignored and an entire area of social research is censored. By doing away with the binary oppositions currently associated with sex materials and sex workers, by not censoring an area of research, we allow for the forceful criticism of sex materials. As feminists we can investigate and address the sexism, racism, homophobia, and classism manifest in some sex materials, including phone fantasy lines, without utilizing binary oppositions. Sexual images are related to a culturally constructed climate which allows for their existence. To construct sex workers as the Other, to discourteously stigmatize them and those who conduct research with them, is to reproduce the climate, not to question or understand it.

Notes

1. Erving Goffman, *Stigma: Notes on the Management of Spoiled Identity* (Englewood Cliffs, N.J.: Prentice Hall, 1963).

2. Arnold Birenbaum, "On Managing Courtesy Stigma," *Journal of Health and Social Behavior* 11 (1970): 196–206.

3. Nancy J. Herman and Larry T. Reynolds, "Family Caregivers of the Mentally Ill: Negative and Positive Adaptive Responses," in *Symbolic Interaction: An Introduction to Social Psychology,* ed. Nancy J. Herman and Larry T. Reynolds (New York: General Hall, 1994), 344.

4. Richard Kirby and Jay Corzine, "The Contagion of Stigma: Fieldwork Among Deviants," *Qualitative Sociology* 4 (1981): 3–20.

5. Kirby and Corzine, "The Contagion," 7.

6. Arlie R. Hochschild, *The Managed Heart* (Berkeley: University of California Press, 1983); Monica J. Hardesty, "Plans and Mood: A Study in Therapeutic Relationships," in *Studies in Symbolic Interaction: The Iowa School,* ed. Carl J. Couch, Stanley Saxton, and Michael A. Katovich (Greenwich, Conn.: JAI Press, 1986), 209–30; Mary Romero, "Chicanas Modernize Domestic Service," *Qualitative Sociology* 11 (1988): 319–33; Wendy Strickland, "Institutional Emotion Norms and Role Satisfaction: Examination of a Career Wife Population," paper presented at the North Central Sociological Association meetings, Dearborn, Mich., April 1991; Martin Tolich, "Alienating and Liberating Emotions at Work," *Journal of Contemporary Ethnography* 22 (1993): 361–81.

7. Hochschild, *Managed.*

8. Hochschild, *Managed.*

9. Hochschild, *Managed,* 105.

10. See, for example, Carolyn Ellis, "Emotional Sociology," *Studies in Symbolic Interaction* 12 (1991): 123–45; Carol Rambo Ronai, "The Reflexive Self Through Narrative: A Night in the Life of an Erotic Dancer/Researcher," in *Investigating Subjectiv-*

ity, ed. Carolyn Ellis and Michael G. Flaherty (Newbury Park, Calif.: Sage, 1992), 102–24; Sherryl Kleinman and Martha A. Copp, *Emotions and Fieldwork* (Newbury Park, Calif.: Sage Publications, 1993).

11. Ellis, "Emotional Sociology," 125.

12. Christine Mattley, "Review of *Emotions and Fieldwork* by Sherryl Kleinman and Martha Copp and *Secrecy and Fieldwork* by Richard G. Mitchell," *Journal of Contemporary Ethnography* 23 (1995): 530–32.

13. Lynn Sharon Chancer, "Prostitution, Feminist Theory, and Ambivalence: Notes from the Sociological Underground," *Social Text* 37 (1993): 143–71.

14. Chancer, "Prostitution," 146.

15. Chancer, "Prostitution," 162, 165.

16. Chancer, "Prostitution," 166.

17. Birenbaum, "On Managing"; Herman and Reynolds, "Family Caregivers."

18. Kirby and Corzine, "The Contagion."

19. Chancer, "Prostitution."

20. Gail Pheterson, "The Whore Stigma: Female Dishonor and Male Unworthiness," *Social Text* 37 (1993): 39–64.

21. Pheterson, "Whore Stigma," 43, 46, 48, emphasis added.

22. I wish to thank Cathy Celebreeze for the term "sex materials."

Drugs and Drug Worlds
Urban and Rural

Researching Crack Dealers Dilemmas and Contradictions

Bruce A. Jacobs

"Yo, Bruce, come on down the set [neighborhood]. Meet where we usually do," Luther said, and hung up the phone.[1] A trusted contact for an ongoing study of street-level crack dealers and a crack dealer himself, I had no reason to question him. "Just another interview," I thought. Notebooks and file folders in hand, I went to the bank, withdrew fifty dollars for subject payments, and drove fifteen minutes to the dope set I was coming to know so well.

Luther flagged me down as I turned the corner. The seventeen-year-old high school drop-out opened the door and jumped in. "Swerve over there." He pointed to a parking space behind the dilapidated three-story apartment building he called home. "Stop the car—turn it off." Nothing out of the ordinary; over the previous three months, we often would sit and talk for a while before actually going to an interview. This time, though, there was an urgency in his voice I should have detected but did not. He produced a pistol from under a baggy white T-shirt. "Gimme all your fuckin' money or I'll blow your motherfuckin' head off!"

"What the fuck's your problem?" I said, astonished that someone I trusted had suddenly turned on me. The gun was large, a six-shooter, probably a long-barrel .45. It was ugly and old looking. Most of its chrome had been scratched off. Its black handle was pockmarked from years of abuse. Why was he doing this? How did I get myself into this situation? It was the kind of thing you hear about on the evening news but don't expect to confront, even though I knew studying active offenders risked such a possibility.

I frantically pondered a course of action as Luther's tone became more and more hostile. He was sweating. "Just calm down, Luther, just calm down—everything's cool," I trembled. "Don't shoot—I'll give you what you want." "Gimme all your fuckin' money!" he repeated. "I ain't fuckin' around—I'll waste you right here!" I reached in my left-hand pocket for the fifty dollars and handed it over. As I did so, I cupped my right hand precariously an inch from the muzzle of his gun, which was pointing directly into my abdomen. I can survive a gunshot, I thought to myself, as long as I slow the bullet down.

He snatched the five, crisp ten-dollar bills and made a quick search of the vehicle's storage areas to see if I was holding out. "OK," he said, satisfied there were no more funds. "Now turn your head around." I gazed at him inquisitively. "Turn your motherfuckin' head around!" For all I knew, he was going to shoot and run; his right hand was poised on the door handle, his left on the trigger. "Just take your money, man, I'm not gonna do anything." "Turn the fuck around!" he snapped. "OK," I implored, "I won't look, just lemme put my hand over my eyes." I left small openings between my fingers to see what he was really going to do. If he were truly going to fire, which he appeared to be intent on doing—the gun was being raised from the down-low position in which it had been during the entire encounter to right below head level—I would smack the gun upward, jump out of the car, and run a half block to the relative safety of a commercial street.

As I pondered escape routes, he jammed the gun into his pants as quickly as he had drawn it, flung open the door, and disappeared behind the tenements. I hit the ignition and drove slowly and methodically from the scene, grateful to have escaped injury, but awestruck by his brazen violation of trust. All I could do was look back and wonder why.

If this were the end of the story, things would have normalized, I would have learned a lesson about field research, and I would have gone about my business. But Luther was not through. Over the next six weeks, he called my apartment five to ten times a day, five days a week, harassing, taunting, irritating, baiting me. Perhaps twice over that six-week period, I actually picked up the phone—only to find out it was he and hang up. Luther would call right back and let the phone ring incessantly, knowing I was there and letting the answering machine do the dirty work. On several occasions, it became so bad that I had to disconnect the line and leave the apartment for several hours.

I'd arrive home to see the answering machine lit up with messages. "I can smell the mousse in your hair—huh, huh, huh," his sinister laugh echoing through the apartment. "I know you're there, pick it up." More often than not, I would hear annoying dial tones. One message, however, caught my undivided attention: "897 Longacre—huh, huh, huh," he laughed as I heard him flipping through the phone book pages and identifying my address. "We'll [he and his homeboys] be over tomorrow." I didn't sleep well that night or for the next six weeks.

What was I to do—report the robbery, and go to court and testify to stop what had become tele-stalking? Some researchers contend that when crimes against fieldworkers occur, staff are to "report them to the police to indicate that such violations will have consequences."[2] I did not feel I had this option. Calling the authorities, no matter how much I wanted to, would not only have endangered future research with Luther's set and those connected to it, but would also have risked retaliation—since Luther's homies knew where I lived and worked.

So I called the phone company and got caller ID, call return, and call block. These devices succeeded in providing his phone number and residence name, which I used to trace his actual address, but I could still do nothing to stop him. Changing my number was the last thing I wanted to do, because those who smell fear often attack. As other researchers have noted, concern about "violence may cause ethnographers to appear afraid or react inappropriately to common street situations and dangers. . . . Fearful behavior is easily inferred by violent persons" and may often lead to violence itself.[3] Thus, Berk and Adams stress the importance of maintaining one's cool when threatened: "The investigator will be constantly watched and tested by the very people he is studying. This is especially true [with] delinquents who . . . value poise in the face of danger."[4] Danger, it must be remembered, is "inherent" in fieldwork with active offenders, "if for no other reason than there is always the possibility of dangerous cultural misunderstandings arising between researchers and subjects."[5] This is especially true of research among active streetcorner crack sellers, who routinely use violence or threats of violence to gain complicity.[6]

After enduring six weeks of this post-robbery harassment, and with no end in sight, I had to do something. I called the police and told them the story. An officer came out and listened to messages I had saved. As he listened, the telephone rang, and Luther's number displayed on the caller ID. "Do you want me to talk to him?" the officer asked sternly. "No," I replied, feeling more confident with a cop three feet away. "Lemme see if I can work things out." I picked up the phone and started talking.

"What do you want?"

"Why do you keep hangin' up on me? All I want is to talk."

"What do you expect me to do, *like* you? [sardonically, on the verge of losing it]. You fuckin' robbed me and I trusted you and now you call me and leave these fuckin' messages and you want me to *talk* to you? [incredulous]"

"I only did that 'cause you fucked me over. I only ganked [robbed] you 'cause *you fucked me*."

"What are you talking about?"

He proceeded to explain that without him, none of the forty interviews I obtained would have been possible. True, Luther was the first field contact to believe that I was a researcher, not a cop. He was my first respondent, and he was responsible for starting a snowball of referrals on his word that I was "cool."[7] But after he could no longer provide referrals, I moved on, using his contacts to find new ones and eliminating him from the chain. My newfound independence was inexplicable to him and a slap in the face. He wanted vengeance; the robbery and taunting were exactly that.[8]

Ethnography and Social Distance?

Such are the risks ethnographers take when studying dangerous, unstable offenders. Although "robbery, burglary, and theft from field staff are uncommon, [they] do occur. In fact, many crack distributors are frequent and proficient robbers, burglars, and thieves."[9] Not so ironically, someone I had trusted and considered a "protector"[10] had become someone to be protected from. Such flip-flops are entirely possible in the world of active offenders, who themselves often admit an inability to control or understand their behavior.

All of this merely underscores the changeable, unpredictable nature of fieldwork relations, especially with active offenders. Johnson notes that "[i]t is incumbent on the investigator to assess the influences of these changes."[11] The important point is for researchers to put themselves in a position where they can do this. Unfortunately, the very nature of criminological fieldwork may work against this.

Much of the problem revolves around the dilemma between social distance and immersion in fieldwork, and the difficulty researchers have in resolving it. The notion of "social distance" is thought to be in some ways foreign to the ethnographic enterprise. Wolff, for example, contends that successful fieldwork inevitably requires surrender—psychological, social, and otherwise—to the setting, culture, and respondents one is studying. It requires "total involvement, suspension of received notions, pertinence of everything, identification, and risk of being hurt."[12] Ethnographers are advised to immerse themselves in the native scene,[13] to become a member of what they are studying.[14] They are told to become an actual physical and moral part of the setting.[15] As Berk and Adams put it, "The greater the social distance between the participant observer and the subjects, the greater the difficulty in establishing and maintaining rapport."[16]

Building rapport with active offenders typically becomes more difficult, though, as the "deviantness" of the population one studies increases.[17] With any offender population, trying to become "one of them" too quickly can be downright harmful. Some contend that the most egregious error a fieldworker can make is to assume that the fieldworker can gain the immediate favor of his or her hosts by telling them that he or she wants to "'become one of them' or by implying, by word or act, that the fact that they tolerate his [or her] presence means that he [or she] is one of them."[18] Similarly, Polsky warns that "you damned well better not pretend to be 'one of them,' because they will test this claim out and one of two things will happen. Either the researcher will get drawn into participating in actions one would otherwise not engage in, or the researcher could be exposed as a result of not doing so, the latter having perhaps even greater negative repercussions."[19] The more attached the researcher gets too early in the process, the more vulnerable she or he may be to exploitation. The researcher is still a researcher, no matter how close the researcher thinks she or he is getting. Subjects know this and may also know there will be few if any serious repercussions if they try to pull something, especially at the beginning of research when the fieldworker tends to be the most desperate for acceptance. Problems are only compounded by the fact that researchers tend to be far more streetwise by the end of fieldwork than they are at the beginning. Perhaps the least important time to be streetwise is at the end; both the number and seriousness of threats tend to decline with time. Where threats are often highest—at the beginning, when the researcher may be labeled a narc, a spy, or simply a suspicious character—the researcher may also be least capable of handling them. This only makes the threats that do materialize more threatening.

Researchers who are victimized at this early stage may often be barred

from reporting it; doing so threatens to breach promises of confidentiality and anonymity made to subjects. The practical matter of being labeled
a narc who "sold someone out" is a separate issue and potentially more
problematic: snitching violates a sacred norm of street etiquette, even if
the person being snitched on is in the wrong. At best, snitching will ter-
minate future chains of respondents. At worst, it will label the researcher
a "rat" and subject him or her to street justice. Both outcomes are of
course undesirable and will likely bring an end to one's research.

Being immersed while remaining to some degree objective is the key.
Some researchers stress the importance of using "interactional devices
and strategies that allow the fieldworker to stay on the edges of unfolding
social scenes rather than being drawn into their midst as a central actor."[20]
Others recommend engaging in a paradoxical and "peculiar combination
of engrossment and distance."[21] Like the Simmelian stranger, researchers
are told to be familiar yet not too familiar, involved yet not too involved,
all the while making the balance seem natural.[22] Some modicum of social
distance is thus critical to the ethnographic enterprise—"as a corrective
to bias and overrapport brought on by too strong an identification with
those studied."[23]

In some sense, then, social distance between the researcher and the
active offenders she or he studies *can* be beneficial. As Wright and Decker
observe, "[T]he secrecy inherent in criminal work means that offenders
have few opportunities to discuss their activities with anyone besides associates, a matter which many find frustrating."[24] By definition, criminal
respondents will often have "certain knowledge and skills that the researcher does not have."[25] This asymmetry may empower them to open
up or to open up sooner than they otherwise would. Offenders may enjoy
speaking about their criminal experiences with someone who is "straight."
Perhaps it is a satisfaction gained from teaching someone supposedly
smarter than they, at least in terms of academic degrees. The fact that respondents may see something in the research that benefits them, or an
opportunity to correct faulty impressions of what it is they actually do,[26]
only facilitates these dynamics.

All of it may come down to dramaturgy. Yet, the very nature of criminological fieldwork dictates that the researcher either can't or won't "act"
in certain ways at certain times. Acting inappropriately can compromise
the research itself, the fieldworker's ability to remain in the setting, or the
ability to remain there safely. The moral and practical conundrum be-

tween social distance, immersion, and "participant" observation in criminological fieldwork may, in many ways, be unresolvable.

My failure to manage the distance/immersion dialectic with Luther appeared to have more to do with a practical shortfall in managing informant relations—a myopia if you will—than with going native. Clearly, I had lost objectivity in the process of "handling" Luther. Whether this was a function of overimmersion is open to question, but it undoubtedly played some role. Whether it was avoidable is also open to question, particularly when one considers the practical and methodological paradoxes involved in fieldwork with active offenders. Although myopic (mis)management led to my exploitation by Luther, without putting myself in such a position, I would never have been able to collect the data I did. In many ways, the "shortfall" was necessary and, at some level, advantageous.

The bottom line is that no matter how deft the fieldworker is at managing relations, he or she ultimately never gains total control. Criminological fieldworkers exist in a dependent relationship with their subjects.[27] This makes one wonder who is indeed the "subject" and what he or she can be "subject to" at any given moment. Some contend that the hierarchical relationship between interviewer and subject in social research is "morally indefensible"[28] and should be thrown out. Perhaps the hierarchy may be jettisoned as a matter of course, by the very nature of the fieldworker-active offender relationship. Luther's actions toward me stand as an exemplary case.[29]

Studying Active Offenders

Studying active drug dealers is problematic precisely because their activity is criminal. Active offenders are generally "hard to locate because they find it necessary to lead clandestine lives. Once located, they are reluctant, for similar reasons, to give accurate and truthful information about themselves."[30] "Outsiders" are often perceived as narcs seeking to obtain damaging evidence for juridical purposes.[31] Indeed, the most common suspicion that subjects have about fieldworkers is that they are spies of some sort. As Sluka notes, "It is difficult to find an [ethnographer] who has done fieldwork who has not encountered this suspicion."[32]

Collecting data from drug dealers, particularly from active ones, is likely to be difficult and dangerous unless one can construct friendships within a dealing community.[33] Because of this difficulty, some researchers target institutional settings.[34] Such settings afford the chance of obtaining data without the risk of physical harm associated with "street" interviews.[35] Unfortunately, collecting valid and reliable data in such settings may not be entirely possible, as criminologists have "long suspected that offenders do not behave naturally" in them.[36] Sutherland and Cressey argue that "[t]hose who have had intimate contacts with criminals 'in the open' know that criminals are not 'natural' in police stations, courts, and prisons and that they must be studied in their everyday life outside of institutions if they are to be understood."[37] Polsky is more emphatic, commenting that "we can no longer afford the convenient fiction that in studying criminals in their natural habitat, we . . . discover nothing really important that [cannot] be discovered from criminals behind bars. What is true for studying the gorilla of zoology is likely to be even truer for studying the gorilla of criminology."[38] There are fundamental qualitative differences between the two types of offenders. Institutionalized drug dealers, for example, may represent those not sophisticated or skilled enough to prevent apprehension, or those who simply do not care about getting caught and who sell to anyone with money. Studies of incarcerated offenders are thus open to the charge of being based on "unsuccessful criminals, on the supposition that successful criminals are not apprehended or are at least able to avoid incarceration." This weakness is "the most central bogeyman in the criminologist's demonology."[39]

Knowing this, I entered the field and began frequenting a district near a major university that is both prestigious and expensive, yet which borders a dilapidated neighborhood with a concentrated African American population and heavy crack sales. A lively commercial district, with restaurants, quaint cafés, bars, theaters, and stores, splits the two. The area is known for racial and ethnic diversity, making it relatively easy for most anyone to blend in. Over a nine-month period, I frequented the area and made myself familiar to the regular crowd of hangers-out in the dividing commercial district. Some of these individuals were marginally homeless and spent entire days in the district smoking, drinking, playing music, and begging. Though not crack dealers themselves, they knew who the dealers were and where they worked. After gaining their trust, I was shown the dealers' congregation spots and quickly took to the area.

At first, I would simply walk by, not explicitly acknowledging that anything was going on. Sometimes I would be escorted by one of the "vagabonds," but most of the time I went alone. My objective was simply to let dealers see me. Over the days and weeks, I walked or drove through slowly to gain recognition, trying to capitalize on what Goffman has called second seeings: "[U]nder some circumstances if he and they see each other seeing each other, they can use this fact as an excuse for an acquaintanceship greeting upon next seeing. . . ."[40] Unfortunately, this did not go as easily as Goffman suggests, as dealers openly yelled "SCAT!"—a term for the police undercover unit—at me.[41] Jump-starting participation was clearly the toughest part of the research because dealers suspected I *was* the police. Ironically, it was the police who gave me my biggest credibility boost.

Police and Credibility

In the second chapter of this volume, "Criminological *Verstehen:* Inside the Immediacy of Crime," Ferrell notes that "a researcher's strict conformity to legal codes can be reconceptualized as less a sign of professional success than a possible portent of methodological failure . . . a willingness to break the law," by contrast, "[opens] a variety of methodological possibilities."

Hanging with offenders on street corners, driving them around in my car, and visiting their homes must have been a curious sight. My appearance is somewhat akin to that of a college student. Shorts, T-shirts, crosstrainers, and ball caps with rounded brims, "just like SCAT wear 'em" (as one respondent put it), make up my typical attire. Further, I am white, clean-cut, and affect a middle-class appearance, traits the relatively poor, African American respondents associated with the police. These traits appeared to make them even more leery that I was SCAT, or that I worked for SCAT in some capacity.

To offenders who hadn't gotten to know me well, or to those waiting to pass judgment, I was on a deep-cover assignment designed to unearth their secrets and put them in jail. To cops on the beat, I was just another college boy driving down to crackville with a user in tow to buy for me. Such relations are commonplace in the street-level drug scene and have generalized subcultural currency: users serve as go-betweens and funnel unfamiliar customers to dealers for a finder's fee, usually in drugs and without the customer's consent, but generally with his or her tacit permission. When cops see a relatively nicely dressed, clean-shaven white boy driving a late-model car (with out-of-state plates, I might add) and a black street person in the passenger seat, they lick their chops.

Several police stops of me in a one-month period lent some credibility to this proposition. I had not obtained, as Wright and Decker had, a "prior agreement with the police" [42] whereby the police knew what I was doing and pledged not to interfere. I chose not to; the last thing I wanted was to let police know what I was doing. As Polsky explains, "Most of the danger for the fieldworker comes not from the cannibals and headhunters but from the colonial officials. The criminologist studying uncaught criminals in the open finds sooner or later that law enforcers try to put him on the spot—because, unless he is a complete fool, he uncovers information that law enforcers would like to know. . . ." [43] Because my grant was not a federal one, I could not protect the identity of my respondents with a certificate of confidentiality (which theoretically bars police from obtaining data as it pertains to one's subjects). My work was undercover in a sense and eminently discreditable. However, contrary to admonitions by some to avoid contact with the police while doing research with dangerous populations, [44] my run-ins with police turned out to be the most essential tool for establishing my credibility.

My first run-in came two weeks after making initial contact with offenders. I was driving Luther through a crack-filled neighborhood—a neighborhood which also happened to have the highest murder rate in a city which itself had the fourth-highest murder rate in the nation. [45] We were approaching a group of ten mid-teen youths and were about to stop when a St. Louis city patrol car pulled behind. Should I stop, as I planned on doing, and get out and talk with these youths (some of whom Luther marginally knew), or would that place them in imminent danger of arrest? Or should I continue on as if nothing was really going on, even though I had been driving stop and go, under ten miles an hour, prior to and during the now slow-speed pursuit? I opted for the latter, accelerating slowly in a vain attempt to reassert a "normal appearance." [46]

Sirens went on. I pulled over and reassured Luther there was nothing to worry about since neither of us had contraband (I hoped). As officers approached, I thought about what to tell them. Should I say I was a university professor doing field research on crack dealers (a part I clearly didn't look), lie, or say nothing at all? "Whatcha doin' down here?" one of the officers snapped. "Exit the vehicle, intertwine your fingers behind your heads, and kneel with your ankles crossed," he commanded. The searing June sidewalk was not conducive to clear thinking, but I rattled something off: "We used to work together at ———. I waited tables, he bussed, and we been friends since. I'm a sociology major up at ——— and he said he'd show me around the neighborhood sometime. Here I am." "Yeah right," the cop snapped again while searching for the crack he thought we already had purchased. Three other police cars arrived, as the cop baited Luther and me as to how we really knew each other, what each other's real names were (which neither of us knew at the time), and what we were doing here. Dissatisfied with my answers, a sergeant took over, lecturing me on the evils of crack and how it would destroy a life others in this very neighborhood wished they had. I found no fault with the argument, listened attentively, and said nothing. After a final strip search in the late afternoon sun revealed nothing, they said I was lucky, vowed to take me in if I ever showed my face again, and let us go.

On a second occasion, Luther and his homie Frisco were in my car when we pulled up to a local liquor store. The two became nervous upon seeing two suits in a "tec" (detective) car parked at the phone booth. I told Luther and Frisco to wait, and I went into the store. As I exited, the two men approached and showed their badges. "What you doin' with these guys—do you know 'em?" "Yes," I said, deciding to tell them who I *really* was and what I was doing. "Mind if we search your car?" one asked. "No problem," I replied. "Go right ahead." As one searched my car (for crack, guns, or whatever else he thought he'd find), his partner cuffed both Luther and Frisco and ran warrants. As I soon learned, both detectives knew the two as repeat violent offenders with long rap sheets. They took Frisco in on an outstanding warrant and let Luther go with me. "I respect what you're doing," the searching officer said as he finished and approached, "but you don't know who you're dealing with. These guys are no good." I told him thanks and promptly left with Luther, feeling remorseful about Frisco being taken in only because he was with me.

On a third occasion, I was sitting on my car making small talk with four or five dealers when a patrol car rolled by. The officers inside gave a stern look and told us to break it up. "All right," I said, not going anywhere. We continued to talk for a few minutes when the officers, clearly agitated, rolled by again and demanded in no uncertain terms, "Break it up and we mean now." I hopped in my car, drove four or five blocks, made a left, and heard sirens. "Here we go again." This time, I was not nearly as nervous as I had been on the other occasions, ready to dispense my professor line, show my consent forms and faculty ID, and see their shocked reaction. "Get out of the car and put your hands on the trunk," the driver predictably ordered as I began my explanation. They searched me anyway, perhaps thinking it was just another mendacious story, but I kept conversing in a relaxed, erudite tone. Cops are known to have perceptual shorthands to render quick and accurate typifications of those with whom they're interacting,[47] and I could tell my conversational style was creating a good impression. I told them that I was doing interviews, that I was paying respondents for their time, and that the research was part of a university grant designed to better understand the everyday lives of urban youth. This was, of course, specious. The study's true purpose was to identify how crack dealers avoid arrest, something I dared not admit, for obvious reasons. "You can do what you want," one of them said, satisfied after a thorough search revealed no contraband, "but if I were you, I'd be real careful. You don't want to mess around with these punks." His words rang all too true several weeks later when Luther pointed the gun at my abdomen.

I did not realize it at the time, but my treatment by police was absolutely essential to my research. Police provided the "vital test"[48] I desperately needed to pass if my study were to be successful. The differential enforcement practices of these police officers (and many others around the country)—in which young, minority males are singled out as "symbolic assailants" and "suspicious characters" deserving of attention[49]—benefited *me* immensely. Police detained *me* because I was with "them." Driving alone in these same areas at the same time, though suspicious, would not likely have attracted nearly as much attention. I was "guilty by association" and "deserving" of the scrutiny young black males in many urban locales receive consistently. For my research, at least, this differential enforcement was anything but negative.

As Douglas notes, it is often necessary for researchers to convince offenders they are studying that the researchers do not represent the authorities.[50] Sluka adds that subjects "are going to define whose side they think you are on. They will act towards you on the basis of this definition,

regardless of your professions."[51] Words may be futile in convincing offenders who or what one really is. Ultimately, "actions speak louder than
words. . . . [T]he researcher will have to demonstrate by . . . actions that he
is on the side of the deviants, or at least, not on the side of the officials."[52]
The police had treated me like just another user, and had done so with offenders present. This treatment provided the "actions" for me, the picture
that spoke a thousand words.

Offenders' accounts of my treatment spread rapidly through the
grapevine, solidifying my credibility for the remainder of the project and
setting up the snowball sampling procedure I would use to recruit additional respondents. Without the actions of *police* I may not have been
accepted by *offenders* as readily as I was or, perhaps, never accepted at all.
A skillful researcher can use the police—indirectly and without their
knowledge or, as in my case, without even the researcher's own intent—
to demonstrate to offenders that the researcher is indeed legitimate and
not an undercover police officer. Often thought to be a critical barrier to
entry, the police may be the key to access. Of course, undercover officers
themselves can manipulate this very dynamic to gain credibility with
those they target—something savvy law enforcement administrators
may exploit by setting up fake arrests in plain view. Such tactics may make
a researcher's identity even more precarious; in my case, though, this did
not occur.

Why police never attempted to confiscate my notes during these
pull-overs I'll never know. Perhaps it was because the notes appeared to be
chicken scratch and were indecipherable by anyone but me. Perhaps it
was because my notes didn't reveal anything the cops did not already
know, or at least thought they knew. Regardless, the law is clearly against
ethnographers, who can be held in contempt and sent to jail for protecting sources and withholding information.[53] As Carey points out, "There
is no privileged relationship between the . . . researcher and his subject
similar to that enjoyed by the lawyer and client or psychiatrist and pa-
tient."[54] This, of course, says nothing about issues of guilty knowledge or
guilty observation.[55] Being aware of dealing operations and watching
transactions take place makes one an accessory to their commission, a
felony whether one participates or not. Fieldworkers are co-conspirators
by definition, no matter their motive or intent. As Polsky concludes, "If
one is effectively to study adult criminals in their natural settings, he

must make the moral decision that in some ways he will break the law himself."[56]

Researching Active Crack Sellers: In Perspective

By definition, criminological fieldworkers regularly intrude into the lives of individuals engaged in felonies—felonies for which these individuals can receive hard time. The more illegal the behavior, the more offenders as research subjects have to lose if found out. Obviously, this makes it tougher—and more risky—for researchers to gain access.

Street-level crack selling is thus a paradox of sorts: there is perhaps no other behavior so openly visible and so negatively sanctioned by law as crack selling. It must be this way for sellers to be available to their customers. This is particularly true in a declining drug market such as St. Louis,[57] where demand is finite and dwindling, while the number of sellers has remained constant or increased. To compete in such conditions, sellers will often stand out longer and in more difficult conditions than they previously would, in greater numbers, and in greater numbers together. Individual sellers also may rush to customers to steal sales from competitors, drawing even more attention. This situation creates ideal conditions for police—or researchers—to identify open-air sellers and infiltrate them.

Access notwithstanding, the importance of a strong indigenous tie to the research setting at the beginning of field relations—as a way of vouching for the researcher—cannot be overstated. Access and safe access are two wholly different notions. In my case, this tie was Luther—or at least so I thought. More generally, it is an indigenous offender or ex-offender turned fieldworker who acts as gatekeeper and protector. Yet, in a twist of sorts, field research with active offenders often requires strong ties in order to generate weak ones—that is, to initiate the methodological snowball. Micro-structurally and methodologically, this is unique; multiple weak ties rather than one or two strong ones are thought to be indispensable for social-network creation.[58] Indeed, one or two strong ties may actually cut off an actor from an entire social network.

In field research, developing strong ties with the wrong person or persons can, at a minimum, bias the sample or, worse, generate no sample at all.[59] Researchers may gain entry, but it may be with the wrong person. As my encounter with Luther attests, the outcome can be far more threatening than obtaining a biased sample or no sample. Perhaps the larger point here is that, no matter how strong or safe one's ties, danger is inherent in fieldwork with active offenders. Nowhere is this more true than among streetcorner crack sellers. Although many dangers can be addressed through planning and preparation, more often than not, danger management hinges on a creative process of "trial and blunder"[60] and results from a combination of skill and luck.[61] As Sluka notes, "[G]ood luck can sometimes help overcome a lack of skill, and well-developed skills can go far to help overcome the effects of bad luck. But sometimes no amount of skill will save one from a gross portion of bad luck."[62] Inevitably, criminological fieldwork is unpredictable and less subject to rational planning than we want it to be. How researchers handle this problem ultimately is a personal choice.

Researching active offenders requires one to balance conflicting agendas. Such agendas emanate from specific audiences—whether police or criminals—each with their own biases toward the ethnographic enterprise. Simply taking sides or currying favor with one audience over the other is not the issue, though this may be done at some point. Research strategies must be weighed carefully because their consequences are inevitably dialectical: police can get you "in" with offenders, but offenders can get you "in trouble" with police. Personal security is dependent on offender acceptance, yet security can be compromised by dependency. Police can be researchers' last bastion of hope against volatile offenders, but reliance on authorities may undermine the very purpose for being in the field. Caught among these contradictions stands the researcher, a true one-person "island in the street."[63] In this lonely position, the researcher must decide when to shade the truth and when to be forthright, when to offer and when to omit, when to induce and when to lie back. Such judgments are subjective and context specific, as any ethnographer will tell you. They must be made with the audience in mind, whether that audience is legal or illegal, academic or social. Each choice affects the kinds of data obtained and revealed. And how far an ethnographer is willing to go to get such data intertwines with the results that ethnographer hopes ultimately to obtain—as my encounter with Luther attests.

Notes

The research on which this chapter is based was funded by Grant No. S-3-40453 from the University of Missouri Research Board. Points of view or opinions expressed in this document are those of the author and do not necessarily represent those of the UMRB. I would like to thank Jeff Ferrell and Richard Wright for their helpful comments and criticisms on an earlier version of this chapter.

1. All names are pseudonyms to protect identities.

2. Terry Williams, Eloise Dunlap, Bruce D. Johnson, and Ansley Hamid, "Personal Safety in Dangerous Places," *Journal of Contemporary Ethnography* 21 (1992): 365.

3. Williams et al., "Personal Safety," 350.

4. Richard A. Berk and Joseph M. Adams, "Establishing Rapport with Deviant Groups," *Social Problems* 18 (1970): 110.

5. Jeffrey A. Sluka, "Participant Observation in Violent Social Contexts," *Human Organization* 49 (1990): 114.

6. Williams et al., "Personal Safety," 347.

7. Patrick Biernacki and Dan Waldorf, "Snowball Sampling," *Sociological Methods and Research* 10 (1981): 141-63.

8. See Harold Garfinkel, "Conditions of Successful Degradation Ceremonies," *American Journal of Sociology* 61 (1956): 420-24.

9. Williams et al., "Personal Safety," 364.

10. Williams et al., "Personal Safety," 350.

11. John M. Johnson, "Trust and Personal Involvements in Fieldwork," in *Contemporary Field Research*, ed. Robert M. Emerson (Prospect Heights, Ill.: Waveland, 1983), 205.

12. Kurt H. Wolff, "Surrender and Community Study: The Study of Loma," in *Reflections on Community Studies*, ed. Arthur J. Vidich, Joseph Bensman, and Maurice R. Stein (New York: Wiley, 1964), 237.

13. Robert H. Lowie, *The History of Ethnological Theory* (New York: Farrar and Rinehart, 1937), 232.

14. Hortense Powdermaker, *Stranger and Friend: The Way of an Anthropologist* (New York: Norton, 1966), 19.

15. E. E. Evans-Pritchard, *Social Anthropology and Other Essays* (New York: Free Press, 1964), 77-79.

16. Berk and Adams, "Establishing Rapport," 103.

17. Berk and Adams, "Establishing Rapport."

18. Rosalie H. Wax, "The Ambiguities of Fieldwork," in *Contemporary Field Research*, ed. Robert M. Emerson (Prospect Heights, Ill.: Waveland, 1983), 195.

19. Ned Polsky, *Hustlers, Beats, and Others* (Chicago: Aldine, 1967), 124.

20. Robert M. Emerson, ed., *Contemporary Field Research* (Prospect Heights, Ill.: Waveland, 1983), 179.

21. Ivan Karp and Martha B. Kendall, "Reflexivity in Field Work," in *Explaining Human Behavior: Consciousness, Human Action, and Social Structure*, ed. Paul F. Secord (Beverly Hills, Calif.: Sage, 1982), 261.

22. Georg Simmel, "The Stranger," in *Georg Simmel*, ed. Donald Levine (Chicago: University of Chicago Press, 1908), 143–49.

23. Emerson, *Contemporary*, 179.

24. Richard T. Wright and Scott H. Decker, *Burglars on the Job: Streetlife and Residential Break-ins* (Boston: Northeastern University Press, 1994), 26.

25. Berk and Adams, "Establishing Rapport," 107.

26. See Polsky, *Hustlers*.

27. Peter K. Manning, "Observing the Police: Deviance, Respectables, and the Law," in *Research on Deviance*, ed. Jack D. Douglas (New York: Random House, 1972), 213–68.

28. Annie Oakley, "Interviewing Women: A Contradiction in Terms," in *Doing Feminist Research*, ed. Helen Roberts (London: Routledge and Kegan Paul, 1981), 41.

29. Luther's stalking came to an end only because police picked him up on two unrelated counts of armed robbery and armed criminal action. He is now serving ten years in a Missouri state penitentiary. With the help of colleagues, I moved. My phone number is now unlisted and unpublished, something I recommend to other ethnographers researching active offenders.

30. John Irwin, "Participant Observation of Criminals," in *Research on Deviance*, ed. Jack D. Douglas (New York: Random House, 1972), 117.

31. See Erich Goode, *The Marijuana Smokers* (New York: Basic, 1970).

32. Sluka, "Participant Observation," 115.

33. See Patricia Adler, *Wheeling and Dealing: An Ethnography of an Upper-Level Drug Dealing and Smuggling Community* (New York: Columbia University Press, 1985).

34. Diana Scully, *Understanding Sexual Violence* (Boston: Unwin Inman, 1990).

35. Michael Agar, *Ripping and Running: A Formal Ethnography of Urban Heroin Addicts* (New York: Seminar Press, 1973).

36. Wright and Decker, *Burglars*, 5.

37. Edwin Sutherland and Donald Cressey, *Criminology*, 8th ed. (Philadelphia: Lippincott, 1970), 68.

38. Polsky, *Hustlers*, 123.

39. George McCall, *Observing the Law* (New York: Free Press, 1978), 27.

40. Erving Goffman, *Relations in Public: Micro Studies of the Public Order* (New York: Basic Books, 1971), 323.

41. SCAT is an acronym for "street corner apprehension team." This fifteen-man undercover team is charged with curbing street-level drug sales by apprehending dealers immediately after sales to one of their "buy" officers. Hiding nearby in unmarked cars, personnel "swoop" down on offenders in an attempt to catch them with marked money just given them by buy officers. This money either has traceable dye or serial numbers previously recorded that link dealers to undercover transactions.

SCAT units were highly feared because they were reportedly merciless in their arrest procedures (i.e., they conducted strip searches).

42. Wright and Decker, *Burglars*, 28.

43. Polsky, *Hustlers*, 147.

44. See Sluka, "Participant Observation."

45. Federal Bureau of Investigation, *Crime in the United States* (Washington, D.C.: Government Printing Office, 1995).

46. See Erving Goffman, *Stigma: Notes on the Management of Spoiled Identity* (Englewood Cliffs, N.J.: Prentice-Hall, 1963).

47. See John Van Maanen, "The Asshole," in *Policing: A View from the Streets*, ed. Peter K. Manning and John Van Maanen (Santa Monica: Goodyear, 1978), 221–38.

48. Erving Goffman, *Frame Analysis: An Essay on the Organization of Experience* (Cambridge, Mass.: Harvard University Press, 1974).

49. See Jerome Skolnick, "A Sketch of the Policeman's 'Working Personality,'" in *Criminal Justice: Law and Politics*, ed. George F. Cole (North Scituate, Mass.: Duxbury Press, 1980).

50. Jack D. Douglas, "Observing Deviance," in *Research on Deviance*, ed. Jack D. Douglas (New York: Random House, 1972), 3–34.

51. Sluka, "Participant Observation," 123.

52. Douglas, "Observing Deviance," 12.

53. Irving Soloway and James Walters, "Workin' the Corner: The Ethics and Legality of Fieldwork among Active Heroin Addicts," in *Street Ethnography*, ed. Robert S. Weppner (Beverly Hills, Calif.: Sage, 1977), 175–76.

54. James T. Carey, "Problems of Access and Risk in Observing Drug Scenes," in *Research on Deviance*, ed. Jack D. Douglas (New York: Random House, 1972), 77.

55. See Adler, *Wheeling*, 24.

56. Polsky, *Hustlers*, 133–34.

57. Andrew Gollub, Farrukh Hakeem, and Bruce D. Johnson, "Monitoring the Decline in the Crack Epidemic with Data from the Drug Use Forecasting Program," Unpublished manuscript, 1996.

58. Mark Granovetter, "The Strength of Weak Ties," *American Journal of Sociology* 78 (1973): 1360–80.

59. Douglas's research on nudist beach goers, for example, was jeopardized because of his early bond with a marginal and generally disliked participant (something Douglas did not know until later)—a participant with whom he was able to bond precisely because of that person's marginality; see Douglas, "Observing Deviance."

60. See Karp and Kendall, "Reflexivity."

61. Robert F. Ellen, *Ethnographic Research: A Guide to General Conduct* (London: Academic Press, 1984), 97.

62. Sluka, "Participant Observation," 124.

63. Martin Sanchez-Jankowski, *Islands in the Street: Gangs in American Urban Society* (Berkeley: University of California Press, 1991).

Marijuana Subcultures Studying Crime in Rural America

Ralph A. Weisheit

The idea of studying domestic marijuana growers came to me by accident. I was watching the ten o'clock local news on an October evening. The state police were conducting a raid on a large marijuana-growing operation and had invited a local television station to cover the event. A father and son were arrested. The father was a farmer who was about sixty years old, and his son, who farmed with him, was about twenty-five years old. Both were long-term residents of the community, wore bib overalls, and looked like stereotypical farmers.

Their marijuana operation was large, over one thousand plants. This meant it required a great deal of labor and a market for the finished product. It was also a relatively sophisticated operation. The plants were cultivated as sinsemilla, a way of growing marijuana in which male plants are killed and the flowering bud tops of the female plants are harvested. This meant these "simple farmers" had a relatively advanced knowledge of marijuana growing.

This was not the first local story about the arrest of a marijuana grower. What drew my attention to this case were the comments of the son. As he stood in handcuffs, a microphone was put in his face and he was asked to comment. His reply: "I just want the people of Illinois to know how professional their police are and what a good job they did investigating this case. The people of this state should be proud of their state police." The comment was odd. He was not saying this with sarcasm or hostility, and he appeared to have little "street smarts" or experience with the police. A later interview confirmed that he was quite naive about the criminal justice process. I asked him if he had any prior contacts with the police, and he said there had been one occasion several years earlier. He and his father were working in the barnyard when his father's heart began causing him problems. He was out of the prescription medicine he needed and sent his son to town to buy more. On the way to town, the son was nervous and in a hurry and didn't stop fully at a stop sign. When the officer pulled him over, the son realized he had forgotten his driver's license. I asked what else happened, and he said that was all—that was the extent of his prior criminality. I could not get those contrasting images out of my mind. On the one hand, he defined this minor traffic incident as prior criminality, but, on the other hand, he had a large and sophisticated marijuana-growing operation. I kept returning to the same question: "How did someone so naive about crime become involved in an operation this large and this complicated?" This apparent incongruity prodded me to learn more about large-scale marijuana cultivators.

Getting Started

I quickly learned that marijuana growers had not been systematically studied. While a number of researchers had addressed drug problems, most of the research had focused on middle-class marijuana users, on hard-core addicts, or on street-level drug dealers. Middle-class users had been the subject of numerous surveys, while hard-core addicts and street dealers had frequently been the subject of field research.

Information about marijuana growers was sparse. Aside from a few brief journalistic accounts, most information about the marijuana industry came from the Drug Enforcement Administration (DEA). I knew from data collected by the DEA that marijuana cultivation took place in every state and that the amount of marijuana seized each year was substantial. For example, in the late 1980s, when the study began, authorities were routinely seizing between five and seven million cultivated plants each year, and they were eradicating well over one hundred million wild marijuana plants each year. Since for many drugs the amount seized by police represents only 10 to 20 percent of the total, the size of the marijuana industry was potentially huge. Even conservative estimates of the numbers of marijuana growers suggested that over one million people might be involved. While these production estimates were useful starting points, they told me nothing about the kinds of people involved or their motivations for entering the business.

I next turned to *High Times* magazine and a number of how-to books on marijuana cultivation. These sources were enormously informative about the mechanics of marijuana cultivation. They said little, however, about the sorts of people involved in growing or about the marijuana industry itself. Neither the development nor the marketing of these how-to-grow materials required a great deal of personal information about marijuana growers. The consumers of these books and magazines, in turn, had good reason not to share much information about themselves. Most copies of *High Times,* for example, are sold anonymously over the counter, rather than by subscriptions. I suspect that many of the subscription sales are to police officers who buy them for their departments in order to keep abreast of developments in marijuana cultivation technology—something many departments in the study did. Ironically, the police in this study were more likely to be regular readers of *High Times* than were the commercial marijuana growers.

My training was in survey research, but it was clear that the problem did not lend itself to study through surveys. There was no ready list of growers; the subject was one that would make growers reluctant to put their behaviors in writing; further, my interest was in dynamic processes and interactions. Most important, a survey was ill suited for a "fishing expedition" into an area about which almost nothing was known. Without a basic understanding of the issues and the people involved, it would have been impossible to know what survey questions to ask and for whom they should be written.

For these reasons I was drawn to field research, which has often been used to develop an understanding of the dynamics of drug use and drug dealing. Field studies had proven fruitful in describing the "drug scene" and had led to a richer understanding of the culture of drug use and drug dealing. Unfortunately, these studies shared a common weakness: with a few exceptions, they were based in urban settings. The culture of drugs in rural areas had remained largely unexplored.

Most commercial marijuana growing takes place in rural areas, and it quickly became apparent that many of the techniques used to study the urban drug problem were either inappropriate in rural settings or had to be substantially modified. This also meant there were few examples of existing research to guide the study. Thus, it was necessary to deal with two unknowns, the *substantive issue* of marijuana cultivation and the *methodological issue* of conducting research in rural areas. I have dealt with the substantive issue of marijuana cultivation elsewhere.[1] While I have also considered methodological issues in rural research,[2] the discussion that follows provides an expanded and personally grounded discussion of these methodological concerns.

A Matter of Perspective

My own methodological experiences have been eclectic. I have utilized a variety of methodologies, depending on the substantive issues and the specific questions to be addressed. For this study I wanted a glimpse into the world of the marijuana grower, but I also wanted to appreciate the larger context in which that everyday world existed, including the world of police who pursued marijuana growers. I believed then, and still believe, that each of those worldviews could be better understood when juxtaposed against the other. While field researchers often tout the advantages of becoming a true insider, it was clear that I could not be a complete insider in the world of the grower and still have good access to the world of the "pot police." That is, full participation in either group would limit my access to the other. Further, given that little field research had been done on rural crime in general and on rural marijuana growers in particular, it was unclear whether intimate access to either group would be possible. My own experiences growing up in rural southern Indiana led me to expect that intimate access would be very difficult to obtain without some kinship tie or some pre-existing connection to a grower.

I resolved to do what I could to maintain the position of neutral observer, while appreciating that few researchers are ever truly neutral. I decided in advance that in my interviews with police and with growers, I would go to their settings to speak with them. Most growers were interviewed in their homes, which allowed me to learn a great deal about them, including the fact that many were amateur gardeners and cultivators of a variety of legal plants. And, since most grew plants in or near their homes, the interview also gave me the opportunity to view the physical setting in which growing took place.

In the interviews I attempted to be sympathetic and nonjudgmental. I did not overtly deceive either growers or the police, although I routinely played the role of naive observer, allowing them to "educate" me about the issues. This required that interviews be rather loosely structured to allow them to flow more like conversations than formal interactions.

The role of neutral observer and "student" of the marijuana issue seemed to work particularly well with growers. Marijuana was an issue that aroused passionate feelings in many of these growers and also in a surprisingly large number of the police. Growers who had been arrested were accustomed to being either villainized by those who had an anti-marijuana agenda or praised by family members or others who had a pro-marijuana agenda. In the aftermath of the disruption and confusion arising from their arrest and conviction, many seemed eager to use the interview as a sounding board in which they could freely express their opinions and feelings. On many occasions I felt more like a visiting therapist than a researcher.

As the research progressed, it became clear that my choice of approach was a good one. While these commercial growers were actively cultivating marijuana, none of them was active in the political movement to legalize marijuana, and only a few became involved in the movement after their arrest. For most growers the arrest was a personal tragedy. Approaching the issue from a broader political position, either pro-legalization or anti-legalization, would have reflected a lack of sensitivity to their individual concerns and probably would have made it more difficult to conduct candid interviews about those concerns.

My decision to play the role of detached observer was also vindicated, in my mind, at the conclusion of the study. I sent copies of my findings to growers, to people connected with the marijuana industry, and to police who have handled marijuana cultivation cases—and all three groups generally agreed that I had presented an accurate picture of commercial marijuana growers. This was no small accomplishment, given their very different perspectives on the issue and the strength of their feelings about it.

The Study

My plan was to select 30 marijuana growers identified by the Illinois State Police as part of the "Cash Crop" program. Using each of these 30 growers as a starting point, I would then use snowballing techniques in which the arrested grower would give me the names of approximately

10 other people in his or her social network. These others would include members of the family, police who investigated the case, community members, and, where applicable, accomplices. Thus, a total of 330 people were to be interviewed: 30 growers and 300 community members. Several factors led to changes in these plans.

First, the state police had originally promised to share their list of arrested marijuana growers, but when it came time to carry out the study they changed their minds. It was explained that officers generally believed that arrested growers would resume growing after their sentences had been served. Authorities were concerned that my interviews would make growers wary of being caught, and some growers would stop cultivating plants, thus depriving the police of another arrest. In other words, the police didn't want my research to discourage criminal activity! This was logic that only a bureaucrat could love. As it happened, it was a fortuitous turn of events. Instead of using the state police files as starting points, letters were sent to the sheriff, the editor of the major newspaper, and the county extension agent of each Illinois county. The letters explained the project and mentioned that a staff member would be calling for information. A month later, similar letters and phone calls were directed to state's attorneys in each county. County extension agents were initially thought to be a good source of information about activities in rural agricultural areas. However, they either did not have or would not share such information. Similarly, small-town newspapers were of little help, although newspapers in larger adjoining communities did provide coverage. Small-town newspapers were generally loath to report news about "bad people" in their community, although they were sometimes quite comfortable running such stories about people in nearby counties. Sheriffs and prosecutors were more helpful, although even for this group there were individuals who were not cooperative.

Through this process seventy-four cases were identified. This was an improvement over the use of state police files in three important ways.

First, I had decided early on to be honest with those I was interviewing. When contacted, nearly all of them wanted to know how I had gotten their names. I could honestly explain that I saw their case in a local paper, and in most cases I had a copy of the story with me. I am convinced I would have had far more refusals had I said their names came from the police. Growers were rightly suspicious of anyone asking questions about their illegal activity. Citing the press gave me a legitimate entree. This same process seemed to facilitate interviews with the police, some of whom seemed far more guarded (or perhaps more paranoid) than the growers.

Second, relying on newspaper accounts to locate cases provided an excellent means for beginning the interviews. I would generally start by saying that according to the newspapers they had an operation of a particular size and of a certain complexity. I sometimes raised other issues, such as the seizure of weapons by the police. The grower would invariably begin his or her response with something like: "Don't believe everything you read in the papers. Let me tell you what my operation was really like," or "Let me explain about those weapons."

Third, as the study drew near its conclusion, the state police did cooperate by providing some sketchy information about arrests over several years, including the date and county of arrest and the number of plants eradicated—but no names of arrestees. Nonetheless, they provided enough information that we could compare their list with ours. While all agencies are expected to report marijuana seizures to the state police, at least 14 of the 74 cases originally identified through our searches were not in state police files. Apparently they were handled locally without a report being forwarded to the state police.

Of the 74 original cases, 19 were excluded for a variety of reasons— some had had their cases thrown out, and others had been found not guilty. Of the remaining 55 growers, 70 percent were listed in the phone book and were contacted by telephone. The remainder were either in prison or had an unlisted number. Of those who were contacted, approximately 60 percent consented to be interviewed. The most common reason for refusing an interview was that their arrest was traumatic and had caused them a great deal of embarrassment in the community, feelings they did not wish to stir up again. Residential stability, listed phone numbers, and concern with community opinion were all factors that were likely more pronounced among these rural growers than would have been true among inner-city street dealers.

By the conclusion of the study, interviews had been conducted with 32 commercial marijuana growers from Illinois, 20 Illinois officials, 13 officials from 5 other states, and over a dozen others from around the country who had some familiarity with marijuana growers. This "other" category included the authors of marijuana cultivation books and magazines, the current and several past directors of the National Organization for the Reform of Marijuana Laws (NORML), defense attorneys, prosecutors, and even a technician who had helped develop satellite imaging to spot outdoor marijuana patches. Missing from the interview group were community residents referred to the interviewer by the grower. The arrest and its aftermath were very sensitive topics among these growers. Most did not want community members to be interviewed about the arrest. While I might have done such interviews without the consent of the growers, such an action would have been insensitive and could have harmed their jobs or their reputations. Further, as discussed below, rural citizens were often hesitant to talk about the illegal activities of members of their own community.

During the course of this study it became obvious that one reason so little was known about marijuana growers was the rural context in which much growing took place. The discussion that follows focuses on methodological issues arising from this rural context.

Drugs in Rural Communities

The scholarly neglect of marijuana cultivation in rural areas cannot be explained solely as a result of the absence of drugs in rural communities. Surveys find that the rate of marijuana use in rural areas has rapidly approached that in urban areas.[3] In addition, rural areas are increasingly used to produce synthetic drugs, such as methamphetamine.[4] Rural areas are also essential in the movement of imported drugs, particularly heroin and cocaine, across the country.[5] Rural Kentucky, for example, is not only a major producer of marijuana, but also has been an important transshipment point for cocaine.[6] The absence of scholarly research on marijuana growers does not result from the absence of drugs in rural areas. A more likely explanation for this lack of research focuses on several features of rural America. These include geography, urban ethnocentrism, and the nature of rural culture.

A Question of Geography

The rural setting in which most large marijuana fields are found presents challenges regarding both geography and culture. Regarding geography, the media, special police drug units, and researchers are all more often centered in urban areas and, consequently, have focused on drug issues in the urban environment. To urban observers of the drug scene, the domestic marijuana industry has been largely invisible.

The wide geographic dispersion of marijuana producers continues to limit research and media attention on the issue and was a major limitation for law enforcement until the mid-1980s. Before then, marijuana detection and eradication were almost exclusively local responsibilities, usually headed by rural county sheriffs, who are among the most underfunded and understaffed of law enforcement agencies. During the 1980s, the federal government became more involved in eradicating domestic marijuana. At the same time, there have been increased cooperative efforts across jurisdictions, such as the formation of task forces which include county sheriffs and the state police. Despite the increased attention to rural drug enforcement, there are still comparatively more drug arrests in urban areas. Castellano and Uchida estimate that the rate of drug arrests in urban areas is nearly four times that in rural counties.[7] They also argue that because most drug enforcement is pro-active, variations in arrest rates among jurisdictions are more the result of differences in enforcement efforts than of differences in consumption patterns. The effect of geography on police operations is well illustrated by the comments of a New Mexico state trooper. Regarding highway accidents in New Mexico, he noted that "[w]hen I was in Vietnam, a medic was never more than 10 minutes away. Here you can wait by a wreck on the highway for 45 minutes before help gets there."[8]

For the media, rural drug cases are simply too scattered and too remote for quick coverage. For example, some of the most potent strains of marijuana developed in the United States were created near Spokane, Washington, which is nearly three hundred miles from Seattle. Major networks and newspapers are not physically positioned to give such developments extensive coverage. Researchers and agencies that fund research are also concentrated in urban areas. In addition, rural marijuana cultivation cases are often widely dispersed, which has meant that studying the problem is very labor intensive. In this study, for example, it was common for a single interview to require two to three hours of travel each way. By comparison the logistics of interviewing drug dealers and users in a single neighborhood or section of a large city are simple.

Geography and the relatively closer social networks in rural communities combine to pose a dilemma for the rural researcher. Geography means that including a large number of cases quickly becomes very labor intensive and expensive. Close social networks mean that an intensive focus on a few individuals will raise problems of confidentiality and of the anonymity of research subjects. Word may quickly spread if an outsider is making a series of visits to a local resident, and citizens may easily recognize themselves or others in written reports, even if names and other identifying information are omitted.

Urban Ethnocentrism

Drugs in rural areas have also been ignored because of an urban bias among researchers, the media, and federal enforcement agencies. The urban bias in much social science research can be seen by walking through any library of a research university. While there are hundreds of books on urban studies, there are relatively few on rural life and culture. Researchers who focus on rural environments have a smaller base of published research experiences from which to work. This is particularly true for those who study drug cultures.

For the national media, an urban bias is partly a result of where television stations, larger radio stations, and major newspapers are located, partly a result of the urban backgrounds of news personnel, and partly a result of "playing" to such large markets as New York, Chicago, and Los Angeles by taking urban problems and portraying them as national problems. This happened in the 1980s when the national media portrayed crack cocaine as a problem which had permeated "main street U.S.A."; in reality, there was little evidence that crack was widespread outside a few large urban areas, and in fact it didn't penetrate rural areas until several years later. Conversely, rural drug problems are more likely to be perceived as isolated problems of little national interest. Because marijuana cultivation is primarily rural, stories about it are more likely to be seen as curiosities which are primarily of local interest. This is particularly ironic since much of the marijuana cultivated in large rural operations is eventually marketed in suburbs and cities.

A similar neglect of rural areas has been noted by Levin and Fox in their study of serial killers.[9] Ed Gein, for example, used the skin and body parts of his victims to make belts, household decorations, masks, and to upholster furniture. Despite the sensational and gruesome nature of the crimes, his killings were given relatively little national attention. Levine and Fox suggest that because his crimes took place in the small town of Plainfield, Wisconsin, they were little noted by the national press: "Outside of Wisconsin, few people had heard of Edward Gein . . . what happens in Plainfield is not nearly as important, at least to the national media, as what happens in a large city like Chicago or New York."[10] It would be a mistake, however, to attribute the neglect of rural drug issues to simple geographic remoteness or low population density. Equally important is the culture of rural communities.

Rural Culture

Aside from geography and urban ethnocentrism, studies of drugs in rural areas must contend with rural culture. Rural culture affects the research process in several ways: (1) rural communities are often closed to outsiders; (2) rural citizens may be particularly reluctant to tell outsiders about local deviants; (3) rural citizens are often suspicious of state and federal governmental agencies, including agencies that fund research; (4) social interactions in rural areas may be less formal and legalistic; and (5) situations which have largely taken-for-granted definitions in urban areas may have very different meanings in rural areas.

Rural Areas Are Often Closed to Outsiders—An example of the self-imposed isolationism of rural areas is given in Kessler's description of the problems in establishing a legal services program in a rural community:

> The norms of cooperation, trust and courtesy shared by members of the local bar apply exclusively to attorneys with strong local roots. In general, the legal community is unreceptive to lawyers from outside the county using their local court. Further, members of the local legal community are suspicious of, if not openly hostile to, lawyers born and raised outside the county opening a practice within the county. The attitudes of the legal community to outsiders are illustrated in the comments of one veteran local attorney: "If you're part of the community, practicing law here can be great. But it's not particularly pleasant for out-of-county people. There's a very tight knit organization over here that doesn't particularly care for the outsider."[11]

Rural areas may be particularly closed to outsiders who are from urban areas. A Missouri Highway Patrol officer told me that rural growers who hired an attorney from the city were often at a disadvantage with a local jury: "You hire a Springfield attorney to go down and try a case in Neosko. For these people in Neosko, it just doesn't set well with them. They say 'we have Neosko attorneys. If they [the growers] are going to spend this kind of big bucks and take the money outside the county, they have got something to hide and they are guilty.'"

Urban drug researchers may find it very difficult to penetrate and understand the rural culture in many parts of the United States. In this study, a local sheriff was reluctant to be interviewed about growers in his area, agreeing only after a state trooper with whom he had worked had recommended me. The sheriff began the interview by vaguely describing a large case and casually throwing out questions to "test" me. For example: "The grower was a sorghum farmer—but being from the city you wouldn't know what that is, would you?" As it turned out I grew up in a rural community and knew something about sorghum farming. Having passed his "test" by answering a series of similar questions, the tone of the interview changed to openness and cooperation. The interview lasted for several hours and was very informative. I left with the clear impression that his concern was that a stranger would be insensitive to local concerns and would paint an inaccurate (and unflattering) picture of the community. It was also my impression that a researcher with little knowledge of rural life would not have gotten very far in the interview, finding the sheriff polite but not very talkative.

In rural areas, outsiders are subject to particular scrutiny. For example, reservations about turning in local growers are not in play when the growers are clearly outsiders. One Minnesota case came to police attention because the new tenants of a local farm seemed to know nothing about farming and their behavior did not fit into that of the local area:

"You could tell they weren't much as farmers. One of the first things they did was to plow under their best alfalfa. That was in late May, just after they moved in," said a neighbor. "We just kind of waited to see what they would do next." "They put up no trespassing signs—five of them right in a row that said 'Keep Out.' That's just not the way we do things up here," said another neighbor.[12]

The tendency to fend off outsiders who would study the seamy side of rural life was also evident in the reactions of faculty in our university's department of agriculture. Early in the process I had requested funding from our college to conduct a pilot study based on the interest kindled by the arrest of the farmer and son described at the beginning of this chapter. I later discovered that a faculty member in the university's department of agriculture tried to block the funding, saying, "No farmer would ever grow marijuana, and if someone is growing marijuana they are obviously not really a farmer." As a follow-up to my study of marijuana growers, I became interested in studying rural crime. When I approached another faculty member in the university's department of agriculture, who also lived in a rural area, about working on the project, he responded, "We don't have crime in rural areas, and when we do have a problem we take care of it ourselves." A colleague at another university whose research includes rural communities has reported similar experiences of paternalism and protective behaviors by academics who study agriculture.

Keeping Things In—Rural areas are not only known for shutting others out, but for keeping things in. There is often a concern that the misbehavior of community members will give the community a bad name. I had expected this based on my childhood experiences, and I saw numerous examples of it while doing my research.

It was originally planned that community members would be interviewed about the effects of arrests on the local area, partly in order to determine the level of local sympathy for growers. This turned out to be extremely difficult. After repeated failed efforts, and a few disappointing interviews, the strategy was stopped. These problems manifested themselves in several ways. In smaller communities, concern with community image was compounded by a hesitation to speak with outsiders and a concern that the grower or his family would be further embarrassed and hurt by any discussion of the case. In her research on marijuana growers in Kentucky, Hafley has also noted this tendency to keep bad news within the community: "The rural central and eastern Kentucky resident relishes socializing with others and discussing activities within the community. However, they will not discuss [with outsiders] illegal activities occurring within the community. For an outsider it can be difficult to get the rural resident to even admit such activities occur in their community. Rural central and eastern Kentucky residents take pride in not divulging the community's business to outsiders. Other residents are aware of those within the community who are or have been participating in illegal activities. It is only the outsider who is deceived by protestations of moral outrage." [13]

The caution shown by these residents is in many ways understandable. Even with assurances of confidentiality, residents and officials from these rural areas did not know the researcher personally and had no way of knowing that their comments would not come back to somehow damage the reputation of the community. On the positive side, difficulties in obtaining the cooperation of citizens illustrated the power of community in these areas. These difficulties also suggest that the field researcher who comes from a rural area and is sensitive to rural culture is at a considerable advantage over the researcher who approaches the study with an urban background. Of course, a distrust of outsiders is not unique to rural communities, but it seems especially pronounced there. Further, in rural areas where the pool of interview subjects is small from the start, the impact on research can be substantial.

For the study of marijuana growers, the tendency of rural citizens to keep silent to outsiders was reinforced by the nature of marijuana growing. Unlike the cocaine dealer, who has the option of possessing the drug for a relatively short period of time, the marijuana grower is bound to his or her product for several months. During this time it may be discovered by either thieves or the police. It is clearly in the grower's best interest to keep quiet about what he or she is doing and where he or she is doing it. While secrecy is an excellent means of self-defense against marijuana thieves and against information being leaked to the police, secrecy is also consistent with rural culture. Kentucky stands as an extreme example. The level of secrecy among growers in Kentucky was particularly strong when dealing with people outside of the local community. For example, at the time I interviewed officials from Kentucky, there had been indictments against seventy people linked to Kentucky's "cornbread mafia." Although each was facing fifteen to twenty years in prison, *none* was willing to provide the names of others connected to the organization. In these cases all of the criminal investigations were conducted by state and federal police with little cooperation from local authorities. An official from another state observed: "People in rural areas tend to be pretty conservative generally and don't want government coming in, or an outsider coming in, or foreigners coming in. They want the status quo and that's it. And when they develop a cancer from within they don't want it going out. They don't want people telling about it and they don't want people rocking the boat. They are the same people who will ostracize members of their society who get caught doing this [marijuana growing]." When cases were originally being located, six sheriffs reported having cases but were unwilling to provide names, even though the arrests and prosecutions were matters of public record.

The secrecy which surrounds commercial marijuana growing — combined with the fact that it largely occurs in rural settings — means that some of the techniques used to study urban drug use and urban drug networks will be less useful for studying rural growers. I had originally planned to begin with a sample of arrested growers, to interview them, and then to use snowball techniques to identify other growers who had never been caught. This strategy proved completely unworkable. Most arrestee growers *could not* give the names of other growers, and most had kept the size and sophistication of their own operations a secret from others. Most were justifiably concerned that if information about their growing operation became known in the community, it would increase the likelihood of theft or arrest. Bragging to others, even close friends, about the size and location of their operation was rare among large-scale growers, making the snowball technique for identifying other growers of questionable value in this population.

Another urban strategy was never tried because of its obvious limitations in rural areas. In their study of daily marijuana users, Henden and his associates located subjects by using newspaper advertisements.[14] Such an approach would not be practical in sparsely populated rural settings in which growers are secretive, widely dispersed, and for whom anonymity would be more difficult to assure.

As noted above, the initial study had proposed short interviews with several citizens from each community in which a grower had been arrested. The intent was to supplement grower reports about community response in order to determine how rural communities support or reject longtime members arrested for growing marijuana. This proved to be the most difficult task of the project, and it was fortunate that the research did not hinge on successful interviews with community members. There were several problems in locating and interviewing community members. The most serious problem was the general unwillingness of citizens in rural communities to talk about the misfortune or misbehavior of fellow community members. In one community, frustration with finding citizens to interview led to a decision to first interview a police officer who was well known and respected in the community and who was familiar with the case. More than two months of repeated efforts failed to produce an interview with the officer. He was willing to be interviewed about police procedure and technical details of the case, but was uncomfortable talking about the community response to the arrest and the way in which citizens changed their views of the offender following the arrest. Requests to the officer's supervisor generated a similar response. In another community, the local sheriff admitted that a farmer had been arrested for growing marijuana in the county, but the sheriff and the local prosecutor had discussed the matter and decided they would not discuss the case, or even give the name of the farmer. In still another instance, a sheriff's deputy was asked about a case for which the researcher had only sketchy information. The deputy replied that his job would be in jeopardy if he discussed the case or even gave the names of the arrested growers, who were two established members of the community.

The reluctance of citizens to talk about the criminal activities of their rural neighbors is not unique to the study of marijuana growers. In his oral history of homicides in rural Kentucky, Montell described the problems of getting citizens to talk about rural homicides, even as much as sixty years after the event.[15] Montell's work also illustrated the importance of informal networks for gaining entry to these groups.

Aside from preserving the community's good name, keeping things in is also a product of strong informal networks in rural areas. These informal networks mean that citizens are likely to know both the offender and the offender's family. Even if there is little sympathy for the offender, rural residents may be reluctant to discuss these cases with outsiders out of concern for the feelings and reputation of the offender's family. Further, if the offender is even a distant relative, a citizen risks damage to her or his own reputation because of the considerable attention rural citizens pay to kinship networks.

Suspicion of Government—While wary of outsiders in general, those in rural areas are often particularly suspicious of government agencies. It is no accident that many militia groups and antitax groups work out of rural areas.[16] Representatives of state and federal agencies are seen as too distant from the people to truly understand their problems, and as unlikely to promote local interests.

One local sheriff spoke about serving on a statewide commission and about his experiences trying to communicate local problems to outsiders:

> I served on a commission. There were twenty-two people on this commission and it was aimed at the production of marijuana. I brought it up that we needed more conservation officers in this area, not only for marijuana but for deer poaching, because we have so many deer. There was no one on that commission but myself who was from southern Illinois. Everybody else was from Chicago and places far away. Their immediate solution was to buy two airplanes. I just sat there and laughed at them. You know, when you fly over my county what you see are the tops of about ten million trees. You cannot find marijuana from the air in my county. They couldn't understand that, so I resigned.

This same sheriff, whose office was chronically understaffed, was asked about utilizing the DEA to assist in marijuana raids:

> I did call the feds in a couple of times. Then I quit. I have no confidence in them. In the first place, they are egomaniacs. They think they are really something on a stick. They come into an area like this, of which they know nothing. They don't know the history of it, the people, the terrain. They can mess up an investigation faster than you can shake a stick at it. I had two unfortunate experiences. One was with this two-and-a-half-million-dollar patch we had. I could see it was quite an important thing; I mean we really needed to catch somebody. So I called in the DEA. You would have thought they were a SWAT team. They came in with all this fancy stuff. You can't imagine the equipment and stuff they had with them. I'm sure, just by the way they approached the plot, they scared the people off. And eventually, all we did was pull all the plants and burn them. I decided after that we would handle it ourselves, because we knew more about the territory than any of them did.

Shortly after my study of marijuana growers, I was working with a sheriff's deputy who was on a fellowship with the Federal Law Enforcement Training Center (FLETC). He was calling rural sheriffs and small-town police chiefs as part of a survey on community policing. When he identified himself as part of a federal agency, rural officials were often reluctant to cooperate. Their attitudes usually changed when he told them he was a sheriff's deputy who was only temporarily working with FLETC. Their attitudes were not based on their direct experiences with FLETC, but on their stereotypes of federal agencies. The researcher who receives federal funding to study rural crime may find that an explicit connection with the federal government limits the cooperation of local residents and authorities.

The belief that state and federal governments are insensitive to local needs, along with a strong sense of autonomy that characterizes many rural areas, may explain why proponents of rural development warn against public policies dictated by a strong central government.[17] Another reflection of these attitudes is the finding that rural residents are generally less supportive than urban residents of government programs which provide welfare, housing, unemployment benefits, higher education, and Medicaid.[18] However, hesitating to accept the help of state and local authorities should not be confused with tolerating crime. To the contrary, rural areas are often less tolerant of deviance.[19] Paternoster, for example, reports that rural prosecutors may be *more* likely to seek the death penalty.[20] Further, when rural justice systems are more lenient, it is less a reflection of tolerance than of the simultaneous operation of *informal* sanctions.[21]

The Informal Nature of Rural Life—Interactions in rural areas are less often formal and legalistic than in urban areas. For example, during the course of the study, several growers expressed annoyance at the manner in which they were arrested. This was particularly true when the arrest was conducted with a team of officers (often drawing in officers from the state police) in a conventional military-style rush of the house. These growers often knew the local sheriff, as did most people in the area, and could not understand why he did not simply call on the phone and ask them to turn themselves in. In fact, there were several cases in which the sheriff did just that! The complaint of these growers was *not* with the fact of their arrest, but with the formal manner in which it was done.

The best police officers knew the area and the people and were sensitive to this issue. One officer, who grew up in a rural area, illustrated this with an example:

> You can't act overly high and mighty with them, you won't get any cooperation. In the big cities, that's what you do, you come on strong, "I'm the boss." That's often a very effective method there, but not out here in the rural areas. . . . This summer I went down and there was a guy with maybe two hundred plants spread out over a small farm. I was fairly confident it was there and I pull up in his driveway. He was unloading wood. I'm in the pickup truck, and obviously he knows who I am. I walked up and told him what I was doing there. I said, "I've come to get your marijuana and we're going to be doing an open field search. We're not going to be going through your barns or anything right now. You've got some marijuana out there and I've just come up here to tell you what I'm doing." I helped him unload his wood and then I said, "I'm going down by the pond and look at this marijuana. I'll be back in a minute." I went down, looked at it and came back up. I said, "Well, your marijuana is down there," and then I went ahead and helped him unload some more wood and talked about it. He went to jail with no problem. I think this was the kind of guy who would have liked to have fought you. But because of the way I handled it, he wasn't going to fight anybody. Because, I didn't go in there and say, "You're a marijuana grower and you're worthless." A lot of times if you're dealing with people in these rural areas, they don't have a problem with you coming in and arresting them. They just want to be treated like human beings.

In the same way, treating subjects with respect and gaining entrance to the research setting through informal channels is important for any type of field research on deviance, but for studying illegal behavior in rural areas it is essential. It is possible not only to insult people as individuals but also as rural residents. Rural citizens are often sensitive to any words or actions they might interpret as urban snobbery or condescension.

The relatively informal nature of interactions in rural areas is also reflected in a stronger system of informal social control. Several studies have found that the justice system in rural areas is less bureaucratic than in urban areas. In the current study, informal social control was reflected in interviews when arrested growers were asked to name the worst consequence of their arrest. For many growers, the toughest part of their arrest and punishment was not their fine or imprisonment, but the damage to their reputation and the shame brought to their families, as the following four accounts attest:

> Being put down for a federal conviction really puts you down into a deep hole. I've had to scratch, and claw, and dig, and try to repair what's left of the family name. And it's made me a lot hungrier for success than before my conviction. So, I have to prove to all these people that I'm not a piece of dirt lowlife, I am a good person, good man, and an excellent manager. And as soon as I get up to success, then I'd have proved them wrong.

> Probably the publicity and the personal effect of it; it still hangs over my head. I'm getting over the money part of it; I mean, everybody gets over the money. For a while I wouldn't even go to town because I just didn't even want to be in town, people looking at you and staring at you. I don't like for people to think that I'm a criminal.

> The fact that I had a good reputation; I worked all my life for this reputation and my standing in the community, and then to just be laughed at. And, I am so disappointed at our legal system; it is such a joke.

> Probably the things that the prosecutor said bothered me. . . . The courtroom was full that day, and a lot of people from our neighborhood were there, a lot of people from the town were there. . . . It was the first time that anybody had ever said things like that. There's one person standing up there in front of everybody saying all that bad stuff about you . . . well, that hurt.

Despite the embarrassment, few had moved from their communities or planned to in the future. Many emphasized the importance of working hard to re-establish their good names: "Well, letting down my friends has probably been the worst. But financially it's been the most devastating in that area. It about wrecks your business. In a big city, it probably wouldn't have made a difference. But in a small town, with professional people where you deal one on one with the same people all the time, it has a big effect. A lot of people say, 'you should move out of here, this is a Peyton Place, and people will never forget.' That's my goal; I may move away eventually, but I'm bound and determined to get my reputation back."

This informal control in turn raised further problems in setting up interviews with members of the grower's community. Several growers, particularly those with no prior arrests, were concerned that community interviews would rekindle public animosity and compel them to relive the public embarrassment of their arrest. Considering the already noted reluctance of citizens to cooperate and the potential harm to growers who had agreed to take part in the study, it was decided to give citizen interviews a low priority.

Rural versus Urban Meanings—The rural environment in which marijuana growing takes place also compels the researcher to rethink definitions which are taken for granted in urban areas. Perhaps the clearest example of this is the possession of weapons. In urban settings (and according to the law), the presence of weapons is synonymous with violence or violent intentions, but in rural areas guns have a very different meaning. While about 75 percent of rural residents own guns, a rate triple that for urban residents, guns are *less likely to be used in a crime in rural areas.* For example, a 1990 report by the Bureau of Justice Statistics found that the rate of crimes committed with handguns was over three times as great in urban areas.[22] Similarly, the *National Crime Victims Survey* reports that in cities 37 percent of rapes are committed with a handgun, compared with only 14 percent of rapes in rural areas.[23]

In the present study there was simultaneously an absence of violence and a presence of weapons among marijuana growers, and this could partly be accounted for by the rural setting in which growing took place. It was around the issue of weapons that the definition of violence used by the law and that used by growers differed. In urban areas, firearms are carried with one main target in mind: other people. Of the growers who did not have guns in their houses at the time of the arrest, most lived in larger communities. In rural areas, however, guns have a very different meaning and a variety of other applications. They are commonly carried when their owners are traveling in remote areas for the purpose of shooting varmints, hunting, and general target practice. State and federal laws regarding carrying firearms during the commission of a crime such as cultivating marijuana, however, are generally based on an urban definition of the function of personal weapons. Growers who carried weapons into the field for sport sometimes faced additional weapons charges, and all those with felony charges faced the loss of their firearm registration cards after their conviction. My interviews reveal this disjunction between urban and rural gun owners:

> Q: You said you had a gun just for sport? A: We would always go out and shoot by the creek [near the patch]. We had a couple of cows down there, and some hogs. Q: So you weren't carrying the gun for self-defense? A: No. They asked me that too. I said, "Hell, I spent a year in Vietnam. I carried an M-16 and a grenade launcher there. Why would I carry a .25 automatic pistol in a tight pair of jeans if I was going to protect myself? I would have carried it in my hand." So, they don't use common sense.

Several growers lamented that their arrest forced them to give up hunting rifles they had used for sport. Despite their fondness for guns used for recreational purposes, some growers tried to avoid trouble by making certain they were unarmed when they tended their crops. Others made it clear that the possibility of violence gave them pause about their growing activities: "Yeah, I was [concerned], because the guy on that farm had an old junk car parked there. He said if anybody tried to rip him off, he'd take that car and he'd crash their cars. That's all he had it for, like a demolition car. If anybody came in there, and I was worried about somebody getting hurt, and I think he had a firearm, too, cause I saw him out shooting something one time. That I didn't go for, that's one of the reasons why I got out of it [commercial growing]."

In this regard, concerns about safety were initially raised by my university's human subjects committee. Ironically, their concerns were over *my* safety, not that of the research subjects. These concerns did not materialize. In only one of the interviews was there any sense that I might be harmed. The subject was one of the few growers who would not allow me to tape the interview. His level of paranoia was very high, but not just about the interview. He suspected that I might be part of a conspiracy to get him—as were, he suspected, some members of his family and others in the community. He also made it clear, repeatedly, that he was willing to use violence against those who would betray him. While he did not want to be taped, he would not stop talking. I spent about three hours with him at his home. During this time I calmly tried to ask as many questions as he could coherently answer. He paced the floor continuously, and he frequently peeked out of the corners of windows to see who might be spying on him. He also engaged in long rants, sometimes coherent and sometimes not. Over the course of the "interview," my mood changed from apprehension to pity, and finally to a mixture of impatience, boredom, and annoyance. This person may have been dangerous, but it was not because of his involvement in marijuana growing; he was psychologically unstable. By the end of the interview, my concerns were less about safety and more about deciding what to do with the information I had obtained during the interview.

Overall, there was little evidence of violence in the cases examined for this study, and little evidence of guns being owned with the intention of using them against people. There was no indication that people prone to violence were drawn to marijuana growing. To the contrary, there was a striking absence of violence, considering the dollar amounts involved and the ease with which violence could have been adopted. Most important, owning weapons in rural areas had a very different meaning from owning them in urban settings, particularly when the weapons were hunting rifles and small-bore pistols.

Variations across Settings

None of the preceding discussion is intended to suggest that rural culture is a completely homogeneous entity. What has been presented is a sketch of rural culture and its effects on the research process. Of course, there are wide variations in rural culture, as there are in urban cultures. In the course of the study it was clear that some of the features of rural culture described here were more pronounced in some portions of the state than others and that some interstate variations existed. Southern Illinois is closer to the pure case of rural culture than is central or northern Illinois. Not surprisingly, then, I found access to interview subjects much more difficult in the south. For example, when comparing interviewed growers with those who refused to be interviewed, the two groups were similar in a variety of ways (in terms of age, sex, number of plants seized, and disposition of case). They differed, however, by region of the state. In the southern part of the state, refusals outnumbered consents by two to one, while in the remainder of the state, consents outnumbered refusals by two to one. To acknowledge variations in rural culture, however, is not to deny that it constitutes a distinct way of life when juxtaposed against the culture of urban areas.

Conclusions

While the context in which people live, work, and engage in crime and deviance is important for many types of research, qualitative research often draws contextual issues into the foreground. Similarly, the importance of community and networks of acquaintanceships in rural areas makes qualitative methods particularly appealing for research in these settings.[24] In other words, understanding context is essential to understanding rural crime, and for this reason qualitative research is a particularly useful tool for research in rural settings. Many important differences between rural and urban settings will not be obvious through more structured approaches such as survey research.

The preceding discussion was intended to illustrate several issues in this regard. First, I wanted to provide a personal illustration of the origins of a research idea and of the ways in which it was turned into a research project. Second, I endeavored to build a case for rural culture as something distinct from urban culture. Finally, I attempted to show how this rural culture, along with other features of the rural setting, influenced my research process. It is not wise to assume that the methods we use to study urban problems will automatically fit rural settings, that the findings of urban research can be assumed to fit rural circumstances, or that the policy implications of urban research must be identical to those for rural settings. Moreover, researchers must be sensitive to differences within and among rural areas. The key is to adapt the methods to the local context, rather than forcing local contexts to fit a single methodology.

Notes

1. Ralph A. Weisheit, *Domestic Marijuana: A Neglected Industry* (Westport, Conn.: Greenwood Press, 1992); Ralph A. Weisheit, "Drug Use Among Domestic Marijuana Growers," *Contemporary Drug Problems* 18 (1991): 191–217; Ralph A. Weisheit, "The Intangible Rewards from Crime: The Case of Domestic Marijuana Growers," *Crime and Delinquency* 37 (1991): 506–27.

2. Ralph A. Weisheit, "Studying Drugs in Rural Areas: Notes from the Field," *Journal of Research in Crime and Delinquency* 30 (1993): 213–32; Ralph A. Weisheit and L. Edward Wells, "Rural Crime and Justice: Implications for Theory and Research," *Crime and Delinquency* 42 (1996): 379–97.

3. Joseph F. Donnermeyer, "The Use of Alcohol, Marijuana, and Hard Drugs by Rural Adolescents: A Review of Recent Research," in *Drug Use in Rural American Communities*, ed. Ruth W. Edwards (New York: Haworth Press, 1992), 31–75.

4. James N. Baker, Patricia King, Andrew Murr, and Nonny Abbott, "The Newest Drug War: In Rural America, Crack and 'Crank' are Now Hot Commodities in the Backwoods," *Newsweek*, April 3, 1989, 20–22; Paul Weingarten, "Profits, Perils Higher for Today's Bootleggers," *Chicago Tribune*, September 14, 1989, 1, 8.

5. Paul Weingarten and James Coates, "Drugs Blaze New Paths: Interstates, Backroads Join Courier System," *Chicago Tribune*, September 12, 1989, 1, 8.

6. Gary Potter and Larry Gaines, "Organizing Crime in 'Copperhead County': An Ethnographic Look at Rural Crime Networks," paper presented at the meeting of the Southern Sociological Association, Louisville, Ky., 1990.

7. Thomas C. Castellano and Craig D. Uchida, "Local Drug Enforcement, Prosecutors, and Case Attrition: Theoretical Perspectives for the Drug War," *American Journal of Police* 9 (1990): 133–62.

8. Peter Applebome, "Some Say Frontier Is Still There, and Still Different," *New York Times*, December 12, 1987, 11.

9. Jack Levin and James Alan Fox, *Mass Murder: America's Growing Menace* (New York: Plenum Publishing, 1985).

10. Levin and Fox, *Mass Murder*, 5.

11. Mark Kessler, "Expanding Legal Services Programs to Rural America: A Case Study of Program Creation and Operations," *Judicature* 73 (1990): 274–75.

12. Karl Karlson, "Strangers Were Too Strange: New Neighbors' Odd Habits Lead to Huge Drug Bust," *Chicago Tribune*, October 28, 1987, 3.

13. Sandra Riggs Hafley, "Rural Organized Crime" (Master's thesis, University of Louisville, 1994), 140–41.

14. Herbert Henden, Ann Pollinger Haas, Paul Singer, Melvin Ellner, and Richard Ulman, *Living High: Daily Marijuana Use Among Adults* (New York: Human Sciences Press, 1987).

15. William L. Montell, *Killings: Folk Justice in the Upper South* (Lexington: University Press of Kentucky, 1986).

16. Ralph A. Weisheit, David N. Falcone, and L. Edward Wells, *Crime and Policing in Rural and Small-Town America* (Prospect Heights, Ill.: Waveland Press, 1996).

17. Donald W. Littrell and Doris P. Littrell, "Civic Education, Rural Development, and Land Grant Institutions," in *The Future of Rural America: Anticipating Policies for Constructive Change*, ed. Kenneth E. Pigg (Boulder, Colo.: Westview Press, 1991), 195–212; Jim Seroka and Seshan Subramaniam, "Governing the Countryside: Linking Politics and Administrative Resources," in *The Future of Rural America: Anticipating Policies for Constructive Change*, ed. Kenneth E. Pigg (Boulder, Colo.: Westview Press, 1991), 213–31.

18. Bert E. Swanson, Richard A. Cohen, and Edith P. Swanson, *Small Towns and Small Towners: A Framework for Survival and Growth* (Beverly Hills, Calif.: Sage, 1979).

19. Thomas C. Wilson, "Urbanism, Migration and Tolerance: A Reassessment," *American Sociological Review* 56 (1991): 117–23.

20. Raymond Paternoster, "Race of Victim and Location of Crime: The Decision to Seek the Death Penalty in South Carolina," *Journal of Criminal Law and Criminology* 74 (1983): 754–85.

21. Barry C. Feld, "Justice by Geography: Urban, Suburban, and Rural Variations in Juvenile Justice Administration," *Journal of Criminal Law and Criminology* 82 (1991): 156–210.

22. Bureau of Justice Statistics, *Handgun Crime Victims*, Special Report for the U.S. Department of Justice, U.S. Department of Justice, Washington, D.C., 1990.

23. Ronet Bachman, *Crime Victimization in City, Suburban, and Rural Areas*, Report for the Bureau of Justice Statistics for the U.S. Department of Justice, U.S. Department of Justice, Washington, D.C., 1992.

24. Weisheit and Wells, "Rural Crime and Justice."

Edgework, Honesty, and Criminality

Honesty, Secrecy, and Deception in the Sociology of Crime Confessions and Reflections from the Backstage

Kenneth D. Tunnell

I'm driving down Highway 41 for a scheduled rendezvous in town with Robert, who then will lead me to his house in the country. I'm running late and pushing hard across the curvy, hilly roads of rural east Tennessee. Finally, I arrive and meet Robert at the appointed spot, his father's business, where he has worked since his release from prison just nine months prior. He looks different than when we first met, as he was nearing the end of his second stint in prison for burglary. On that late evening, we had spent two or three hours together in a small office normally used by prison counselors, but made available to us for my interview with him. Then, he seemed small, drawn, and pale with his hair slicked back; but today he seems different, in ways evidently characteristic of recent freedom—well fed, tanned, erect, with his hair stylishly cut.

I follow as he leads the way through town and across winding country roads. We arrive at a nearly new mobile home on a large, shaded lawn of maples and oaks, behind a clearly middle-class home—his father's, as I later discovered. Once inside we make small talk for a while and he offers me a beer, which I accept. "Where can you get beer around here on Sundays?" I query, for I had tried buying some for the drive back but learned it was not available. "Ah, you can git it, butcha gotta know the local bootlegger," he explains. We both sit on the couch and, after I've reminded him of his rights as a participant and assured him of confidentiality, I turn on the tape recorder and begin the interview. Just more than an hour into it, the beer necessitates a pause. I turn off the tape recorder, and Robert, pointing to it, says, "I don't know about you, but that thing makes me nervous as hell." "Why don't we keep it off and just talk a bit?" I suggest. "Great," he replies, then asks, "Wanna burn one?" I feel inclined, and we sit smoking and sharing stories of our childhoods in similar parts of the mountainous areas of rural east Tennessee. As we talk, he opens up and speaks of matters more central to the research. He describes his large number of marijuana plants growing in the nearby hills, the small select clientele to whom he sells, and his casual and ongoing operation of buying and selling stolen goods. Ironically, just shortly before turning off the tape recorder, he had assured me that he had been involved in no illegalities since his release from prison. But now there must be something about the intimacy, the real freedom to talk without words being captured on cassette, and the loosening effects of a couple of beers and a joint that provides a setting for some honest interaction, and some revelations of crime after prison and of his difficulty in doing straight time.

There I was, in the living room of a twice-convicted felon, an ex-con, surrounded by electronic and decorative items collected from previous burglaries, smoking dope, and being made privy to his recent crimes. There was something surreal about this, but also something deviant, for I was actively engaging in a crime of ceremony with him and hearing of his wrongdoings after prison. Perhaps turning off the tape recorder and turning on with him were necessities for establishing that level of trust, closeness, and rapport. After we returned to the recorded interviewing, he seemed more relaxed, up front, reflective, and, at the same time, less cautious than earlier. I felt that I came away with some excellent data made possible by a connection established through methods other than those promulgated by hard science, objectivity, and researcher neutrality—a connection lubricated by weed and drink. I had participated in human rather than stereotypical interviewer/participant exchange; he had willingly detailed activities that others had guarded. Departing from a science of distancing oneself from others allowed the human qualities, interactions, and rationales of doing crime to emerge.

This chapter is my confessional of participating in illegalities, intentionally taking sides, withholding information, deceiving, and lying to authorities, all while engaged in qualitative research into the decision making of property offenders and in a lengthy case study of a specific violent crime.[1] I engaged in some of these actions as manifestations of siding with the underdog, and because I determined such actions would mostly benefit the research participants. Never were they intended to harm anyone, least of all the respondents, and I fully believe that no harm resulted from my decisions and actions. This essay reflects my "coming clean" by articulating these actions and the relationships between the participants and myself.[2] Such actions are probably not that unusual, for the reflexive dynamics of human interaction within research settings often yield problems the solutions of which are not covered in the latest methodological treatises (and today are best confronted in feminist methodologies). The unusual quality is that such confessions rarely appear in print. Indeed, the methodologies of "muddy boots" and "grubby hands" implicitly mean taking sides, recognizing the politics of one's research, engaging in impression management, and hedging the truth.[3] But actually writing about such things is, at some level, liberating, and it is indicative of political acts and decisions—a confessional, so to speak, as things are revealed that usually don't appear on the front stages of scholarly publications and that are tangential to other research strategies.[4]

Deception and Lying

Whenever we as researchers gain entree into the world of deviants and personally learn the activities of hustlers, thieves, and drug peddlers, for example, we become privy to information normally accessible only to occupants of such trades. A resultant problem, and one described by other ethnographers, is that legal authorities may learn of the research and exact damning information from researchers.[5] During my interview research with property criminals, I was aware of the possibility that crime-control managers might demand access to the data. After all, I had information about crimes (and in several cases violent ones) that remained unsolved.

To ensure that such access was never gained and to maintain confidentiality, I initiated certain safeguards. For example, I never spoke participants' names during the recorded interviews, which were themselves quickly transcribed and the tapes erased. Although I kept an identifier list and assigned numbers to pertinent information obtained from individuals' case files, names were not connected to the information from the files or interviews. If, by chance, legal authorities learned of the project, realized that I had information about crimes that had not been cleared, decided to subpoena my records, and in the end actually gained access to them, they would have only nameless files. If ordered to court and directed to relate a particular transcript to an individual participant, I was prepared to lie by claiming that it was simply impossible to connect specifics to a single person from the dozens interviewed. This was a calculated strategy to minimize risks to the participants, to myself, and to the success of this research. I was prepared to deceive and lie to authorities if ever questioned about the particulars of my research, and, as the following reveals, I did just that.

During the property offender study, I interviewed an individual in prison who, I discovered afterwards, had assumed the identity of a man who actually had died in the mid-1960s (I will refer to him as Jimmy Morini).[6] Everyone believed he was Morini. His case files used that name, prison administrators called him Morini, and, in the end, his false identity played a significant part in his early release from prison and placement in a halfway house. I learned of his charade within a week of the interview but immediately decided to keep the information to myself. If prison authorities became suspicious of him on their own, I had decided, they would have to discover his true identity without my assistance. Not long after his placement in the halfway house, he and the director appeared unannounced at my office and asked when I would interview him for the second and final time. Not wanting to reveal information to someone with power over his post-prison life, I simply told them that I believed we had gathered enough information from his first interview and that his services no longer were needed.

That seemed to satisfy them both for a time. Another member of the research staff, though, casually told someone that we knew this man was not Morini. Word then spread to the halfway house director, who shortly afterward phoned and confronted me with this information. I denied it was true and claimed that he had been misinformed. I lied. I lied and was glad that I did. I lied and today remain happy that I did. Although the director was only one bureaucrat among many, I presumed that he, nonetheless, would be compelled to report the truth as I knew it about Jimmy, and that those with decision-making powers would then have reason to adversely affect his confinement. I thought too about the raw emotional response likely to result from authorities' realization that the entire corrections department had been duped by a three-time loser. Their response,

I feared, would be quick, decisive, and repressive. Thus, I intentionally deceived state agents. I deceived them not necessarily because I endorse or practice a conflict methodology, but because I believed providing them with accurate information was (1) irrelevant to the research and (2) not my responsibility, since it was easily available to state managers just as it had been to me.[7] Furthermore, revealing the truth as I knew it to state officials was and is completely contrary to my personal position as a sociologist in the study of crime. These concerns with safeguarding data were heightened during later research.

During a rather lengthy case study that a colleague and I conducted, public defenders, after learning of our research, threatened to subpoena our interview audiotapes, to petition the courts to issue an injunction against us, and to question us under oath about our conversations with our interviewees. Their threats centered on a murder case that we were researching. The defendant, their client, was on death row for the murder. The public defenders had hoped that their appeal, which was in its initial stages, would proceed quietly and remain unknown to the small yet emotionally charged community where the murder had occurred. They feared that our involvement likely would arouse public curiosity about their legal proceedings. When they learned of our case study, they assumed the worst-case scenario and, to prevent our research from becoming known to the wider community, thought it best to silence us — to bring our study to a halt. During a heated two-hour conversation, the attorneys told us that in order to prevent (1) the state's investigation of some of our interview participants, (2) an injunction, and (3) a suit from being filed against us, we must cease the research and, furthermore, deliver to them all materials requested, including specific field notes, interview audiotapes, and interview transcripts. With all of this coming from an office whose work actually had our support and sympathy, we felt we had been blindsided. No matter how much we explained that our raw data simply would not be made available, we had no impact on the attorneys. We left their office having resolved nothing except to reconvene in a few days.

We were faced with a moral dilemma because we had approached the appellate lawyers and elicited their participation in our research, believing that it was important to interview them and hoping that they would arrange an interview with their client. We had intended to win their confidence and support. Suddenly we were confronted with the realization that neither was likely and that they were engaged in an all-out assault on our research and academic freedom.

In the interim, we devised a strategy to minimize risks to our interview participants (to whom we felt indebted; indeed, I had become close with one specific individual), to ourselves, and to the integrity of our study. We had no choice but to refuse to surrender anything—field notes, participants' names, or interview transcripts. We thus decided simply to lie and tell the attorneys that, due to their threats, we had destroyed the tapes and transcripts in question. Furthermore, we decided to let them know that our research would proceed, that their threats of an injunction and lawsuit instilled no fear in us whatsoever, and that if their desire was to have a quiet appeal, then intimidating us likely would produce just the opposite. We believed a good poker face would conceal our nervousness and our concerns that they just might initiate the threatened legal proceedings.

When we later met and stated our position, they were angered but realized we had called their bluff and there was little they could do. We had anticipated this reaction. Still, we had taken a calculated risk, since they very well could have engaged in the legal jockeying they had intimated. The risk was especially grave because our university had refused to support our research, having defined the case as a political lightning rod due to public outrage about the murder and its position in the appellate process. This was a painful time during an otherwise rewarding case study, when the potential for risk to our participants, our academic freedom, and ourselves was very real. We proceeded with the case study, and published three manuscripts from it; the attorneys' client won a new trial on appeal.[8]

Much of our concern during the case study had centered on one specific participant—an attorney who had first represented their client. Forrest had been the first person interviewed during this case study, and he was the person with whom I had established a long-term friendship. He had given us information that probably violated a lawyer-client confidence (as the appellate lawyers had claimed), but he was committed to this case and to saving the defendant's life. He believed, as did medical professionals, that the offender was insane, that justice had not been served, and that this case represented a story deserving of academic investigation. Forrest was first an interviewee, but he became my friend throughout our several other meetings about this case and also in our time together apart from this research. We had become close, and getting close to participants means confronting, with head and heart, the myth of value-free sociology, for it was no longer possible to be simply objective toward this participant.[9] He had become nonnegotiable. Much of my decision to safeguard him and our secrets was not based on some rational standard of scientific evaluation. Rather, it was based on "emotion work," an "intentional display of affect that is self-induced and managed in accordance with others' expectations."[10] We were and are friends, which means emotion was crucial to the ongoing conflicts over this research, the data, our academic freedom, participant protection, and confidentiality. Thus, lying and deceiving those in positions of power over Forrest, the research, and myself became the only choice. There was no calculation, no debate. The decision was a simple one.

Deception, which is central to a sociology of crime, is two-pronged: it involves misleading participants and duping those with only peripheral affiliation to the research. Regarding the first, there is widespread support for being truthful with participants and making them aware of research objectives, confidentiality, and their roles.[11] Some researchers, though, have used deception to gain entree and knowledge not possible otherwise, and have apparently caused no harm to the deceived; without a charade, they were powerless to access the worldview that participants suspiciously guard.[12] Others advocate deception; while they claim that bureaucratic, informed consent and human-rights processes are liberal intrusions into the world of social science, they also maintain the objectives of learning and of avoiding harm, injury, or exposure to participants.[13]

The second form is deceiving those whose positions of official power (e.g., legal authorities) allow them to adversely affect participants, researchers, and researchers' work. Prison guards, university administrators, bureaucrats, and attorneys each possess the power to make life miserable for participants and researchers alike. In some cases, it becomes necessary for researchers to deceive those individuals who are not central to the study; at other times, such deception is not only necessary but also laudable. In both cases, power differentials are at work. And in both scenarios, participants, in the final analysis, are those most at risk and with the most to lose.

I did not have to contemplate deceiving participants to win their cooperation. They assessed the research, its objectives, its legitimacy, and me as one to be or not to be trusted. A precontractual solidarity, so to speak, was at work in our agreeing to certain conditions. I did deceive others who attempted to exercise their power over the research and participants. I believed it necessary, indeed commendable, and in the best interests of the research, the participants, confidentiality, and issues central to academic freedom.

Frontstage/Backstage

Analogous to the theatre, social rituals are composed of interactional performances and are typically stratified within distinct classes and power differentials.[14] Research, like most social rituals, also is stratified and includes the crucial elements of cooperation, negotiation, communication, and power. The qualitative research strategy of interviewing implicitly contains ritualistic behaviors, props, roles, impression management, and frontstage/backstage distinctions.[15] In qualitative inquiries, researchers seek information while participants judge and evaluate the questioning, the questioner, and just what is at stake. Each party engages in frontstage/backstage behavior, assuming a role for the other without revealing the complexities of the whole self, which is managed backstage. Interview research is based, in part, on maintaining this distinction, for while rapport and trust are essential to successful interviews, the conversation is usually unidimensional, as the researcher questions and the participant answers, yielding, submitting, and revealing whatever it may be that the researcher elicits and whatever the participant is willing to bring to center stage. Researchers (in some cases) maintain a professional frontstage appearance that guides directed conversation with a specific objective — vastly different from a conversation among friends, for example. Participants also maintain a frontstage role, fully aware that an interview, rather than a friendly conversation, is in progress. Thus, that which is exposed by participants is no doubt qualitatively different from revelations occurring in more intimate and informal contexts. A participant's presentation of self is guided by the context, purpose, and power differentials at work within the social ritual of interviewing.

Interviewing which is satisfying and fulfilling to researchers and participants involves a process where participants move from the frontstage of presentation of self to the backstage, through the backdrops and heavy curtains of suprapersonal insulation, to yet other backstages. On these backstages are acknowledged those thoughts, actions, motives, and rationales that typically are not revealed on the frontstage, where maintaining an appropriate and ideal image of self is all-important. On these extreme backstages, reflection and rapport in interviewing are at their best. This is where Robert and I traveled — or I should say, where he took me. Making the trip was no easy feat. I could not have forced him along. Nor could I have deceived him into making the passage. I believe the gist of explaining the journey lies in the social moment, the very essence of human interaction that is unique among (to state only a few) social settings and conditions, individual characteristics, social chemistry, and even mind-altering substances. And perhaps by engaging in the ritual of marijuana smoking with Robert and responding casually to his admitted illegalities, I had been recast from simply "researcher" into someone whom he could trust, a co-participant. Traveling to these backstages is the raison d'être of interview research, and a process where the rich methods of reflexivity and *verstehen* are fundamental.

Reflexivity and Verstehen

Reflexivity is a fundamental component of the sociological tradition. Little progress toward developing full understandings of the textures of crime and its seductions is possible without a critical, reflexive methodology. This approach enlightens definitions of crime, revealing dimensions of pleasure, meaning, or expressiveness that otherwise likely would remain unknown. The participant's view (i.e., the emic) and the outsider's perspective, abstractions, and scientific explanations (i.e., the etic) are both essential to a sociology of crime. Good qualitative research is the mixture of the two, as researchers become integrated into the knowledge that is constructed and produced, as the "how" and the "why" of doing sociology become intertwined.[16] As a result, researcher and respondent become co-participants in qualitative strategies that allow movement from frontstages to backstages, that enable rich understandings of the subjects' worldviews to emerge, and that place researchers in arenas where the lines of doing science while maintaining an objective distance from subjects become blurred.

A sociological *verstehen* of crime means accepting the subjective viewpoint and understanding actors' states of mind while rejecting the notion that science can deliver a complete or ontological reality. It also implicitly means that empirical knowledge is subjective and typically reflects (among other things) investigators' interests, values, and biases. As a result, a sociological *verstehen* of crime recognizes that relativity is central to doing social science.[17] The interpretive requisite for sociology lies in making sense of rational action; for a sociology of crime, the focus is instrumentally rational action (i.e., *Zweckrationalität*), characterized most typically by behaviors aimed at attaining calculated, hedonistic, short-term goals. Understandings of those rich and subtle qualities of behaviors that are subjective, spontaneous, and situationally bounded—actions indicative of property criminals' performances, for example—are best gained through sociological *verstehen*.[18]

Among Weber's dichotomy, it is *"erklarendes verstehen"* (as opposed to *"aktuelles"*) that is central to interviewing strategies regarding crime and criminals, for this methodology places particular acts within "a broader context of meaning involving facts which cannot be derived from immediate observation of a particular act or expression."[19] Although interview accounts are retrospective, we arrive at an explanatory understanding of motives, decisions, and rationales, for example, that emerge within a particular context of meaning and that are significant to and reflective of the individual whose action is being studied. This does not imply that the real and unequivocal truth is attained, for subjective self-reflection is relative. Rather, what is attained is a subjective truth that gets closer to realities and intended meanings, as subjects define them, than does the data generated by other methodologies. Although inherently incomplete, such an approach nonetheless produces rich explanations which represent the defining characteristics of action communicated by researchers' co-participants.[20] In other words, what emerges from a sociological *verstehen* of crime are reflections on backstage behaviors. But as such reflections emerge, researchers often discover, as I did with Robert and Forrest, that sides must be taken.

Taking Sides

Taking sides does not necessarily mean siding with the underdog (as those who take sides are nearly always accused of—such "subjectivity"of course rarely is applied to sociologists who overtly take sides when serving as the system's lackeys).[21] Perhaps those groups most commonly seen as underdogs are oppressed peoples — racial minorities, women, prisoners of conscience, and the dispossessed and powerless. But the concept is not solely applicable to those groups. Clearly, the new religious right, the moral majority, and antichoice movements all represent underdogs in one fashion or another. There is a distinction then in siding with the underdog and with particular kinds of underdogs. The point with regard to taking sides, as I see it, is advancing a humanist sociology which promotes definitions of crime and criminality that reflect efforts at humanizing the crime control industry, gaining economic parity, and lessening racist, sexist, and oppressive social behaviors.[22] Sociological traditions from Comte to Durkheim, from Marx to Sutherland, from the Schwendingers to current feminist and peacemaking sociologies of crime, have called for praxis, that is, for siding with particular kinds of underdogs with the objective of advancing human-centered explanations and solutions for social problems. As this chapter attests, I have done my fair share of taking sides while engaged in the sociology of crime. An additional confession further illustrates this.

In one inhospitable county jail where a research participant found himself incarcerated only three months after his release from prison, I witnessed his confronting the ugly realities of racism. I knew from personal experiences that this county was known for having a racist history and culture. The participant, a black male, expressed anger over his treatment and resentment over the racist policing (as he defined it) in that part of the state. I too was treated unkindly and with grave suspicion by jail officials, because it was he I had come to interview.

Beyond the formal interview, I witnessed this man personally struggle against the injustices of a generations-long tradition, an overtly hostile criminal justice system, and the harsh realities of racist selective incapacitation. During our conversation, we talked more about race than crime; more of injustice than justice; more of empowerment than acquiescence. I surmised that discussing these issues was as important, perhaps more important, than focusing explicitly on the interview. The next day, I ventured out to a local used book store and bought copies of *Manchild in a Promised Land* and *The Autobiography of Malcolm X* and mailed them to him, while wondering if he would receive them or if they would be intercepted by jail authorities. The brief time that we spent together, our com-

mon concerns of ongoing racism, our conversations about power and imprisonment, and the simple task of buying him two used books are but
modest examples of taking sides on a particular issue and with a particular individual. But beyond that, he had a profound impact on me, reinforcing the axiom that qualitative research is a social process and, as feminist
methodologies remind us, is both personal and political.[23] In that situation, not taking sides would have represented a valueless cop-out.[24]

Regarding my choices, one may say, "You sided with known felons
who duped state officials"—a point I cannot deny. I sided with those men
because I believed I owed them greater allegiance than I did to crime control industry officials. They were co-participants in ongoing studies who
had been guaranteed confidentiality and who had placed their faith in
my assurances. I had promised state officials nothing. My research sought
the cooperation of both authorities and participants, but I only pledged
allegiance to the latter. Contrary to the tenets of a conflict-oriented
methodology, my purposes were largely benign. My intentions were to
avoid conflict with legal authorities and the conditions that would compel me to deceive them intentionally, or to simply withhold information
that I determined they had no business knowing. Furthermore, I believed
some deception acceptable, especially in cases where being forthright
would have adversely affected participants. My decisions to take sides did
not simply result from ideology, praxis, or commitment, although each
was pertinent to my decisions to engage in the actions described here. My
choices were shaped by my own personal limitations, experiences, values,
and interpretations. Sociology, happily, is not value free, but is filtered
through human qualities and emotions and, as a result, is both limited
and liberated by the human state.[25]

Conclusion

These reflections on doing the sociology of crime illustrate some of
the benefits and rewards involved in qualitative research—a strategy that
is both liberating and restrictive. While survey research certainly mini-
mizes the risks and conundrums described here, the rich, insightful explanations that emerge from qualitative methods remain unparalleled.
Doing sociology is greater than simply learning about a particular problem or population. It is an ongoing lesson in how to relate to divergent
groups of people, establish rapport, win confidence, and assist participants

in opening up and revealing those subtle complexities of social life that are most fully tapped through qualitative methodologies. Such strategies demand that researchers take risks, weigh ethical considerations, ponder just what assurances of confidentiality actually mean, and question just how far they are willing to go to obtain data while at the same time protecting their data, their academic integrity, and their co-participants. Such strategies are the heart and soul of qualitative sociology and are those characteristics that set it apart from other, perhaps less eventful, methodologies.

As I personally have learned, sociologists engaged in the study of crime are particularly vulnerable and often find themselves on the wrong side of the law simply by doing their research. These problems are indicative of the micro-politics of social research and point to political constraints on social scientists' willingness to truly confess revelations about their investigations, their participants, and their interpersonal relationships.[26] Knowledge of criminal/deviant activities alters researchers' performances, as selective revelations are made publicly on the frontstages of scholarly publications, and as allegiances and relationships are maintained on the backstages, all within the negotiated politics of the sociology of crime.

Some sociologists have admitted (sometimes more explicitly than others) that their work has taken them to the edges of crime and, at times, beyond. Others have witnessed crimes as they unfold, and still others have heard admissions of crimes that remain unsolved. Doing the sociology of crime and deviance often places researchers in situations where there is no neutral ground. We become enmeshed in personal contradictions and are caught between dual worlds as values that are not meant to be relevant become germane. Ideological, political, ethical, and scientific decisions are made; choices are weighed; lines are drawn; sides are taken. The choices we make speak loudly about each of us as individuals, our relationships to our participants, and how we choose to live as qualitative researchers—for sociology or off of it.

Notes

1. Robert was selected as a participant in the property criminal study through the Tennessee Board of Parole. After reviewing his case file and determining that he

fit the criteria for sample selection, I wrote to him and later visited him at his place of confinement, where he agreed to participate in that interview and in the follow-up interview after his release from prison. See Kenneth D. Tunnell, *Choosing Crime: The Criminal Calculus of Property Offenders* (Chicago: Nelson-Hall, 1992). Regarding the lengthy case study, see Terry C. Cox and Kenneth D. Tunnell, "Competency to Stand Trial or the Trivial Pursuit of Justice?" *Homicide: The Victim-Offender Connection,* ed. Anna Wilson (Cincinnati: Anderson, 1993), 415–40; Kenneth D. Tunnell and Terry C. Cox, "Applying a Subculture of Violence Thesis to an Ongoing Criminal Lifestyle," *Deviant Behavior* 16 (1995): 373–89; Kenneth D. Tunnell and Terry C. Cox, "Sexually Aggressive Murder: A Case Study," *Journal of Contemporary Criminal Justice* 7 (1991): 232–44.

2. Maurice Punch, *The Politics and Ethics of Fieldwork* (Thousand Oaks, Calif.: Sage, 1986), 15.

3. Punch, *Fieldwork;* Maurice Punch, "Politics and Ethics in Qualitative Research," in *Handbook of Qualitative Research,* ed. Norman K. Denzin and Yvonna S. Lincoln (Thousand Oaks, Calif.: Sage, 1994), 95.

4. Even in the hard sciences, similar confessions are appearing regarding the creativity that often emerges from mistakes made while doing research; see, for example, Ronald Hoffman, *The Same and Not the Same* (New York: Columbia University Press, 1996).

5. See, for example, Laud Humphreys, *Tearoom Trade: Impersonal Sex in Public Places* (Chicago: Aldine, 1970); and Patricia A. Adler, *Wheeling and Dealing: An Ethnography of an Upper-Level Drug Dealing and Smuggling Community* (New York: Columbia University Press, 1985).

6. Tunnell, *Choosing.*

7. Jack Douglas, *Introduction to the Sociologies of Everyday Life* (Boston: Allyn and Bacon, 1974).

8. Although their client won a new trial on appeal, in a controversial decision he was determined competent to stand trial (just as in the first trial), found guilty, and sentenced to death. See Cox and Tunnell, "Competency"; Tunnell and Cox, "Sexually Aggressive Murder"; Tunnell and Cox, "Applying a Subculture."

9. Alvin Gouldner, "Anti-Minotaur: The Myth of Value-Free Sociology," *Social Problems* 9 (1962): 199–213.

10. Arlie Hochschild, *The Managed Heart* (Berkeley: University of California Press, 1983); see Richard G. Mitchell, *Secrecy and Fieldwork* (Thousand Oaks, Calif.: Sage, 1993), 7.

11. Adler, *Wheeling;* Thomas Mieczkowski, "Geeking Up and Throwing Down: Heroin Street Life in Detroit," *Criminology* 24 (1986): 645–66; Tunnell, *Choosing Crime;* Jeff Ferrell, *Crimes of Style: Urban Graffiti and the Politics of Criminality* (Boston: Northeastern University Press, 1996); Mark S. Hamm, *American Skinheads: The Criminology and Control of Hate Crime* (Westport, Conn.: Praeger, 1993).

12. See, for example, Mitchell, *Secrecy;* Erving Goffman, *Asylums* (New York: Doubleday, 1961); Humphreys, *Tearoom Trade.*

13. Mitchell, *Secrecy.*

14. Randall Collins, *Four Sociological Traditions* (New York: Oxford University Press, 1994), 219.

15. Erving Goffman, *The Presentation of Self in Everyday Life* (Garden City, N.Y.: Doubleday, 1959).

16. For a succinct comparison of participant observation and interviewing, see Howard S. Becker and Blanche Geer, "Participant Observation and Interviewing: A Comparison," in *Issues in Participant Observation,* ed. George J. McCall and J. L. Simmons (Reading, Mass.: Addison-Wesley, 1969), 322–31. See also Martyn Hammersley and Paul Atkinson, *Ethnography: Principles in Practice* (London: Tavistock, 1983).

17. Max Weber, *The Theory of Social and Economic Organization* (New York: Oxford University Press, 1947), 87.

18. Malcolm Waters, *Modern Sociological Theory* (Thousand Oaks, Calif.: Sage, 1994); Max Weber, *Economy and Society* (Berkeley: University of California Press, 1978).

19. Weber, *Theory,* 94.

20. Jeff Ferrell and Clinton R. Sanders, eds., *Cultural Criminology* (Boston: Northeastern University Press, 1995), 304–8.

21. See, for example, Howard S. Becker, "Whose Side Are We On?" *Social Problems* 14 (1967): 239–47.

22. See, for example, Ronald C. Kramer, "Defining the Concept of Crime: A Humanistic Perspective," *Journal of Sociology and Social Welfare* 12 (1985): 469–87.

23. See, for example, Joyce McCarl Nielsen, *Feminist Research Methods* (Boulder, Colo.: Westview, 1990).

24. See, for example, Aaron Cicourel, *Method and Measurement in Sociology* (New York: Free Press, 1964).

25. See, for example, Thomas C. Hood, "The Practical Consequences of Sociology's Pursuit of 'Justice for All,'" *Social Forces* 74 (1995): 1–14.

26. See, for example, Punch, *Fieldwork.*

Dangerous Methods
Risk Taking and the Research Process

Stephen Lyng

My first experience in the instant after crossing the threshold was confusion. I didn't quite know where I was, although I was sure I had remained conscious while passing over. I was aware of a strange noise—a rhythmic whooshing sound, deep and somehow reassuring even as it defied my attempt at definition. Some long minutes of studying the mysterious sound finally brought me to an awareness of my new location in time and space. I realized after a while that I was listening to my own breathing, magnified and distorted by the fiberglass and foam-rubber confines of my motorcycle helmet. With this recognition came another sobering realization: "Man, I've gotten myself into some serious shit now."

As I lay bleeding and shattered, squashed like a bug in the dirt and weeds, I was struck by the dramatic contrast between where I had been in the minutes just before crossing over and where I was now. It was as if a mighty implosion had just occurred, like a spent star collapsing in on itself to become a black hole. In the before-time, I was dancing on the far edge of the universe—screaming through an S-curve at 120 miles per hour, running on a mixture of heavy fuel and weed, leaning hard off the right side of the motorcycle, inches away from the pavement. In the after-time, my entire world had been reduced to the quiet space inside my helmet where the only action was the slow swoosh of air moving in and out of punctured lungs now beginning to fill with blood. The line separating the before and after was no stranger to me, having devoted so much time to analyzing its nature, writing about it, and seeking greater clarity by moving as close to it as I could on many occasions.[1] But what I did not completely understand until months later was the methodological significance of the line, how imploding into the small space of my helmet was the inevitable end-point of a research process started many years before.

My place on the other side of this threshold offers a distinctive vantage point for thinking about the nature of research problems that can be addressed only by employing "dangerous methods"—techniques of data collection and analysis that force the researcher to assume moral and physical risks. Through an account of my own experience, I will suggest that many important empirical and theoretical problems taken up in the social sciences can be thoroughly and honestly studied only by placing oneself in situations that may compromise safety and security in a normative or corporeal sense. Moreover, researchers who take these risks present their professions with some difficult dilemmas: should they be supported or shunned when their research activities involve violations of normative and legal standards or decisions to take "crazy" risks that may lead to bodily injury? And how do we address this problem in professional training and socialization if we know that researching certain issues of vital interest to social science will inevitably harm those who study such problems? Thus, my reflections here focus on a type of social analysis that puts researchers—and sometimes people connected to them—in harm's way, on a form of research that often creates difficult and unavoidable professional and ethical problems.

The Starting Point: Edgework and the Participant Observation Method

To explain how I came to the black hole inside my motorcycle helmet, I must first describe the development of my initial research interest in the "edgework" experience. The edgework project emerged out of serendipitous circumstances that existed during my graduate education. As a student working on a doctoral degree in sociology, I was introduced to the subcultural world of skydivers through weekend employment as a commercial pilot for a local sport parachute center. My relationship to this group was, at first, strictly pecuniary—I earned a meager salary as a teaching assistant in the sociology department, and so I took advantage of an opportunity to earn some extra money by working as a part-time "jump pilot." After a year of continuous contact with skydivers in this capacity while undergoing intensive training and socialization in academic sociology, several converging forces engendered a more personal and intellectual interest in the world of skydiving.

More than anything else, I found myself drawn to the core group of "serious" skydivers—individuals who organized all aspects of their life around weekend jumping activities. Much to my surprise, I discovered that these individuals shared some of my deepest intellectual concerns, an unexpected turn because of the significant differences in our institutional locations. Although several of the skydivers were either pursuing or had completed undergraduate degrees, most had not advanced beyond high school education and were employed in trade occupations or as marginal, unskilled laborers. In my interactions with most group members, I found nothing to indicate an interest in the work of academicians or even a remote understanding of the structure of academic institutions. They knew I was a student and worked for the university in some capacity but were unclear on, and largely uninterested in, the nature of sociology, the difference between a Ph.D. and other university degrees, or the activities of university faculty. But while we were worlds apart in this respect, I soon discovered that I could participate in a rich and sophisticated discourse with these individuals on issues central to my intellectual agenda.

What connected their subcultural world to my intellectual preoccupations was our common fascination with varieties of "anarchy" in human affairs. My initial interest in this subject had been stimulated by several intellectual traditions I had been exposed to in my graduate training—the writings of well-known political anarchists such as Emma Goldman, Peter Kropotkin, Leon Trotsky, and Michael Bakunin, as well as varieties of conceptual anarchism advocated by such figures as Paul Feyerabend, Carlos Castaneda, and others.[2] The skydivers were primarily interested in "experiential anarchism," but they had developed an analytical orientation to this subject as a result of their exposure to several key documentary sources, the most influential of which was the writing of the infamous "gonzo" journalist, Hunter S. Thompson.[3] Through his articulate and engaging treatment of various forms of experiential anarchy conceptualized as "edgework," Thompson offered a way to define what some skydivers regarded as the essential character of their sport.

Thus, one way that I connected with certain key members of the group was through ongoing reading and discussion of Thompson's work, an exchange that eventually led me to explore the sociological potential

of Thompson's edgework concept for understanding a wide range of voluntary risk-taking activities.[4] But once I made the decision to begin field
research on the skydiving group, I immediately ran into problems. Despite intensive discussions of Thompson's writings on edgework with the
skydivers, I was constantly frustrated in my data-collection efforts when
I inquired about the nature of *their* edgework experiences. In order to
construct a comprehensive social psychological explanation of edgework
behavior, I needed to capture the phenomenological aspects of the risk-
taking experience — the feelings and sensations that high-risk situations
generate. But when this topic was broached, most of my subjects had little to say. I later discovered that the reluctance to talk about the experience is common to participants in almost all forms of voluntary risk
taking, a finding which led me to identify "ineffability" as one of the
defining characteristics of edgework.[5]

My inability to assemble the phenomenological evidence I needed
was the starting point of the long journey to the liminal event that completed one important phase of my research project, and changed my life
profoundly. More precisely, the journey began with a specific statement
from one of my subjects: when I asked him to talk about the freefall experience,[6] he responded, "If you want to know what it's like, then do it!" It
became clear that the nature of my study would dictate the use of research
methods oriented to the lived experience of my subjects. I would have to
become a participant observer in order to penetrate the meaning structures surrounding these activities.

This decision was not motivated by any illusions about my capacity as a researcher to discover the essence of the phenomenon through
individual immersion in the experience. My research was rooted in the
theoretical principle that individual experience is symbolically mediated
through interactional exchanges between co-present social actors. Embodied within this conceptual orientation is an elegant theoretical justi-
fication for the participant observation method. In order to "understand"
(in the Weberian sense of "*verstehen*") human conduct in the ongoing flux
of everyday life, subjects must instruct researchers in how their worlds are
made meaningful. This is accomplished through the same interactional
processes that allow any group of two or more people to establish intersubjectivity: shared categories of meaning symbolically organize the ongoing flow of existential forces and events. Considering the nature of this

interactional process, there can be no doubt that the depth of understanding is related to the degree of "co-presence" between subjects and researchers.

A high degree of co-presence means not only occupying the same spaces and experiencing the same events as one's subjects but also sharing the circumstances of their lives with a constitutional stance that matches theirs as closely as possible. This ideal is captured metaphorically by the phrase "getting inside the skin of one's subjects"—that is, when the researcher's experience of the external events, places, and people that constitute the subjects' world is embedded in the emotions, sentiments, and physical/mental states that shape their responses to this world. Thus, to record faithfully the lived experience of people who routinely manage their daily affairs deprived of adequate amounts of food or sleep and stressed by interpersonal crises, for example, participant observers must immerse themselves in these same conditional circumstances. In some cases, the cultivation of a mind/body state that matches one's subjects can be accomplished with little normative dissonance. But when dealing with social actors engaged in marginal enterprises, as in my study of edgeworkers, establishing a high degree of co-presence with one's subjects gives rise to difficult personal and normative dilemmas.

Spiraling into the High-Risk Lifestyle—In my case, these dilemmas began to crystallize as I developed a more thorough understanding of the nature of edgework, both as a general phenomenon and as practiced by members of the skydiving group. As noted in my main report on edgework, a common pattern among risk takers is to increase the risks of dangerous activities artificially by incapacitating themselves in various ways, as when mountain climbers make an ascent without oxygen tanks or rock climbers scale cliffs without safety ropes.[7] The point of such imprudence is to get as close as possible to the "edge" separating life and death, the place where edgework sensations are most pronounced. In the case of the skydivers I studied, this involved practices such as "pulling low" (deploying one's parachute at a low altitude), parachuting in marginal conditions (low clouds, high winds, etc.), or jumping under the influence of intoxicating substances. Within the subcultural framework, these sorts of activities delimited the boundaries of "true" edgework, as distinct from the more institutionalized and routinized forms of skydiving practiced by mainstream jumpers.

It became increasingly clear that I would not be able to assemble the phenomenological data I needed to construct a social psychological explanation of voluntary risk taking unless I was prepared to share in the indiscretions that were crucial to the edgework enterprise. Obviously, I could not be a co-present participant in all of the skydivers' activities. I did complete a parachute training course and made several jumps, but I lacked the time and financial resources needed to reach the skill level of the elite cadre of jumpers. Consequently, I had to find other ways to get as close as possible to the phenomenological core of their collective life—the experience of "crowding the edge."

This was not an especially difficult task due to another special characteristic of edgework subcultures. Documentary and interview data relating to the specific physical and mental skills typically employed in edgework reveal a widely held belief among participants in the notion that true edgeworkers possess a "survival instinct"—an innate ability to successfully negotiate all varieties of risk-taking situations.[8] Thus, accomplished risk takers in one domain often seek out other avenues for exercising their survival skills. The jumpers were no exception in this respect, and their lives were filled with a wide variety of high-risk behavior. They adopted a way of life that resembles the "transcendent" lifestyle pattern of professional criminals. As Jack Katz notes, these individuals' primary criminal activities (stickups, shoplifting, etc.) are usually combined with various forms of illicit "action" involving "the routine integration of illicit sex, use of intoxicating substances, and high-risk methods of committing a variety of property crimes in an overall way of life."[9] To my knowledge, though none of the skydivers was involved in any form of street crime, they did tend to gravitate toward many of these same forms of illicit action/edgework. Moreover, this lifestyle pattern seemed to serve the same function in both domains: the "connections among various forms of illicit action [create] the possibility of constructing a *transcendent* way of life," which sustains the motivation to undertake the main form of action/edgework.[10]

Thus, in the five years that I conducted field research on this group, I became increasingly immersed in the high-risk action of jumpers and other types of edgeworkers who were a part of the skydivers' extended network. This pattern evolved through regular weekday contacts with members of the group in bars, restaurants, and residences, as well as through the weekend jumping activities consisting of dawn-to-dusk sky-diving operations (when weather permitted) and heavy partying into the night after jumping had ceased for the day. As I became more entangled in the skydiver network, I found myself involved in a continuing round of high-intensity anarchistic pursuits, although the demands of graduate school and my normative and ethical priorities set limits on how far I was willing to move in this direction.

Typical of this pattern were the standard preparations for the weekend jumping activities. Members of the group regularly gathered at a favorite bar after work on Friday afternoon to begin a long night of heavy drinking and smoking, moving from place to place in search of action. Early the next morning, jumpers would assemble at the local airport "drop zone" to begin the day's jumping activities, usually with only a few hours of sleep (or no sleep at all) and nursing bad hangovers. For me, the routine was more coerced than self-motivated. Many of my weekend mornings during the field research period began with irate phone calls from jumpers anxious to make the day's first jump. They would scream, "Where the hell are you?!" as I lay in bed, paralyzed from lack of sleep and the after-effects of the previous night's activities. As one of the primary jump pilots, the operation depended upon my presence, and they expected me to perform my duties regardless of my state of mind or body. Claiming incapacitation did not absolve me of my responsibilities. I discovered early on that emphasizing the need to conduct safe operations would be met with derision: "You wimp! If we can skydive with bad hangovers, you can fly the airplane that way!"

I must acknowledge that I experienced a significant amount of dissonance in negotiating these kinds of exchanges with the group. Their approach to the skydiving enterprise seemed to reflect traditional male gender-role attributes—in particular, a rather "macho" commitment to proving one's toughness and willingness to take unnecessary risks. Although this orientation was embraced with equal enthusiasm by both men and women in the group, it seemed to be rooted in a masculine stereotype that offended my "progressive" sensibilities. Moreover, I found that my moral and practical judgment was constantly being tested by the jumpers. For instance, it was not uncommon for a group of skydivers to "blow a joint" while we climbed to jump altitude, and at some point they would pass it to me. When I would refuse to join them in "getting high while we get high" and admonish them for their illicit behavior, they would respond by saying, "Other jump pilots do it! What's the big deal, can't you handle it?"

These normative challenges were daunting from the very beginning of my field research, and they eventually led to the first of several transformations of self I would experience during the project. I discovered early on it would be necessary to segment parts of myself in relation to the radically different social spheres delimited by the research setting and by my academic network. My deepest values were rooted in my status as an aspiring academic sociologist. In this role, I was committed to the use of sociological knowledge for emancipatory purposes, to a personal and professional agenda for transcending oppressive institutional patterns within both the interpersonal and macro-structural domains, an agenda to which I have maintained continued allegiance. Although my research experience with the skydivers and other edgework groups placed me in circumstances that constantly challenged my core values and normative standards, I was able to participate in some of their activities by drawing on an "impulsive self" that existed apart from my "institutional self."[11] This "impulsive self" existed only in residual form before I began the research project, but, as I will document, the demands of field research led to a further transformation of self in which the impulse dimension became a more pronounced part of who I was. Like many other "mutable selves" populating the postmodern landscape, I began to take on multiple and, to a certain degree, contradictory self-definitions.[12] But in my case, these contradictions of self emerged as a direct consequence of my desire to acquire a thorough understanding of the risk experience.

The depth and variety of high-risk activities that were practiced by members of the network during these years was quite astounding. I will describe this action only in general terms, as a web of illicit activities (involving drugs, sex, and deviant behaviors) combined in endless variegation with dangerous activities such as freefall relative work,[13] BASE jumping,[14] airplane piloting, high-speed motorcycle riding, and similar pursuits. My connection to the skydivers also led indirectly to contacts with other high-risk subcultures, most notably outlaw biker groups and a loosely connected network of motorcycle racers. These additional contacts led me to broaden the focus of my research beyond the early emphasis on skydiving,[15] eventually culminating in the development of a general theory of voluntary risk taking.[16] But my relations with other types of edgeworkers also inspired me to undertake an even more intensive search for a pure expression of the edgework experience.

Motorcycle Anarchy—Though the diffuse structure of edgework and action within my extended network of contacts offered numerous opportunities for personal immersion in the edgework experience, high-speed motorcycle riding proved to be the most accessible of these risk-taking activities. After being introduced to motorcycling by a colleague early in my graduate training, I became an enthusiastic follower of the sport. My interest in motorcycling took a new and fateful turn when several members of the skydiving group I was studying also acquired motorcycles and began to use riding as another way to conduct edgework. At this point, motorcycling took on greater significance for me—it became one of the primary experiential focal points for the collective signification of the edgework phenomenon.

The motorcycle became a crucial research tool for several reasons. First, it served as the principal vehicle, literally speaking, for establishing a co-presence with some of the skydivers in the edgework experience. Although I was intimately involved in skydiving activities in my role as a jump pilot, I could not share in the critical threshold events that constituted the transcendent experience of freefall edgework. My co-presence with the jumpers came to an abrupt end when they exited the airplane, a barrier I confronted repeatedly as I watched them dropping away, human bodies slowly transforming into black dots, disappearing into the contours of the landscape below before re-emerging as flowering parachute canopies. But when we rode motorcycles together, I was there with them as we moved into the liminal terrain, close enough for exchanged glances at crucial points during the approach—acts of signification that can transmit more meaning than a thousand words. Even when I explored this terrain alone, I was able to maintain a type of co-presence with the jumpers by establishing a phenomenological reference for a retrospective interpretation of the edgework experience. As stated above, a large variety of edgework opportunities existed during the field research period, and I took advantage of many of them. But none of these high-risk explorations were as ontologically significant as the experience of motorcycle anarchy.

Another way that my motorcycling activities contributed to the field research program was in confirming to the inner circle of jumpers that I was a person who could understand the nuances of the edgework experience. As noted earlier, individuals who routinely engage in high-risk pursuits often see themselves as special people with innate survival skills that apply to many different situations. In the face of an experience that they regard as largely ineffable, edgeworkers feel that little can be gained from discussing the phenomenon with nonpractitioners. Thus, while one did not have to be experienced in freefall edgework to win the skydivers' confidence, demonstrating the capacity for *some* form of edgework was a prerequisite for participating in any collective discourse on this subject.

These were the methodological considerations that pushed me further and further into the dangerous territory of motorcycle anarchy. As with most other forms of voluntary risk taking, my riding career consisted of a progressive movement toward more extreme and varied risks as my skill level increased. In the beginning, the primary constraint on the risks that members of the riding group could explore were the performance limitations of our motorcycles. Most of the members of our loose-knit group owned Harley-Davidsons, machines that are known less for acceleration rates and top speed than for soulfulness in sound and feel. To be sure, the Harleys were challenging enough at first; after an initial period of cautious riding while developing our skills, we were soon blasting down hill-country roads and practicing open-highway speed runs in excess of a hundred miles per hour. But by the end of the first year of riding, we began to feel a need to push beyond the threshold defined by the machines' capabilities. Following the lead of the skydiving elite, we succeeded in redrawing this line by mixing our motorcycle edgework with various forms of intoxication and incapacitation.

By moving in this direction, the group followed a pathway carved out by various types of edgeworkers, both criminal and noncriminal, seeking to maintain feelings of transcendence in their lives. Like Katz's stickup professionals, some members of the group came to regard intoxication as a valuable background condition for conducting the main risk-taking activity because this was a seductive way to "stay in the action." [17] After mastering the skills required for high-speed riding in full control of their faculties, the new challenge was to negotiate the edge with those faculties chemically altered. The sensual payoff for success in this endeavor was enormous. As most substance users know, the sensual pleasures of even quite pedestrian activities, such as listening to music or meditation, are greatly enhanced in an altered state of consciousness. But when the mix involves psychoactive chemicals and edgework, one moves beyond euphoria to a realm of transcendence and personal metamorphosis.

The "drinking and riding" pattern started with spontaneous forays during or after parties attended by members of the skydiver network. Our motorcycle clique gained a certain notoriety within the skydiving group after a few months, and it became a routine practice for individuals to request rides at some point during skydiver parties. Most often, we would depart as a group with passengers in place, conducting high-speed runs "in formation" so as to simulate the experience of freefall relative work. The connection between riding and skydiving was an ever-present theme in these activities. When the formation of motorcycles reached triple-digit cruising speed, we would move close enough for passengers to touch one another across the roaring windblast—in the same way that jumpers grasp one another in relative work formations. This is a tricky procedure that can be safely accomplished only by individuals who understand the aerodynamics of the human body, knowledge grounded in the performance of freefall maneuvers.

The party context accounted for the relatively high intoxication levels of participants in these "runs," although this began to change in later months. For the skydivers who were either "pilots" or passengers on the motorcycles, the party rides provided a way to stay in the action after skydiving activities had ceased for the day. Increasingly, however, some members of the riding clique began to make substance use a routine part of their activities even when the motorcycle run was the central event and not merely ancillary to a party. In this new stage, day-long runs were organized in the tradition of the European "café racers" of the 1950s and 1960s—road racing from one café or bar to another, stopping for refreshment before racing to the next place to refuel body and machine.

Though racing big motorcycles under the influence of powerful intoxicants is a terrifying thing to contemplate, it must be noted that the group did manage to negotiate this challenge successfully—not a single accident occurred in five years of riding. This can be attributed, in part, to the "professional" orientation of group members. As experienced edgeworkers in other domains, these individuals possessed a keen sense of the magnitude of the risks they were taking, even as they sought to *increase* the risks by incorporating intoxicants into the action. As noted above, edgeworkers often seek more purified forms of the experience by artificially increasing the risks — to get as close as possible to the edge without going over it. Thus, members of the motorcycle group succeeded in maintaining a high level of vigilance and control in their riding in spite of the alterations of consciousness.

For my part, the connection to the group proved to be a crucial resource for advancing the edgework research project. In addition to experiencing firsthand the various sensations generated by the close encounter with life extinction,[18] I was able to gain the complete confidence of all varieties of risk takers I had contacted. They now regarded me as a member of their tribe, as someone who could be trusted with the secrets of the marginal reality to which they were drawn. They assumed that anyone who was not a regular visitor to this place could only understand their actions in terms of the irrational behavior of half-wits or insane individuals. Hence, they would share their interpretations of the experience only with someone they knew had also danced to the siren's song at the edge.

My field research on the skydivers ended after about five years of regular contact with the group when I reached the end of my graduate education and accepted a full-time academic appointment in another region of the country. Although I had sporadic contacts with other skydiving groups, outlaw biker clubs, and motorcycle racing networks in my new location, my research focus shifted from systematic field research on edgeworkers to assembling and analyzing secondary data sources relating to a broader range of high-risk activities.[19] The primary task at this point in the project was to broaden the empirical base of my study and include data that would allow me to draw on a "distanced" view of voluntary risk taking to complement insights deriving from the "close" contact of field research.[20] But as I moved into this new phase of the project, I continued to maintain an experiential connection to edgework through motorcycle riding. Thus, an important legacy of the field research period was further personal metamorphosis: what had started as an intellectual quest to understand the edgework phenomenon became a sensual attraction to the experience itself. The impulse nexus, which had constituted only a small part of my self-concept in the years before I began this research project, grew in relation to the other dimensions of self as I became increasingly addicted to edgework.

The pattern of "pushing the envelope" in my riding habits thus continued well past the field research period. In addition to employing earlier methods of risk escalation, I also began to explore the limits of dangerous motorcycle technologies. When my original Harley-Davidson Sportster was stolen, I replaced it with an older Harley "Panhead." In contrast to the Sportster, which was essentially a stock motorcycle with modern suspension and brakes (front and rear), the Panhead was configured as an "outlaw" bike with a rigid frame (no suspension), a "suicide" foot clutch, an oversized "springer" front end (minimal suspension), and a single mechanical rear brake (no front brake). This type of motorcycle design is notoriously dangerous, even for the more staid, "cruising" riding style practiced by most Harley owners. My own riding, however, consisted primarily of high-speed roadwork which, on this machine, required the maximum use of my riding skills. Riding the Panhead this way allowed me to experience a kind of perverse pleasure that derives from combining the thrill of motorcycle edgework with the challenge and outrageousness of using a most ill-equipped machine for doing it. It was something akin to flying around the world in a pre-war biplane—to complete the journey at all is a significant feat, but to do it with equipment that is as stylistically unique as it is technologically inferior constitutes a singular achievement.

I experienced many moments of terror and exhilaration on the Panhead, but, consistent with the logic of edgework, I soon felt compelled to take further steps in the exploration of dangerous motorcycle technologies. In the end, I found myself increasingly drawn to the most pure form of motorcycle anarchy—that which pushes the outer limits of speed and riding agility. During the many years of riding Harleys, I had always felt a nagging "need for speed" that could not be fulfilled with the machines I owned. I knew that my riding skills exceeded the Harley's performance limits, and therefore I resolved to acquire at some point in my riding career a motorcycle that would fully challenge those skills. That opportunity finally arrived when I decided to do a complete restoration of the Panhead, a complicated task that would take many months to complete. To avoid a riding hiatus, I began looking for another motorcycle, one with performance characteristics that would allow me to fully develop and explore my riding abilities.

My fateful choice was the ultimate "bullet bike," a machine that motorcycle magazines refer to as the "king of speed." I purchased a Kawasaki

ZX-11 ("Ninja"), which, at this writing, remains the fastest stock production motorcycle ever built, with the quickest acceleration rate and
highest top speed (176 mph) of any motorcycle currently on the market.
Although I had minimal experience with full-blown road racers, I felt a
certain urgency about getting beyond any technological limitations on
my ability to do edgework. Hence, I decided to go to the highest possible
performance level. The ZX-11 would be the quickest way there.

The ascending curve of escalating risks that the Ninja offered me constituted the final chapter of the edgework project, the denouement of a research adventure that had started many years before. The pattern of
behavior leading up to the final cataclysmic event was a familiar one: a period of cautious riding in which I became acquainted with the machine
and honed my skills, followed by a sober exploration of extreme riding,
and a gradual turn to the most illicit form of motorcycle anarchy—the
deadly mix of psychoactive chemicals and silk-smooth speed at the high
end of the Ninja's range. Thus, the methodological strategy I had adopted
some years before to generate data essential to my research project set in
motion a logic that led inevitably to an endpoint with extreme personal
consequences: nine broken bones, serious internal injuries, permanent
disability, and a body held together with steel straps and screws. But the
most important consequence of this event was the closure it brought to
my search for knowledge about the nature of this marginal reality and
how social actors manage it. As Hunter Thompson noted in his early ru-
minations on "The Edge," "There is no honest way to explain it because
the only people who really know where it is are the ones who have gone
over."[21]

Negotiating the Personal and the Methodological

This journey beyond the edge points to the complex interrelations
between the theoretical, methodological, and professional problems associated with the study of certain domains of social life. Drawing on the
field research experiences described here, I want especially to direct attention to the multiple and mutually reinforcing risks and ethical challenges that researchers confront when they take up certain problems for
study. These problems have been almost entirely ignored as a topic of formal discussion within the social sciences, even though they are largely

unavoidable consequences of some crucial lines of sociological inquiry. The time for initiating a discussion of the many difficult dilemmas tied to this type of research is long past due.

My experience in conducting research on voluntary risk taking speaks directly to a principal theme of this volume—the documentation and interpretation of the personal and ethical challenges involved in criminological field studies. For as distant as I seemed to be from the field of criminological research in the beginning of the edgework project, the decision to study this phenomenon eventually led to immersion in behavior that was clearly criminal in nature. As noted above, edgeworkers typically fall into a pattern of escalating risks that propels them toward a spiral of illicit action. For the subjects of my study, most of this illicit action had no potential for harming anyone other than themselves. The one exception to this, of course, was the illicit action that eventually put me over the edge—the danger posed to others by the potentially lethal combination of intoxicating substances and high-speed roadwork.

I want to be clear on this matter: I embrace without reservation the view that operating a motor vehicle while intoxicated is a criminal act, even in the face of persistent public ambivalence on this issue as revealed in the continuing high rates of drunk-driving violations in the United States. This statement is not merely an acknowledgment of the formal legal sanctions against driving while impaired. Rather, it reflects an understanding of the risks that chemically impaired drivers pose not only to themselves but also to others who use public highways. Drunk drivers were responsible for approximately 120,000 deaths and over a million disabling injuries on U.S. highways in the last ten years.[22] The logic of viewing the mayhem caused by impaired drivers as no less criminal than victimization by users of other "deadly weapons" cannot be reasonably questioned.

Thus, in the spirit of confession that anchors this volume, I must admit to a type of legal and moral transgression that cannot be excused as a "victimless" crime, although I am profoundly relieved that no one else was actually physically injured by my actions. But as uncomfortable as it is for me to acknowledge publicly my participation in this type of criminal activity, it is necessary to do so in order to argue that involvement in such behavior is a likely, if not inevitable, consequence of the search for valid knowledge about important dimensions of social life. In making this argument, I do not seek to justify my actions. Rather, I seek to call attention to difficult issues relating to the transgressing of normative boundaries in the research process, as a means of achieving deep insight into human affairs.

Transaction and the Participant Observation Method—In discussing the complex issues surrounding field studies of criminal subcultures and other marginal groups, I will begin by examining the methodological problems presented by this kind of research and then consider the ethical and moral dimensions of such research as a separate issue. I first want to extend the earlier discussion of participant observation as a methodological approach that is particularly well suited for studying the phenomenological dimensions of marginal social enterprises. Having previously outlined the theory of intersubjectivity that undergirds this method, I will now delve more deeply into the theoretical foundations of the approach in order to argue for a radical form of participant observation.

By returning to the older theoretical tradition that helped spawn contemporary symbolic interactionism—the pragmatist perspective advanced by Dewey, Peirce, Mead, and other members of the Chicago School—it is possible to pose an ontological argument in support of a participant observation method that transcends the boundaries set by current professional norms. In the pragmatist framework, capturing the lived experience of social actors requires that researchers be socially situated to act within the constraining conditions (broadly defined) of the subjects' world and to confront the resistance of these conditional factors to our actions. Meaning is certainly generated from the process of symbolic interaction with co-present individuals; but it also depends to an equal degree on social actors *transacting* with elements of the existential world that are the focus of collective concern.

The pragmatist concept of "transaction," as developed by Dewey (in 1925) and Dewey and Bentley (in 1949),[23] refers to the interpenetration of organism and environment whereby the sensitivities of the organism and "objects" within the organism's environment emerge in relation to one another. Everything that we take as self-contained in both the subjective and objective sense is understood in this perspective to be "relational" in nature. Indeed, the dualistic opposition between subject and object is rejected by pragmatists in favor of a dialectical view of these two domains as opposing dimensions existing in necessary relation to one another. Subject and object are joined through manipulative action which, in pragmatist terms, constitutes the real meaning of "transaction." As Dewey and Bentley note in describing the character of transaction, "[T]he interpenetration of the old dualism is revealed by avoiding the tendency to name characteristics of organisms alone, or environments alone, in every case they name the *activity* that occurs of both together."[24]

Thus, pragmatism offers an ontological frame for viewing environmental objects "as those features that *answer to* or sustain the particular capacities of the organism to act toward them."[25] Similarly, subjective sensitivities and cognition must also be seen as phases or dimensions of the act that precede and follow adaptive behavior *toward* something in the external environment.[26] This emphasis on the dialectical interpenetration between subject and object serves as a counterweight to the subjectivist thrust of modern symbolic interactionism. By stipulating a determinant influence for the material world in symbolically mediated human action, Mead and the other pragmatists hoped to give equal measure to objectivism and subjectivism in their epistemological framework.

The transactional ontology broadens the theoretical foundations for the participant observation method considerably while also raising practical questions about the actual use of this method. In theoretical terms, we find an even more powerful argument as to why researchers must actively participate in the construction of meaning in order to generate data relevant to the lived experience of the groups they study. While it is important for researchers to learn the categories of meaning with which subjects symbolically construct their worlds, they must also understand how these categories relate to the existential conditions acted upon by the group.

Social actors do not construct symbolic systems in a materialistic vacuum. As the ongoing flow of symbolic interaction proceeds, symbolically driven actions are either sustained or resisted by the existential conditions acted upon. Consequently, to capture socially situated realities faithfully, researchers must participate in interactional exchanges with group members as they deal with the problems and constraints imposed by their material circumstances. Adopting this approach puts researchers in touch with dimensions of their subjects' experience that constitute critically important forms of data—the contradictions and discontinuities of symbolic construction, on the one hand, and the reflexive power of pragmatic certainties, on the other.[27]

The importance of such data can be seen in the edgework project. As noted in the first published research on the skydiving group I studied,[28] the conceptualization of skydiving as "edgework" emerged out of a framework of situated meaning created by the subjects themselves, one of three distinct "vocabularies óf motive" that held sway at different times during my five-year association with the group.[29] Each of the motivational complexes or subcultural orientations, which included the "hedonistic" and "countercultural" orientations along with the "edgework" perspective, was represented in a distinct pattern of banter, rhetoric, literature, and rituals used to socialize new members of the group. These motivational complexes fulfilled multiple functions: in addition to serving as a source of motivational vocabulary for "explaining" their participation in skydiving to outsiders, they were used by group members to justify continued participation to one another and to themselves. Hence, the subcultural orientations were crucial for sustaining the jumpers' commitment to the skydiving enterprise.

More important, all three subcultural orientations "worked" at some level as symbol systems that signified crucial aspects of the skydivers' collective experience, allowing them to pursue group goals and mediate common problems. For instance, the hedonistic stance reflected in the often-used skydiver maxim "Eat, Fuck, Skydive!" produced a motivational rhetoric focused on the sensual nature of the freefall experience.[30] Treating freefall as a sensual activity was, in fact, a crucial requirement for being able to undertake it successfully. In this subcultural context, one learned to approach freefall in the same way one approaches sexual intercourse. By giving oneself up to the experience, avoiding established formulae and not trying too hard to make it happen, one could develop a natural "feel" for air and move in a fluid and coordinated way in relation to others in the formation. Hence, skydivers achieved a degree of pragmatic certainty by conceptualizing freefall as a sensual activity because this construction allowed them to deal effectively with practical problems of concern to the group, problems that ranged from how to achieve lateral movement in freefall to justifying one's decision to jump out of an airplane in the first place (e.g., "We value the experience in the same way that we value eating and intercourse"). And, once established, this pragmatic principle became the basis of a more extensive subcultural complex as the sensuality motif was elaborated into other domains of group activity.

Like all subcultural orientations (and symbol systems in general), the hedonistic perspective incorporated pragmatic contradictions as well as pragmatic certainties. What could not be reconciled with the hedonistic orientation were the various dimensions of the freefall experience that clearly detracted from its sensuality — moments of intense fear, the need for constant vigilance, the careful preplanning required to make a jump, and many other features associated with the inherent dangers of the sport. This contradiction helped fuel new subcultural constructions (in particular, the "countercultural" and "edgework" perspectives)[31] that revealed their own pragmatic certainties and contradictions.

The key point here is that the certainties and contradictions of each subcultural perspective were "revealed" to me only after I became deeply involved in risk-taking activities myself. Though the financial circumstances of my life during this period precluded any serious commitment to sport parachuting, my active participation in the other varieties of action undertaken by members of the group — most important, motorcycle racing — allowed me to grapple with the existential challenges they routinely faced in edgework. As I joined the group in other risk-taking pursuits, I found them negotiating the practical problems of each new risk activity by drawing on the same subcultural vocabularies used to symbolically construct the skydiving experience. Thus, after high-speed motorcycle riding was incorporated into the mix of group activities, members of the riding group began drawing parallels between freefall and riding by referencing each of the three motivational vocabularies at different points in time, with the "hedonistic" perspective dominating in the early stages of field research and the "countercultural" and "edgework" perspectives becoming more influential during the middle and end of the five-year period. By participating in the motorcycle action with this group, I was able to experience firsthand the practical consequences of constructing the risk experience in terms of each of these perspectives.

Thus, my early experiences with extreme riding confirmed for me the practical benefits of approaching our high-speed motorcycle runs as a sensual activity, consistent with the "hedonistic" orientation. As with freefall relative work, collective performance was enhanced considerably by negotiating the experience in the same way one would approach sexual intercourse. So, in the face of intense environmental stimuli flooding in at speeds of one hundred miles per hour or more, one had to remain relaxed and not try to "force" the action in the unfolding sequence of events. Also, by attending to feelings of "connectedness" to one's machine and to other persons and machines in the group, high-speed maneuvering relative to one another could be accomplished with smoothness, fluidity, and coordination. Of greatest importance, though, was the way in which our common system for signifying the experience helped to maintain the solidarity of the group. Trust in one another's ability to act appropriately in circumstances of high risk could be maintained because we were all operating by the same symbolic "logic." Of course, this feature was not unique to the hedonistic orientation since the other perspectives functioned in precisely the same way at other points in time.

This involvement in the activities of my subjects under the constraints imposed by the existing material circumstances was crucial to my ability to understand the emergence and use of situated knowledge by the group. As we acted collectively to solve the multitude of practical problems associated with conducting high-speed motorcycle runs, the verities and fallacies of our group vocabularies became apparent. This is what it means to participate in the social construction of meaning—researchers must transact with the material world just as their subjects do in order to understand fully the complexities involved in the symbolic constructions of this world.

Extensive involvement in the action played a crucial role in my decision to explore the nomothetic potential of the edgework orientation for the purpose of constructing a general theory of voluntary risk taking. As I struggled to document the various vocabularies of motive employed by my subjects while, at the same time, becoming more entangled in high-risk activities, it became increasingly obvious that the edgework orientation succeeded as a pragmatic conceptualization of risk taking in ways that the competing subcultural orientations did not. Talking and thinking about our collective actions in terms of an approach to the line separating order and chaos—the "edge," as it were—contributed to a higher level of performance and a more comprehensive organization of sensations. Moreover, further research revealed that the risk-taking rhetoric of individuals operating in many other domains could be easily subsumed within the edgework schema.[32] Thus, because the environmental patterns signified by the edgework vocabulary sustained our risk-taking action in such a powerful way (e.g., the effects of maintaining vigilance at the edge, keeping focused on essential objects, etc.), I became convinced that this subcultural orientation could be elaborated into a useful social science narrative on voluntary risk taking.

But, as I have documented here, the realization of these intellectual and disciplinary goals through this radical form of participant observational research often gives rise to serious moral dilemmas with powerful personal consequences for researchers who choose to study marginal groups or criminal subcultures. I am convinced that negotiating the material contingencies of my subjects' world, including induced alterations of mind and body, was an essential step in the construction of the edgework model. The significant sacrifice of moral and physical integrity required to attain this knowledge was, however, a high price to pay.

Ethics, Morality, and Criminological Verstehen—How are we to approach the study of deviant or criminal groups if the theoretical and methodological precepts discussed here are valid? Those who call for "criminological *verstehen*"[33] or a study of the "phenomenological foreground"[34] of the criminal experience advocate, either directly or indirectly, a redistribution of role patterns for criminological researchers leading to greater immersion in groups or events under study. This shift, of course, contributes to a decline in the professional insularity so many academic researchers experience today as they construct questionnaires or surveys in university offices and research facilities far removed from the social domains they study.

It also brings increased attention to ethical challenges that academic professionals have largely ignored in the past. Clearly, field researchers often feel it necessary to transgress normative and legal boundaries in conducting their research, and they may develop an attraction to such illicit behavior as a consequence of the research experience. My story illustrates how the allure of a powerful marginal experience can contribute to the maintenance of a pattern of legal and moral transgression long after the field research has been completed. Participant observers of groups operat-

ing on the edges of the normative and existential order often must be prepared to embrace serious normative or physical risks themselves and to
confront the ethical consequences of doing so.

Having discussed the epistemological justifications for my illicit behavior in the edgework study, I now want to address a more difficult
issue—the problem of determining when ethical concerns about conducting this type of research outweigh epistemological considerations.
For whatever leads a researcher to violate the law in studying a particular
problem, it must be granted that this decision can have many different
consequences, some more troubling than others. Breaking laws designed
to protect property, institutionalized power, or established custom constitutes a different matter than violating laws that protect innocent people
against physical or psychological harm. Some researchers may wish to
avoid any imputation of ethical impropriety by abstaining from all forms
of criminal conduct in the course of conducting their research. I cannot
endorse this position because, like some other social scientists, I believe
that "higher-order" moral considerations can sometimes justify violations of legal codes protecting established power and privilege. At the
same time, however, I believe that we must endeavor to draw a line between laws that protect people from mental and bodily harm and those
that do not. Clearly, the violation of laws belonging to the former category is ethically inappropriate behavior for researchers.

In the course of conducting my research on risk takers, I crossed into
this forbidden domain. My task here has been to account for the powerful
and perplexing forces that led me to this end—issues of method and epistemology combined with the internalization of a symbol system I was
seeking to describe and the subsequent slide into edgework addiction. I
do not present these complicating factors as excusing the failure of ethical judgment on my part. Rather, I offer my account as a cautionary tale to
others who confront similarly powerful but subtle forces that may push
them in the direction of moral compromise.

Researchers who conduct field studies on marginal or criminal groups
could benefit, perhaps, from some conceptual guidance in dealing with
the ethical dimensions of their work. At a minimum, decisions about participation in illegal acts should be made with reference to a hierarchy
of consequences that would classify, in general terms, the moral conse-

quences of various types of illegal behavior. At the top of this hierarchy are illegal acts that lead unambiguously to the harming of others, in either a physical or psychological sense. So, for example, we could say that a researcher even tangentially involved in street crime (e.g., "aiding and abetting" a mugger as part of a study of stickup professionals) is engaging in unethical behavior. At the other end of the continuum are illegal acts that clearly do not injure others and may contribute to a political/moral agenda that the researcher embraces. A researcher who participates in an act of civil disobedience (e.g., blocking traffic in a busy intersection to attract media attention for a political cause) as part of a social movement study would illustrate this type of illegal behavior. In my view, a researcher's involvement in crimes of the latter type is entirely ethical.

Of course, the most difficult task in constructing a hierarchy of consequences is to fill the space between these two extremes. This task is complicated by inherent problems such as identifying the precise criteria by which to judge one's actions as harmful (physically or psychologically) to others. Is a researcher who participates in drug use with his or her subjects acting ethically when children are offered drugs in the researcher's presence? The researcher's participation in this activity may indirectly encourage drug use by children, leading to injurious consequences for them. Additionally, determining the consequences of illegal acts is always complicated by the "externalities" associated with behavior directed by situationally specific considerations. While a researcher may feel morally comfortable engaging in drug use with a group of experienced adult subjects, his or her participation in the purchase and use of illicit drugs helps to sustain an illegal drug trade in which people are routinely injured and killed. Failing to consider this consequence in assessing the ethical implications of one's research protocol would constitute a serious oversight.

Any attempt to establish the unambiguous distinctions needed for a hierarchy of consequences is greatly complicated by these sorts of problems, and, therefore, the overall task will require the collective effort of an entire community of social scientists and ethicists. In the present context, I can perhaps best contribute to such an effort by orienting the discussion of consequences to my own illegal actions. Unquestionably, the most important *personal* consequence of my final encounter with the edge was a new set of pragmatic problems that would force me to reconsider the ethical and epistemological issues involved in my research effort. I thus return to the moments after my motorcycle wreck, and the dense space within my helmet.

The Journey Back—As my account reveals, I have been compelled on numerous occasions to "cross the line" in seeking to understand the special attraction that edgework holds for those who practice it. Each of these crossings altered my understanding of the phenomenon and myself. But it was the final line, crossed in the inversion from pure anarchy to the black hole, that was most consequential in the search for certainty and self.

In that moment of implosion, the logic that had driven me to the outer edge was inverted: from that point on, my most intense efforts and deepest satisfactions would be focused not on finding the far edge of experience, but on successfully negotiating the most mundane aspects of living. I was forced to start over, to undergo a rebirth of sorts not unlike our first entry into the world—working one's way out of a quiet, dark space into conscious and physical engagement with the world of lived experience.

The new script began to take shape for me as I lay in the weeds listening to my own breathing. A half hour or so of drifting on that enveloping sound gave way to the realization that the crash had not been observed by anyone, that I was invisible to the passing traffic, and that I would not be rescued unless I somehow managed to stand up. This mundane act—standing up—became the most important challenge of my life because I knew I would bleed to death if I failed. Many unsuccessful tries followed and then, suddenly and much to my surprise, I was upright, hobbling back to the place on the highway where I had catapulted into the darkness. The next half hour was spent on the shoulder of the highway trying to flag passing cars with limbs that wouldn't work, confronting another mundane problem of comic/tragic proportions: standing beside a busy highway with bone shards protruding from my arms, and no one to stop and give me a lift. A bad hitchhiking experience, to be sure.

Someone did eventually stop—a stranger who kept a safe distance and agreed to call for help at the next exit, a person I never saw again but who rescued me at a point of near collapse. In the days, weeks, and months that followed, my life was filled with the kind of mundane challenges that seriously injured and disabled people routinely face, from the struggle to sit up in bed, get out of the wheelchair, and feed and bathe oneself, to the even greater challenge of returning to the day-to-day routines of work and family life, experiences that sustain our identities more than we normally realize. And like many people who have had a close brush with death, my sense of the importance of so much that I had previously taken for granted was radically transformed. The assumed inevitability of mundane pleasures was supplanted by profound feelings of gratitude for these experiences.

The new pragmatic certainty that emerged as the governing logic of my post-crash existence is clear: when you pass beyond the established contours of familiar social space and slip over the edge—and if you're lucky enough to make it back alive—you begin the life journey all over again, moving from the experience of mastering and savoring the most mundane of human acts to feeling, once again, the constraints of institutional routines and the allure of transcendent experiences. But this time, you make the trip with a clear sense of what it's like to cross the line from form into formlessness—a realm that Hunter Thompson has described as "the place of definitions."[35]

The new definitions formed at this crossing led me to some important insights about the risk experience and the ethical consequences of choosing to study it in the way I did. Although I was fortunate to escape the worst potential outcome of my actions in an ethical sense—the chance that the accident could have resulted in the death or injury of other motorists or their passengers—I realized in the aftermath that I had indeed victimized other individuals. By crossing the line, I had forced a larger network of people to deal with the consequences of my individual risk taking, from a family who had to live with the pain and incapacities of a loved one to insurance policyholders who helped pay the hugely inflated medical expenses arising from the accident. These individuals paid a price for my actions and, therefore, were victims of my failure to set limits on how far I would go to experience and understand edgework as my subjects do.

Perhaps I could have anticipated these consequences by being more reflective about my research activities, a vigilance I hope to inspire in others with this "confession." The greatest challenge we face in achieving this vigilance, however, lies in coming to terms with powerful social and cultural forces acting on both researchers and subjects as they calculate the consequences of individual risk taking. In the context of the radical individualism of contemporary American culture, it is not surprising that people often make decisions about risks based on individual considerations alone. Yet, in crossing the line, I have acquired a deeper appreciation of the crucial distinction between the individual and collective orientation for calculating risks and rewards. A sociologically informed study of risk treats not the individual, but the group—whether subculture or society—as the basic unit of analysis, forming a perspective on risk that should figure, most certainly, into all deliberations about the ethical consequences of criminological field research.

My sensitivity to these issues and the new lines of inquiry to which they point are direct consequences of having passed through the "place of definitions." The new insights have come at a high price, both literally and figuratively. Furthermore, while the combination of experiential, intellectual, and personal transcendence achieved in that moment of pure anarchy justifies the price *I* had to pay, I cannot say that it would be worth any actual or potential sacrifices by those who may suffer the consequences of my actions, for it is not my right to impose such costs upon others. And therein lies a fundamental dilemma for the field researcher who seeks knowledge at the ragged edges of social life.

Conclusions

In choosing to confess publicly my transgressions as a researcher, I have endeavored to contribute to a discourse on the methodological and ethical problems faced by field researchers who study criminal and other marginal groups. This very personal way of conducting my role as a professional sociologist certainly contradicts the dominant normative principles of the modern, bureaucratic order; it also reflects my belief in the wisdom of recent calls for more reflexive methodologies in social scientific research.[36] As presently articulated, the reflexive approach embodies an obligation by researchers to describe their social, normative, and, in some cases, emotional relations to the subjects, problems, and data they study. In other words, researchers must explicitly identify themselves as an active part of the research process.

Although the most common way to implement the reflexive approach is to identify one's social and personal relations to subjects, problems, and evidence prior to the collection or interpretation of data, much can be gained from "retrospective reflexivity" as well. Here, the task is to make the research process itself the object of analysis through a retrospective exploration of one's personal experience as a researcher. As we have seen, complex issues of method and morality, epistemology and ethics are directly manifested in the personal traumas and transformations that researchers experience in studying some forms of human conduct. Consequently, retrospectively analyzing the personal tribulations of doing research can advance our understanding of the research process in important ways.

In addition to informing us about the nature of the research process, retrospective reflexivity allows us to explore another crucial issue that must be addressed by academic professionals in search of criminological *verstehen.* Anyone who chooses to conduct field research must pay heed to the powerful dialectic that exists between the researcher and the research process. For just as we should acknowledge the ways in which the actions of a thoroughly immersed researcher transform empty symbolic categories into pragmatic certainties and contradictions, it is also important to realize that the field experience also inevitably transforms the researcher. The actions involved in generating data about complex human affairs are also actions that lead to transformations of self. Thus, researchers who make use of field methods must be made aware of this dialectic and must be willing to accept the transformative consequences of the research experience.

To some, the foregoing account may represent little more than an expression of contrition by an irresponsible thrill seeker who took a bad fall. But along with sounding some cautionary notes about the corporeal and ethical dangers of field research on marginal groups, I have tried also to convey a sense of the anguish and revelry that often attends the intellectual quest to know all there is to know about certain dimensions of human experience. In the common view, academic intellectuals live quite pedestrian lives, housed in "ivory towers" where they are shielded from the moral ambiguities and pragmatic contradictions of the real world by neatly constructed conceptual systems and moral codes that form the corpus of their knowledge. Perhaps this is an accurate depiction of the lifestyle of many academics. But for those driven by a deep curiosity about their experience of the world, the "life of the mind" is filled with moral and conceptual ambiguity, self-contradiction, and anomic terror, combined with instances of pure insight and personal transcendence.

The pattern of life to which I refer is certainly not unique to highly educated individuals or people who identify themselves as intellectuals; the basic curiosity that produces this life experience is often found in people who are poorly educated and who may feel entirely divorced from the intellectual world. What they share with some intellectuals is an all-encompassing reflexivity about themselves and others, which often drives them to a marginal status within the social order. As "intellectual edgeworkers," who take nothing for granted and are always ready to step into the conceptual void in search of truth, they sometimes threaten individuals who prefer to operate with established formulae and familiar cosmologies. In some social sectors, they form an avant-garde; in other domains, they are bohemians; and in the broad mainstream of American culture, they are often labeled as misfits in search of unnecessary conflict and trouble.

The fact that intellectual edgeworkers, of whatever stripe, are often a danger to themselves and others should come as no surprise. Their desire to understand and explain human experience in all of its complexity propels them into unexplored places and often forces them to abandon accepted frames of reference that fail to capture critical aspects of this uncharted terrain. Of course, exploring unfamiliar dimensions of human experience without the security of a well-established conceptual and normative apparatus for ordering and integrating this reality is akin to shooting heroin for the first time. The experience is intense, thrilling, enlightening, anomic, scary, and, above all else, dangerous—to oneself and eventually to others.

And so it is that moral people are sometimes led by their curiosity to embrace a situated logic that finally results in immoral actions. Such behavior can never be excused; but neither can it be eliminated in a universe of human affairs where moral and conceptual certainties remain forever just beyond our reach.

Notes

The author wishes to thank David Croteau, David Courtney, and Gideon Sjoberg for their comments on an earlier draft of this chapter. Special thanks go to Jeff Ferrell for his encouragement of this project, and the inspiring example of his search for the experiential and intellectual edge.

1. Stephen Lyng, "Edgework: A Social Psychological Analysis of Voluntary Risk Taking," *American Journal of Sociology* 95 (1990): 851–86; Stephen Lyng, "Dysfunctional Risk Taking: Criminal Behavior as Edgework," in *Adolescent Risk Taking*, ed. Nancy J. Bell and Robert W. Bell (Newbury Park, Calif.: Sage Publications, 1993), 107–30; Stephen Lyng and David A. Snow, "Vocabularies of Motive and High-Risk Behavior: The Case of Skydiving," in *Advances in Group Processes*, vol. 3, ed. Edward J. Lawler (Greenwich, Conn.: JAI Press, 1986), 157–79; Stephen Lyng and Mitchell L. Bracey, Jr., "Squaring the One Percent: Biker Style and the Selling of Cultural Resistance," in *Cultural Criminology*, ed. Jeff Ferrell and Clinton R. Sanders (Boston: Northeastern University Press, 1995), 233–76.

2. Emma Goldman, *Anarchism and Other Essays* (New York: Dover, 1969); Peter Kropotkin, *The Essential Kropotkin*, ed. Emile Capouya and Keitha Tompkins (New York: Liveright, 1975); Leon Trotsky, *The Permanent Revolution and Results and Prospects* (New York: Pathfinder Press, 1969); Michael Bakunin, *Statism and Anarchy*, ed. M. S. Shatz (Cambridge: Cambridge University Press, 1990); Paul Feyerabend, *Against Method: Outline of an Anarchistic Theory of Knowledge* (London: Verso, 1978); Carlos Castaneda, *A Separate Reality: Further Conversations with Don Juan* (New York: Simon and Schuster, 1971). As suggested by this mix of citations, various lines of intellectual and political thought have claimed the anarchist designation, so it is impossible to speak of a single anarchist tradition. I have identified only a few of the better-known anarchist theorists here.

3. Hunter S. Thompson, *Hell's Angels: The Strange and Terrible Saga of the Outlaw Motorcycle Gangs* (New York: Ballantine Books, 1966); Hunter S. Thompson, *Fear and Loathing in Las Vegas: A Savage Journey to the Heart of the American Dream* (New York: Warner Books, 1971); Hunter S. Thompson, *The Great Shark Hunt: Strange Tales from a Strange Time* (New York: Warner Books, 1979). For a discussion of the theoretical basis for conceiving of voluntary risk taking as "experiential anarchy," see Lyng, "Edgework," 869–82.

4. Lyng, "Edgework."

5. Lyng, "Edgework," 861.

6. "Freefall" refers to the period of time during which the skydiver is falling at the maximum downward velocity, or "terminal velocity" (calculated to be about 120 mph), and can maneuver laterally by making slight changes in body position. The length of the freefall stage varies, depending on the altitude from which the skydiver exits the aircraft, but it usually lasts from forty-five to sixty seconds.

7. Lyng, "Edgework," 862.

8. For many edgeworkers, beliefs about the "survival instinct" are protected by an interesting tautology: when edgeworkers are killed in a high-risk activity, it is taken as evidence by other edgeworkers that they did not possess the instinct and therefore were not true edgeworkers; see Lyng, "Edgework," 859–60.

9. Jack Katz, *Seductions of Crime: Moral and Sensual Attractions in Doing Evil* (New

York: Basic Books, 1988), 196–98. The term "action" was coined by Erving Goffman in his classic essay "Where the Action Is," in *Interaction Ritual* (Garden City, N.Y.: Doubleday, 1967).

10. Katz, *Seductions*, 198, emphasis in original; Lyng, "Dysfunctional."

11. Ralph H. Turner, "The Real Self: From Institution to Impulse," *American Journal of Sociology* 81 (1976): 989–1016.

12. Louis A. Zurcher, *The Mutable Self: An Adaptation to Accelerated Socio-Cultural Change* (Beverly Hills, Calif.: Sage, 1977).

13. Relative work is a form of skydiving in which four or more jumpers typically exit the aircraft together and maneuver in freefall to create a series of group formations.

14. BASE jumping is an extremely dangerous activity in which one jumps off of skyscrapers, radio or television antennae, high bridges, or cliffs in order to receive the BASE (an acronym for "Buildings, Antennae, Spans, Earth") designation.

15. Lyng and Snow, "Vocabularies."

16. Lyng, "Edgework."

17. Katz, *Seductions*, 205.

18. For a description of these sensations, see Lyng, "Edgework," 860–63.

19. The secondary data sources are described in Lyng, "Edgework," 856.

20. While I argue strongly in this essay for the importance of active participation by researchers in the lived experience of their subjects, this should not be construed as an effort to promote a form of methodological essentialism. In studying edgework, I have used a variety of data sources to construct a general theory of voluntary risk taking that links micro-sociological factors in the "phenomenological foreground" with macro-sociological "background factors" tied to the political economy of late capitalism. This mixed methodological strategy allows one to identify common or homogeneous empirical patterns by moving from subjective perceptions emerging within a particular field experience to empirical commonalities found in a broader range of similar cases. As Jeff Ferrell notes, such an approach forces one to "play out a set of tensions and contradictions: between stepping into the nuances of each case and stepping back to look for commonalities and patterns between cases; between a research methodology of firsthand immersion and a theory-building technique of secondhand appropriation; between the primacy of ethnographic particulars and the elegance of theoretical models" ("Making Sense of Crime," *Social Justice* 19 [1992]: 114). See also Katz, *Seductions*, 312.

21. Thompson, *Hell's Angels*, 345.

22. H. Laurence Ross, *Confronting Drunk Driving: Social Policy for Saving Lives* (New Haven, Conn.: Yale University Press, 1992), 38.

23. John Dewey, *Experience and Nature* (New York: Dover, 1925 [1958]); John Dewey and Arthur F. Bentley, *Knowing and the Known* (Westport, Conn.: Greenwood Press, 1949).

24. Dewey and Bentley, *Knowing*, 69, emphasis added.

25. David D. Franks, "Thoughts and Deeds: Toward a Typology of Action for G. H. Mead's Social Behaviorism," unpublished manuscript, 1987, 13. Emphasis in original.

26. Paul Tibbetts, "Mead's Theory of the Act and Perception: Some Empirical Confirmation," *The Personalist* 55 (1974): 69; Franks, "Thoughts," 16.

27. See Dmitri N. Shalin, "Critical Theory and the Pragmatist Challenge," *American Journal of Sociology* 98 (1992): 237–79.

28. Lyng and Snow, "Vocabularies."

29. C. Wright Mills, "Situated Actions and Vocabularies of Motive," *American Sociological Review* 5 (1940): 904–13.

30. Lyng and Snow, "Vocabularies," 164–66.

31. For a description of these two complexes, see Lyng and Snow, "Vocabularies," 166–73.

32. I emphasize again the importance of using many different kinds of data for theory construction and verification, a mix of empirical evidence incorporating both firsthand observations and secondary data. In adopting this approach, I have endeavored to avoid an essentialist view of what constitutes reliable data for sociological analysis.

33. Jeff Ferrell, "Criminological *Verstehen:* Inside the Immediacy of Crime," *Justice Quarterly* 14 (1997): 3–23.

34. Katz, *Seductions.*

35. Thompson, *Hell's Angels,* 345.

36. Shulamit Reinharz, *On Becoming a Social Scientist* (New Brunswick, N.J.: Transaction Books, 1984).

Conclusions
and Prospects

Confessions of Danger and Humanity

Have you read any criminological texts? They are staggering. How can they go on at this level without producing a theoretical framework . . . or even a coherent framework?
—Michel Foucault, *Power/Knowledge: Selected Interviews and Other Writings, 1972–1977*

You might need somethin' to hold on to
When all the answers they don't amount to much.
Somebody that you can just talk to
And a little of that human touch.
—Bruce Springsteen, "Human Touch"

Mark S. Hamm

Jeff Ferrell

In *The Structure of Scientific Revolutions,* Thomas Kuhn distinguishes between normal science and revolutionary science.[1] In normal science, scientists generally build on the work of others, expanding existing paradigms to account for acknowledged phenomena in greater detail. In revolutionary science, scientists forsake aspects of existing paradigms and participate in a paradigm shift as a way of constructing new understandings of the world.

This book participates in an ongoing paradigm shift in criminology and sociology. In the tradition of Howard S. Becker's *Outsiders,* Ned Polsky's *Hustlers, Beats, and Others,* Jack Katz's *Seductions of Crime,* and other works, it takes the much-explored question of why people engage in crime and deviance and turns it on its head: this work asks how it is that crime and deviance attract people.[2] Where much normal or mainstream social science explains crime and deviance in positivist or structural terms or, by default, provides a simplistic theory of rational choice, this alternative approach attempts to identify the situated social, psychological, and cultural forces that draw people into behavior which violates social and legal norms. From this view, structural factors like alienation and inequality may well set the context for crime and deviance; but it is the human taste for danger, pleasure, and excitement that fills that context with meaning.

Accordingly, people are driven to crime and deviance out of desperation less than they are enticed into it by the "sneaky thrills," "adrenalin rushes," and "edgework" associated with the war on the streets, by the sensual terrors and pleasures of everyday violence, and by the tantalizing allure of the forbidden. These powerful, collective emotions can be seen swirling inside many of today's major social problems. They attract thousands of American youth into the "slangin', hangin', and bangin'" world of urban street gangs, into all-night graffiti crews, into cults, and into violent paramilitary subcultures. They draw thousands more to the consumptive thrills of shoplifting and property offending. And, of course, they lure countless others into the often deadly haze of the crack trade and the crack pipe.

The method undergirding this alternative analytic paradigm is ethnography—that is, a researcher's attentive, expressive immersion in the situated dangers and sensual dynamics which construct deviance and crime. Drawing from the Greek *ethnos,* "people," and *graphein,* "depict," ethnography is in some sense as old as human curiosity about, and attentiveness to, the lives of others.[3] Yet this book *does* offer something new concerning the ethnographic study of crime and deviance: it explores the ways in which the practice of "depicting people" involved in risky behaviors is, appropriately, grounded in personal risk and involvement on the part of the researcher. Because, as the essays collected here have shown, types of research risk and danger vary—ranging from ostracism by academic colleagues to the threat of assault by violent street toughs—they necessarily have variable effects on the research process itself. Simply put, various forms of personal and professional danger exist for ethnographers of crime and deviance as a serious, yet potentially productive, dimension of the research process. To engage effectively in such research, then, is to confront and negotiate the situated dangers and dangerous thrills which shape both the subject and method of study.

A Typology of Research Dangers and Solutions

The contributors to this volume have negotiated their way through a veritable mine field of research dangers. In so doing, they have relied on a host of survival skills rooted in gendered identities, professional expertise, and personal conceptions of adventure, art, citizenship, and spirituality. In demonstrating how these individual characteristics and experiences shape the research process, this collection has moved each researcher's personal experiences from the periphery to the center of the research enterprise; along the way, it has discarded the myth of researcher neutrality and objectivity and reconstructed each researcher as inescapably human. These experiences have in turn given rise to something remarkable—the intellectual insights that blossom from the application of particular human survival skills in times of personal and methodological crisis. Carl Sagan once wrote that the scientific method is characterized by "two uneasily cohabitating modes of thought"—skepticism and wonder.[4] This book has been primarily concerned with the latter.

By establishing researchers' identities and experiences as essential components of the research process, the paradigm utilized here thus points toward the great need for a diversity of identities that can be brought to bear in the ongoing ethnographic study of crime and deviance. If we take seriously the model of ethnography and criminological *verstehen* developed throughout this collection—a model which highlights the insights gained from the researcher's own empathic understanding of and emotional participation in the subject of study—we cannot afford the fiction that researcher identities somehow stand outside this process. Instead, we must acknowledge that different researcher identities generate different insights and that a diversity of researcher identities thus opens avenues into a diversity of research settings and understandings. According to the old myths of objective social science, researcher identities wouldn't (or at least shouldn't) much matter, subsumed as they are within the uniformity of scientific method; neither would it matter, then, that criminology and sociology today remain all too white, too male, too straight, too middle class. Within the paradigm used here, though, these issues matter profoundly. Within this paradigm, diversity exists not only as a humanist goal; diversity exists as methodology. The diverse dangers faced by this collection's different ethnographers of crime and deviance, and the diversity of their responses to these dangers, provide a dramatic demonstration of this notion.

Legal Danger—A first danger encountered is legal in nature, as exemplified by Ferrell's journey into the graffiti underground and Weisheit's excursions into rural marijuana-growing subcultures. Here, the researchers faced the dilemma of finding a dialectical balance between pursuing personal involvement with criminals and maintaining observational perspective. On the one hand, deep involvement is vital to providing a sympathetic and detailed understanding of the criminal events in question. On the other, a certain observational perspective is necessary to maintain the ability to analyze and critique—to conduct what Jim Thomas calls "critical ethnography."[5] Because *total* involvement and *total* detachment are mutually exclusive, an accommodation must be made in the research process. Ferrell adopts a relatively anarchistic, go-for-broke approach, deciding that he will not "hide behind the cloak of researcher or scholar, but rather . . . participate as fully as possible in these risky social processes. . . ." Weisheit takes a more reserved approach. Adopting as best he can the role of "neutral observer and 'student,'" he uses press clippings and the telephone book, eventually wins the confidence of thirty-two marijuana growers, and conducts qualitative interviews with them and with state officials.

These methodological decisions regarding blurring the researcher/subject distinction are made, of course, in the context of variable legal danger. Ferrell's participant observation with graffiti writers most likely involved the relatively minor risks of a short jail stay, a small fine, and probation, even in the hyped atmosphere of an aggressive anti-graffiti campaign being waged by local legal officials at the time. Were Weisheit to have "participated as fully as possible" with his marijuana growers, on the other hand, he would have risked—under the penalties of the contemporary "war on drugs"— a twenty-five-year prison sentence, the certain loss of employment, and the forfeiture of his personal property.

Both researchers, in turn, relied on a set of personal survival skills, which became a crucial subtext of the research. They gave shape to the authors' research experiences and to their true confessions here. In Ferrell's case, one does not fully participate in an outlaw artistic subculture unless one has both artistic abilities related to that subculture and intimate knowledge of the cultural and aesthetic norms of the subculture. Hence, in the tradition of this century's earlier sociological ethnographers,[6] Ferrell draws on a body of knowledge that lies beyond the orbit of traditional academic discourse—in this case, a knowledge of contemporary art, popular culture, and youth subcultures. Clearly, this knowledge base is linked to social theory and research methods, but perhaps more so to the researcher's broader social and existential identity.

Weisheit also relies on knowledge beyond the orbit of academic discourse. Whereas Ferrell traversed the often treacherous world of late-night back alleys, railroad yards, and gang turf, Weisheit found it necessary to call on his own personal history and thereby to immerse himself in the gentle folkways of rural America. While Ferrell and his outlaw artists weighed the subtle merits of Krylon paint and graffiti murals, Weisheit came to appreciate the complex world of hydroponic growing techniques, sinsemilla cultivation, alfalfa farming, and rural weaponry. Here we see an important theme that unites these two very different research projects: both criminal subcultures, it seems, were best inhabited and understood by researchers who could reflexively appreciate the dynamics by which people came to join and enjoy them.

Sutherland and Cressey argued that two conditions are necessary for successful criminality: skill and ideology.[7] Though Ferrell's and Weisheit's studies are distinguished by modes of personal and professional survival, they share a competency in understanding the skills and ideologies of their respective criminal collectives. Again, such competency is rarely gleaned from academic journals and books. Instead, it is learned through lived experience, through an appreciation of certain types of adventure, and—above all else—through skills in interpersonal communication that inspire trust and mutual respect between researcher and subjects of study. Moreover, such situated competency requires researchers to move beyond notions of objectivist detachment and to confront their own humanity in relation to their subjects of study. "They just wanted to be treated like human beings," said a police officer of Weisheit's marijuana growers. The same holds true for the subjects of Ferrell's study, and countless others as well.

Stigma Danger—One of life's most painful experiences is to become the brunt of prejudice and discrimination based on stereotypical views of one's identity or group affiliation. Sadly—but, we must emphasize, predictably—this is precisely what happened to the two female ethnographers whose work is represented in this collection. In their critical feminist research on the sex industry, both Kane and Mattley were made to suffer the indignities of the whore stigma—Kane from hotel owners and pawnshop managers she encountered in the course of her field research, Mattley from her own academic colleagues. Their true confessions here offer powerful testimonies to the degradation of personal and professional identity that regularly haunts the work of female ethnographers—and especially those who dare investigate not only crime and deviance, but also the frameworks of gendered inequality in which it emerges.

For Kane, the whore stigma played itself out in the male gaze. In a Belizean bar, "he looked at me with a glance of utter disgust"; in a Chicago pawnshop, the managers glance at her "like I was a piece of slime on the floor." In both cases, Kane notes, she "feel[s] the sickness that is racism and sexism." For Mattley, the whore stigma was served up by her academic colleagues, both male and female, who implied that she was conducting research on phone sex operators "because it was titillating," and because it allowed Mattley to indulge her own "perverted voyeuristic tendencies." The result was emotional and professional dislocation. The harsh sibilance of workplace giggles, double entendres, and references to dirty movies in her presence stripped Mattley of her identity as a sociologist, reducing her to nothing more than a "great voice."

Meda Chesney-Lind and Barbara Bloom argue that feminist scholars shoulder many burdens, but perhaps the most daunting is the task of "investigating aspects of women's oppression while seeking at the same time to be a part of the struggle against it."[8] Significantly, this dynamic of investigation and resistance was played out not only in Kane's and Mattley's choice of research topics and analytic frameworks, but also in the very process of conducting research and responding to research danger.

Kane confronts situations of gender oppression in her research with bravado, street smarts, and more than a little serendipity. "Doing this work solo was rough," she says of her research into prostitution and AIDS transmission. Attempting to anticipate and defuse the salacious gaze of male bar patrons, Kane dresses in "the unsexiest tropical clothing I could find." Confronting the condescending questions of two barroom bouncers, Kane lets them have it with both barrels: "Yes, thank you, I know where the fuck I am." And following a similar incident on the mean streets of South Chicago, Kane returns to admonish those involved that "they had no right to look at a person like they looked at me."

But it is kinship with others, across fault lines of gender and ethnicity, that provides Kane her greatest survival skill. Kane ("a white woman ethnographer," by her own identification) discovers a community of understanding not only in the research and writing of African American

feminist scholars, but in the African American men of her ethnography—
black street poets like Loki, who "cared about me as a friend," and gave
their toasts to her as gifts of "friendship and artful speech." From them,
and from a folklorist colleague, she comes to understand that, while such
toasts regularly incorporate misogynist images, they also invert and undermine gendered hierarchies, and thus draw their "emotional power
from love, humor, and adventure, *not* degradation." As Kane emphasizes,
contradictions, ambiguities, and mistaken and misplaced identities per-
meate the experience of field research—and at the same time often provide the insights which emerge out of it.

Contradictions also shaped Mattley's field research, her stigmatization, and her resistance to it. Because universities employ faculty who are
highly educated, it is assumed that academe will also produce a high degree of social tolerance. Yet, as Mattley confesses, "I found labeling of me
just as, if not more, problematic among academics than among nonacademics." While her co-sex workers "treated me as they treated the other
women," Mattley's university colleagues reacted to her study with disdain, "laughing and teasing me about it." Moreover, while Mattley found
that, among colleagues, "the reactions to my research were (and are) gendered," they were not gendered neatly. Some women expressed genuine
interest in Mattley's research; others reacted with dichotomized assumptions about good and evil and with disgust. Some men responded with in-
fantile and inappropriate questions; others (one an "experienced field
researcher and feminist") served as essential sounding boards and sources
of intellectual support. But perhaps the most revealing contradiction centered on the source of Mattley's insight into her subjects, and into her
own experiences as an ethnographer; as she says, "[T]alking with other
[sex] workers about the stigmas they endured helped me recognize the
one applied to me."

Ethical Danger—Sociologists or criminologists who rely directly or
indirectly on official sources of data are likely to encounter ethical conflicts between their roles as researchers and their roles as citizens. While
the *researcher* must cooperate with public officials to gain access to data,
the *citizen* may discover during the course of research instances of social
injustice—often orchestrated by these same public officials—and become inspired to fight such injustices. For ethnographers especially, this
conflict often begins with an affinity researchers develop with their sub-

jects. Few have articulated the conflict as succinctly as the high priest of criminological ethnography, Ned Polsky: "If one is effectively to study adult criminals in their natural settings, he must make the moral decision that in some ways he will break the law himself. He need not be a 'participant' observer and commit the criminal acts under study, yet he has to witness such acts or be taken into confidence about them and not blow the whistle. That is, the investigator has to decide that when necessary he will 'obstruct justice' or have 'guilty knowledge' or be an 'accessory' before or after the fact, in the full legal sense of those terms."[9]

This conflict lies at the heart of Tunnell's confession. Relying on his contacts with local criminal justice agents, Tunnell travels to the hills of Tennessee, where he meets a property offender who becomes "nervous as hell" about Tunnell's use of a tape recorder. In response, Tunnell shuts the thing off, pops a beer, and fires up a joint, engaging in a "crime of ceremony" with his subject. As a result, Tunnell gains more insightful biographical data on this offender—including information on such ongoing criminal activities as commercial marijuana growing and trading in stolen property—than could ever have been achieved through conventionally "objective" research methods.

Yet the bounty of ethnographic data which Tunnell generates from this and other research situations comes at a heavy price. Upon learning of one study, criminal justice officials waged "an all-out assault" on Tunnell's research by requesting field notes, subjects' names, and interview transcripts. Turning over this information to authorities could have led to severe sanctions against Tunnell's subjects, including felony time in prison. Tunnell thus faced a dilemma not unlike the one encountered by Arrigo in his re-evaluation of his research role inside a residential facility for the homeless. At base, both researchers found themselves face to face with their own sense of citizenship. Polsky asked: "But what of one's duty as a citizen? Shouldn't that take precedence? Well, different types of citizens have different *primary* duties. And our very understanding of 'citizenship' itself is considerably furthered in the long run if one type of citizen, the criminologist, conceives his primary duty to be the advancement of scientific knowledge about crime even when such advancement can be made only by 'obstructing justice' with respect to particular criminals in the short run."[10]

In the context of this dilemma, Arrigo and Tunnell turn to survival skills situated in the research moment and in their sense of justice. Growing increasingly dissatisfied with the routine collection of records required by his job as principal researcher, the bureaucrat Arrigo crosses the line into "research deviance" and humanitarian citizenship by participating with residents in the generation of "nonobjective," but potentially life-saving, data. In the process, Arrigo embarks on a "journey of fellowship and belonging." Tunnell also crosses the line and, much like Ferrell and Kane, makes few apologies for it. When faced with the officials' request for his data, Tunnell and a colleague "decided simply to lie and tell the attorneys that, due to their threats, we had destroyed the tapes and transcripts in question," and to defiantly add that "their threats of an injunction and lawsuit instilled no fear in us whatsoever. . . ."

Tunnell and Arrigo therefore confirm the importance of the sort of "emotion work" that Mattley describes in her chapter. In Tunnell's words, this involves "confronting, with head and heart, the myth of value-free sociology." It involves seeking a subjective truth that comes closer to the actual politics and morality of crime and deviance than conventionally objective methods would allow. Once more, it requires a human touch.[11]

Emotional Danger—Emotion work can create an intensity of passion in a variety of directions.[12] As pointed out by Kraska, Fleisher, and Hamm, confronting the human appetite for violence "with head and heart" can at times evoke empathy with the lived experiences of criminals, their victims, or agents of the criminal justice system. At other times, though, it can lead to hatred, to loathing, and to experiences that can shake researchers to the very core of their existence. Along with Lyng's work in this volume, these authors show that criminology can be experienced with the body as well as the mind.

To gain access to paramilitary police units, Kraska engages in some industrial-strength male bonding by relying on "hypermasculine signifiers" from his past—Alaskan Bush Guide, Shotgun Warrior, and Gun Worshiper. This allows Kraska to develop rich experiential insights into the social, cultural, and technological forces that now undergird such policing mainstays as "crack raids" and "dynamic entrances." In reaching out and touching this institutionalized aggression, however, Kraska discovers that he "unreflectively re-emerged as a co-conspirator" in the militarized use of deadly force. He is at once emotionally disturbed and fascinated by this. "I drifted back and forth between enjoyment and alarm," he confesses. But ultimately this experience led Kraska to confront his own citizenship.

Returning from what he calls "the edge of legitimate and illegitimate behavior," the author finds solace in a higher humanitarian ideal: exposing for the rest of us the pervasive social network of violence that permeates paramilitary subcultures and paramilitary policing. By reflexively importing macro-meanings into his micro-level experiences, Kraska not only unpacks the masculine construction of white paramilitary violence, but also uses this intellectual filter as an emancipatory education for his own personal and existential survival. "The theoretical and personal," Kraska concludes, "thus merge with the political."

It is devotion to a higher humanitarian ideal that also sustains Fleisher through his nightmares and his growing "coldness" associated with studying street gangs in Kansas City. Like Kraska, Fleisher confesses that he actually enjoys the "risk and excitement" of hanging out with gang members in dangerous neighborhoods where "drive-by shootings occur as regularly as Little League games." However, such enjoyment clearly does not compensate for the existential pain Fleisher feels as he watches their daily lives unfold. "I pay a heavy price," he says.

Fleisher's pain is rooted not only in the lives of these young people, but also in other scholars' lack of interest in them, along with misguided public policies and out-of-touch politicians who have no effective plans for achieving social and economic justice on their behalf. Essentially, Fleisher concludes, nobody cares. This leads to the widespread use of coercive social control that ultimately "destroys lives" instead of saving them. Fleisher finds shelter from this destructive storm in a sort of scholastic activism. He begins by abandoning objectivist detachment and colorless crime statistics, which only serve to protect "us, the onlookers, from the horror of the real lives criminals live." Instead, Fleisher becomes a citizen and a friend to his subjects. He effects a "marriage" between himself and the gang members of his study. This allows Fleisher to "see things other researchers never see, ask questions others never ask, get answers others never get."

This privileged information about "drug addiction and . . . trafficking, teenage prostitution, blood spilled on the ground, and tearless teenagers" has one overriding purpose for Fleisher: the possibility that "maybe [my] writing will effect some change, some day." The same holds true for Hamm's humanistic account of "the blood that has dried on the codes of law" in the Oklahoma City bombing case. Relying on citizenship forged through poetry, music, and his own secular spirituality, he works through a ton of existential pain to tell the story of Timothy McVeigh "as clearly as possible."

Physical Danger—The research conducted by Jacobs and Lyng demonstrates perhaps most clearly the physical dangers inherent in the ethnography of crime and deviance. The life-threatening situations faced by both researchers emerged, however, in very different ways.

Knowing perhaps not enough about the dynamics of social distance, the culture and rhythms of black street life, and the pharmacological effects of crack cocaine, Jacobs began his field research by recruiting Luther, a teenage crack dealer from the grim ghettos of St. Louis, to serve as a contact, respondent, and research assistant in his study of street-level crack dealing. Luther's job was to introduce Jacobs to other crack entrepreneurs for the purpose of conducting interviews and "collecting data." For this service, Jacobs paid Luther in cash. This seemingly professional relationship was freighted with problems, however—problems which Erving Goffman might well characterize as stemming from a mutual (mis)presentation of self.[13]

Jacobs writes that Luther was his first respondent and "was responsible for starting a snowball of referrals" that eventually led to some forty interviews conducted by Jacobs. He continues: "But after [Luther] could no longer provide referrals, I moved on, using his contacts to find new ones and eliminating him from the chain." Jacobs explains this error as "a practical shortfall in managing informant relations." For Luther, something far more personal was going on.

In essence, Jacobs had violated a fundamental moral presupposition: he had used Luther as a means to an end. In his famous categorical imperative, Immanuel Kant wrote: "Act so that you treat humanity, whether in your own person or in that of another, always as an end, never as a means only."[14] Not surprisingly, then, Luther—rejected, unstable, perhaps loaded on crack—wound up pointing a .45 revolver at Jacobs, shouting: "I'll blow your motherfuckin' head off!" From there, the research danger continued, with Luther mounting a six-week campaign of terror against his former employer. The following telephone conversation, quoted verbatim from Jacobs's chapter, speaks volumes about the dangers of doing field research during a breakdown in human relations:

Luther: "Why do you keep hangin' up on me? All I want is to talk."

Jacobs: "What do you expect me to do, *like* you? [sardonically, on the verge of losing it]. You fuckin' robbed me. . . ."

Luther: "I only did that 'cause you fucked me over. . . ."

Alternatively, this volume concludes with an extraordinary example of human relations forged in the fire of shared experience. In his chapter on edgework, Lyng offers a brilliant explication and critique of "dangerous methods"—a form of data collection and analysis that forces researchers to confront the moral and physical imperatives of their field-work investigations. Rather than treating his subjects as a means to an end, Lyng finds in the skydivers and motorcycle riders of his study "individuals [who] shared some of my deepest intellectual concerns." Moreover, Lyng becomes connected to this subcultural world through a common fascination with anarchy in human affairs. This in turn leads Lyng to research experiences that are largely "ineffable." And that is the crowning achievement of Lyng's study: he at least begins to explain the unexplainable.

For Lyng, it was the need to forge a deep human connection that both preceded and followed his edgework experience. He began his study of skydivers by trying to share "the circumstances of their lives [and] a con-stitutional stance that matches theirs as closely as possible." Few have paid such a heavy price for total immersion in the lives of those they study. Not only does the author share a host of mind-altering substances with his subjects ("indiscretions that were crucial to the edgework experi-ence"), but he also thoroughly immerses himself in the "survival in-stincts" of motorcycle anarchy as well. Lyng is unambiguous about the short-term purpose of all this: "[D]emonstrating some form of edgework," he writes, "was a prerequisite for participating in any collective discourse on the subject." He is equally clear about the long-term purpose: "[T]he research . . . [was] a means of achieving deep insight into human affairs," he confesses.

At the peak of his research experience, Lyng offers a very real repre-sentation of the human touch, as we join him and his motorcycle com-patriots blasting down the highway at one hundred miles an hour. "[W]e would move close enough for passengers to touch one another across the roaring windblast," he writes—the experiential equivalent of a researcher shooting heroin in order to describe yet another ineffable state. Such risk taking paid off, of course, and the motorcycle anarchists accepted Lyng as "a member of their tribe . . . someone who could be trusted with the secrets of the marginal reality to which they were drawn."

But then came the soul sacrifice, as sacrifice must inevitably come to those who push the outer edges. And with blood filling his punctured lungs, slipping into the darkness with broken bones protruding from his leather jacket, Lyng brings us fully into the sheer terror of the ethnographic moment.

The Promise

We have offered in this collection a particular sociological and methodological paradigm of human danger. This paradigm seems supremely suited to the subject matter. Crime is certainly a dangerous enterprise for its perpetrators. It is becoming increasingly dangerous for victims. And for those of us who take to the field and study it, crime has certainly never been more dangerous. As we have also shown, though, this danger can be confronted and even lessened to some degree if researchers rely on their methodological skills, their personal and professional identities, their colleagues, and their shared humanity. In the words of Richard Quinney, the contributors to this volume have grounded their studies in a "belief in the unity of the human race, and the potential of human beings to be perfected by their own efforts."[15] While some may criticize this humanism on the grounds that it is sentimental and unscientific, the fact that an identifiable human touch shows up among the different researchers represented here—from diverse backgrounds, with different skills, and in various research settings—speaks more to its academic consistency than to its scholastic weakness.

Not only is danger at the center of the research experience for criminological ethnographers; it is gaining recognition among researchers of other methodological persuasions as well. James Q. Wilson, among today's most frequently cited contemporary American criminologists (and one who works primarily with official statistics and secondary, quantitative sources), leaves no doubt about the prominence of danger in contemporary criminality: "Crime . . . was not a major issue in the 1984 election and had only begun to be one in the 1988 contest; by . . . 1994 it dominate[d] all other matters. The reason, I think, is that Americans believe something fundamental has changed in our patterns of crime. They are right. . . . [W]e are terrified by the prospect of innocent people being gunned down at random, without warning and almost without motive, by youngsters who afterwards, show us the blank, unremorseful face of a seemingly feral, presocial being." [16]

Drawing on the extant literature, Wilson concludes that "criminology has learned a great deal of who these people are." [17] Perhaps it has. But much more can be learned through the paradigm of human danger and its attendant methodologies of ethnography and criminological *verstehen*. Wilson argues, for example, that "[t]hey [offenders] tend to have criminal parents"—yet we know little about the particular ways in which criminal skills and ideologies are in reality passed from one generation to the next. "[They] live in cold or discordant families," he continues—but much work remains to be done on unraveling the lived connections between family dysfunction and criminality. After all, nearly half of all marriages now end in divorce; yet, according to Wilson's count, only 6 percent of the U.S. male population commits fully half of all serious crime. What situated dynamics keep the majority of child divorce victims away from crime? What other dynamics seduce the minority into it? Clearly, researchers can go a long way toward answering these sorts of questions by situating *themselves,* as best they can, inside the lives of families, inside the interactions of fathers and sons, inside divorce courts and family service agencies, where they can better understand the lived immediacy and meaning of "discordant families" and "dysfunction," and their relationship to criminality.

Wilson further argues that most criminals "have a low verbal intelligence quotient and do poorly in school." But what exactly does Wilson know about the subtlety of day-to-day student/teacher relationships in these schools? What does he know about the daily degradations, about the institutional racism and cultural intolerance, to which many inner-city students must submit as part of their "education"? And how in fact *does* "low verbal intelligence" manifest itself in the elaborate skills and ideologies, in the localized vocabularies of motive, necessary for ongoing criminality?

Criminals tend to be "emotionally cold and temperamentally impulsive," says Wilson, a conclusion based on surveys of criminals before or after the criminal events in question. But what emotional and temperamental patterns emerge inside the criminal moment, in the phenomenology of the event? If we have learned anything from years of field research, it is that crime and violence tend to be anything but emotionally cold. Thumping hearts, adrenalin rushes, and heated exchanges accompany the violent edgework of a strong-arm robbery or a drive-by shooting. At the same time, there may be little that is "temperamentally impulsive" about successful street-level drug dealing, carefully planned commercial marijuana growing (currently the largest cash crop in the United States), the billion-dollar sex trade industry, or long-plotted eruptions of paramilitary violence and mass murder. In every case, attentive field research seems to promise a better avenue for unraveling the emotional complexity of criminality—and the emotional capacity of criminals—than does secondhand generalization.

Yet, before this promise can be realized, field researchers must deal with a problem—a problem which Kuhn would remind us is endemic to all science. They must overcome the gatekeepers of the dominant paradigm.

Hotel Criminology

In their introductory comments to this book, Patricia and Peter Adler argue that criminological ethnography has entered a Dark Ages of legal constraint and institutional disrespect. They are right. Ethnographic studies are seldom found in mainstream books or journals on crime and deviance. Such studies are routinely overlooked in the annual reviews of research, and they receive only scant attention in many textbooks. Perhaps as a result of this academic neglect, field studies are largely ignored by government research agencies on the grounds that ethnography does not produce results of major policy significance. In 1997 alone, the U.S. Congress appropriated more than sixty million dollars for research on crime and justice, and another fifty million dollars for terrorism research. The vast majority of these funds were earmarked for developing new technologies to deter violence and to enhance criminal justice capacities to incarcerate offenders.[18] As in previous years, little of this money will be used to support ethnographic research.

Moreover, ethnographic studies—with their emphasis on attending to and explaining the behaviors of people—are regularly shunned in favor of quantitative studies, with their unyielding emphasis on predicting the behavior of numbers. Finally, adding insult to injury, field researchers and their work are routinely disparaged by their quantitative-oriented colleagues on grounds of bias, overinvolvement, even immorality.

Such are the gatekeepers of the Dark Ages. They seem primarily interested in creating and enforcing artificial, hierarchical divisions between types of scholars and scholarship, and then using those divisions to play a zero-sum game of in-group/out-group politics. Through their politics of exclusion, their disdain of ethnography as a legitimate research method, and their outright professional meanness, the gatekeepers install a bright and authoritarian demarcation within the fields of criminology and sociology.

On the out-group side of it all, ethnographers have learned to hunker down, stay warm, and get on with their work as best they can. For them, academic criminology and sociology have come to resemble what Henry James called Hotel Civilization—a social order characterized by too much stale comfort, void of the subtle shadows of everyday life.[19] Like the great Beat poets of the 1950s, the ethnographers of the Dark Ages long to step outside the hotel—to be wrapped in the mystery of those shadows, in the power of what can't be easily seen, in the dangerous beauty of unnoticed alternatives. Interestingly, the architecture of Hotel Civilization, of Hotel Criminology, was described decades ago by Max Weber in *The Protestant Ethic and the Spirit of Capitalism.* "No one knows who will live in this cage in the future," said Weber, "or whether at the end of this tremendous development entirely new prophets will arise or there will be a great rebirth of old ideas, or, if neither, mechanized petrification, embellished with a sort of compulsive self-importance. For of this last stage it may truly be said, 'Specialists without spirit, Sensualists without heart; this nullity imagines that it has attained a level of civilization never before achieved.'"[20]

In our ongoing ethnographies of crime and deviance, and in this collection, we seek to create human alternatives to the mechanized petrification of data sets and statistics, to serve if nothing else as troublingly human ghosts inside the machinery of modern criminology and sociology. We work to remind academic specialists of a world that continues to emerge outside their specialization, to fill the nullity of abstract social science with the heart, spirit, and sensuality of crime and deviance. And in all of this, we employ another of Weber's great insights: the notion that shared emotion and understanding, *verstehen,* can in turn shape understandings of crime, deviance, and ourselves.

In preface to *Let Us Now Praise Famous Men,* his passionate ethnography of southern sharecroppers, James Agee proposed "a test":

> Get a radio or phonograph capable of the most extreme loudness possible, and sit down to listen to a performance of Beethoven's Seventh Symphony or of Schubert's C-Major Symphony. But I don't mean just sit down and listen. I mean this: Turn it on as loud as you can get it. Then get down on the floor and jam your ear as close into the loudspeaker as you can get it and stay there, breathing as lightly as possible, and not moving, and neither eating nor smoking nor drinking. Concentrate everything you can into your hearing and into your body. You won't hear it nicely. If it hurts you, be glad of it. As near as you will ever get, you are inside the music; not only inside it, you are it; your body is no longer your shape and substance, it is the shape and substance of the music.[21]

We invite the residents of Hotel Criminology to undertake a similar test. Leave the hotel for a while. Go out in the streets, into living rooms and corporate boardrooms, into juvenile lockups. Situate yourselves as close as you can to the perpetrators of crime and deviance, to the victims, to agents of legal control; put yourselves, as best you can and for as long as you can, inside their lives, inside the lived moments of deviance and crime. You won't experience it nicely, and if the danger and hurt become too much, be glad of it. Because as near as you will ever get, you have found your way inside the humanity of crime and deviance.

Afterword

As a quick glance at the biographical notes on this book's contributors will confirm, we too live in Hotel Criminology — not in its penthouse suites, of course, and perhaps not contentedly, but there nonetheless. We are thus well aware of one further danger not yet discussed: the danger which a book of this sort may pose to our continued residence. More than one contributor to this volume has asked whether a chapter here would more likely enhance an academic career or end it. Regarding a collection in which illegal drug use, drunk driving, weapons violations, obstruction of justice, arrest, and various other "unprofessional" behaviors are confessed, this does not appear an unreasonable question. It is also a revealing one. For it seems entirely appropriate that a book on edgework and danger should itself become a sort of dangerous edgework—that a book on the risks of ethnographic research into crime and deviance should reproduce those risks in its execution.

Notes

1. Thomas S. Kuhn, *The Structure of Scientific Revolutions* (Chicago: University of Chicago Press, 1970).

2. Howard S. Becker, *Outsiders: Studies in the Sociology of Deviance* (New York: Free Press, 1963); Ned Polsky, *Hustlers, Beats, and Others* (Chicago: Aldine, 1967); Jack Katz, *Seductions of Crime: Moral and Sensual Attractions in Doing Evil* (New York: Basic Books, 1988). Among the many other examples, see Jeff Ferrell, *Crimes of Style: Urban Graffiti and the Politics of Criminality* (Boston: Northeastern University Press, 1996); Mark S. Hamm, *American Skinheads: The Criminology and Control of Hate Crime* (Westport, Conn.: Praeger, 1993); Stephen Lyng, "Edgework: A Social Psychological Analysis of Voluntary Risk Taking," *American Journal of Sociology* 95 (1990): 851–86; Pat O'Malley and Stephen Mugford, "Crime, Excitement, and Modernity," in *Varieties of Criminology,* ed. Gregg Barak (Westport, Conn.: Praeger, 1994), 189–212.

3. Richard P. Appelbaum and William J. Chambliss, *Sociology* (New York: Longman, 1997).

4. Carl Sagan, *The Demon-Haunted World: Science as a Candle in the Dark* (New York: Random House, 1995), xiii.

5. Jim Thomas, *Doing Critical Ethnography* (Newbury Park, Calif.: Sage, 1993).

6. See, for example, Becker, *Outsiders;* Alfred R. Lindesmith, *The Addict and the Law* (Bloomington: Indiana University Press, 1965); William F. Whyte, *Street Corner Society: The Social Structure of an Italian Slum* (Chicago: University of Chicago Press, 1943).

7. Edwin Sutherland and Donald Cressey, *Principles of Criminology* (New York: J. B. Lippincott, 1970).

8. Meda Chesney-Lind and Barbara Bloom, "Feminist Criminology: Thinking About Women and Crime," in *Thinking Critically About Crime,* ed. Brian D. MacLean and Dragan Milovanovic (Vancouver: Collective Press, 1997), 47.

9. Polsky, *Hustlers,* 139.

10. Polsky, *Hustlers,* 143, emphasis in original.

11. For a remarkable example of this humanist approach to the ethnography of crime and deviance, see Leon E. Pettiway, *Honey, Honey, Miss Thang: Being Black, Gay, and on the Streets* (Philadelphia: Temple University Press, 1996).

12. See Richard G. Mitchell, *Secrecy and Fieldwork* (Thousand Oaks, Calif.: Sage, 1993).

13. Erving Goffman, *The Presentation of Self in Everyday Life* (Garden City, N.Y.: Anchor, 1959).

14. Immanuel Kant, *Fundamental Principles of the Metaphysics of Morals* (Indianapolis: Bobbs-Merrill, 1949), 47.

15. Richard Quinney, "Socialist Humanism and Critical/Peacemaking Criminology: The Continuing Project," in MacLean and Milovanovic, *Thinking Critically About Crime,* 116.

16. James Q. Wilson, "Crime and Public Policy," in *Crime,* ed. James Q. Wilson and Joan Petersilia (San Francisco: ICS Press, 1995), 491–92.

17. All further quotations by Wilson appear in "Crime and Public Policy," 492.

18. U.S. Department of Justice, *Building Knowledge About Crime and Justice* (Washington, D.C.: National Institute of Justice, 1997).

19. Henry James, *The Portrait of a Lady* (New York: Modern Library, 1881).

20. Max Weber, *The Protestant Ethic and the Spirit of Capitalism,* trans. Talcott Parsons (New York: Scribner and Sons, 1958), 182.

21. James Agee and Walker Evans, *Let Us Now Praise Famous Men* (New York: Ballantine, 1960), 14–15.

References

Abrahams, Roger. 1963. *Deep Down in the Jungle: Negro Narrative Folklore from the Streets of Philadelphia.* Chicago: Aldine.

Adler, Patricia A. 1985. *Wheeling and Dealing: An Ethnography of an Upper-Level Drug Dealing and Smuggling Community.* New York: Columbia University Press.

Adler, Patricia A., and Peter Adler. 1987. *Membership Roles in Field Research.* Newbury Park, Calif.: Sage.

Adorno, Theodore. 1967. *The Jargon of Authenticity.* New York: Continuum.

———. 1976. *Negative Dialectics.* New York: Continuum.

Agar, Michael. 1971. "Folklore of the Heroin Addict: Two Examples." *Journal of American Folklore* 84: 175–85.

———. 1973. *Ripping and Running: A Formal Ethnography of Urban Heroin Addicts.* New York: Seminar Press.

Agee, James, and Walker Evans. 1960. *Let Us Now Praise Famous Men.* New York: Ballantine.

Agger, Ben. 1992. *The Discourse of Domination: From the Frankfurt School to Postmodernism.* Evanston, Ill.: Northwestern University Press.

Alasuutari, Pertti. 1995. *Researching Culture: Qualitative Method and Cultural Studies.* Thousand Oaks, Calif.: Sage.

Althusser, Louis. 1971. *Lenin and Philosophy.* New York: Monthly Review.

American Sociological Association. 1996. *Code of Ethics.* Washington, D.C.: American Sociological Association.

Anaya, Rudolfo. 1995. "Foreword: The Spirit of the Place." In David King Dunaway, ed., *Writing the Southwest,* ix–xvi. New York: Plume.

Anderson, Elijah. 1976. *A Place on the Corner.* Chicago: University of Chicago Press.

———. 1990. *Streetwise: Race, Class, and Change in an Urban Community.* Chicago: University of Chicago Press.

Anderson, Nels. 1923. *The Hobo: The Sociology of the Homeless Man.* Chicago: University of Chicago Press.

Appelbaum, Richard P., and William J. Chambliss. 1997. *Sociology.* New York: Longman.

Applebome, Peter. 1987. "Some Say Frontier is Still There, and Still Different." *New York Times,* December 12, 11.

Armstrong, Gary. 1993. "Like that Desmond Morris?" In Dick Hobbs and Tim May, eds., *Interpreting the Field: Accounts of Ethnography,* 3–43. Oxford: Clarendon.

Arrigo, Bruce. 1994. "Rooms for the Misbegotten: Social Design and Social Deviance." *Journal of Sociology and Social Welfare* 24 (1): 95–113.

———. 1994. "Legal Discourse and the Disordered Criminal Defendant: Contributions from Psychoanalytic Semiotics and Chaos Theory." *Legal Studies Forum* 18 (1): 93–112.

———. 1995. "The Peripheral Core of Law and Criminology: On Postmodern Social Theory and Conceptual Integration." *Justice Quarterly* 12 (3): 447–72.

———. 1995. "New Directions in Crime, Law, and Social Change: On Psychoanalytic Semiotics, Chaos Theory, and Postmodern Ethics." *Studies in the Social Sciences* 33: 101–29.

———. 1996. "A Preliminary Investigation of the 'Modest Needs' Homeless Family Phenomenon: Agenda for Research, Policy, and Practice." Unpublished manuscript. Institute of Psychology, Law, and Public Policy, Fresno, Calif.

———. 1996. "Recommunalizing Drug Offenders: The 'Drug Peace' Agenda." *Journal of Offender Rehabilitation* 24 (3/4): 83–106.

———. 1996. *The Contours of Psychiatric Justice: A Postmodern Critique of Mental Illness, Criminal Insanity, and the Law.* New York: Garland.

———. 1997. "Dimensions of Social Justice in an SRO: Contributions from Chaos Theory, Policy, and Practice." In Dragan Milovanovic, ed., *Chaos, Criminology, and Social Justice,* 139–54. New York: Greenwood.

Arrigo, Bruce, and T. R. Young. 1997. "Chaos, Complexity, and Crime: Working Tools for a Postmodern Criminology." In Brian MacLean and Dragan Milovanovic, eds., *Thinking Critically About Crime,* 77–84. Vancouver: Collective Press.

Associated Press. 1995. "Researcher on Prostitution Slain." *Arizona Republic,* September 29, A5.

Bachman, Ronet. 1992. *Crime Victimization in City, Suburban, and Rural Areas.* Report for the Bureau of Justice Statistics for the U.S. Department of Justice. U.S. Department of Justice, Washington, D.C.

Bahr, Howard M. 1968. *Homelessness and Disaffiliation.* New York: Columbia University Bureau of Applied Social Research.

Baker, James N., Patricia King, Andrew Murr, and Nonny Abbott. 1989. "The Newest Drug War: In Rural America, Crack and 'Crank' Are Now Hot Commodities in the Backwoods." *Newsweek,* April 3, 20-22.

Bakunin, Michael. 1990. *Statism and Anarchy.* M. S. Shatz, trans. and ed. Cambridge: Cambridge University Press.

Balkin, Jean M. 1987. "Deconstructive Practice and Legal Theory." *Yale Law Journal* 96 (4): 743-86.

Barak, Gregg. 1991. *Gimme Shelter: A Social History of Homelessness in Contemporary America.* New York: Praeger.

Barak, Gregg, and Robert Bohm. 1989. "The Crimes of the Homeless or the Crime of Homelessness?" *Contemporary Crises* 13: 275-88.

Barthes, Roland. 1988. *The Semiotic Challenge.* New York: Hill and Wang.

Baudrillard, Jean. 1983. *Simulacra and Simulations.* P. Foss, P. Patton, and Philip Beitchman, trans. New York: Semiotext(e).

———. 1988. *Selected Writings.* Mark Poster, ed. Stanford: Stanford University Press.

Bayer, Robert. 1989. *Private Act, Social Consequence: AIDS and the Politics of Public Health.* New York: Free Press.

Becker, Howard S. 1963. *Outsiders: Studies in the Sociology of Deviance.* New York: Free Press.

———. 1967. "Whose Side Are We On?" *Social Problems* 14: 239-47.

———. 1992. "Cases, Causes, Conjunctures, Stories, and Imagery." In Charles C. Rarin and Howard S. Becker, eds., *What Is a Case? Foundations of Social Inquiry,* 205-16. New York: Cambridge University Press.

Becker, Howard S., and Blanche Geer. 1969. "Participant Observation and Interviewing: A Comparison." In George J. McCall and J. L. Simmons, eds., *Issues in Participant Observation,* 322-31. Reading, Mass.: Addison-Wesley.

Begley, Adam. 1994. "The I's Have It." *Lingua/Franca* 4: 54-59.

Benhabib, Seyla. 1986. *Critique, Norm, and Utopia: A Study of the Foundations of Critical Theory.* New York: Columbia University Press.

Berk, Richard A., and Joseph M. Adams. 1970. "Establishing Rapport with Deviant Groups." *Social Problems* 18: 102-17.

Bernard, H. Russell. 1994. *Research Methods in Cultural Anthropology.* Newbury Park, Calif.: Sage.

Bernstein, Richard. 1978. *The Restructuring of Social and Political Theory.* Philadelphia: University of Pennsylvania Press.

———. 1983. *Beyond Objectivism and Relativism: Science, Hermeneutics, and Praxis.* Philadelphia: University of Pennsylvania Press.

———. 1992. *The New Constellation: The Ethical-Political Horizons of Modernity/Postmodernity.* Cambridge, Mass.: MIT Press.

Bhaskar, R. 1986. *Scientific Realism and Human Emancipation.* London: Verso.

Biernacki, Patrick, and Dan Waldorf. 1981. "Snowball Sampling." *Sociological Methods and Research* 10: 141–63.

Birenbaum, Arnold. 1970. "On Managing Courtesy Stigma." *Journal of Health and Social Behavior* 11 (3): 196–206.

Bishop, K. 1990. "Military Takes Part in Drug Sweep and Reaps Criticism and a Lawsuit." *New York Times,* August 10, A11.

Bittner, Egon. 1973. "Objectivity and Realism in Sociology." In George Psathas, ed., *Phenomenological Sociology,* 109–25. New York: John Wiley.

Bogue, Donald J. 1961. *The Homeless Man on Skid Row.* Chicago: Tenants Relation Bureau, City of Chicago.

———. 1963. *Skid Row in American Cities.* Chicago: University of Chicago Press.

Bourdieu, Pierre. 1977. *Outline of a Theory of Practice.* London: Cambridge University Press.

———. 1991. *Language and Symbolic Power.* Cambridge, Mass.: Harvard University Press.

———. 1993. *Sociology in Question.* Thousand Oaks, Calif.: Sage.

Bourdieu, Pierre, and Jean Claude Passeron. 1977. *Reproduction in Education, Society and Culture.* London: Sage.

Bourgois, Philippe. 1989. "In Search of Horatio Alger: Culture and Ideology in the Crack Economy." *Contemporary Drug Problems* 16: 619–49.

———. 1995. *In Search of Respect.* New York: Cambridge University Press.

———. 1996. "Confronting Anthropology, Education, and Inner-City Apartheid." *American Anthropology* 98 (2): 249–58.

Brajuha, Mario, and Lyle Hallowell. 1986. "Legal Intrusion and the Politics of Fieldwork: The Impact of the Brajuha Case." *Urban Life* 14: 454–78.

Briggs, Charles L. 1990. *Learn How to Ask.* Cambridge: Cambridge University Press.

Briggs, John, and F. David Peat. 1989. *Turbulent Mirror.* New York: Harper and Row.

Burawoy, Michael, Alice Burton, Ann Arnett Ferguson, Kathryn J. Fox, Joshua Gamson, Nadine Gartrell, Leslie Hurst, Charles Kurzman, Leslie Salzinger, Josepha Schiffman, and Shiori Ui. 1991. *Ethnography Unbound: Power and Resistance in the Modern Metropolis.* Berkeley: University of California Press.

Bureau of Justice Statistics. 1990. *Handgun Crime Victims.* Special Report for the U.S. Department of Justice. U.S. Department of Justice, Washington, D.C.

Carey, James T. 1972. "Problems of Access and Risk in Observing Drug Scenes." In Jack D. Douglas, ed., *Research on Deviance,* 71–92. New York: Random House.

Carr, Wilfred, and Stephen Kemmis. 1986. *Becoming Critical.* London: Falmer Press.

Castaneda, Carlos. 1971. *A Separate Reality: Further Conversations with Don Juan.* New York: Simon and Schuster.

Castellano, Thomas C., and Craig D. Uchida. 1990. "Local Drug Enforcement, Prosecutors, and Case Attrition: Theoretical Perspectives for the Drug War." *American Journal of Police* 9: 133–62.

Caton, Catherine. 1990. *Homeless in America.* New York: Oxford University Press.

Caulfield, Susan, and Nancy Wonders. 1994. "Personal and Political: Violence Against Women and the Role of the State." In Kenneth Tunnell, ed., *Political Crime in Contemporary America: A Critical Approach,* 79–100. New York: Garland.

———. 1994. "Gender and Justice: Feminist Contributions to Criminology." In Gregg Barak, ed., *Varieties of Criminology,* 213–29. Westport, Conn.: Praeger.

Chancer, Lynn Sharon. 1993. "Prostitution, Feminist Theory, and Ambivalence: Notes from the Sociological Underground." *Social Text* 37 (Winter): 143–71.

Chesney-Lind, Meda. 1989. "Girls' Crime and Woman's Place: Toward a Feminist Model of Female Delinquency." *Crime and Delinquency* 35: 5–29.

Chesney-Lind, Meda, and Barbara Bloom. 1997. "Feminist Criminology:

Thinking About Women and Crime." In Brian D. MacLean and Dragan Milovanovic, eds., *Thinking Critically About Crime,* 45–55. Vancouver: Collective Press.

Christie, Nils. 1994. *Crime Control as Industry: Toward Gulags, Western Style.* New York: Routledge.

Churchill, Lindsey. 1978. *Questioning Strategies in Sociolinguistics.* Rowley, Mass.: Newbury House.

Cicourel, Aaron. 1964. *Method and Measurement in Sociology.* New York: Free Press.

———. 1971. *Cognitive Mappings.* New York: Free Press.

Clifford, James, and George E. Marcus. 1986. *Writing Culture: The Poetics and Politics of Ethnography.* Berkeley: University of California Press.

Clough, Patricia. 1992. *The End(s) of Ethnography: From Realism to Social Criticism.* Newbury Park, Calif.: Sage.

Collins, Randall. 1994. *Four Sociological Traditions.* New York: Oxford University Press.

Cox, Terry C., and Kenneth D. Tunnell. 1993. "Competency to Stand Trial or the Trivial Pursuit of Justice?" In Anna Wilson, ed., *Homicide: The Victim-Offender Connection,* 415–40. Cincinnati: Anderson.

Cressey, Donald. 1954. "The Differential Association Theory and Compulsive Crime." *Journal of Criminal Law and Criminology* 45: 49–64.

Cressey, Paul G. 1932. *The Taxi Dance Hall.* Chicago: University of Chicago Press.

Cuomo, Mario M. 1983. *1933/1983—Never Again.* A Report to the National Governors' Association Task Force on the Homeless, Portland, Maine.

Daly, Kathleen, and Meda Chesney-Lind. 1988. "Feminism and Criminology." *Justice Quarterly* 5: 497–535.

Davis, Mike. 1992. *City of Quartz.* New York: Vintage.

Derrida, Jacques. 1973. *Speech and Phenomena.* Evanston, Ill.: Northwestern University Press.

———. 1976. *Of Grammotology.* Baltimore: Johns Hopkins University Press.

Deutsch, Albert. 1937. *The Mentally Ill in America: A History of Their Care and Treatment from Colonial Times.* New York: Columbia University Press.

Dewey, John. 1958. *Experience and Nature.* New York: Dover Publications.

Dewey, John, and Arthur F. Bentley. 1949. *Knowing and the Known.* Westport, Conn.: Greenwood Press.

Dews, Peter. 1987. *Logics of Disintegration: Post-Structuralist Thought and the Claims of Critical Theory.* New York: Verso.

DiCristina, Bruce. 1995. *Method in Criminology: A Philosophical Primer.* New York: Harrow and Heston.

Donnermeyer, Joseph F. 1992. "The Use of Alcohol, Marijuana, and Hard Drugs by Rural Adolescents: A Review of Recent Research." In Ruth W. Edwards, ed., *Drug Use in Rural American Communities,* 31–75. New York: Haworth Press.

Donziger, Steven. 1995. *The Real War on Crime.* New York: Harper Perennial.

Douglas, Jack D., ed. 1972. *Research on Deviance.* New York: Random House.

———. 1972. "Observing Deviance." In Jack D. Douglas, ed., *Research on Deviance,* 3–34. New York: Random House.

———. 1974. *Introduction to the Sociologies of Everyday Life.* Boston: Allyn and Bacon.

———. 1976. *Investigative Social Research.* Beverly Hills, Calif.: Sage.

Douglas, Jack D., and Paul Rasmussen. 1977. *The Nude Beach.* Beverly Hills, Calif.: Sage.

Drew, P. 1984. "Speakers' Reportings in Invitation Sequences." In J. Maxwell Atkinson and J. Heritage, eds., *Structures of Social Action.* Cambridge: Cambridge University Press.

Eco, Umberto. 1976. *Theory of Semiotics.* Bloomington: Indiana University Press.

———. 1984. *Semiotics and the Philosophy of Language.* London: Macmillan.

Edgerton, Robert B. 1992. *Sick Societies: Challenging the Myths of Primitive Harmony.* New York: Free Press.

Ellen, Robert F. 1984. *Ethnographic Research: A Guide to General Conduct.* London: Academic Press.

Ellis, Carolyn. 1991. "Emotional Sociology." *Studies in Symbolic Interaction* 12: 123–45.

Emerson, Robert M., ed. 1983. *Contemporary Field Research.* Prospect Heights, Ill.: Waveland.

Enloe, Cynthia. 1980. *Police, Military and Ethnicity.* New Brunswick, N.J.: Transaction.

————. 1993. *The Morning After: Sexual Politics at the End of the Cold War.* Berkeley: University of California Press.

Evans, David. 1977. "The Toast in Context." *Journal of American Folklore* 90: 129–49.

Evans-Pritchard, E. E. 1964. *Social Anthropology and Other Essays.* New York: Free Press.

Fay, Brian. 1987. *Critical Social Science: Liberation and Its Limits.* New York: Cornell University Press.

Feagin, Joe R., Anthony M. Orum, and Gideon Sjoberg, eds. 1991. *A Case for the Case Study.* Chapel Hill: University of North Carolina Press.

Feagin, Joe R., Anthony M. Orum, and Gideon Sjoberg. 1991. "Conclusion: The Present Crisis in U.S. Sociology." In Joe R. Feagin, Anthony M. Orum, and Gideon Sjoberg, eds., *A Case for the Case Study,* 269–78. Chapel Hill: University of North Carolina Press.

Federal Bureau of Investigation. 1995. *Crime in the United States.* Washington, D.C.: Government Printing Office.

Feld, Barry C. 1991. "Justice by Geography: Urban, Suburban, and Rural Variations in Juvenile Justice Administration." *Journal of Criminal Law and Criminology* 82: 156–210.

Ferrell, Jeff. 1992. "Making Sense of Crime." *Social Justice* 19: 110–23.

————. 1993. *Crimes of Style: Urban Graffiti and the Politics of Criminality.* New York and London: Garland.

————. 1994. "Confronting the Agenda of Authority: Critical Criminology, Anarchism, and Urban Graffiti." In Gregg Barak, ed., *Varieties of Criminology,* 161–78. New York: Praeger.

————. 1995. "Culture, Crime, and Cultural Criminology." *Journal of Criminal Justice and Popular Culture* 3: 25–42.

————. 1995. "Urban Graffiti: Crime, Control, and Resistance." *Youth and Society* 27: 73–92.

————. 1995. "True Confessions: Law, Crime, and Field Research." Paper presented at the meetings of the Academy of Criminal Justice Sciences, Boston.

————. 1996. *Crimes of Style: Urban Graffiti and the Politics of Criminality.* Paperback ed. Boston: Northeastern University Press.

————. 1997. "Against the Law: Anarchist Criminology." In Brian MacLean and Dragan Milovanovic, eds., *Thinking Critically About*

Crime, 146–54. Vancouver: Collective Press.

———. 1997. "Criminological *Verstehen:* Inside the Immediacy of Crime." *Justice Quarterly* 14: 3–23.

———. Forthcoming. "Anarchism and Justice." In Bruce Arrigo, ed., *Justice at the Margins.* Belmont, Calif.: Wadsworth.

Ferrell, Jeff, and Clinton R. Sanders, eds. 1995. *Cultural Criminology.* Boston: Northeastern University Press.

Feyerabend, Paul. 1978. *Against Method: Outline of an Anarchistic Theory of Knowledge.* London: Verso.

Fine, Gary Alan. 1993. "Ten Lies of Ethnography: Moral Dilemmas in Field Research." *Journal of Contemporary Ethnography* 22 (3): 267–94.

Fleisher, Mark S. 1989. *Warehousing Violence.* Newbury Park, Calif.: Sage.

———. 1995. *Beggars and Thieves: Lives of Urban Street Criminals.* Madison: University of Wisconsin Press.

———. 1997. *Parents, Kids, and Gangs.* Madison: University of Wisconsin Press.

———. In Press. "Guns, Drugs, and Gangs: Kids on the Streets of Kansas City." *Valparaiso Law Review* 31.

———. In Press. "How to Break the Criminal Lifestyle." *USA Today Magazine.*

———. 1998. *Dead End: Lives of Urban Gang Kids.* Madison: University of Wisconsin Press.

Fonow, Mary Margaret, and Judith A. Cook, eds. 1991. *Beyond Methodology: Feminist Scholarship as Lived Research.* Bloomington: Indiana University Press.

Foucault, Michel. 1965. *Madness and Civilization: A History of Insanity in the Age of Reason.* New York: Pantheon.

———. 1972. *The Archeology of Knowledge.* New York: Pantheon.

———. 1985. *The Use of Pleasure.* New York: Pantheon.

———. 1990. *The History of Sexuality, Volume 1: An Introduction.* New York: Vintage.

Franks, David D. 1987. "Thoughts and Deeds: Toward a Typology of Action for G. H. Mead's Social Behaviorism." Unpublished manuscript.

Fraser, Nancy. 1994. "Foucault on Modern Power." In Stuart Henry, ed., *Social Control: Aspects of Non-State Justice,* 3–20. Aldershot, UK: Dartmouth.

Freeman, Charles R. 1980. "Phenomenological Sociology and Ethnomethodology." In Jack D. Douglas, ed., *Introduction to the Sociologies
of Everyday Life,* 114–30. Boston: Allyn and Bacon.

Galliher, John. 1995. "Chicago's Two Worlds of Deviance Research:
Whose Side Are They On?" In Gary Alan Fine, ed., *A Second Chicago
School? The Development of a Postwar American Sociology.* Chicago:
University of Chicago Press.

Gamson, Joshua. 1991. "Silence, Death, and the Invisible Enemy: AIDS
Activism and Social Movement 'Newness.'" In Michael Burawoy
et al., *Ethnography Unbound,* 35–57. Berkeley: University of California Press.

Garfinkel, Harold. 1956. "Conditions of Successful Degradation Ceremonies." *American Journal of Sociology* 61: 420–24.

———. 1967. *Studies in Ethnomethodology.* Englewood Cliffs, N.J.: Prentice-
Hall.

Geertz, Clifford. 1988. *Works and Lives: The Anthropologist as Author.*
Stanford: Stanford University Press.

Geis, Gilbert. 1991. "The Case Study Method in Sociological Criminol-
ogy." In Joe R. Feagin, Anthony M. Orum, and Gideon Sjoberg, eds.,
A Case for the Case Study, 200–223. Chapel Hill: University of North
Carolina Press.

Gelsthorpe, Loraine. 1990. "Feminist Methodologies in Criminology." In
Loraine Gelsthorpe and Allison Morris, eds., *Feminist Perspectives in
Criminology,* 89–106. Milton Keynes, UK: Open University Press.

Gerth, Hans H., and C. Wright Mills, eds. 1946. *From Max Weber: Essays
in Sociology.* New York: Oxford University Press.

Gibson, James W. 1994. *Warrior Dreams: Manhood in Post-Vietnam America.* New York: Hill and Wang.

Giddens, Anthony. 1990. *The Consequences of Modernity.* Stanford: Stanford University Press.

Gleick, James. 1987. *Chaos: Making a New Science.* New York: Penguin
Books.

Goffman, Erving. 1959. *The Presentation of Self in Everyday Life.* Garden
City, N.Y.: Anchor/Doubleday.

———. 1959. *The Presentation of Self in Everyday Life.* London: Allen Lane.

———. 1961. *Asylums.* New York: Doubleday.

———. 1961. *Encounters: Two Studies in the Sociology of Interaction.* New York: Bobbs-Merrill.

———. 1963. *Stigma: Notes on the Management of Spoiled Identity.* Englewood Cliffs, N.J.: Prentice-Hall.

———. 1967. *Interaction Ritual.* Garden City, N.Y.: Doubleday.

———. 1971. *Relations in Public: Micro Studies of the Public Order.* New York: Basic Books.

———. 1974. *Frame Analysis: An Essay on the Organization of Experience.* Cambridge, Mass.: Harvard University Press.

Goldman, Emma. 1969. *Anarchism and Other Essays.* New York: Dover.

Gollub, Andrew, Farrukh Hakeem, and Bruce D. Johnson. 1996. "Monitoring the Decline in the Crack Epidemic with Data from the Drug Use Forecasting Program." Unpublished manuscript.

Goode, Erich. 1970. *The Marijuana Smokers.* New York: Basic Books.

Gouldner, Alvin. 1960. "The Norm of Reciprocity." *American Sociological Review* 25: 161–78.

———. 1962. "Anti-Minotaur: The Myth of Value-Free Sociology." *Social Problems* 9: 199– 213.

Granovetter, Mark. 1973. "The Strength of Weak Ties." *American Journal of Sociology* 78: 1360–80.

Greimas, Algirdas. 1987. *On Meaning.* Minneapolis: University of Minnesota Press.

———. 1990. *The Social Science: A Semiotic View.* Minneapolis: University of Minnesota Press.

Grob, Gerald. 1973. *Mental Institutions in America: Social Policy to 1875.* New York: Free Press.

Habermas, Jürgen. 1975. *Legitimation Crises.* Boston: Beacon Press.

———. 1984. *Theory of Communicative Action, Vol. 1, Reason and the Rationalization of Society.* T. McCarthy, trans. Boston: Beacon Press.

———. 1987. *Theory of Communicative Action, Vol. 2, Lifeworld and System: A Critique of Functionalist Reason.* T. McCarthy, trans. Boston: Beacon Press.

Hafley, Sandra Riggs. 1994. "Rural Organized Crime." Master's thesis, University of Louisville.

Hagedorn, John M. 1990. "Back in the Field Again: Gang Research in the Nineties." In C. Ronald Huff, ed., *Gangs in America,* 240–59. Newbury Park, Calif.: Sage.

Hallowell, Lyle. 1985. "The Outcome of the Brajuha Case: Legal Implications for Sociologists," *Footnotes* 13 (9): 1.

Hamm, Mark S. 1993. *American Skinheads: The Criminology and Control of Hate Crime.* Westport, Conn.: Praeger.

———. 1993. "State Organized Homicide: A Study of Seven CIA Plans to Assassinate Fidel Castro." In William J. Chambliss and Marjorie S. Zatz, eds., *Making Law: The State, The Law, and Structural Contradictions,* 315–46. Bloomington: Indiana University Press.

———. 1994. "No Sense Makes Sense: The Paradox of Prosecuting Bias-Motivated Cult Crime." *American Journal of Criminal Justice* 19: 145–60.

———. 1995. *The Abandoned Ones: The Imprisonment and Uprising of the Mariel Boat People.* Boston: Northeastern University Press.

———. 1995. "Hammer of the Gods Revisited: Neo-Nazi Skinheads, Domestic Terrorism, and the Rise of the New Protest Music." In Jeff Ferrell and Clinton R. Sanders, eds., *Cultural Criminology,* 190–212. Boston: Northeastern University Press.

———. 1996. "Doing Gang Research in the 1990s." In J. Mitchell Miller and Jeffrey P. Rush, eds., *Gangs: A Criminal Justice Approach,* 17–32. Cincinnati: ACJS/Anderson.

———. 1996. *Terrorism, Hate Crime, and Anti-Government Violence.* Washington, D.C.: National Research Council.

———. 1997. *Apocalypse in Oklahoma: Waco and Ruby Ridge Revenged.* Boston: Northeastern University Press.

Hamm, Mark S., and Jeff Ferrell. 1994. "Rap, Cops, and Crime: Clarifying the 'Cop Killer' Controversy." *ACJS Today* 13: 1, 3, 29.

Hamm, Mark S., and John C. Kite. 1991. "The Role of Offender Rehabilitation in Family Violence Policy: The Batterers Anonymous Experiment." *Criminal Justice Review* 16: 227–48.

Hammersley, Martyn, and Paul Atkinson. 1983. *Ethnography: Principles in Practice.* London: Tavistock.

Handel, William H. 1982. *Ethnomethodology.* Englewood Cliffs, N.J.: Prentice-Hall.

Hardesty, Monica J. 1986. "Plans and Mood: A Study in Therapeutic Relationships." In Carl J. Couch, Stanley Saxton, and Michael A. Katovich, eds., *Studies in Symbolic Interaction: The Iowa School,* 209–

30. Greenwich, Conn.: JAI Press.

Harris, Marvin. 1981. *Why Nothing Works*. New York: Touchstone.

Heidegger, Martin. 1962. *Being and Time*. New York: Harper and Row.

Henden, Herbert, Ann Pollinger Haas, Paul Singer, Melvin Ellner, and Richard Ulman. 1987. *Living High: Daily Marijuana Use Among Adults*. New York: Human Sciences Press.

Heritage, Jeremy. 1984. *Garfinkel and Ethnomethodology*. Cambridge: Polity.

Herman, Nancy J., and Larry T. Reynolds. 1994. "Family Caregivers of the Mentally Ill: Negative and Positive Adaptive Responses." In Nancy J. Herman and Larry T. Reynolds, eds., *Symbolic Interaction: An Introduction to Social Psychology*, 342–50. New York: General Hall.

Hobbs, Dick, and Tim May. 1993. *Interpreting the Field: Accounts of Ethnography*. Oxford: Clarendon Press.

Hoch, Charles, and Richard Slayton. 1989. *New Homeless and Old: Community and the Skid Row*. Philadelphia: Temple University Press.

Hochschild, Arlie R. 1979. "Emotion Work, Feeling Rules, and Social Structure." *American Journal of Sociology* 85: 551–75.

———. 1983. *The Managed Heart*. Berkeley: University of California Press.

Hoffman, Ronald. 1996. *The Same and Not the Same*. New York: Columbia University Press.

Hood, Thomas C. 1995. "The Practical Consequences of Sociology's Pursuit of 'Justice For All.'" *Social Forces* 74: 1–14.

hooks, bell. 1990. *Yearning: Race, Gender, and Cultural Politics*. Boston: South End Press.

Hopper, Kim, and Jan Hamberg. 1985. *The Making of America's Homeless: From Skid Row to the New Poor, 1945–1984*. New York: Community Services Society.

Humphreys, Laud. 1970. *Tearoom Trade: Impersonal Sex in Public Places*. Chicago: Aldine.

———. 1975. *Tearoom Trade: Impersonal Sex in Public Places*, enlarged ed. New York: Aldine de Gruyter.

Husserl, Edmund. 1962. *Ideas: General Introduction to Pure Phenomenology*. New York: Collier.

———. 1965. *Phenomenology and the Crisis of Philosophy*. New York: Harper and Row.

———. 1973. *The Phenomenology of Internal Time-Consciousness*. Bloomington: Indiana University Press.

Hymes, Dell H. 1972. "Models of the Interaction of Language and Social Life." In John H. Gumperz and Dell H. Hymes, eds., *Directions in Sociolinguistics: The Ethnography of Communication,* 35–71. New York: Holt, Rinehart, and Winston.

Inciardi, James A. 1993. "Some Considerations on the Methods, Dangers, and Ethics of Crack-House Research." In James A. Inciardi, Dorothy Lockwood, and Anne E. Pottieger, *Women and Crack Cocaine,* 147–57. New York: Macmillan.

Inciardi, James A., Dorothy Lockwood, and Anne E. Pottieger. 1993. *Women and Crack-Cocaine.* New York: Macmillan.

Irigaray, Luce. 1985. *This Sex Which Is Not One.* Ithaca, N.Y.: Cornell University Press.

———. 1993. *Je, Tu, Nous.* New York: Routledge.

Irwin, John. 1972. "Participant Observation of Criminals." In Jack D. Douglas, ed., *Research on Deviance,* 117–37. New York: Random House.

Jackson, Bruce. 1972. "Circus and Street: Psychological Aspects of the Black Toast." *Journal of American Folklore* 85: 123–39.

———. 1974. *Get Your Ass in the Water and Swim Like Me: Narrative Poetry from Black Oral Tradition.* Cambridge, Mass.: Harvard University Press.

———. 1975. "A Response to 'Toasts: The Black Urban Poetry.'" *Journal of American Folklore* 88: 178–82.

Jacobs, Bruce A. 1994. "Anticipatory Undercover Targeting in High Schools." *Journal of Criminal Justice* 22: 445–57.

James, Henry. 1881. *The Portrait of a Lady.* New York: Modern Library.

Jenkins, Pamela J., and Steve Knoll-Smith, eds. 1996. *Witnessing for Sociology: Sociologists in Court.* Westport, Conn.: Praeger.

Johnson, John M. 1983. "Trust and Personal Involvements in Fieldwork." In Robert M. Emerson, ed., *Contemporary Field Research,* 203–15. Prospect Heights, Ill.: Waveland.

Kane, Stephanie. 1990. "AIDS, Addiction and Condom Use: Sources of Sexual Risk for Heterosexual Women." *Journal of Sex Research* 27 (3): 427–44.

———. 1991. " HIV, Heroin and Heterosexual Relations." *Social Science and Medicine* 32 (9): 1037–50.

———. 1993. "Prostitution and the Military in Belize: Planning AIDS Intervention in Belize." *Social Science and Medicine* 36 (7): 965–79.

———. 1993. "Race, Sex Work and Ethnographic Representation; Or, What to Do About Loki's Toast." *Canadian Folklore canadien* 15 (1): 109–17.

Kant, Immanuel. 1949. *Fundamental Principles of the Metaphysics of Morals.* Indianapolis: Bobbs-Merrill.

Kappeler, Victor, Richard Sluder, and Geoffrey Alpert. 1994. *Forces of Deviance.* Prospect Heights, Ill.: Waveland.

Karlson, Karl. 1987. "Strangers Were Too Strange: New Neighbors' Odd Habits Lead to Huge Drug Bust." *Chicago Tribune,* October 28, 3.

Karp, Ivan, and Martha B. Kendall. 1982. "Reflexivity in Field Work." In Paul F. Secord, ed., *Explaining Human Behavior: Consciousness, Human Action, and Social Structure,* 249–76. Beverly Hills, Calif.: Sage.

Kasinitz, Paul. 1984. "Gentrification and Homelessness: The Single Room Occupant and the Inner City Revival." *Urban and Social Change Review* 17: 3–18.

Katz, Jack. 1988. *Seductions of Crime: Moral and Sensual Attractions in Doing Evil.* New York: Basic Books.

Kerouac, Jack. 1970. *The Scripture of the Golden Eternity.* New York: Corinth.

Kessler, Mark. 1990. "Expanding Legal Services Programs to Rural America: A Case Study of Program Creation and Operations." *Judicature* 73: 273–80.

Kirby, Richard, and Jay Corzine. 1981. "The Contagion of Stigma: Fieldwork Among Deviants." *Qualitative Sociology* 4: 3–20.

Kleinman, Sherryl, and Martha A. Copp. 1993. *Emotions and Fieldwork.* Newbury Park, Calif.: Sage.

Kotarba, Joseph A., and Andrea Fontana, eds. 1984. *The Existential Self in Society.* Chicago: University of Chicago Press.

Kramer, Ronald C. 1985. "Defining the Concept of Crime: A Humanistic Perspective." *Journal of Sociology and Social Welfare* 12: 469–87.

Kraska, Peter B. 1993. "Militarizing the Drug War: A Sign of the Times." In Peter B. Kraska, ed., *Altered States of Mind: Critical Observations of the Drug War,* 159–206. New York: Garland.

———. 1996. "Collaboration Between the Military and Criminal Justice Industrial Complexes: From Ideological to Material Connections." Paper presented at the meetings of the Academy of Criminal Justice Sciences, Las Vegas, Nev.

———. Forthcoming. "The Military as Drug Police: Exercising the Ideology of War." In Peter B. Kraska and Larry K. Gaines, eds., *Drugs, Crime, and Justice.* Prospect Heights, Ill.: Waveland.

Kraska, Peter B., and Louis J. Cubellis. Forthcoming. "Paramilitary Policing in Small U.S. Localities: A National Study." *Justice Quarterly.*

Kraska, Peter B., and Victor E. Kappeler. 1995. "To Serve and Pursue: Exploring Police Sexual Violence Against Women." *Justice Quarterly* 12 (1): 85–111.

———. 1997. "Militarizing American Police: The Rise and Normalization of Paramilitary Units." *Social Problems* 44 (1): 1–18.

Kress, June. 1994. "Homeless Fatigue Syndrome: The Backlash Against the Crime of Homelessness in the 1990s." *Social Justice* 21: 85–108.

Krieger, Susan. 1985. "Beyond 'Subjectivity': The Use of the Self in Social Science." *Qualitative Sociology* 8: 309–24.

Kristeva, Julia. 1980. *Desire in Language.* New York: Columbia University Press.

———. 1984. *Revolution in Poetic Discourse.* New York: Columbia University Press.

Kropotkin, Peter. 1975. *The Essential Kropotkin.* Emile Capouya and Keitha Tompkins, eds. New York: Liveright.

Kuhn, Annette. 1985. *The Power of the Image: Essays on Representation and Sexuality.* New York: Routledge and Kegan Paul.

Kuhn, Thomas S. 1970. *The Structure of Scientific Revolutions.* Chicago: University of Chicago Press.

Lacan, Jacques. 1975. *Encore.* Paris: Edition du Seuil.

———. 1977. *Ecrit: A Selection.* A. Sheridan, trans. New York: W. W. Norton.

Lakoff, George, and Mark Johnson. 1980. *Metaphors We Live By.* Chicago: University of Chicago Press.

Lamb, Richard H. 1984. "Deinstitutionalization and the Homeless Mentally Ill." *Hospital and Community Psychiatry* 35: 899–907.

Landesco, John. 1925. "The Criminal Gang." Report to Local Community Research Committee. Charles E. Merriam Papers, University of Chicago Archives, Chicago, Ill.

———. 1929. *Organized Crime in Chicago.* Chicago: Illinois Association for Criminal Justice.

Lee, Raymond M. 1993. *Doing Research on Sensitive Topics.* London: Sage.

———. 1995. *Dangerous Fieldwork.* Thousand Oaks, Calif.: Sage.

Leo, Richard A. 1995. "Trial and Tribulations: Courts, Ethnography, and

the Need for an Evidentiary Privilege for Academic Researchers."
American Sociologist 26: 113–34.

Levin, Jack, and James Alan Fox. 1985. *Mass Murder: America's Growing Menace.* New York: Plenum.

LeVine, Robert A. 1973. *Culture, Behavior, and Personality.* Chicago: Aldine.

Liebow, Elliot. 1967. *Tally's Corner.* Boston: Little, Brown.

Lindesmith, Alfred R. 1965. *The Addict and the Law.* Bloomington: Indiana University Press.

Littrell, Donald W., and Doris P. Littrell. 1991. "Civic Education, Rural Development, and the Land Grant Institutions." In Kenneth E. Pigg, ed., *The Future of Rural America: Anticipating Policies for Constructive Change,* 195–212. Boulder, Colo.: Westview Press.

Lofland, John. 1966. *Doomsday Cult.* Englewood Cliffs, N.J.: Prentice-Hall.

———. 1969. *Deviance and Identity.* Englewood Cliffs, N.J.: Prentice-Hall.

Lowie, Robert H. 1937. *The History of Ethnological Theory.* New York: Farrar and Rinehart.

Lyng, Stephen. 1990. "Edgework: A Social Psychological Analysis of Voluntary Risk Taking." *American Journal of Sociology* 95: 851–86.

———. 1993. "Dysfunctional Risk Taking: Criminal Behavior as Edgework." In Nancy J. Bell and Robert W. Bell, eds., *Adolescent Risk Taking,* 107–30. Newbury Park, Calif.: Sage.

Lyng, Stephen, and Mitchell L. Bracey, Jr. 1995. "Squaring the One Percent: Biker Style and the Selling of Cultural Resistance." In Jeff Ferrell and Clinton R. Sanders, eds., *Cultural Criminology,* 235–76. Boston: Northeastern University Press.

Lyng, Stephen, and David Snow. 1986. "Vocabularies of Motive and High-Risk Behavior: The Case of Skydiving." In Edward J. Lawler, ed., *Advances in Group Processes,* 157–79. Greenwich, Conn.: JAI.

Lyotard, Jean-Francois. 1984. *The Postmodern Condition: A Report on Knowledge.* Minneapolis: University of Minnesota Press.

Mandelbrot, Benoit. 1983. *The Fractal Geometry of Nature.* New York: W. A. Freeman.

Manning, Peter K. 1972. "Observing the Police: Deviance, Respectables, and the Law." In Jack D. Douglas, ed., *Research on Deviance,* 213–68. New York: Random House.

———. 1977. *Police Work: The Social Organization of Policing.* Cambridge, Mass.: MIT Press.

———. 1988. "Community Policing as a Drama of Control." In Jack R. Greene and Stephen D. Mastrofski, eds., *Community Policing: Rhetoric or Reality*, 27–46. New York: Praeger.

———. 1992. "Economic Rhetoric and Policing Reform." *Criminal Justice Research Bulletin* 7 (4): 1–8.

Marcuse, Herbert. 1964. *One-Dimensional Man.* Boston: Beacon.

———. 1972. *Counterrevolution and Revolt.* Boston: Beacon.

Mark, A., R. Kleiman, and K. D. Smith. 1990. "State and Local Drug Enforcement: In Search of a Strategy." In Michael Tonry and James Q. Wilson, edg., *Drugs and Crime: Vol. 13*, 69–108. Chicago: University of Chicago Press.

Marquart, James. 1986. "Doing Research in Prison: The Strengths and Weaknesses of Participation as a Guard." *Justice Quarterly* 3: 15–32.

Martin, Madeline A. 1987. "Homeless Women: A Historical Perspective." In Rick Beard, ed., *On Being Homeless: Historical Perspectives*, 112–43. New York: Museum of the City of New York.

Marx, Gary. 1988. *Undercover: Police Surveillance in America.* Berkeley: University of California Press.

Mattley, Christine. 1995. "Review of *Emotions and Fieldwork* by Sherryl Kleinman and Martha Copp and *Secrecy and Fieldwork* by Richard G. Mitchell." *Journal of Contemporary Ethnography* 23: 530–32.

McCall, George. 1978. *Observing the Law.* New York: Free Press.

McCarthy, Bill. 1995. "Not Just 'For the Thrill of It': An Instrumentalist Elaboration of Katz's Explanation of Sneaky Thrill Property Crimes." *Criminology* 33: 519–38.

McKinney, John C. 1966. *Constructive Typology and Social Theory.* New York: Appleton-Century-Crofts.

Mead, George H. 1934. *Mind, Self, and Society.* Chicago: University of Chicago Press.

Merleau-Ponty, Maurice. 1962. *Phenomenology of Perception.* New York: Humanities Press.

———. 1983. *The Structure of Behavior.* Alden L. Fisher, trans. Bloomington: Indiana University Press.

Mieczkowski, Thomas. 1986. "Geeking Up and Throwing Down: Heroin Street Life in Detroit." *Criminology* 24: 645–66.

Miller, James. 1993. *The Passion of Michel Foucault.* New York: Simon and Schuster.

Miller, Walter. 1958. "Lower Class Culture as a Generating Milieu of Gang Delinquency." *Journal of Social Issues* 14: 5–19.

Millett, Kate. 1994. *The Politics of Cruelty: An Essay on the Literature of Political Imprisonment.* New York: Norton.

Mills, C. Wright. 1940. "Situated Actions and Vocabularies of Motive." *American Sociological Review* 5: 904–13.

———. 1970. "The Power Elite" and "The Structure of Power in American Society." In Marvin Olsen, ed., *Power in Societies,* 241–61. New York: Macmillan.

Milovanovic, Dragan. 1992. *Postmodern Law and Disorder: Psychoanalytic Semiotics, Chaos Theory, and Juridic Exegesis.* Liverpool: Deborah Charles.

———. 1993. "Lacan, Chaos, and Practical Discourse in Law." In Roberta Kevelson, ed., *Flux, Complexity and Illusion in Law,* 311–37. New York: Lang.

Minh-ha, Trinh. 1989. *Woman, Native, Other: Writing Postcoloniality and Feminism.* Bloomington: Indiana University Press.

Mitchell, Richard G. 1993. *Secrecy and Fieldwork.* Thousand Oaks, Calif.: Sage.

Montell, William L. 1986. *Killings: Folk Justice in the Upper South.* Lexington: University Press of Kentucky.

Morgan, Gareth. 1986. *Images of Organization.* Beverly Hills, Calif.: Sage.

Morrow, Raymond A. 1994. *Critical Theory and Methodology.* Thousand Oaks, Calif.: Sage.

National Institute of Justice. 1995. "Technology Transfer from Defense: Concealed Weapon Detection." *National Institute of Justice Journal* 229: 35–38.

Nehring, Neil. 1993. *Flowers in the Dustbin: Culture, Anarchy, and Postwar England.* Ann Arbor: University of Michigan Press.

New York City Welfare Council. 1949. *Homeless Men in New York City.* New York: City Welfare Council.

Nielsen, Joyce McCarl. 1990. *Feminist Research Methods.* Boulder, Colo.: Westview.

Oakley, Annie. 1981. "Interviewing Women: A Contradiction in Terms." In Helen Roberts, ed., *Doing Feminist Research.* London: Routledge and Kegan Paul.

O'Malley, Pat, and Stephen Mugford. 1994. "Crime, Excitement, and

Modernity." In Gregg Barak, ed., *Varieties of Criminology,* 189–212. Westport, Conn.: Praeger.

Outhwaite, William. 1976. *Understanding Social Life: The Method Called Verstehen.* New York: Holmes and Meier.

Padilla, Felix M. 1992. *The Gang as an American Enterprise.* New Brunswick, N.J.: Rutgers University Press.

Palmer, C. Eddie. 1991. "Human Emotions: An Expanding Sociological Frontier." *Sociological Spectrum* 11: 213–29.

Paternoster, Raymond. 1983. "Race of Victim and Location of Crime: The Decision to Seek the Death Penalty in South Carolina." *Journal of Criminal Law and Criminology* 74: 754–85.

Pepinsky, Harold E., and Richard Quinney, eds. 1991. *Criminology as Peacemaking.* Bloomington: Indiana University Press.

Pettiway, Leon E. 1996. *Honey, Honey, Miss Thang: Being Black, Gay, and on the Streets.* Philadelphia: Temple University Press.

Pheterson, Gail. 1993. "The Whore Stigma: Female Dishonor and Male Unworthiness." *Social Text* 37 (Winter): 39–64.

Police Executive Research Forum. 1990. *Issues Paper: Metropolitan Police Department.* Unpublished manuscript.

Pollner, Michael. 1970. "On the Foundations of Mundane Reason." Ph.D. diss., University of California.

Polsky, Ned. 1967. *Hustlers, Beats, and Others.* Chicago: Aldine.

———. 1969. *Hustlers, Beats, and Others.* Garden City, N.Y.: Anchor.

Potter, Gary, and Larry Gaines. 1990. "Organizing Crime in 'Copperhead County': An Ethnographic Look at Rural Crime Networks." Paper presented at the meeting of the Southern Sociological Association, Louisville, Ky.

Powdermaker, Hortense. 1966. *Stranger and Friend: The Way of an Anthropologist.* New York: Norton.

Presdee, Mike. 1994. "Young People, Culture, and the Construction of Crime: Doing Wrong versus Doing Crime." In Gregg Barak, ed., *Varieties of Criminology,* 179–87. Westport, Conn.: Praeger.

Prigogine, Ilya, and Isabelle Stengers. 1984. *Order Out of Chaos.* New York: Bantam Books.

Prus, Robert. 1991. "Encountering the Marketplace: Achieving Intimate Familiarity with Vendor Activity." In William B. Shaffir and Robert B. Stebbins, eds., *Experiencing Fieldwork: An Inside View of Qualitative Research,* 120–30. Newbury Park, Calif.: Sage.

Punch, Maurice. 1986. *The Politics and Ethics of Fieldwork.* Thousand Oaks, Calif.: Sage.

———. 1994. "Politics and Ethics in Qualitative Research." In Norman K. Denzin and Yvonna S. Lincoln, eds., *Handbook of Qualitative Research,* 83–97. Thousand Oaks, Calif.: Sage.

Quinney, Richard. 1975. *Criminology.* Boston: Little, Brown.

———. 1997. "Socialist Humanism and Critical/Peacemaking Criminology: The Continuing Project." In Brian D. MacLean and Dragan Milovanovic, eds., *Thinking Critically About Crime,* 114–17. Vancouver: Collective Press.

Ragin, Charles C., and Howard S. Becker. 1992. *What Is a Case? Foundations of Social Inquiry.* New York: Cambridge University Press.

Reason, Peter. 1994. *Participating in Human Inquiry.* Thousand Oaks, Calif.: Sage.

Redhead, Steve. 1995. *Unpopular Cultures: The Birth of Law and Popular Culture.* Manchester and New York: Manchester University Press.

Redmond, Sonja P., and Joan Brackman. 1990. "Homeless Children and Their Caretakers." In Jamshid Momeni, ed., *Homelessness in the United States,* 123–32. New York: Praeger.

Reinharz, Shulamit. 1984. *On Becoming a Social Scientist.* New Brunswick, N.J.: Transaction.

Reynolds, Anthony. 1974. "Urban Negro Toasts: A Hustler's View from L.A." *Western Folklore* 33: 267–300.

Riemer, Jeffrey. 1981. "Deviance as Fun." *Adolescence* 16: 39–43.

Ringenbach, Peter T. 1973. *Tramps and Reformers 1873–1916: The Discovery of Unemployment in New York.* Westport, Conn.: Greenwood Press.

Ritzer, George. 1993. *The McDonaldization of Society: An Investigation into the Changing Character of Contemporary Social Life.* Thousand Oaks, Calif.: Pine Forge Press.

Rochford, E. Burke, Jr. 1985. *Hare Krishna in America.* New Brunswick, N.J.: Rutgers University Press.

Rock, P. 1979. *The Making of Symbolic Interactionism.* London: Macmillan.

Rohner, Ronald P. 1975. *They Love Me, They Love Me Not: Worldwide Study of Parental Rejection.* New Haven, Conn.: HRAR Press.

Rojek, Chris, and Brian S. Turner. 1993. *Forget Baudrillard?* New York: Routledge.

Romero, Mary. 1988. "Chicanas Modernize Domestic Service." *Qualitative Sociology* 11 (4): 319–33.

Ronai, Carol Rambo. 1992. "The Reflexive Self Through Narrative: A Night in the Life of an Erotic Dancer/Researcher." In Carolyn Ellis and Michael G. Flaherty, eds., *Investigating Subjectivity*, 102–24. Newbury Park, Calif.: Sage.

Rosenau, Pauline M. 1992. *Post-Modernism and the Social Sciences: Insights, Inroads, and Intrusions*. Princeton: Princeton University Press.

Ross, H. Laurence. 1992. *Confronting Drunk Driving: Social Policy for Saving Lives*. New Haven, Conn.: Yale University Press.

Rothman, David J. 1971. *The Discovery of the Asylum*. Boston: Little, Brown.

———. 1980. *Conscience and Convenience: The Asylum and Its Alternatives in Progressive America*. Boston: Little, Brown.

———. 1987. "The First Shelters: The Contemporary Relevance of the Almshouse." In Rick Beard, ed., *On Being Homeless: Historical Perspectives*. New York: Museum of the City of New York.

Ruefle, William, and Kenneth Reynolds. 1995. "Curfews and Delinquency in Major American Cities." *Crime and Delinquency* 41: 347–63.

Sagan, Carl. 1995. *The Demon-Haunted World: Science as a Candle in the Dark*. New York: Random House.

Sanchez-Jankowski, Martin. 1991. *Islands in the Street: Gangs in American Urban Society*. Berkeley: University of California Press.

Sanders, Clinton R. 1995. "Stranger than Fiction: Insights and Pitfalls in Post-Modern Ethnography." *Studies in Symbolic Interaction* 17: 89–104.

Sayer, Andrew. 1992. *Method in Social Science: A Realist Approach*, 2d ed. London: Routledge.

Scarce, Rik. 1994. "(No) Trial (But) Tribulations: When Courts and Ethnography Conflict." *Journal of Contemporary Ethnography* 23 (1): 123–49.

———. 1995. "Scholarly Ethics and Courtroom Antics: Where Researchers Stand in the Eyes of the Law." *American Sociologist* 26: 87–112.

Schegloff, Edward, and Howard Sacks. 1974. "Opening Up Closings." In Robert Turner, ed., *Ethnomethodology*, 147–68. Baltimore: Penguin.

Scheper-Hughes, Nancy. 1994. "Embodied Knowledge: Thinking with the Body in Critical Medical Anthropology." In Robert Borofsky, ed., *Assessing Cultural Anthropology*, 229–42. New York: McGraw-Hill.

Schiffman, Josepha. 1991. "Fight The Power: Two Groups Mobilize for

Peace." In Michael Burawoy et al., *Ethnography Unbound*, 58–79. Berkeley: University of California Press.

Schutz, Alfred. 1962. *Collected Papers I: The Problem of Social Reality.* Maurice Natanson, ed. The Hague: Martinus Nijhoff.

———. 1964. *Collected Papers II: Studies in Social Theory.* Maurice Natanson, ed. The Hague: Martinus Nijhoff.

———. 1966. *Collected Papers III: Studies in Phenomenological Philosophy.* Maurice Natanson, ed. The Hague: Martinus Nijhoff.

———. 1967. *The Phenomenology of the Social World.* Evanston, Ill.: Northwestern University Press.

Scott, Marvin. 1968. *The Racing Game.* Chicago: Aldine.

Scully, Diana. 1990. *Understanding Sexual Violence.* Boston: Unwin Inman.

Seroka, Jim, and Seshan Subramaniam. 1991. "Governing the Countryside: Linking Politics and Administrative Resources." In Kenneth E. Pigg, ed., *The Future of Rural America: Anticipating Policies for Constructive Change*, 213–31. Boulder, Colo.: Westview Press.

Shaffir, William B., and Robert A. Stebbins, eds. 1991. *Experiencing Fieldwork: An Inside View of Qualitative Research.* Newbury Park, Calif.: Sage.

Shalin, Dmitri N. 1992. "Critical Theory and the Pragmatist Challenge." *American Journal of Sociology* 98: 237–79.

Shaw, Clifford. 1930. *The Jack Roller.* Chicago: University of Chicago Press.

Shostak, Arthur B. 1996. *Private Sociology: Unsparing Reflections, Uncommon Gains.* Dix Hills, N.J.: General Hall.

Siegal, Harvey. 1978. *Outpost of the Forgotten.* New Brunswick, N.J.: Transaction.

Simmel, Georg. 1908. "The Stranger." In Donald Levine, ed., *Georg Simmel*, 143–49. Chicago: University of Chicago Press.

Sjoberg, Gideon, ed. 1967. *Ethics, Politics, and Social Research.* Cambridge, Mass.: Schenkman.

Skolnick, Jerome H. 1980. "A Sketch of the Policeman's 'Working Personality.'" In George F. Cole, ed., *Criminal Justice: Law and Politics*, 3d ed. North Scituate, Mass.: Duxbury Press.

Slobin, Kathleen. 1995. "Fieldwork and Subjectivity: On the Ritualization of Seeing a Burned Child." *Symbolic Interaction* 18 (4): 487–504.

Sluka, Jeffrey A. 1990. "Participant Observation in Violent Social Contexts." *Human Organization* 49: 114–26.

Small, Stephen. 1983. *Police and People in London II: A Group of Black Young People.* London: Policy Studies Institute.

Smith, Charles D. 1995. "Taking Back the Streets." *Police Magazine: The Law Officer's Magazine* 19 (9): 36–40, 82.

Smithers, Jan. 1985. *Determined Survivors: Community Life Among the Urban Elderly.* New Brunswick, N.J.: Transaction.

Solenberger, Andrew W. 1911. *One Thousand Homeless Men.* New York: Russell Sage Foundation.

Soloway, Irving, and James Walters. 1977. "Workin' the Corner: The Ethics and Legality of Fieldwork among Active Heroin Addicts." In Robert S. Weppner, ed., *Street Ethnography,* 159–78. Beverly Hills, Calif.: Sage.

Spillers, Hortense. 1984. "Interstices: A Small Drama of Words." In Carole Vance, ed., *Pleasure and Danger: Exploring Female Sexuality,* 73–100. London: Pandora.

Spradley, James P. 1970. *You Owe Yourself a Drunk: An Ethnography of Urban Nomads.* Boston: Little, Brown.

Stanley, Chris. n.d. *Outwith the Law.* Ph.D. thesis, University of Kent.

Strickland, Wendy. 1991. "Institutional Emotion Norms and Role Satisfaction: Examination of a Career Wife Population." Paper presented at the meetings of the North Central Sociological Association, Dearborn, Mich.

Sudnow, David, ed. 1972. *Studies in Social Interaction.* New York: Free Press.

Sutherland, Edwin, and Donald Cressey. 1970. *Principles of Criminology,* 8th ed. Philadelphia: Lippincott.

Swanson, Bert E., Richard A. Cohen, and Edith P. Swanson. 1979. *Small Towns and Small Towners: A Framework for Survival and Growth.* Beverly Hills, Calif.: Sage.

Tayler, Avril. 1993. *Women Drug Users: An Ethnography of a Female Injecting Community.* Oxford: Clarendon Press.

Taylor, Steven, and Robert Bogden. 1984. *Introduction to Qualitative Research Methods: The Search for Meanings.* New York: Wiley.

Thomas, Jim. 1993. *Doing Critical Ethnography.* Newbury Park, Calif.: Sage.

Thompson, Hunter S. 1966. *Hell's Angels: A Strange and Terrible Saga.* New York: Ballantine.

———. 1971. *Fear and Loathing in Las Vegas: A Savage Journey to the Heart of the American Dream.* New York: Warner Books.

——. 1979. *The Great Shark Hunt: Strange Tales from a Strange Time.* New York: Warner Books.

Thornberry, Terence. 1994. "Violent Families and Youth Violence." Office of Juvenile Justice and Delinquency Prevention, Fact Sheet #21 (December).

Thrasher, Frederic. 1927. *The Gang.* Chicago: University of Chicago Press.

Tibbetts, Paul. 1974. "Mead's Theory of the Act and Perception: Some Empirical Confirmation." *The Personalist* 55: 68–71.

Tifft, Larry, and Lynn Markham. 1991. "Battering Women and Battering Central Americans: A Peacemaking Synthesis." In Harold Pepinsky and Richard Quinney, eds., *Criminology as Peacemaking,* 114–53. Bloomington: Indiana University Press.

Tolich, Martin. 1993. "Alienating and Liberating Emotions at Work." *Journal of Contemporary Ethnography* 22: 361–81.

Trotsky, Leon. 1969. *The Permanent Revolution and Results and Prospects.* New York: Pathfinder Press.

Truzzi, Marcello. 1974. *Verstehen: Subjective Understanding in the Social Sciences.* Reading, Mass.: Addison-Wesley.

Tunnell, Kenneth D. 1992. *Choosing Crime: The Criminal Calculus of Property Offenders.* Chicago: Nelson-Hall.

Tunnell, Kenneth D., and Terry C. Cox. 1991. "Sexually Aggressive Murder: A Case Study." *Journal of Contemporary Criminal Justice* 7: 232–44.

——. 1995. "Applying a Subculture of Violence Thesis to an Ongoing Criminal Lifestyle." *Deviant Behavior* 16: 373–89.

Turner, Ralph H. 1976. "The Real Self: From Institution to Impulse." *American Journal of Sociology* 81: 989–1016.

Turner, Steve. 1996. *Angelheaded Hipster: A Life of Jack Kerouac.* New York: Viking.

U.S. Department of Justice. 1997. *Building Knowledge About Crime and Justice.* Washington, D.C.: National Institute of Justice.

Van Maanen, John. 1978. "The Asshole." In Peter K. Manning and John Van Maanen, eds., *Policing: A View from the Street,* 221–38. Santa Monica, Calif.: Goodyear.

——, ed. 1995. *Representation in Ethnography.* Thousand Oaks, Calif.: Sage.

——. 1995. "An End to Innocence: The Ethnography of Ethnography."

In John Van Maanen, ed., *Representation in Ethnography,* 1–35. Thousand Oaks, Calif.: Sage.

Vaughn, Ted R., Gideon Sjoberg, and Larry T. Reynolds, eds. 1993. *A Critique of Contemporary American Sociology.* Dix Hills, N.Y.: General Hall.

Vigil, James Diego. 1988. *Barrio Gangs: Street Life and Identity in Southern California.* Austin: University of Texas Press.

Vigil, James Diego, and John M. Long. 1990. "Emic and Etic Perspectives on Gang Culture: The Chicano Case." In C. Ronald Huff, ed., *Gangs in America,* 55–68. Newbury Park, Calif.: Sage.

Vila, Bryan J. 1993. "Is the War on Drugs an Example of a Runaway Cultural Process?" In Peter Kraska, ed., *Altered States of Mind: Critical Observations of the Drug War,* 11–48. New York: Garland.

Wallace, Michele. 1990. *Invisibility Blues: From Pop to Theory.* New York: Verso.

Wallace, Samuel E. 1965. *Skid Row as a Way of Life.* Totowa, N.J.: Bedminster Press.

Waters, Malcolm. 1994. *Modern Sociological Theory.* Thousand Oaks, Calif.: Sage.

Wax, Rosalie H. 1993. "The Ambiguities of Fieldwork." In Robert M. Emerson, ed., *Contemporary Field Research,* 191–202. Prospect Heights, Ill.: Waveland.

Weber, Max. 1947. *The Theory of Social and Economic Organization.* New York: Oxford University Press.

———. 1949. *The Methodology of the Social Sciences.* Edward A. Shils and Henry A. Finch, trans. New York: Free Press.

———. 1958. *The Protestant Ethic and the Spirit of Capitalism.* Talcott Parsons, trans. New York: Scribner and Sons.

———. 1978. *Economy and Society.* Berkeley: University of California Press.

Weigert, Andrew. 1981. *Sociology of Everyday Life.* New York: Longman.

Weinberg, Daniel. 1987. "Rural Pockets of Poverty." *Rural Sociology* 52: 398–408.

Weingarten, Paul. 1989. "Profits, Perils Higher for Today's Bootleggers." *Chicago Tribune,* September 14, 1, 8.

Weingarten, Paul, and James Coates. 1989. "Drugs Blaze New Paths: Interstates, Backroads Join Courier System." *Chicago Tribune,* September 12, 1, 8.

Weisheit, Ralph A. 1991. "Drug Use Among Domestic Marijuana Growers." *Contemporary Drug Problems* 18: 191–217.

———. 1991. "The Intangible Rewards from Crime: The Case of Domestic Marijuana Growers." *Crime and Delinquency* 37: 506–27.

———. 1992. *Domestic Marijuana: A Neglected Industry.* Westport, Conn.: Greenwood Press.

———. 1993. "Studying Drugs in Rural Areas: Notes from the Field." *Journal of Research in Crime and Delinquency* 30: 213–32.

Weisheit, Ralph A., and L. Edward Wells. 1996. "Rural Crime and Justice: Implications for Theory and Research." *Crime and Delinquency* 42: 379–97.

Weisheit, Ralph A., David N. Falcone, and L. Edward Wells. 1996. *Crime and Policing in Rural and Small-Town America.* Prospect Heights, Ill.: Waveland Press.

Wepman, Dennis, Ronald Newman, and Murray Binderman. 1974. "Toasts: The Black Urban Folk Poetry." *Journal of American Folklore* 87: 208–24.

———. 1976. *The Life: The Love and Folk Poetry of the Black Hustler.* Philadelphia: University of Pennsylvania Press.

Whyte, William F. 1943. *Street Corner Society: The Social Structure of an Italian Slum.* Chicago: University of Chicago Press.

Williams, Richard. 1988. *Hard Labor.* Atlanta: Southern Regional Council.

Williams, Terry, Eloise Dunlap, Bruce D. Johnson, and Ansley Hamid. 1992. "Personal Safety in Dangerous Places." *Journal of Contemporary Ethnography* 21 (3): 343–74.

Willis, Paul. 1977. *Learning to Labour.* New York: Columbia University Press.

Wilson, James Q. 1995. "Crime and Public Policy." In James Q. Wilson and Joan Petersilia, eds., *Crime,* 489–507. San Francisco: ICS Press.

Wilson, Thomas C. 1991. "Urbanism, Migration, and Tolerance: A Reassessment." *American Sociological Review* 56: 117–23.

Wiseman, Jacqueline P. 1970. *Stations of the Lost.* Englewood Cliffs, N.J.: Prentice-Hall.

Wolf, Daniel R. 1991. "High-Risk Methodology: Reflections on Leaving an Outlaw Society." In William B. Shaffir and Robert A. Stebbins, eds., *Experiencing Fieldwork: An Inside View of Qualitative Research,* 211–23. Newbury Park, Calif.: Sage.

Wolff, Kurt H. 1964. "Surrender and Community Study: The Study of Loma." In Arthur J. Vidich, Joseph Bensman, and Maurice R. Stein, eds., *Reflections on Community Studies,* 233–63. New York: Wiley.

Wright, John D. 1988. "The Mentally Ill Homeless: What is Myth and What is Fact." *Social Problems* 35 (4): 133–45.

———. 1989. *Address Unknown: The Homeless in America.* New York: Aldine de Gruyter.

Wright, Richard T., and Scott H. Decker. 1994. *Burglars on the Job: Street-life and Residential Break-ins.* Boston: Northeastern University Press.

Wright, Richard T., Scott H. Decker, Allison K. Redfern, and Dietrich L. Smith. 1992. "A Snowball's Chance in Hell: Doing Fieldwork with Active Residential Burglars." *Journal of Research in Crime and Delinquency* 29: 148–61.

Yablonsky, Lewis. 1966. *The Violent Gang.* New York: Macmillan.

Young, T. R. 1991. "Chaos and Crime: Nonlinear and Fractal Forms of Crime." *Critical Criminologist* 3 (2): 3–4, 10–11.

———. 1991. "The ABC's of Crime: Attractors, Bifurcations, Basins, and Chaos." *Critical Criminologist* 3 (4): 3–4, 13–14.

———. 1992. "Chaos Theory and Human Agency: Humanist Sociology in a Postmodern Age." *Humanity and Society* 16 (4): 441–60.

Young, T. R., and Bruce Arrigo. 1997. *Chaos and Crime: From Criminal Justice to Social Justice.* Albany: SUNY Press.

Zurcher, Louis A. 1977. *The Mutable Self: An Adaptation to Accelerated Socio-Cultural Change.* Beverly Hills, Calif.: Sage.

Contributors

Peter and Patricia A. Adler received their doctorates in sociology from the University of California, San Diego. He is professor of sociology at the University of Denver, where he was chair of the department from 1987 to 1993. She is associate professor of sociology at the University of Colorado, Boulder. They have written and worked together for over twenty-five years. Their interests include qualitative methods, deviant behavior, sociology of sport, sociology of children, and work and leisure. They have published numerous articles and books, including *Momentum* (Sage, 1981), *Wheeling and Dealing* (Columbia University Press, 1985), *Membership Roles in Field Research* (Sage, 1987), *Backboards and Blackboards* (Columbia Univer-sity Press, 1991), and *Peer Power* (Rutgers University Press, 1998). The Adlers have served as editors of the *Journal of Contemporary Ethnography* (1986–94) and as the founding editors of *Sociological Studies of Child Development* (1985–92).

Bruce A. Arrigo received his Ph.D. from the Pennsylvania State University in the administration of justice. He is professor of forensic psychology and criminology and the director of the Institute of Psychology, Law, and Public Policy at the California School of Professional Psychology—Fresno. He has published some forty monographs, peer-reviewed articles, and academic book chapters dealing with issues in crime, law, justice, and community. His most recent books include *The Contours of Psychiatric Justice* (Garland, 1996); the anthology *Justice at the Margins: The Maturation of Critical Theory in Law, Crime, and Deviance* (Wadsworth, 1997); and, with T. R. Young, *Chaos and Crime: From Criminal Justice to Social Justice* (SUNY Press, 1997). Recent articles have appeared in *Justice Quarterly;* the *Journal of Offender Rehabilitation; Critical Criminology; Criminal Justice and Behavior; Crime, Law, and Social Change;* and *Theoretical Criminology.* Professor Arrigo is also the editor of the social science quarterly *Humanity and Society.*

Jeff Ferrell is professor of criminal justice at Northern Arizona University. He received his Ph.D. in sociology from the University of Texas at Austin. Ongoing research interests include the intersections of criminal and cultural processes, the uses of qualitative methods in criminology, and criminological theory. He is author of *Crimes of Style: Urban Graffiti and the Politics of Criminality* (Garland, 1993; Northeastern University Press, 1996), and lead editor, with Clinton R. Sanders, of *Cultural Criminology* (Northeastern University Press, 1995), the finalist for the 1996 Michael J. Hindelang Award, presented by the American Society of Criminology for the Most Outstanding Contribution to Criminology. He currently serves as an associate editor for the journal *Justice Quarterly.*

Mark S. Fleisher is a cultural and linguistic anthropologist and an anthropologically trained ethnographer. He has done ethnographic and linguistic fieldwork in Mexico, Guatemala, Indonesia, on the northwest coast of North America among Salish- and Nootkan-speaking peoples, and in state and federal prisons and high-crime urban gang neighborhoods. Fleisher has written three books: *Warehousing Violence* (Sage, 1989); *Beggars and Thieves: Lives of Urban Street Criminals* (University of Wisconsin Press, 1995); and *Dead End: Lives of Urban Gang Kids* (University of Wisconsin Press, 1998), as well as journal articles and book chapters on federal prison industries, prison organizational culture and development, correctional management assessment, and youth gangs and crime policy. Fleisher is a site evaluator in a national, multisite youth gang intervention project funded by the U.S. Department of Justice, Office of Juvenile Justice and Delinquency Prevention. He has served as a consultant on managing gangs and deviant groups at the National Institute of Corrections and is a consultant to the Illinois attorney general on gang crime, gang intervention, and community mobilization. He is an associate editor on law and justice for *USA Today Magazine.*

Mark S. Hamm is professor of criminology at Indiana State University. He is the author of *American Skinheads: The Criminology and Control of Hate Crime* (Praeger, 1993); *Hate Crime: International Perspectives on Causes and Control* (Anderson, 1994); *The Abandoned Ones: The Imprisonment and Uprising of the Mariel Boat People* (Northeastern University Press, 1995); and *Apocalypse in Oklahoma: Waco and Ruby Ridge Revenged* (Northeastern University Press, 1997). He is the recipient of the 1993 Frederic Milton Thrasher Award for Outstanding Gang Scholarship and the 1996 Critical Criminologist of the Year Award from the American Society of Criminology. He continues his work on apocalyptic violence in contemporary America, and on the collection of quality Grateful Dead tapes.

Bruce A. Jacobs is assistant professor of criminology at the University of Missouri—St. Louis. His research explores the use, distribution, and control of illicit drugs. Recent papers appear in *Criminology* (1996), *Justice Quarterly* (1996), *Sociological Quarterly* (1996), and the *British Journal of Sociology* (1997). He is currently completing a book on the social organization of street-level crack sales entitled *Selling Crack: Trade and Tradeoffs* (under contract with Northeastern University Press).

Stephanie Kane is an assistant professor in the department of criminal justice at Indiana University. She is the author of *The Phantom Gringo Boat: Shamanic Discourse and Development in Panama* (Smithsonian Institute Press, 1994) and is working on a second book, entitled *AIDS Alibis: Sex and the Drug War in the Americas*. Her current ethnographic research is a comparative study of the criminalization of intentional HIV transmission in the United States and the Netherlands.

Peter B. Kraska is associate professor of police studies at Eastern Kentucky University. His most recent research documents and theorizes on the militarized nature of governmental crime and drug control efforts in the post–cold war era. Professor Kraska and Vic Kappeler have recently published a piece concerning the militarization of police in the journal *Social Problems* ("Militarizing American Police: The Rise and Normalization of Paramilitary Units"); another article examining trends in paramilitarism is forthcoming in the journal *Justice Quarterly* ("Militarizing Mayberry: Trends and Issues in Paramilitary Policing").

Stephen Lyng is associate professor of sociology and director of graduate studies in sociology at Virginia Commonwealth University. His research on voluntary risk taking, social movements, social policy, and health care has appeared in a variety of journals, including *Social Forces,* the *American Journal of Sociology,* the *Journal of Applied Behavioral Science,* and *Humanity and Society,* and in various edited books. He is author of *Holistic Health and Biomedical Medicine: A Countersystem Analysis* (SUNY Press, 1990).

Christine Mattley is associate professor of sociology at Ohio University, where she teaches courses in social psychology, gender inequality, the sociology of emotion, and research methods. Her research interests include gender identity, battered women, emotion work and the self, and the emotion work of sex workers. The author of numerous articles and book chapters, her work has appeared in such journals as *Symbolic Interaction* and the *Journal of Family Violence.* Her current work focuses on phone sex workers.

Kenneth D. Tunnell is an associate professor at Eastern Kentucky University. His work has appeared in a variety of sociology, criminology, and popular culture periodicals. His books include *Choosing Crime* (Nelson-Hall, 1992), an ethnography of property criminals, and *Political Crime in Contemporary America* (Garland, 1993). His ongoing research interests include qualitative approaches to understanding crime and justice and the political economy of crime and punishment.

Ralph A. Weisheit is professor of criminal justice at Illinois State University, where he has taught since 1982. He is the author of seven books, including *Domestic Marijuana: A Neglected Industry* (Greenwood, 1992) and, with David N. Falcone and L. Edward Wells, *Crime and Policing in Rural and Small-Town America* (Waveland, 1996). His research has covered a variety of topics, including rural police, illegal drugs, juvenile justice, the insanity defense, the impact of going to jail, women and crime, and women as criminal justice professionals. He has been named Outstanding University Researcher at Illinois State University and has received the Academy Fellow Award from the Academy of Criminal Justice Sciences for distinguished teaching and scholarly achievement.

Index

CPSIA information can be obtained at www.ICGtesting.com
Printed in the USA
BVOW05s1628040915

415738BV00002B/5/P